# Survival of the
# African American Family

# Survival of the
# African American Family

*The Institutional Impact of
U.S. Social Policy*

K. SUE JEWELL

Westport, Connecticut
London

**Library of Congress Cataloging-in-Publication Data**

Jewell, K. Sue.
  Survival of the African American family : the institutional impact of U.S. social policy /
K. Sue Jewell.
    p. cm.
  Includes bibliographical references (p.) and index.
  ISBN 0–275–95769–1 (alk. paper)—ISBN 0–275–95779–9 (pbk. : alk. paper)
  1. African American families. 2. African American families—Government policy.
3. African Americans—Social conditions—1975– 4. Family policy—United States.
5. United States—Social policy—1993– 6. United States—Race relations—Political
aspects. I. Title.
E185.86.J485 2003
306.85'089'96073—dc21          2003052895

British Library Cataloguing in Publication Data is available.

Library of Congress Catalog Card Number: 2003052895
ISBN: 0–275–95769–1
       0–275–95779–9 (pbk.)

First published in 2003

Praeger Publishers, 88 Post Road West, Westport, CT 06881
An imprint of Greenwood Publishing Group, Inc.
www.praeger.com

Printed in the United States of America

The paper used in this book complies with the
Permanent Paper Standard issued by the National
Information Standards Organization (Z39.48–1984).

10  9  8  7  6  5  4  3  2  1

For SiSi, Curtis II, and Valerie

# Contents

# Preface

The primary focus of this book is on the limited progress that African American families have made several decades after the implementation of liberal social policies in the 1960s and 1970s. I also examine the continued hope and high aspirations of African American families who have remained committed to the belief that Democratic administrations will represent their interests and understand and attempt to remedy their continued experiences as the targets of institutional racial inequality, injustices, and even aggression. However, I present irrefutable evidence that these expectations and hopes are dashed as new administrations become even less committed to the elimination of institutional racial discrimination and structural barriers that prevent African American families from participating fully in mainstream American institutions, and that make them victims of institutional and individual racial inequality, which have a profound adverse effect on the stability of African American families. Institutional policies and practices such as racial profiling; financial institutions that deny mortgage loans to creditworthy African Americans; police brutality; policymakers permitting the increasing presence of predatory lenders in lower-income inner-city neighborhoods where African Americans become their chief prey; the mainstream media's continued practice of vilifying African American males and devaluing and negatively stereotyping and objectifying African American females; and the poor quality of urban education and health care–delivery systems provided to African American families are presented as further evidence of the deprivation, humiliation, and inequalities that African American families encounter on a daily basis. I also explore how some of the most harmful, yet deeply entrenched, myths regarding the inferiority of African Americans have been dispelled as well as the myth that racism is no longer a problem as it has been virtually eliminated in American society. Nevertheless, African American families continue to suffer denigration and subordination through racial discrimination, inextricably integrated into institutional policies, practices, and laws. While acknowledging the importance of African Americans establishing coalitions and alliances with other marginalized groups, I believe that the impetus for change must come from within the African American community and that well-designed strategies will serve as the catalyst for meaningful, progressive, and effective social policies. Therefore, I propose practical approaches and solutions that must emanate from within the African American community, namely through the efforts of African American institutions, with African American families in the vanguard, as key agents of social change.

# Acknowledgments

I would like to thank Jim Sabin, former Director of Academic Research and Development at Greenwood Publishing Group, for his patience and assistance in the preparation of this manuscript. I would also like to express my sincere appreciation to SiSi Jewell, Curtis Jewell II, Valerie Warren, Kathy Warren, and Michael Warren for their unconditional support, understanding, and patience, which has contributed significantly to the completion of this book.

# CHAPTER 1

# Introduction

Recently, when I began to reflect on recurrent issues that were the focus of news reports, it became apparent that African American families were experiencing innumerable incidents involving racial, sex, and class inequality. What became increasingly obvious is that even African American families who are in the middle class and upper-middle class, like others within the African American community, were the objects of institutional forms of race and sex inequality individually and collectively. In fact, I was quite surprised at the systematic methods of oppression that were being perpetrated against African American families and their members.

For example, the fact that African Americans were upwardly mobile; secured high-income, prestigious positions; and operated successful businesses did not shield them from assaults and abuses from societal institutions. For example, the practice of racial profiling affects all African Americans without regard to their socioeconomic status. Being denied loans for mortgages to purchase and refinance homes disproportionately affects African Americans who have higher incomes than African Americans who are less economically advantaged. In addition, ongoing microaggressions directed at African Americans, like rebuffs from teachers, scowls on the faces of judges, and the inability of African American men to hail taxis in major metropolitan areas, have made it increasingly obvious how the very oppressions that we had anticipated would be eliminated with social policies, laws, and executive orders generated during the 1960s and 1970s—the era of liberal social policy—appear to be increasing. It is also the case that while many liberal social policies were rescinded and their effects minimized during the Reagan-Bush administrations, they have not been restored, replaced, or made more effective in subsequent Democratic administrations, as many African Americans had expected. Consequently, I realize that the problems and challenges facing African American families remain. And their attempt to enjoy the same rights and privileges as their white counterparts is still elusive, not because of their lack of aspirations, motivations, or efforts, but due to a monopoly of power and wealth by a small minority of Americans who unquestionably influence policies and practices of societal institutions as well as laws that are enacted in American society. Moreover, the unequal distribution of power and wealth in America manifests itself in wealthy families and corporations receiving an inordinate share of the resources, while others, especially African American families and other families positioned lower on the racial/ethnic hierarchy, receive considerably less. And despite their investment in terms of time, commitment, and playing by the rules, the rewards that African American families and their members receive are rarely commensurate with their efforts.

Accepting this premise, I examine liberal social policy along with subsequent social-policy reforms and their effects on African American families, as well as the extent to which new social policies and laws must be formulated and enacted respectively. Finally, I explore those actions that must originate in the African American community to bring about meaningful change that is necessary to stabilize African American families and other institutions within the African American community, and to consolidate the resources in our community to assuage the institutional assaults and various forms of cultural humiliation that have been directed at African American families and their members over the past 25 years.

Because I believe that socially and politically it is imperative for African Americans to identify their origins, rather than to have them inaccurately imposed as commencing during slavery in America, I use the cultural appellation *African American* throughout the book. Unlike numerous other families who have migrated to the United States and can identify a country from which they originated along with customs, traditions, values, and beliefs, most African American families have been denied this most valuable and cherished entitlement, yet we are able to identify Africa as our continent of origin, which means that we have a heritage, pride, and connection that is our birthright. However, on occasion, the cultural label *black* is used in discussing various institutions and organizations that continue to be identified with this label within the African American community.

## LIBERAL SOCIAL POLICY DEFINED

Social policy is a topic that has joined the ranks of religion and politics in contemporary society, able to polemicize discussions among seemingly homogeneous, congenial segments of the population. Perhaps one reason for the volatility that is apt to be generated by discussions of social policy, which on the surface appears to be an innocuous issue, is the direction it took in the 1960s and the constituency for which it became intended. Because African Americans petitioned the government to develop mechanisms to eliminate the barriers that prevented their participation in societal institutions, the government became involved in formulating, funding, and monitoring social and economic programs. In effect, a major goal of liberal social policy was to elevate the status of African American families in the United States. The scope of social and economic programs was not limited to African Americans but was extended to poor families irrespective of race or ethnic background. However, since an inordinate number of African American families were represented among the nation's poor, liberal social policy was by design intended to meet their needs.

While definitions of *liberalism* vary, here defined, it is a belief system that embraces the precept that the federal government has a responsibility to do all within its power to ensure that all its people receive equitable treatment and are given equal opportunities to participate fully in social, political, and economic institutions. Moreover, *liberalism* refers to the federal government's attempt to effect social justice for historically disenfranchised groups (such as African Americans, the poor, women, and other racial and ethnic minorities) by implementing and expanding social-service programs, passing civil rights legislation, and exercising rigorous enforcement powers. Liberal social policy, which is commonly associated with the period ranging from 1960 to the late 1970s but more accurately reflects a more expansive era beginning in the mid 1950s, is generally credited/faulted with having brought about major progress or major problems for African American families.

Heated debates that revolve around social policy surround efforts in the 1980s, 1990s, and the twenty-first century to rescind liberal policies and practices. The social conservatism characteristic of the 1980s set the climate for discussions regarding the effectiveness of liberal social policy, the benefits, and the costs.

This book examines the impact of liberal social policy on African American families in America. In so doing, I accept the premise that African American families have always been affected by social policy, even though, until the 1960s (with the exception of a brief period following emancipation), they had never been the intended recipients of a national social policy in this country. It is obvious that African American families, as well as families with membership in other racial and ethnic groups, are affected to some degree by any form of domestic policy. Due to their economically depressed status and inextricably related to their systematic exclusion from traditional institutions, African American families have been especially vulnerable to public policy changes, as well as to fluctuations in other social, economic, and political events. Furthermore, social policy affects not only the structure of African American families but the dynamics as well. Just as social systems on a macro level are sustained and perpetuated by their interdependent relationships, institutions within the African American community are also mutually dependent. What affects one institution will surely impact to some extent on another. For example, when social policy impacts the African American family, one can be relatively sure that other institutions in the African American community (such as the Black Church, African American–owned businesses, etc.) are also affected. In addition to altering the structure of African American families, social policy also has had a profound effect on the dynamics of these institutions. An elaborate and complex series of adaptive mechanisms has evolved for the purpose of ensuring the survival and progress of African American families. Many of these systems and patterns of interaction emerged in response to the absence of a national social policy that would have provided essential goods and services to African American families. Mutual-aid networks, which represent a mechanism for the exchange of valuable commodities, are an example of one such process that has been responsible for the ability of African American families to function largely without support from sources external to the African American community.[1]

In discussions of liberal social policy, there is a tendency to confuse social welfare policy with more global social-policy initiatives. Furthermore, as with the stereotyped image of social welfare programs, the misconception that African American people have been the sole beneficiaries of liberal social and economic programs is quite pervasive. In this examination of liberal social policy I am referring to those programs that include social welfare services but that are not limited to public assistance alone. In the main, I am exploring those social and economic programs that were developed and expanded during the 1960s and 1970s. While I recognize that some of these programs were first developed in the 1930s, and that others were created in the decade preceding 1960, the primary focus is on the 1960s and 1970s because of the infusion of relatively large amounts of government funds into these programs during these two decades. Further, this period, unlike others, was marked by a more liberal pattern of administration, policies, and practices, which resulted in services being extended to larger numbers of individuals. It is important to note that although the period under consideration was, on balance, characterized by liberal policies, the entire time span was not. The Nixon and Ford administrations contained elements of both liberalism and conservatism, with emphasis on the latter. However, despite the interlude of the Nixon and Ford administrations, this new thrust in monetary allocations, innovative policy initiatives, and extended benefits encompasses our definition of liberal social policy. Further, the scope of my analysis of the impact of social policy on African American families includes the passage of laws that were also designed to give disenfranchised groups access to institutions that had, prior to the 1960s, maintained a position of exclusivity and rigidity, thereby limiting the participation of African Americans, women, Hispanics, and other racial and ethnic minorities. Legislation that falls within this realm includes affirmative action; the voting rights act; fair housing legislation; *Brown v. Board of Education*, which made school segregation unconstitutional; and other laws passed to guarantee that all U.S. citizens are accorded the same opportunities for institutional participation.

When in this work reference is made to government involvement being "great" or "massive," it is done with a historical perspective in mind. While there is disagreement over what constitutes "great" or "massive" with respect to monetary allocations and total governmental involvement, the sheer magnitude of the investment made by the federal government during the 1960s and 1970s was unprecedented. It is with this knowledge that I use these descriptive terms. In this same vein, I remain cognizant of the fact that the percentages of moneys spent for federal programs must be viewed relative to other government expenditures during the period under consideration. It is not within the purview of this book to examine social policy within the context of its effectiveness or capacity to fulfill a social obligation based on monetary appropriations alone. This is not to suggest that the government's commitment to eradicate social injustices and to enable African American families to reach economic parity with white families is somehow unrelated to the amounts of money committed for such an endeavor. However, the ability of liberal social policy to effect necessary changes in the status of African American families and their members extends beyond the funds that the federal government has committed. In fact, the allocation of monies to social and economic programs is but one manifestation of the government's perception of its obligation.

The question addressed in this book is, Why did liberal social policy in the United States fail? If, as I believe, liberal social policy *was* ineffective, the questions I seek to answer are, Why? and, What evidence is there to substantiate this claim? Another question I shall attempt to answer is, What has been the overall effect of liberal social policy on the status of African American families? Finally, I explore those conditions that must be present if a social policy is to effectively enhance the status and functioning capacity of African American families and their members.

My premise that liberal social policy, as enacted in the United States, was unsuccessful is not intended to mean that liberal social policy enacted in parts of Europe, or that may emerge in other forms in the United States, is or will be ineffective. As such, inferences to that effect are unacceptable and not representative of my position. What I propose is that liberal social policy initiated in the 1950s and expanded during the 1960s and 1970s did not accomplish the mission for which it was intended. Succinctly stated, social and economic programs that evolved from liberal social policy in the United States have failed to eventuate in full participation for African American and poor families in mainstream institutions. Although these programs had a broader-based constituency, the focus will be placed on the effects of these programs on African American families. My rationale for focusing on African American families is that inherent in my thesis is the belief that race was and continues to be a salient factor in determining an individual's life chances in America. Consequently, a holistic or generic perspective, designed to explain why social policy failed to prevent the perpetuation and growth of underclass families in general, would not sufficiently address racially based factors, which have systematically precluded African Americans from gaining equal access to opportunity structures. And to do so would be, in theory, to ignore a major purpose for which liberal social policy was designed. Before the 20-year period was over, a number of other disenfranchised groups, including Hispanics, American Indians, and white women, also became contenders for the redistribution of power and wealth initially sought by African Americans in the civil rights movement. Although these groups share a commonality of interests with African Americans in that they have all experienced systematic forms of social inequities, there are distinct historical experiences that have resulted in coping strategies that are somewhat unique to each group. It is these adaptive strategies developed by African American families, which encompass family structure and dynamics, that have been a response to social policy; as social policy has changed, the strategies have been changed as well.

## THE GOVERNMENT'S ROLE IN SOCIAL POLICY

By explaining the effect that liberal social policy has had on African American families, I do not argue for the divestment of the federal government or any other levels of government in the funding, development, and supervision of social and economic programs. In fact, I maintain that government participation in the development, funding, and enforcement of social and economic programs is not only important but also essential if African American families are to substantially increase their level of participation in societal institutions throughout the United States.

Accordingly, the issue is not whether the government has a responsibility for ensuring that African American families—and all families—have an equal opportunity to participate fully in social institutions. Rather, the issue is identifying the most expedient way in which the government should fulfill its obligation to guarantee that all groups, irrespective of race, ethnicity, or gender, are granted fundamental civil rights.

The neoconservatives, who have vociferously attacked the government's involvement in social policy, have done so for the purpose of eliminating social and economic programs. Members of this political interest group offer diverse reasons for the failure of liberal social policy to result in economic independence for African American and poor families. Diverse as they are, these arguments are designed with one goal in mind: the radical revision of social policy in general and social welfare policy in particular. This "either-or" approach to social policy is an approach of no utility to the government, the recipients of such programs, or society at large. Few enterprises conduct business in this fashion; to do so would undoubtedly have devastating consequences. Instead, the goal of a well-run business is to enhance function to an optimal level through carefully calculated change. Accordingly, functional features or system components should remain, and those that do not function properly must be either modified and retained or defined as possessing little value and discarded. Rarely is a total system that has salvageable components defined as being of no utility and completely eliminated. Yet, in the 1980s conservatives proposed that liberal social policy was detrimental to recipients, as well as to the general population whose tax dollars supported social and economic programs. Blaming liberal social policy for a high federal deficit and an inadequate national security, conservatives pushed for a drastic reduction in funding and the complete elimination of social and economic programs.

## THE AFRICAN AMERICAN FAMILY AND SOCIAL POLICY: ASCRIBING RESPONSIBILITY

Clearly, the factors identified as causing the failure of liberal social policy dictate the nature of the solution. For those who see the government as too permissive and African American families as the problem, understandably the solution is the elimination of such programs. Conversely, when the failure of liberal social policy is more correctly attributed to misconceptions regarding the recipients of social and economic programs, faulty planning, poor administration, ineffective enforcement, and the inability to develop mechanisms for overcoming institutional resistance, appropriate solutions focus on modifying the programs and identifying strategies that will make social policies and practices more efficacious.

Irrespective of factors that militated against social and economic programs achieving their desired ends, little benefit can be derived from ascribing blame for their failures. As such, what I offer in this discussion is a form of social criticism, not condemnation. Though the latter approach may be feasible for partisan politics, it is of no utility to those who are committed to developing strategies that will ameliorate social and economic conditions for African American families in the United States. In fact, a nonpartisan effort is a requisite for the formulation of a social policy that will possess the capacity for the ongoing formation, implementation, and assessment of social and economic programs.

Perhaps one of the most rudimentary steps toward establishing an effective social policy is the reassessment of the positive and negative consequences of past social and economic programs. Before one can effectively develop a social policy designed to assure that African American families and their members are able to participate fully in social institutions, the plethora of data generated by past social and economic programs must be analyzed. Interestingly, those who oppose liberal social policy on the grounds that the government's involvement was tantamount to intrusion in the open market have been eager to conduct inquiries to determine the outcomes of such programs. While their findings are likely to be similar to those of liberals who advocate government involvement in social-service delivery, the interpretation and recommendations are generally quite different.

While polarization exists among various segments of the population regarding the role of government toward improving the plight of African American and poor families, there is a surfeit of individuals who have not yet established a firm position and for whom no answer is readily available. It has been argued that historically the masses have remained ambivalent regarding social policy and the plight of the less economically advantaged.[2] Much of this uncertainty is related to the adversarial nature of social policy. To a great extent, the proliferation of diametrically opposed views has confused the issue for the public. However, since the inception of liberal social policy, uncertainty over what should be done to improve the economic position of African American families has shifted to whom is responsible for doing so. In some quarters, the federal government is considered the entity that should assume this responsibility. Others maintain that African American families must resolve their own problems. And still there is the position that the problem cannot be adequately improved in light of available resources and the magnitude and institutionalization of the problem, and without the collaborative efforts of the government, African American families, and micro- and macroinstitutions. It is the last position that is set forth in this book.

## THE ROLE OF ACADEME

In seeking solutions to social problems, policymakers have relied on academic scholarship. Although academic scholarship is intended to influence public policy, the converse is not without precedent. Thus, social policy has also served as the impetus for research, which tends to corroborate a priori social-policy decisions. It is difficult to conceive how those who utilize this approach can consider it a reliable method for formulating social policy. Though academicians use scientific methods and instruments to gather data pertinent to social-policy decision making, the extreme divergence in interpretation of this data is reflected in contradictory findings and policy recommendations. While it is not realistic to assume that social scientists should agree on all or even most policy issues, the degree of disparity is far too great in general policy issues as well as in areas of specificity. This pronounced lack of agreement among academicians regarding social policy tends to be exacerbated when the unit of analysis is social policy within the African American community. While polarization is understandable within the larger society, where there is overt and conscious variability in terms of political interests, the role of objectivity and adherence to scientific rigor should result in more uniformity in the academy. Regrettably, such is not the case.

There appear to be two major perspectives in academe, which mirror those within the larger society. As such, academicians tend to be proponents of either the liberal or conservative persuasion. Those who subscribe to the former generally express unswerving support for social and economic programs implemented in the 1960s and 1970s. In the other school of thought are conservatives, who oppose liberal social policy and believe that it is decidedly perilous to tamper with the open-market system. Split along these same lines are academicians who differentially assign responsibility for improving the economically dependent status of African American families: liberals expect societal institutions to improve conditions for African Americans while conservatives insist that African Americans must reach parity with whites through their own efforts, without government support. A careful analysis of the literature is likely to reveal considerable disagreement among scholars regarding the functions of various structures and dynamics within institutions in the African American community and the larger society. Clearly, if academic scholarship is to influence social policy within the African American community, it must overcome this impasse. To do so, however, means that academicians must become less vulnerable to the political pressures that exist within both the larger society and the academy. As such, those who are exponents of the liberal persuasion should have little difficulty identifying policy recommendations that entail the use of African Americans' assets, regardless of how infinitesimal. Moreover, scholars who adhere to the conservative viewpoint must be ready to concede that government involvement in the open-market system is sometimes imperative if other means of increasing private-sector participation have met with limited success. From this vantage point comes the recognition that academic scholarship should play a salient role in the formulation of social policy, rather than social policy affecting academic scholarship.

Academic scholarship relative to the study of any problem is dynamic and not static. The evolutionary nature of academic scholarship is rarely questioned when scientific investigation in the physical sciences leads to policy decisions that later undergo modification, as improved measurement techniques are developed and new data are generated. But academic scholarship that results in policy decisions in the arena of social policy is, oftentimes, expected to be absolute, firm, and unchanging. Whether in the physical or social sciences, academic scholarship should operate within the same parameters. Accordingly, when changes occur that warrant new social-policy recommendations, researchers should willingly make changes without reluctance.

## SOCIAL POLICY BY DEFAULT: ANOTHER BASIS FOR FAILURE

Social policy and the African American family were topics that had received considerable attention for many years. A significant portion of these discussions focused on the necessity for liberal social policy, which would reduce African American family dependency and enhance stabilization. As problems became apparent and the structure of African American families and other institutions in the African American community began to reflect the negative impact of liberal social policy, academicians and nonacademicians increased their examination of these phenomena. However, because liberal social policy evolved out of protests and demands of the 1960s, its proponents—whether academicians, policymakers, administrators, or recipients—have been placed in a position of defensiveness. Therefore, criticisms of liberal social policy by its advocates were generally considered self-defeating. Liberals refrained from criticizing social policies and practices, fearing that their opponents would consider such self-criticism a justification to eradicate social and economic programs and to eliminate government involvement. Equally important is the fact that those aspects of liberal social policy that were damaging to African American institutions, including the African American family, remained virtually unchanged.

The precariousness of this situation, whereby any criticism of liberal social policy was likely to be interpreted as total program failure, is evident in the appearance of problems that, with intervention, could have been prevented. Trepidation on the part of advocates of liberal social policy to enunciate the emergence of problems and the need for policy and administrative change represents an inherent flaw in liberal social policy in the United States. For this reason alone, it is unlikely that liberal social policy could have achieved the goals for which it was designed. This is not to imply that changes did not occur in the policies and administration of social and economic programs. But the belief, on the part of administrators, academicians, and supporters of liberal social policy, that the identification of problems in social and economic programs would have jeopardized components in need of modification or elimination and would have imperiled social and economic programs in their entirety militated against the success of these endeavors.

The fact that liberal social policy was not able to elevate African American families to a position of economic independence is an issue that all too often is overlooked. Moreover, problems that have increased for African American families during the era of liberal social policy are not spuriously but highly correlated with the nature of programs developed and their administration. To continue to ignore the debilitating effects of these programs is likely to be even more devastating to the future of African American families and other African American institutions.

Thus, I undertake the task of dispelling the misconception that liberal social policy, in general, was beneficial to African American families. Associated with the myth that liberal social policy has been advantageous to African American families is the myth that institutions within American society are no longer exclusive but offer to African Americans, women, and members of all racial and ethnic groups equal opportunities to compete for societal rewards. Though changes were made in the practices of major institutions to afford access to minority groups, discriminatory practices, which continue to limit the participation of African Americans as a cultural group, remain. At the same time, there are African Americans who experienced individual success.[3] Ostensibly, upward mobility for those individuals and families was also mitigated. Because an image of institutional cooperation emerged from government efforts to ensure social equity, African American families that are poor continue to be blamed for their social and economic status. Similarly, this sentiment is applied to African American families across all socioeconomic levels. Coupled with the fact that government efforts were devoted to seeking and implementing forms of redress for past racial injustices, some people feel that African American families have received special favors or opportunities denied to others. The combined effect attributes failure to African Americans for not taking advantage of these opportunities but does not recognize that liberal social policy failed to accomplish its objectives. Moreover, this notion of institutional cooperation belies the underrepresentation of African Americans in high-level occupations, business ownership, and other positions of power and wealth throughout the United States.

## A PLURALISTIC APPROACH

Although most analyses of this kind focus almost exclusively on the economic consequences of social policy, it is important that the social-psychological implications of social policy also be examined. It is far too simplistic to limit an assessment of the impact of liberal social policy on

African American families to one dimension alone. And to a large extent, the assumptions upon which social policy is based are sociological. To be sure, perceptions of African American families as structurally and functionally dysfunctional have been at the basis of both conservative and liberal social policy. While the failure of social and economic programs to overcome structural barriers has had a devastating impact on African American families, the perception of their social inadequacy also contributed significantly to the destabilizing effect of liberal social policy. Clearly, an effective social policy must eliminate societal barriers and do so by acknowledging the strengths of African American families.

## NOTES

1. Andrew Billingsley and Jeanne M. Giovannoni, *Children of the Storm: Black Children and American Child Welfare* (New York: Harcourt Brace Jovanovich, 1972), p. 46; Robert Hill, *The Strengths of Black Families* (New York: Emerson Hall, 1972), p. 56; Robert Hill, *Economic Policies and Black Progress: Myths and Realities* (Washington, D.C.: National Urban League, 1981), p. 79; Robert Hill, *Self-Help Groups in the African-American Community: Current Organization and Service* (unpublished paper, University of North Carolina School of Social Work, 1987), pp. 4–5; Carol Stack, *All Our Kin: Strategies for Survival in a Black Community* (New York: Harper & Row, 1974), p. 28; Herbert Gutman, *The Black Family in Slavery and Freedom: 1750–1925* (New York: Pantheon Books, 1976), pp. 213–214; Harriette Pipes McAdoo, "Black Mothers and the Extended Family Support Network," in *The Black Woman*, ed. La Frances Rodgers-Rose (Beverly Hills, Calif.: Sage, 1980), pp. 125–127; Carrie Allen McCray, "The Black Woman and Family Roles," in *The Black Woman*, ed. La Frances Rodgers-Rose (Beverly Hills, Calif.: Sage, 1980), pp. 70–73; and K. Sue Jewell, "Use of Social Welfare Programs and the Disintegration of the Black Nuclear Family," *Western Journal of Black Studies* 8 (winter 1984): 193–195.

2. "Reagan's Polarized America," *Newsweek*, 5 April 1982, p. 19.

3. Derrick A. Bell Jr., *Race, Racism and American Law* (Boston: Little Brown & Company, 1980), p. 43.

# CHAPTER 2

# Social Policy and African American Family Structure

A discussion of the effects of social policy on the formation, maintenance, and dissolution of African American family structures can best be understood through a historical analysis of African American family patterns. The focus of this chapter is on the period covering the 1960s to the 1980s. In later chapters the effects of social policy on African American family structures in the 1990s and the twenty-first century are explored. Although U.S. liberal social policy contributed to the erosion of African American two-parent and extended families, conservative social policy and the absence of a national public policy that addressed the needs of African Americans have been responsible for the emergence and disintegration of other types of African American family arrangements.[1] Unquestionably, the absence of a national social policy resulted in the development of structures among African American families that influence their many configurations today. Interestingly, there exists a considerable lack of agreement among scholars regarding the origins and causes of African American family structures. Essentially two major perspectives relative to etiology and causation of African American family structures have been advanced.

## THEORETICAL PERSPECTIVES ON THE STRUCTURE OF THE AFRICAN AMERICAN FAMILY

According to Herskovits and Nobles, the contemporary African American family is predicated on precolonial African culture, with its emphasis on the clan.[2] Conversely, Frazier, Elkins, Moynihan, and Rainwater and Yancey argued that the vicissitudes of slavery destroyed African familial structures and gave rise to a multiplicity of African American family constellations that continue to exist today.[3] Accordingly, the matrifocal character of African American families is offered as evidence that the patriarchal nature of traditional African families was submerged during slavery. Related to this perspective is the thesis of matriarchy as the primary cause of intergenerational poverty, crime, and other forms of social disorganization among African American families. Popularized in 1965 by Daniel P. Moynihan, then the secretary of labor, the analysis of African American family structures as a determinant of economic dependence served as a buttress for the reformulation of social policy. The myriad social welfare programs that ensued were based on Moynihan's research, which polemicized the issue of societal versus matriarchal culpability for the depressed economic status of African Americans. Although social programs were developed and expanded in direct response to the belief in African American family disorganization, there has never been any consensus regarding African American family structure, its origins, causes, or the ability of African American families to perform the functions to which they have been assigned. In fact, the debate over whether African American families are matriarchal and the extent to which they conform to the traditional nuclear family continues more than 25 years later.

In sum, two major disparate theoretical formulations have been proffered. On one hand, African American families are perceived as deviations from the normative family arrangement—that is, the nuclear family—because slavery destroyed the traditional African family. The opposing view holds that in general African American families are primarily nuclear, and that African American nuclear families represent variations brought about due to harsh social and economic conditions. Sudarkasa cites the validity in both models and suggests that a thorough study of African American family organizations be undertaken.[4]

In either case, the controversy surrounding African American family structure is related to the inordinate proportion of African American families with female heads. The fact that African American families have always had a larger percentage of females maintaining households than white families has raised numerous questions regarding its functioning capability, particularly in the area of socializing male children.[5] Yet, concern over the ability of African American families to function at a level comparable to white middle-class families has not been limited to African American families maintained by females. Augmented, extended, and other variations of African American families have also been characterized by some social scientists as being incapable of performing at a level on par with the traditional nuclear family.[6]

Over the last two decades, a considerable amount of time and energy has been devoted to arguments and counterarguments as to whether African American family structure is deviant, variant, or congruent with the idealized nuclear family. Even more alarming is the recognition that social policy has been predicated on these apparent inconsistencies and misconceptions, which plague African American family studies. Whatever their theoretical perspective, social scientists representing both schools of thought have attempted to verify or refute the matriarchal culpability theory. In the past, many liberal sociologists who challenged the matriarchal culpability theory, which placed the onus for African American deprivation on female-controlled African American families, accurately repudiated the prevalence of matriarchy.[7]

Frequently, efforts to confirm or deny the prevalence of African American matriarchy has led to the systematic comparing of African American families to white families, for the purpose of establishing gross similarities or differences in terms of structure and functioning. Still, a thorough analysis of the structure and dynamics of African American families has yet to be conducted. Clearly, scholars who have developed elaborate paradigms in defense of African American family structures, comparing them to white families and explaining variability as solely due to economic factors, are as guilty of proliferating misconceptions about African American family structure as are those who attribute social ills confronting African Americans to African American families alone. Whether one subscribes to the belief that African American family structures are matriarchal, predicated on African cultural tradition, or hybrids of white American familial structures, it is difficult to refute that African American families are unique and do not conform to the traditional nuclear model.

The failure on the part of social scientists to develop a conceptual model that explains the causes and nature of African American family structures and the dynamics that affect the maintenance of African American families is due largely to continuous efforts to analyze African American families using the normative paradigm. Theoreticians, those in the cultural deviance and relativism schools, continue to examine African American families using a middle-class, nuclear model as the barometer. But not all factors that affect white family structures impact similarly upon the structures of African American families. The primary difference is that African American families, because of social and economic hardships, developed unique family arrangements.[8] Hence, African American families became dependent upon external informal support systems to a greater extent than did their white counterparts.[9] Even the most progressive and upwardly mobile African American families have achieved success due to social-support systems that are outside their immediate families. In other words, African American families have not been autonomous units; rather they have historically relied on informal social-support systems for survival. Thus, to compare African American families to white families, either to confirm or rebut theories purporting deviance or relativism, is akin to comparing apples to oranges.

Clearly, social policy dictates the availability of fundamental resources and strongly mediates the provision of goods and services by institutional and noninstitutional service providers. Because African American families, like white families, are dependent on external sources for survival, the survival of all families is to a greater or lesser degree inextricably related to social policy. However, because race is a salient factor that determines differential access to economic opportunity structures, social policy is likely to have a greater impact on African American families. Whether social policy is conservative or liberal, African American families must rely on entities outside of their primary familial unit for essential goods and services. But social policy can and does alter the nature of the exchange relationship between the African American family and institutional and informal social-support systems. In the case of liberal social policy, in which numerous social and economic programs were developed and entitlement was liberalized, government social welfare programs replaced mutual-aid networks, transferring dependency from noninstitutional support systems to institutional ones. In theory, governmental agencies were neither intended nor designed to supplant these informal social-support systems but were developed as emergency measures to bring about economic independence by supplementing existing informal social-support systems.

In addition to their failure to bring about social and economic parity, social welfare programs drastically altered noninstitutional support systems and modified value and belief systems, thereby accelerating the demise of African American two-parent and extended families and the growth of African American female-headed families. Moreover, the introduction of a plethora of social programs did more than modify the structure of African American families. It radically changed the life cycle of African American families.

Before explaining the process by which the structure and life cycle of the African American family adversely underwent modification, it is necessary to dispel two common myths regarding African American families. First is the myth that African American and white families are similar in terms of structure and dynamics. This notion came about largely as a means of refuting the thesis of the matriarchal character of African American families. Still, there is no empirical evidence to support this contention. As early as 1932, when E. Franklin Frazier criticized lower-class African American families for the disproportionate number of female-maintained families, scholars were quick to note that the majority of African American families, like white families, were nuclear.[10] Later, when

Moynihan advanced his thesis on the matriarchal character of African American families, a number of sociologists hastily pointed to the majority of African American families that, they argued, were like white families relative to their nuclear structural arrangement. Gutman added further corroboration to the argument that African American families should not be labeled social anomalies and pathological, based on the fact that many were headed by females; he used census data to establish that as early as 1890, 90 percent of all African American families were of the nuclear type. Unlike many social scientists, Gutman's use of the concept "nuclear type" also implied that African American and white family structures must be considered in relative and not absolute terms.[11]

Although some researchers have gone to great lengths to establish that the African American family is typically structured like the white family, in many instances subfamilies and variable forms are mentioned. For example, Billingsley developed an extensive composite of familial constellations that exist as autonomous units or within African American families.[12] For instance, female-headed families have been found to coexist within a nuclear or extended structure. When subfamilies are found to coexist with nuclear families, the entire structure is redefined, becoming an extended or augmented nuclear family. In fact, the various types of African American familial arrangements that are found independently or within another family arrangement are too numerous to mention. The issue is not that these structures are not found among whites, for they are. Instead, the controversy is over the prevalence of diverse structural arrangements within the African American community. According to traditionalists, the larger the percentage of families of the simple nuclear type, the greater is conformity to societal expectations. Conversely, the lower the percentage of nuclear families, the greater is the use of the deviance label in describing these families.[13] Understandably, the desire to identify African American family structure with that of white families, thereby employing the cultural equivalent perspective, is related to eliminating the deviance label assigned to African American families. If African American families do not differ significantly from white families, then social scientists, policymakers, and society at large would have difficulty maintaining negative labels and stereotypes that affect the treatment of African Americans in society.

There is a surfeit of evidence suggesting that African American families are unique, and while they may approximate those of white families, they are different in composition, structure, and dynamics over the life cycle of the family unit. In addition to Gutman, researchers including Billingsley and Hill recognized that while African American families were largely nuclear in type, their structures did not strictly conform to that of the traditional white nuclear family.[14] Ostensibly, occupants of a socially and economically disadvantaged status are not in a position to maintain an autonomous structural arrangement such as the nuclear family ad infinitum. Therefore, although husband and wife may be present in the home, African American families in general have not conformed to the ideal "nuclear" type of familial structure. Perhaps one major reason for the unique qualities of African American nuclear-type families has been their willingness to modify their structure based on the needs of their consanguine and fictive kin. Thus, referring to African American families with both husband and wife present as nuclear generally requires qualification. Until recently, white families defined as nuclear were more likely to contain a husband, wife, and children over a longer period of the family life cycle than corresponding African American families.

The second misconception about African American families is that their structures are static. Heretofore, African American families have been viewed as static. While it is true that white families, until the 1970s, have been relatively static, African American family structures have been transitory. Over the African American family life cycle, a variety of changes are likely to occur within the family structure. While the frequency of structural change is related to socioeconomic status, African American families are characterized by changing structures across all social classes. Hence, a developmental approach is a necessity for analyzing African American family structure.

According to Billingsley and Hill, the diversity of African American family structures represents adaptations that are necessary to ensure survival.[15] Thus, it is important to note that African American families, with their flexible and dynamic structures, have manifested optimal levels of functioning. Despite adverse social and economic forces, the flexibility of the African American family has ensured its stability and perpetuation. Failure to understand African American families and the propensity among policy makers and social practitioners to mold African American families into an ideal nuclear model through liberal social and economic programs contributed to the deterioration of viable African American family structures.

When the federal government began massive intervention into social-service delivery to ensure equity and equal access to opportunities for African Americans and the poor, there was little agreement on or understanding of the social forces that had created African American family structures. Policymakers and human-service administrators did not understand that the absence of social policy and later the trend toward conservative policy, in conjunction with limited opportunities for African Americans to achieve economic independence, had created African American families that were malleable and mutually dependent on informal support systems for survival and progress. In the case of the majority of African American families that were labeled "nuclear," there was also a failure to recognize that these families, while appearing on the surface to be structured according to the idealized family model, were more likely to undergo structural change over time. And they, like other African American families, were held intact by dependence on noninstitutional support systems. In effect, the thread that kept African American families together was a social-exchange network embedded in a value and belief system based on the norm of reciprocity. It was also this commitment to collective cooperativism that eventuated in the unique structures and dynamics characteristic of African American families. Taking in new members and permitting the coexistence of subfamilies is evidence of the interdependent relationships of African American families and members of informal support systems.[16]

The foregoing myths, along with the misconception of the matriarchal character of African American families, became firmly entrenched in social policy in the 1960s and served as the basis for government expansion of social programs. Thus liberalization of social policy was designed to bring about economic independence by transforming matriarchal African American families into patriarchal structures, with African American males legitimately usurping power from African American women through economic privilege. Regrettably, social programs, while based on the need to destroy what was purported to be the African American matriarchy, ironically created it. In so doing, African American institutions and cultural value systems, which were responsible for keeping African American two-parent families intact, were undermined.

## DEVELOPMENTAL CHANGES IN AFRICAN AMERICAN FAMILY STRUCTURES

In 1960, before the liberalization of social policy, 74 percent of all African American families were maintained by a husband and wife, 22 percent were headed by women, and the remaining 4 percent were families maintained by African American males.[17] By 1980, approximately two decades after the introduction and expansion of social programs, African American families had undergone considerable change. A dramatic increase in the rate of marital dissolutions through separation and divorce resulted in the decline of African American husband-wife families and the growth of African American families headed by women. The percentage of African American families maintained by married couples had declined to 55 percent in 1982, while the number of African American women heading families rose to 41 percent in this same period. In roughly 10 years following the implementation of a plethora of social programs (designed to stabilize African American and poor families), the divorce rates for African American couples escalated from 104 per 1,000 in 1970 to 220 divorces per 1,000 married couples in 1982. By 1980, divorce had become endemic to African American couples, with African American college-educated women being the most likely to occupy a divorced status.[18] The alarming increase in divorce among African American men and women was not the only reason that the structure of African American families began undergoing change. Separation, the most common method of marital dissolution among low-income African Americans, and out-of-wedlock births also had a significant impact on African American family structure, as evidenced by the growing number of female-maintained families. Despite the fact that African American women who give birth to children out of wedlock eventually marry, the percentage choosing to remain single and maintain families independent of a husband has increased drastically. Of African American families with a female head, 12 percent of the female heads of household had never married in 1960; however, the proportion of African American families headed by a woman who had never married reached 32 percent by 1982.[19]

Between 1960 and 1980 other changes in African American families became apparent, suggesting that the life cycle of African American families had been seriously altered.

### Restructuring

Gutman, in his examination of African American family structures from 1750 to 1925, alludes to the necessity for social scientists to explore the changing nature of African American families.[20] However, social scientists have identified numerous patterns of African American families, considering each as static and independent of all others. When researchers have attempted to scientifically investigate variations in African American family structure over the family life cycle, there has been little theoretical basis for doing so.[21] Specifically, Billingsley, in refuting the generalizability of deviance to all African American families, enumerated a number of African American family structures. He argued that these familial constellations reflected the resiliency of African American families, which were able to adapt and survive in the face of inexorable social and economic conditions. In testing Billingsley's model, Williams and Stockton found that there were still other family structures not encompassed in this elaborate model.[22] The notion of the fluidity and malleability of African American family structures serves to enlighten these discussions. While there is an abundance of evidence giving credence to the existence of a multiplicity of family structures, constant changes in African American families have received little attention.

Moreover, before the 1960s, African American families that conformed somewhat to the definition of the simple nuclear family were still likely to undergo more structural changes during the family life cycle than were similarly situated white families. In either case this occurs by the addition or loss of a member to the family structure.

Structural changes in existing families, caused by modifying the composition of family and nonfamily members, are not peculiar to African American families. Indeed, white families also undergo change during the family life cycle. What is unique to African American families is the frequency and causes of restructuring or modifying the original family structure. Allowing new members to become a part of the family unit and later depart is due to economic exigency, more so for African American families than for white families. In general, the most common reason for altering an existing family structure is maturation. At this point in the family life cycle, children leave to establish independent living arrangements, or a family member is lost through death. Historically, African American families restructured for economic expediency as well as maturation of their members. Essentially, white family restructuring has been characterized more by the latter than by financial exigency.

Restructuring families is not a recent phenomenon for African Americans. Gutman found the existence of subfamilies, extended families, and various other forms of African American families existing following slavery.[23] In many instances, these variant family units reflected the modification of existing family structures.

One common reason for family restructuring is the proportion of African American females with children born out of wedlock. Hill and Gutman argue that African American women, while having a relatively high rate of births outside the legal confines of marriage, generally do marry.[24] When the out-of-wedlock child is born, the existing family is modified to accommodate the new child. During the interim between out-of-wedlock births and marriage, many African American women and their children remain in their preexisting family of orientation, thereby creating subfamilies. Thus, from the original family structure emerges a new family constellation. Following marriage, the African American female and her offspring leave her family of orientation, and the structure once again undergoes modification.

Other causes for restructuring include taking in relatives (extended), nonrelatives (augmented), marital dissolution (incipient nuclear), maturation of children, and death. Fluctuations in family structures are indeed normative for African American families.

The creation and expansion of social welfare programs has definitely altered the causes, frequency, and tenure of African American family restructuring. Prior to 1960, a larger proportion of the African American elderly lived in extended families. But in the 1950s Social Security was amended to cover a broader range of occupations in which African Americans were employed, and federally subsidized housing for the elderly was increased; therefore, there was no longer a great need for African American families to provide living accommodations for older relatives.

In addition, public welfare provides various types of public assistance to female single parents. In effect, this assistance decreases dependence on relatives and promotes autonomous living, thereby reducing the period of time a female single parent and her offspring must reside with her family of orientation. The temporal nature of African American family restructuring has also undergone modification. In the absence of social welfare programs, when African American families were restructured the length of time the modified structure remained stable was generally determined by the African American female becoming economically independent of her family due to marriage or employment. In general, these were the dynamics that were likely to restore the family of origin to its status. In general, restructuring of African American families typically resulted in members adapting to a new family constellation for an indefinite period of time.

Of equal importance is the acceleration of changes in the African American family life cycle. Because of the relatively high number of births to unmarried African American adolescents, the process of restructuring has been accelerated. In 1983, 55 percent of all African American children were born out of wedlock. Fifty-seven percent of these children were born to females under the age of 17, and one-third of these births were to African American teens 15 to 17 years of age. Moreover, 36 percent were first births.[25]

Undoubtedly, large numbers of African American families undergo restructuring to accept related children. The actual duration of such living arrangements, with the mother and her children living within an established family, is an area that requires empirical research. Although a large percentage of out-of-wedlock births are to teenage mothers the availability of social welfare programs tends to lessen the period of time during which the African American female and her children must be dependent on her family of orientation.[26]

Once we recognize the changing nature of African American families, it becomes clear that comparing African American family structures to those of white families is of little utility. This was especially true before the 1970s, when white families were primarily restructuring due to marriage, maturation of children, and death of family members. Today, as in African American families, marital dissolution is increasingly becoming a frequent cause of restructuring among white families. Conditions that give rise to family restructuring for African Americans, while including the reasons that white families restructure, continue to be closely related to economic factors. Restructuring out of economic necessity as well as for maturation has been a salient characteristic of African American families. Moreover, the economically depressed status of African American families, linked with the absence of a national social policy designed to promote economic independence, has served to facilitate the establishment of a complex social-exchange system. Thus, the formation of self-help networks led ultimately to the malleability of African American family structures. The African American family's readiness to absorb individuals in need of food, clothing, shelter, and the like set the stage for the continuous reshaping of African American families. It is important to note that prior to liberal social policy, African American families were restructured to ensure stability. After the enactment and expansion of liberal social policy, African American families have increasingly undergone restructuring as a result of marital instability. Furthermore, since the inception of liberal social policy, African American families have rarely needed to accommodate elderly relatives and nonrelatives, so family restructuring began to occur almost exclusively to accommodate women and children.

### Serial Families

The movement from one family structure to another, or serial families, is also common among the African American population. Historically, family mobility among African Americans has occurred because of economic hardships and to maintain marital stability. More recently, serial families, like restructuring for African Americans, tends to be related to marital instability. Since two out of three marriages among African American couples end in divorce, and a larger number of lower-income African American families prefer separation as a method of resolving marital inharmony, the maritally disrupted African American female and her children frequently become displaced.[27] Typically, when marriages are dissolved, the African American female and her children return to her family of orientation. There she receives the emotional and financial support necessary to reduce stresses associated with uncoupling. Once the African American female is financially and emotionally capable of social reintegration, she leaves with her children to establish an independent living arrangement. Because of the tenuous nature of employment, lower wages for African American women, inflationary costs of living, and noncompliance with child-support payments, independent living for the separated or divorced African American female with children is precarious at best. Thus, it is understandable that African American female single parents are forced to move between family structures, establishing and reestablishing a temporary residence within their families of orientation. Moreover, since health insurance is not universally available, unexpected medical expenses can also trigger serial families, forcing African American women and their children to resume dependence on relatives and friends for shelter and other basic physiological needs.

The phenomenon of moving from one family structure to another among African American families is not new. Shortly after emancipation and throughout the mass migration of African Americans to the North, prior to World War I and again at the time of World War II, entire African American families in search of employment and improved living conditions established a pattern of serial families.

Billingsley and Billingsley state that African American men and women wandered from town to town establishing temporary living arrangements with various African American families.[28] These contacts were made possible by social networking. When a friend or relative in the South recommended an individual to a family in the North it was highly probable that the family would "put the individual up" until he or she could secure employment.

A resurgence of serial family structuring has paralleled the increase in the rate of marital dissolution among African Americans. Once separated or divorced, African American female single parents discover their standard of living decreases substantially, making it necessary for them to return to their families of orientation until they can financially afford independent living. Because of occupational segregation and lack of salable job skills, African American female single parents have financial difficulties that affect the maintenance of independent households. Consequently, for some African American single women and their children, particularly unwed adolescents, serial families are an integral part of life.

## ABSENCE OF SOCIAL POLICY AND THE VARIABILITY OF AFRICAN AMERICAN FAMILY STRUCTURES

Aside from a brief time during Reconstruction, when the Freedmen's Bureau provided goods and services to African American men, women, and children, African American families received a modicum of institutional support until the 1960s.[29] Because of strong public opposition to the federal government providing aid to the needy, the Freedman's Bureau was disbanded in 1872, seven years after its inception. With the exception of short periods of high employment, African American men in the United States have experienced unusually high rates of unemployment. Faced with joblessness, underemployment, and limited job skills, African American men, women, and children were compelled to modify existing family structures and to move often between families. Unquestionably, restructuring and serial families enabled African American families to remain intact and to cope with dire social and economic conditions.

Because social welfare services were unavailable to augment subsistence-level incomes, African American families relied almost exclusively on informal social-support systems for their survival. During the period following Emancipation and throughout the 1940s, African American families expanded and contracted as members, both relatives and nonrelatives, arrived and departed. Augmenting families with new members to consolidate and preserve resources proved to be an efficacious adaptive mechanism and served to preserve the basic two-parent structure of the African American family.

## FEDERALIZING SOCIAL POLICY

It was not until 1935 that the federal government was forced to formulate a national social policy to relieve economic pressures brought about by the Depression. The passage of the Social Security Act in 1935 marked the federal government's first attempt since Emancipation to address the needs of the economically disadvantaged on a massive scale. Until then, states and voluntary organizations had provided fragmented social welfare services to the poor. Because of racial discrimination in the administration of social services, African American families had difficulty receiving public assistance.[30] By creating social insurance, public assistance, and health and welfare services under the Social Security Act, the federal government temporarily restored productivity necessary for consumption. The government's action helped restore the people's confidence in the private enterprise system. This thrust toward providing for the "deserving poor" and ensuring economic well-being for the masses was directly related to social unrest.[31] To take the drastic measure of enacting a national policy to provide assistance to individuals who were unable to care for themselves represented a radical shift in public policy. Indeed, the federal government's posture at that time corroborates the supposition advanced by Piven and Cloward: that social policy is formulated on the basis of interest group politics, and when the populace demonstrates unrest, social programs are created.[32] Conversely, when social order is restored, social programs are rescinded.

In effect, the federal government had moved from the absence of social policy—a laissez-faire attitude—to liberal social policy. Despite the far-reaching effects of these social programs, African American families benefited little from the federal government's involvement in social welfare programs at this time.

Benefits derived from Social Security were not extended to individuals employed in service industries and agricultural occupations, thereby excluding the majority of African American men and women. When the social-insurance program was first instituted, only workers in industry and commerce were entitled to benefits. At that time, 34 percent of all African American workers were employed in service jobs and another one-third were farm workers.[33]

Similarly, the Aid to Dependent Children (ADC) program did not significantly affect the stability of African American two-parent families, including those with unemployed male heads. Initially, since the beneficiaries of ADC were children, both husbands and wives were excluded

from obtaining monetary benefits. Therefore, there was no exclusion of
the father. Hence, there was no social welfare policy that excluded males,
thereby disrupting the family. To support this contention, at the end of
the decade, there was even a slight increase in the percentage of African
American families with both husband and wife present. In 1940, 77 percent of all African American families contained two parents, compared to
77.7 percent in 1950. Besides, the administration of social welfare programs remained decentralized at the state level, where differential administration continued to result in the exclusion of African Americans.[34]

A decrease in the proportion of African American families headed by
women is further evidence that the new ADC program had virtually no
effect on African American family stability. In 1940, 17.9 percent of African
American families had female heads, compared to 1950 when African
American women maintaining families accounted for 17.6 percent of all
African American families.

African American unemployment rose to 50 percent in the peak of the
Depression, while the corresponding rate was 25 percent for whites. Although African Americans suffered significantly higher rates of joblessness and poverty than whites, in 1933 only 18 percent of African American
family heads of households and 15 percent in 1935 had been certified by
the government for relief.[35] Moreover, in 1940 three out of four African
Americans lived in the rural South, where racial discrimination was more
pronounced in the administration of social welfare programs. As a consequence, the formulation of a national social policy to provide assistance
to the old and new poor had little effect on the socioeconomic status or
structure of the African American family. In essence, the initial consequences of early social welfare programs for African American families
was tantamount to the earlier period, when a national social policy was
nonexistent.

With a commitment to the free enterprise system, the federal government had little interest in maintaining or expanding social welfare services. Most efforts designed to bring about economic independence for
poor families were considered emergency measures, and by the mid-1940s
many federal appropriations to social programs created under the New
Deal had been reduced.[36] African American families derived few benefits
from these innovative social programs, for attached to these temporary
emergency measures was the nineteenth-century philosophy that poverty
was inextricably related to character flaws and personal turpitude.[37] Racial
stereotypes categorizing African Americans as lazy and shiftless created
negative sentiments toward African American families as recipients of
public assistance. Further, these beliefs prevented many African American
families from receiving services that they needed and to which they were
entitled. Consequently, African American families' dependence on infor-

mal social-support systems accelerated during the Depression years, as did their needs.

## QUASI CONSERVATISM

Social scientists have characterized the period from the mid-1940s throughout the 1950s as one of political conservatism and economic growth.[38] During this period, there were no catastrophic changes in social welfare policy or in the structure of African American families. In general, changes in policy and African American family structures were incremental in nature. Major social welfare programs legislated in the 1940s and 1950s were the National School Lunch Program in 1946, the Hill-Burton Hospital Construction Bill in 1946, and a special Milk Program in 1954. Moreover, Congress legislated the incorporation of disability insurance in Social Security programs, a new category of public assistance for the disabled, medical assistance to families receiving public assistance, and the expansion of the ADC program to include a relative with whom the child was living (Aid to Families with Dependent Children—AFDC).

The 1950s brought legislation that increased the number of potential beneficiaries and liberalized benefit payments through modifications in benefit formulas. Although several new welfare programs were instituted, this era represented economic growth and an attitude of social complacency.[39] Despite the institution and expansion of social welfare programs, administration of these programs was conservative, if not reactionary. Nowhere was this more noticeable than in the public disaffection with public assistance, particularly the AFDC program. Throughout the country, states implemented punitive policies and procedures for limiting welfare rolls. Only social policies intended to enhance the lives of the middle class met with public approval.

"Man-in-the-house," "suitable home," and residency policies were adopted by numerous states to remove welfare recipients from the rolls. Of all the policies, the one used most effectively to eliminate African Americans as welfare recipients was the requirement that welfare recipients be a resident of the state. By enforcing residency policies, states were able to prevent African American migrants who moved from the South to the North from acquiring public assistance.

Midnight raids to determine if welfare mothers were ineligible for aid by virtue of living with a related or nonrelated man occurred with frequency. Despite the intended deterrent effect of these policies, the number of beneficiaries of public assistance grew 13 percent between 1950 and 1960. Much of this growth occurred in the AFDC program. The proportion of AFDC families that were African American, according to Handel, increased from 36 percent in 1953 to 43 percent in 1961.[40] The elderly and widows with children received aid from Social Security, and the AFDC program became widely associated with mothers and children with absent fathers. Although white females and their children constituted a numerical majority of recipients, the program was viewed as one for African American families deserted by husbands and for African American women with illegitimate children. This labeling occurred because two-thirds of African American welfare families resided in central cities of metropolitan areas, while white families were dispersed throughout small towns and were less visible.[41]

The first real indication that a relationship existed between social welfare programs and the stability of African American families became apparent in the 1950s. Gradually, observable changes in African American family structures began to take place. For most of the decade, African American male employment was unusually high. During the Korean War, between 1951 and 1953, the jobless rates for African Americans were the lowest (ranging from approximately 4.5 percent to 5.4 percent).[42] Still, the proportion of welfare recipients who were African American mothers and children increased. This growth was largely due to a drastic increase in the ratio of African American children born out of wedlock, which climbed from 71.2 per 1,000 in 1950 to 98.3 per 1,000 unmarried women in 1960. Earlier changes in social policy, and those legislated during this decade, set the trend for major changes in African American family structure.

The African American extended family also began to undergo structural changes. As more and more African American males experienced a shift in occupation from farm worker to unskilled laborer, a larger number of African Americans were entitled to Social Security benefits. Furthermore, Congress moved to extend coverage to occupations that had initially been excluded. This had a definite impact on enabling the elderly to become less dependent on their children and permitted the establishment of independent living arrangements. Throughout the general population, the number of related subfamilies declined from 2.5 million in 1950 to 1.5 million in 1960. Likewise, unrelated subfamilies decreased from 465,000 to 207,000 during the same 10-year period. Moreover, the number of subfamilies continued to decline until the mid-1970s.[43] Equally important was the amendment to the Social Security Act entitling relatives of dependent children to receive public assistance.

Together these new laws were responsible for altering the African American family structure and life cycle. These policies resulted in the attenuation of extended and augmented families and subfamilies. Also, amendments to Social Security, increasing benefits to the disabled, had an impact on the structure of African American families. Hence, a decline in African American extended and augmented families and subfamilies took place.

Although liberal social welfare legislation created economic independence for the elderly, conservative administration of social welfare programs, especially in the AFDC program, promoted marital conflict, as welfare policies and practices required male absence as a condition for eligibility. Hence, through overt and covert practices, social welfare agencies, not African American wives, forced men out of the home. Thus, the African American female-headed household, created through separation, divorce, or nonmarriage, has been system precipitated. One could expect an escalation in the dissolution of marriages among African Americans and an increase in the number of African American women with children who choose to permanently forego marriage. The trends in both of these areas were initiated in the 1950s and became firmly established by the 1980s. By excluding African American males through the institution of the "man-in-the-house" policy in the 1950s and maintaining this policy in the 1960s and 1970s, and by systematically entitling women, and not their husbands, to benefits, African American two-parent families were undermined.

Overall, the decade of the 1950s, while defined as a period of social conservatism, had manifestations of liberalism. As further evidence of the quasi-conservative nature of this era was the *Brown v. Board of Education* Supreme Court decision, in which the court ruled that "separate but equal" in educational institutions was unconstitutional. Although this decision was liberal, for the time the court assumed a conservative stance relative to enforcing compliance.[44] Taylor states that it was not until more than 15 years later, in 1971, that the court determined that mandatory desegregation (including busing, if necessary) was the only way to end segregation.[45] This aura of conservatism belies the passage of liberal social welfare policies and the expanded role of the federal government in social-service delivery. Despite moderate to high rates of employment for African American males, African American family structure began reflecting the adverse impact of liberal social policy. Although the African American elderly began acquiring economic independence because of policy initiatives, underclass African American women with children began to transfer their dependence from informal social-support systems and their spouses to social welfare agencies. What this suggests is that extreme measures to deter potential recipients were essentially ineffective. For African American families, restructuring and serial families took on new dimensions.

## EXPANSION OF LIBERAL SOCIAL POLICY: A SOCIAL EXPERIMENT THAT FAILED

As William Graham Sumner said, "It is dangerous to tinker with societies in the same way we carry out experiments in the medical field. When you experiment on an individual the worst that can happen is that the person will die. But society is an eternal organism. When you experiment on it, whatever the results, it is going to live on."[46]

The experiment that took place encompassed far more than the "great experiment" examined by Charles Murray.[47] Murray limits his discussion to an actual study, the Negative Income Tax Experiment (NIT), which failed to prove that a guaranteed income would not adversely affect adult family members' desire to work. Nor am I referring to the plethora of scientific investigations on the relationship between social welfare programs and family stability.[48]

The "social experiment" to which I refer was poorly conceptualized, had conflicting hypotheses, and had numerous uncontrolled variables, not to mention diverse methodologies. The purpose of this experiment was to explain, predict, and control poverty and its adverse effect on the dynamics and structure of families in America. Different underlying assumptions regarding the etiology of poverty, formulated on the basis of socioeconomic class, political persuasion, and other social and economic factors, led to the social experiment more commonly known as liberal social policy.

The gradual expansion in the 1950s of the federal government's role in social-service delivery set the stage for major changes that took place throughout the 1960s and 1970s. Responding to the demands of the civil rights movement and other social activists, the federal government developed public policies (initiated in the Kennedy administration and expanded under President Johnson's War on Poverty) that made it the focal point for funding, developing, and monitoring social welfare services. Moreover, the liberalization of eligibility, which was legislated in the 1950s, was further revised to enable even larger numbers of persons to benefit from social programs. Civil disorders, protest movements, African American population growth, and a sharp increase in African American unemployment rates between 1958 and 1963 contributed to the drastic reformulation of social policy. Unlike the policies of the New Deal, social policy enacted during this twenty-year period was designed for the "old" poor, in which African American families were overrepresented. For the second time in the history of this country, policymakers, heavily influenced by the Johnson administration and the vociferous African American populace, made monetary allocations and proposals for the express purpose of creating stability among poor and African American families. The basis for the specific agenda of social and economic programs, proposed and implemented, was a report reflecting the status of African American families conducted by Moynihan. In effect, the Johnson administration, relying heavily on Moynihan's findings, set out to change the structure of African American families to make them conform to the middle-class nuclear model. At the time, the probability and consequences of failure of this experiment were not considered. Although the details of these programs will be explored in a later chapter, a preliminary discussion is presented here. Moreover, African Americans, the largest single minority recipient class, were not integral to the planning, implementing, or evaluating of these programs.

According to Alexander and Weber, the period beginning in the early 1960s marked the most comprehensive revision of social welfare programs since 1935.[49] Many social programs, while designed to aid poor families irrespective of race or ethnicity, were developed specifically to improve the social and economic plight of African American families by remedying past social injustices. These programs included financial assistance, housing subsidies, food stamps, child-development centers, medical care, youth programs, work-training opportunities, and numerous other programs. In addition, civil rights legislation such as affirmative action laws, the voting rights act, and fair housing legislation were designed to bring about social and economic parity for African Americans.

As social programs were instituted and expanded, the hopes and aspirations of African American men and women were raised. But they were not alone in expecting that social and economic programs would be cost effective and ultimately elevate the socioeconomic status of African American families. That expanded liberal social policy would contribute to the disintegration of African American two-parent families and the creation of a permanent underclass was neither intended nor projected.[50] It is extremely important to note that although many liberal social policies were designed to elevate the status of African American and poor families, there were numerous unintended effects. The fact that social policies can and do have such consequences was recognized by Robert Merton, a sociologist, as early as 1936, and by Walter Williams, an economist, and later by Robert Hill, a sociologist.[51] While many lauded the inventive, comprehensive planning and administration of social and economic programs, others cautioned that the government's increased involvement in social-service delivery could have fissiparous consequences for the African American family. In this vein, McCray warned of the potential threat to the mutual-aid network's ability to continue to influence the maintenance of the African American two-parent family. She stated, "For African American families and African American people, there is but one danger, if these informal adaptive and coping mechanisms are pulled into the bureaucratic structure, the informal nature of the network and the network itself could be destroyed."[52]

Liberal social policy, expanded in the 1960s and continued throughout the 1970s, did create divisiveness within African American institutions and noninstitutional support systems. In spite of oppressive social and economic conditions, high rates of unemployment, inadequate housing, and racial discrimination, African American two-parent families in various forms had remained intact prior to the 1950s. Until the expansion of liberal social policy, informal social-support systems, led by the Black Church, espoused the importance of sharing and caring among African American families. Keeping African American two-parent families intact was the primary objective of these self-help networks. However, the government through the sponsorship of social welfare agencies created the following conditions, which contributed to the disintegration of African American two-parent families:

1. Traditional African American institutions were replaced by white institutions (e.g., schools, colleges, businesses).
2. The influence of the Black Church and mutual-aid network was usurped by the federal government.
3. The African American family's value orientation was transformed from cooperative collectivism to competitive individualism.
4. The valuation of an individual's worth was based on the acquisition and possession of material wealth, rather than traditional criteria, whereby personal worth and esteem were predicated on helping others.
5. The transformation of overt discriminatory practices to covert forms of racial inequities led to institutional racial discrimination.

In addition to contributing to the decline of mutual-aid networks, liberal social programs designed to effect racial integration served to facilitate the decline of African American institutions. These institutions had assumed prominence and viability by functioning as secondary socializing agents. Before the 1960s, African American students who were enrolled in colleges and universities generally attended predominantly African American institutions. In addition, public schools that were highly segregated provided moral support as well as academic preparation for African American children. These social systems served as buffers. They shielded African American youth from social injustices while providing them with valuable information on how to interact effectively in dual worlds. One other important function of traditional African American institutions was to inculcate African American children with a sense of cultural pride and self-worth. Traditional African American institutions, as agents of socialization, imbued African American children with self-esteem through positive reinforcement and African American adult role models. Since most individuals employed by these institutions were African American, they acted as positive and constructive role models for African American children to emulate. The advent of liberal social policy should have enhanced such systems rather than establishing substitutes for them. One of the most devastating consequences of liberal social policy is that it attempted to recreate African American culture in terms of both structure and dynamics. In effect, African American colleges—which had historically depended on African Americans for support, mainly because African Americans had few alternatives—lost that support as African American youth began to transfer en masse to predominantly white public schools and colleges. Now, African American institutions and African American families are not as mutually supportive as in the past. In this case, the African American family, which relied heavily on educational institutions to help socialize their offspring, was placed at a disadvantage. However, this problem should come as little surprise; W.E.B. Du Bois warned of this possibility some years ago. He cautioned that integration alone would result in an environment that was likely to impede the educational process for African American youth.[53]

Moreover, the Black Church and mutual-aid network, which prescribed behavior for African American family members, began to lose its influence on African American two-parent families as the government became the chief service provider. Added to the declining influence of these systems was the societal imperative that African Americans become more culturally integrated, thereby abandoning traditional African American values and accepting majority cultural values and norms. Thus, the government acquired control over African American family structure and dynamics. Unlike the Black Church and mutual-aid network, the government mandated that the husband be absent as a condition for recipiency. Given what appeared to be a surfeit of educational, training, and employment opportunities generated by increased federal money to social programs, African American families expected to derive enormous benefits and elevate their socioeconomic status. As a result, African American families began to incorporate competitive individualism—a value characteristic of the larger society—into their own value orientation. It was believed that this mainstream ideology was necessary if African Americans were to transform their families into autonomous nuclear family units.

Equally devastating to African American families was the acceptance by African Americans of a new set of criteria for measuring an individual's worth. Before the liberalization of social welfare services, African American families ascribed status to individuals based on their willingness to help others.[54] In many ways, this method of determining a person's worth conflicted with capitalism, with its emphasis on competition as the means of acquiring wealth. On the basis of the capitalistic value orientation, the worth of an individual is commensurate with the amount of wealth that he or she possesses. Since African American families were often extended or augmented or consisted of subfamilies, material possessions were important to the extent that they were shared with others.[55] Thus, family members who shared their resources were accorded status and esteem.

Competitive individualism as a value system had greater applicability to white families with a male head, since he was the most likely family member to be involved in competition in the labor force. Hence, resources were initially acquired and mediated by the male head of the household and later shared with members of his nuclear family. Because African American two-parent families, for the most part, have been characterized by dual wage earners and extended, augmented, and subfamilies, sharing and merging resources took precedence over a monopoly of resources by any one family member. In effect, structural barriers resulted in African American families subscribing to cooperative collectivism for the purpose of survival and advancement. Operating under the premise that social obstacles were being removed, African American families began to embrace values inherent in the larger society.

Differential progress of African American females and African American males in educational and occupational arenas between 1960 and 1980 led to the further devaluation of African American males. In effect, a greater number of African American women than men received college degrees. Further, more African American women moved into white-collar occupations than did their male counterparts. The higher rate of occupational mobility among African American women versus African American men added to the belief that African American males who were unable to acquire wealth were to blame, not society. The message that was propagated throughout society, as a result of the new social and economic programs, was that those who did not experience economic mobility had simply failed to take advantage of these opportunities.

Among the conditions that led in the 1960s to the social revolution and liberal social policy were blatant discriminatory practices, to which African Americans were subjected throughout the country. Although these practices varied from region to region and were more pronounced in the South, the fact that African Americans were victims of social injustices could not be denied. Because the federal government incorporated a fairly rigorous system for monitoring and enforcing affirmative action programs and the fair administration of all social programs, efforts to deny African Americans, women, and other minorities equal access to opportunities became insidious and difficult for any external monitoring agent to prove. What has yet to occur is a systematic method by which these groups can efficiently substantiate claims of institutional discrimination.

Ostensibly, liberal social policy did not bring about economic independence for African American families. In light of this unanticipated outcome, African American families more than ever needed the support of African American institutions and informal support systems. Since the government had replaced the Black Church and facilitated the decline of mutual-aid networks, African American families had little choice but to increase their dependency on the government. Thus, the continuous, yet invidious, exclusion of African Americans from full and equal participation in the economic system and the African American families' acceptance of a new value system has resulted in the deterioration of African

American two-parent families and other salient institutions in the African American community. Not all African American families are recipients of social welfare, yet middle-class African Americans also failed to experience the economic gains that should have been forthcoming.

Unfortunately, African American families, regardless of socioeconomic status, did not experience the economic growth that had been projected. Raised expectations caused by liberal social policy remained unfulfilled. In general, underclass African American families did not move to the middle class, and middle-class African American families did not become members of the upper class. Although some families did experience upward mobility and become members of the middle class, it is also the case that some African American families descended the socioeconomic ladder, as the economy became inflationary and old-line industries declined.[56] The failure to meet these expectations was equally devastating to African American middle-class families. In spite of affirmative action programs and educational loans and grants, African American working-class and middle-class families made modest gains. And while many solidified their economic status, there is little evidence to suggest that a substantial percentage of African American families were elevated to a higher stratum. In the aftermath of liberalism, the failure to convert underclass African American families to stable and viable economic units is still attributed, by many, to the African American family.[57]

One of the greatest tragedies during the era of liberal social policy was the failure of scholars, policymakers, and practitioners to recognize the adverse effects of social programs on African American family structure. Instead, there were arguments for the defensibility of these programs, despite growing evidence of their debilitating impact. Perhaps the conviction that social programs were long overdue and that something was better than nothing, as well as the fear that criticism would bring about the elimination of social and economic programs, clouded the signs of the deterioration of the African American family and other microcultural institutions and silenced individuals who would have otherwise raised these issues. A number of social, economic, and political processes prevented the necessary revision of social and economic programs, but leaving these programs basically unaltered has contributed to the demise of African American two-parent and extended families, as well as other African American institutions.

What happened to African American family structures in the 1980s, when the country entered a true period of social conservatism, both in terms of legislation and administration of social programs, is examined in chapter 7. And a close examination of African American family structure in the twenty-first century, in chapter 10, reveals marked changes as African American families continue to be affected by institutional race, sex, and class inequality that neither liberal social policy as it was formulated nor more conservative policies that followed failed to eliminate or significantly diminish.

## NOTES

1. K. Sue Jewell, "Use of Social Welfare Programs and the Disintegration of the Black Nuclear Family," *Western Journal of Black Studies* 8 (winter 1984): 196.

2. Melville Herskovits, *The Myth of the Negro Past* (Boston: Beacon, 1970), pp. 182–184; and Wade Nobles, "Africanity: Its Role in Black Families," *Black Scholar* 9 (June 1974): 10–17.

3. Stanley Elkins, *Slavery: A Problem in American Institutional and Intellectual Life* (New York: Grosset & Dunlap, 1963); E. Franklin Frazier, *The Free Negro Family* (Nashville: Fisk University Press, 1932); E. Franklin Frazier, *The Negro Family in Chicago* (Chicago: University of Chicago Press, 1932); E. Franklin Frazier, *The Negro Family in the United States* (Chicago: University of Chicago Press, 1939); Daniel P. Moynihan, *The Negro Family: The Case for National Action* (Washington, D.C.: U.S. Government Printing Office, 1965); and Lee Rainwater and William Yancey, *The Moynihan Report and the Politics of Controversy* (Cambridge, Mass.: M.I.T. Press, 1967).

4. Niara Sudarkasa, "Interpreting the African Heritage in Afro-American Family Organization," in *Black Families*, ed. Harriette Pipes McAdoo (Beverly Hills, Calif.: Sage Publications, 1981), pp. 37–40.

5. Herbert Gutman, *The Black Family in Slavery and Freedom: 1750–1925* (New York: Pantheon Books, 1976), p. 633.

6. J. Allen Williams Jr. and Robert Stockton, "Black Family Structures and Functions: An Empirical Examination of Some Suggestions Made by Billingsley," *Journal of Marriage and the Family* 35 (February 1973): 48.

7. Donna Franklin, *Ensuring Inequality: The Structural Transformation of the African American Family* (New York: Oxford University Press, 1997), pp.153–181; and Robert Hill, *The Strengths of Black Families* (New York: Emerson Hall, 1972), p. 18.

8. Andrew Billingsley, *Black Families in White America* (Englewood Cliffs, N.J.: Prentice-Hall, 1968); and Hill, *The Strengths of Black Families*, p. 5.

9. Carol Stack, *All Our Kin: Strategies for Survival in a Black Community* (New York: Harper & Row, 1974), p. 25; Carrie Allen McCray, "The Black Woman and Family Roles," in *The Black Woman*, ed. La Frances Rodgers-Rose (Beverly Hills, Calif.: Sage Publications, 1980), p. 70.

10. Frazier, *The Negro Family in Chicago*; and Frazier, *The Free Negro Family*.

11. Gutman, *The Black Family in Slavery and Freedom, 1750–1925*, pp. 432–460.

12. Billingsley, *Black Families in White America*.

13. Talcott Parsons, "Age and Sex in the Structure of the United States," *American Sociological Review* 7 (1942): 604; and Talcott Parsons and Robert F. Bales, *Family, Socialization and the Interaction Process* (Glencoe, Ill.: Free Press, 1955), p. 10.

14. Billingsley, *Black Families in White America*; and Hill, *The Strengths of Black Families*, p. 5.

15. Ibid.

16. Hill, *The Strengths of Black Families*, pp. 5–8.

17. U.S. Bureau of the Census, *The Social and Economic Status of the Black Population in the United States: An Historical View, 1790–1978*. Series P-23, No. 80 (Washington, D.C.: U.S. Government Printing Office, June 1979), p. 103.

18. U.S. Bureau of the Census, *America's Black Population, 1970 to 1982: A Statistical View*. Series P-10/POP 83-1 (Washington, D.C.: U.S. Government Printing Office, July 1983), p. 18.

19. Ibid., pp. 17–18.

20. Gutman, *The Black Family in Slavery and Freedom, 1750–1925*, pp. 432–460.

21. Ann Fischer, Joseph Beasley, and Carl Harter, "The Occurrence of the Extended Family of Procreation: A Developmental Approach to Negro Family Structure," *Journal of Marriage and the Family* (May 1968): 291.

22. Williams and Stockton, "Black Family Structures and Functions," p. 47.

23. Gutman, *The Black Family in Slavery and Freedom, 1750–1925*, pp. 1–44.

24. Gutman, *The Black Family in Slavery and Freedom, 1750–1925*, pp. 363–460; and Hill, *The Strengths of Black Families*, pp. 17–26.

25. "What Must Be Done About Children Having Children?" *Ebony*, March 1985, p. 76.

26. Ibid., p. 78.

27. Billingsley, *Black Families in White America*; and James McGhee, "The Black Family Today and Tomorrow," in *The State of Black America*, ed. National Urban League (New York: National Urban League, 1985).

28. Andrew Billingsley and Amy Billingsley, "Negro Family Life in America," *Social Service Review* 39 (September 1965): 310.

29. Andrew Billingsley and Jeanne Giovannoni, *Children of the Storm* (New York: Harcourt, Brace, Jovanovich), pp. 1–18, 41–43.

30. June Axinn and Herman Levin, *Social Welfare* (New York: Dodd, Mead and Company, 1975).

31. Carolyn Bell, *The Economics of the Ghetto* (New York: Pegasus, 1970).

32. Frances Piven and Richard Cloward, *Regulating the Poor: The Functions of Public Welfare* (New York: Vintage, 1971), pp. 3–41.

33. U.S. Bureau of the Census, *The Social and Economic Status of the Black Population*, p. 62.

34. Axinn and Levin, *Social Welfare*.

35. Ibid.

36. Robert McElvaine, *The Great Depression: America, 1929–1941* (New York: Times Books, 1984), pp. 306–332.

37. Gerald Handel, *Social Welfare in Western Society* (New York: Random House, 1982), pp. 41–73.

38. McElvaine, *The Great Depression*, pp. 323–349.

39. Axinn and Levin, *Social Welfare*.

40. Ibid.

41. Ibid.

42. U.S. Bureau of the Census, *The Social and Economic Status of the Black Population*, p. 61.

43. U.S. Bureau of the Census, *Statistical Abstract of the United States: National Data Book and Guide to Sources*, 106th ed. (Washington, D.C.: U.S. Government Printing Office, 1986), p. 39.

44. William. L. Taylor, "Access to Economic Opportunity: Lessons Since Brown," in *Minority Report: What Has Happened to Blacks, Hispanics, American Indians and Other Minorities in the Eighties*, ed. Leslie W. Dunbar (New York: Pantheon Books, 1984), pp. 36–37.

45. Ibid.

46. William Tucker, "Kindness Is Killing the Black Family," *This World*, January 1985, p. 7.

47. Charles Murray, *Losing Ground: American Social Policy, 1950–1980* (New York: Basic Books, 1984), pp. 147–153.

48. Marjorie Honig, "AFDC Income, Recipient Rates, and Family Dissolution," *Journal of Human Resources* 9 (summer 1974): 302; Mary Jo Bane, *Economic Influence on Divorce and Remarriage* (Cambridge, Mass.: Center for the Study of Public Policy, 1975); Heather L. Ross and Isabel V. Sawhill, *Time of Transition: The Growth of Families Headed by Women* (Washington, D.C., Urban Institute, 1975); Oliver C. Moles, "Marital Dissolution and Public Assistance Payments: Variation among American States," *Journal of Social Issues* 32 (winter 1976): 87; and Stephen Bahr, "The Effects of Welfare on Marital Stability and Remarriage," *Journal of Marriage and the Family* 41 (1979): 553.

49. Chauncey A. Alexander and David N. Weber, "Social Welfare: Historical Dates," *Encyclopedia of Social Work*, no. 17 (1977): 1487–1503.

50. Douglas Glasgow, *The Black Underclass* (New York: Vintage Books, 1981), pp. 3–4.

51. Robert K. Merton, "The Unanticipated Consequences of Purposive Social Action," *American Sociological Review* 1 (1936): 894–904; Walter E. Williams, *The State against Blacks* (New York: McGraw-Hill, 1982), pp. 67–73; and Robert B. Hill, "Economic Forces, Structural Discrimination, and Black Family Instability," in *Black Families*, ed. Harold E. Cheatham and James B. Stewart (New Brunswick, N.J.: Transaction Publishers, 1997), pp. 87–105.

52. McCray, "The Black Woman and Family Roles," p. 77.

53. Meyer Weinberg, *A Chance to Learn* (Cambridge, England: Cambridge University Press, 1977), p. 87.

54. McCray, "The Black Woman and Family Roles," pp. 70–71.

55. Ibid.

56. "America's Underclass, Broken Lives: A Nation Apart," *U.S. News and World Report*, 17 March 1986), p. 20; and Robert B. Hill, *Economic Policies and Black Progress: Myths and Realities* (Washington, D.C.: National Urban League, 1981), pp. 22–26.

57. George Gilder, *Wealth and Poverty* (New York: Basic Books, 1981); Murray, *Losing Ground*; and Lawrence Mead, *Beyond Entitlement* (New York: Free Press, 1986).

# CHAPTER 3

# Informal Social-Support Systems

Although we live in a society that stresses individual and familial autonomy, few families are able to function without external support. Despite a societal philosophy of individualism and an emphasis on the nuclear family as an ideal prototype, white families, like their African American counterparts, have had to rely on social-support systems for their survival. One major difference has been the source and nature of support available to African American and white families. Until the 1960s, African American families depended almost exclusively on informal social-support systems or mutual-aid networks for primary and secondary goods and services. Conversely, white families have had both institutional and noninstitutional support systems as providers of essential goods and services. While African American and white families have relied to a greater or lesser extent on these external sources for assistance, formal agencies have tended to systematically exclude African American families. As a result, an interdependent relationship was established between African American families and members of informal helping networks.

The African American family's ability to make positive contributions to society and to successfully socialize its offspring, while confronted with social barriers, has necessitated its dependence on sources outside the two-parent family unit. For years, the great demand and need for goods and services and the relative absence of aid from formal social-service agencies prevented African American families from embracing the precepts of social isolation and independence, which had gained widespread acceptance as large numbers of African American families gravitated to urban areas during and after the American industrial revolution. According to McCray, it was this "sense of caring and social responsibility in the Black community, plus strong kinship bonds and other reinforcements that kept black families together and strengthened their functioning."[1]

Interestingly, even for white families, the notions of autonomy, privacy, and the use of institutional and noninstitutional support systems have frequently undergone modification. Clearly, a cyclical pattern, representing varying degrees of familial dependence on formal and informal agencies, has evolved throughout American society.[2] Many consider the passage of the Elizabethan Poor Laws in 1601 to be the historical event that had the most profound influence on the formulation of American ideology regarding social welfare policy.[3] The initial shift from informal to formal social-support systems, designating responsibility to the government, was inextricably related to the passage of this legislation. Specifically, by mandating that towns and localities assume responsibility for their poor and creating institutions (almshouses) to care for the indigent, the Elizabethan Poor Laws set a precedent for government involvement in social-service delivery that continues today. Followed by a series of laws passed during the eighteenth, nineteenth, and twentieth centuries, institutions were further obligated to provide social services. Of equal importance, the government's expanded role in social-service delivery during the Great Depression of the 1930s firmly positioned federal, state, and local governments in the role of social-service providers.

Nevertheless, before the 1960s African American families, unlike white families, were seldom given the option of receiving diverse goods and services on an ongoing basis from formal social-service agencies. Thus, the emergence of massive governmental involvement in the provision of social services during the 1960s and early 1970s resulted in an increase in the percentage of African American families who could rely on formal social-service agencies to meet their needs. Indeed, the advent of this phenomenon was revolutionary for African American families.

## ORIGINS OF AFRICAN AMERICAN MUTUAL-AID NETWORKS

For some, it is difficult to conceive an informal self-help network for African American families that predates Emancipation. Accordingly, references to African American mutual-aid networks tend to focus on informal social-support systems following slavery. Nevertheless, historians allude to mutually dependent relationships among slave families. Evidence of the existence of mutual-aid networks during slavery can be found in communal cooking, child care, sewing, and other cooperative activities that occurred in and around slave quarters. Moreover, collective responsibilities assumed by African American families during slavery transcended the boundaries of the plantation to create what Sudarkasa refers to as "transresidential cooperation."[4] Seemingly, the exchange of goods and services involved the young and old, house slaves and field slaves, as well as African American freedmen and freedwomen. Oftentimes they exchanged intangible as well as tangible goods, such as valuable information that facilitated the flight of runaway slaves. Hence, the survival of African American families in America has always been predicated to some extent on the interdependence of members of the African American community.

In spite of this collective sharing, African American families were forced to rely on the slave owner as their primary source of goods and services. Even though the quantity, quality, and frequency of exchange of fundamental goods and services differed from plantation to plantation, the provision of life-sustaining commodities rested ultimately with the slave owner. As such, it is fair to say that although informal social-support systems existed, slaves depended primarily on an institutional support system, that institution being what John Hope Franklin termed the "peculiar institution of slavery."[5] However, the degree to which slave families received basic commodities from their masters depended in large measure on the slave owner's resources and sense of moral obligation.[6]

Following slavery, the abrupt change in the dependent status of African Americans warranted and resulted in massive governmental assistance to African American families. Established and administered by the federal government, the Freedmen's Bureau aided newly freed African American men, women, and children by providing food, clothing, shelter, and vital information about consumerism, land acquisition, labor contracts, and so on. By and large, the limited governmental assistance African Americans received during Reconstruction represented the only form of generic institutional support that African Americans would receive for an extended period of time. More unfortunate than the modicum of support the government provided to African American families was the fact that these services were offered for a mere seven years, from 1865 to 1872, before the Freedmen's Bureau was dismantled. Both before and after government services were offered, mutual-aid networks were mandatory for African American family survival.

In the absence of social institutions designed to address the needs of African American family members, informal mutual-aid networks were established. These networks provided basic goods and services such as food, shelter, clothing, and the like. In addition to providing goods and services for physical survival, they also offered guidance and counseling regarding personal and family matters. Mutual-aid networks enabled African American men and women to identify strategies for ensuring the survival of the two-parent family. Billingsley states that following the period after slavery, when the Freedmen's Bureau was disbanded, social services were not provided by the larger society. And the African Amer-

ican community, through "informal neighbor to neighbor" systems, had
to provide resources for the care of children.[7] This ability of mutual-aid
networks to provide the necessary elements for keeping African American
families intact during unusually stressful conditions is cogently documented by Gutman. He states that approximately 90 percent of all African
American families following slavery were intact two-parent families.[8]

Essentially, the mutual-aid networks' positive impact on the African
American family can be attributed to the composition of the networks,
nature of the commodities exchanged, conditions for exchanging goods
and services, and the limited availability of alternative sources of support
for African American families.

## MUTUAL-AID NETWORKS: COMPOSITION AND COMMODITIES

Despite copious research in the area of networking, "mutual-aid networks" and "self-help groups" are concepts that continue to be elusive.
Factors that distinguish one form of networking from another are ambiguous and overlapping. In addition, sophisticated and complex networking
designs have yet to result in an agreed-upon definition of "social support."[9] Maguire suggests that social support is a feeling and attitude, as
well as an act of concern and compassion. It is what friends, good neighbors, and relatives provide. When these kith and kin link together for the
purpose of helping, they form a social-support network.[10]

In general, informal social-support systems may be comprised of any
number of individuals. Not only do the number of members vary in any
given self-help network, there are also differences in the relationships of
individual members to each other and differences in their giving behavior.[11] Ideally, mutual-aid networks contain family members, as well as
friends, neighbors, relatives, and fellow church members. Among the
many factors that determine the effectiveness of informal social-support
systems are size, basis of the relationship, capabilities, resources, and level
of willingness of the network's members.[12] Moreover, attrition based on
geographic and social mobility can have a decisive impact on the viability
of social-support systems. That is, when individuals move from one community to another, they are likely to establish new relationships, which
alter the original structure of the network. In addition, upward mobility
can result in new friendships and organizational affiliations that also serve
to modify the initial components of the mutual-aid network. Consequently, physical and social mobility have a definite effect on informal
social-support systems. Another common quality of mutual-aid networks
is that they tend to be homogeneous on the basis of race, ethnicity, and
social class. Other factors that affect the structure of mutual-aid networks
are age and marital status.[13]

The systematic exclusion of African Americans from major societal institutions has limited the resources that the members of African American mutual-aid networks have to exchange. This is particularly important, as limited information and contacts with key members of networks within the majority society would undoubtedly facilitate economic progress for African American families and their members. Until a larger number of African Americans are placed in authority positions within the larger society, members of African American mutual-aid networks will not have enough inside knowledge needed to access social systems. African Americans will continue to be excluded from larger informal networks, which are essential for the upward mobility of African American families. In effect, the systematic exclusion of African Americans from mainstream participation, which is manifested as institutional segregation, continues to inhibit the effectiveness of African American mutual-aid networks. For example, in 1982 only 13 percent of African American males and females held baccalaureate degrees, compared to 25 percent of white males and females.[14] This alone is limiting in terms of the proportion of African Americans who possess the knowledge necessary for accessing institutions of higher learning. Thus, an African American youth seeking information, through his or her informal social-support system, regarding college admission policies, financial aid, and other nuances of matriculating in a college or university will find a dearth of members available to provide this vital information. Further, the likelihood that such an individual is a member of any given mutual-aid network is even slighter when one considers geographic residence and social class. For instance, if this same youth resides in the inner city, it is even more improbable that valuable information about colleges and universities will be obtained from the individual's mutual-aid network. This is particularly true since ascension to a higher social class, or success in general, is typically accompanied by the acquisition of certain status symbols. Generally, these include relocating from urban to suburban areas and interacting socially with others whose educational and occupational experiences are similar. As a consequence, informal social-support systems for African American urban dwellers are likely to be devoid of middle-class members who possess invaluable information on accessing social systems.

In addition, a hierarchical system for the informal exchange of goods and services characterizes white mutual-aid networks more than African American ones. The exclusivity and control that white males maintain over educational, economic, political, and religious institutions results in white males' possessing copious resources—the old-boy network. This has been and continues to be an issue of great concern in our society. In fact, one of the most ardent positions assumed by African Americans, feminists, and other contenders for social power has been their disaffection with the old-boy network. Such a structural arrangement, with men controlling material and monetary resources and women and minorities mediating a modicum of such commodities, has clearly been to the detriment of African American families and other minorities, whose race and gender inhibit their full participation in American institutions. Undoubtedly, there is a strong relationship between formal and informal social-support systems. Control over informal social-support systems is certainly correlated with power and authority in social, economic, and political systems. Moreover, it is widely accepted that decisions that appear to have been made in the boardroom were arrived at on the golf course or at some other informal gathering attended by members of a mutual-aid network.

Historically, African American women have occupied a key role in exchanging monetary, material, and other goods and services in mutual-aid networks.[15] Following Emancipation, when African American women secured employment as domestics and African American males were systematically excluded from full labor market participation, African American women were invaluable to the mutual-aid network.[16] During this era, African American women participated in self-help networks to perform the critical service of child care, which enabled them to secure and retain employment at a time when jobs for African American men were virtually nonexistent. In all, the African American mutual-aid network had the capacity for meeting the holistic needs of African American families.

## ROLE OF THE BLACK CHURCH

The entity most responsible for keeping the mutual-aid network intact and functioning properly was the Black Church. The Black Church has been in the vanguard of mutual-aid networks as one of the chief providers of goods and services. Accordingly, schools, job training programs, credit unions, and related economic and educational institutions have been founded and administered by Black Churches. In addition to making food, shelter, and clothing available to African American families, the Black Church has encouraged African American families to engage in cooperative sharing and mutual responsibility. Functioning as one of the network's chief service providers, the Black Church prescribed certain behaviors to be followed by African American families and other members of the network. In total, the Black Church has been instrumental in social-service delivery.[17]

The Black Church's commitment to ensuring the survival and progress of African American families, in conjunction with the strong religious orientation of African American families, gave the Black Church a position of prominence and influence over African American men, women, and children.[18] However, this close affiliation with and dependency on the

Black Church allowed the church to exercise considerable control over the lives of African American families and their members. In effect, the Black Church used religious meetings, the mutual-aid network, and its own resources as a means of establishing and reinforcing values, beliefs, and behaviors. Similar to other social institutions, the Black Church became a mechanism for cultural transmission and social control. Blassingame substantiates the historic significance of the Black Church when he states that the Black Church served as an agency of social orientation, providing encouragement, guidelines, and reinforcement for the traditional values of marriage, family, morality, and spirituality in the face of the devastating effects of slavery.[19]

Since the Black Church occupied an honored position in the African American community, African American families adhered to its tenets of family cohesiveness and unity. With its high degree of integration in the Black Church, the mutual-aid network reinforced values, beliefs, and behaviors governing social interaction between husbands, wives, and children. These beliefs were grounded in theological principles that stressed traditional male and female roles.[20] Thus, African American family members received positive or negative sanctions, depending on their willingness to exhibit prescribed behaviors. Nonconformity to established norms could result in the withholding of goods and services, or some other form of social sanctioning. With the ultimate goal being the maintenance of African American two-parent families, it is little wonder that husbands and wives confronted with family or marital problems sought and utilized strategies for problem resolution that seldom included separation or divorce.

Later, as the government began to provide massive social services, the Black Church began to lose its authority. Furthermore, the mutual-aid network began to decline. At that time, African American families were faced with weighing the latent, as well as the material and monetary, advantages and disadvantages of relying almost entirely on mutual-aid networks versus receiving support from the government. On one hand, the African American mutual-aid network espoused philosophical issues inextricably related to the religious doctrine of the Black Church, such as mutual dependence, collective responsibility, and cooperation. By contrast, the government, like other institutions in the larger society, embraced an ideology of autonomy, social isolation, and individualism. The African American family's decision to utilize formal social-support systems was largely based on monetary and material supply and demand. Ostensibly, the government's resources, to which African Americans were entitled, were far more abundant than those possessed by informal social-support systems. However, a greater reliance on the government to meet fundamental needs had implicit ideological implications.

## DYNAMICS OF EXCHANGE

To some extent, when examining African American mutual-aid networks I am forced to speak in the past tense. As was mentioned in the previous chapter, changes have occurred in the functioning of these complex informal social-support systems. Some changes were due to structural forces and others to the assimilation of African Americans into the larger society. Basically, the "mainstreaming" of African Americans resulted in the acquisition of a new value system, which has brought about changes in the dynamics of mutual-aid networks. These changes necessitate that distinctions be made in mutual-aid networks that existed before the 1960s and those that functioned afterward.

One important aspect of mutual-aid networks is the nature and quantity of the resources possessed by individual members. Figuratively, in terms of monetary and material resources, African American mutual-aid networks have not had an inexhaustive supply to distribute to African American families. In spite of this fact, the support African American families received and gave to each other enabled the mutual-aid network to fulfill its mission of keeping African American families together. Over time, the resources of the mutual-aid network became insufficient to meet the growing demands of African American families. This condition was brought on by the mass migration of African American families to the North, the higher cost of urban living, and the impersonal nature of city dwelling, and it put a strain on the functioning capacity of African American mutual-aid networks. Increasingly, to give to others meant the depletion of one's own resources. Furthermore, obtaining resources from the mutual-aid network had always been a highly capricious endeavor. Frequently, it meant soliciting assistance from several members before obtaining needed goods and services. As Stack indicated in her study of the urban poor, the African American mutual-aid network is extremely complex.[21] Like other informal social-support systems, the linkages and actual networking relative to primary and secondary networks is sophisticated and intricate.[22]

In traditional and contemporary African American mutual-aid networks, members change roles frequently. African American men and women move with fluidity in assuming the role of provider and recipient. Individuals discharge their indebtedness as a recipient by becoming a provider. Indeed, the norm of reciprocity governs the entire exchange process.[23] Giving invokes an automatic system of exchange. This form of informal social support did more than promote African American family stability; it also generated a collective sense of responsibility, which Herskovits, Blassingame, Sudarkasa, and others attribute to precolonial African culture.[24] It is this sense of mutual responsibility that extends beyond consanguineal boundaries that African American scholars have labeled an important African value.[25]

Though mutual-aid networks were designed primarily to keep African American families intact, they by no means delimited their goods and services to African American nuclear-type families. The exclusion of single-parent families, extended families, or other variations of African American family structures did not occur. Single-parent and two-parent families as members of mutual-aid networks were both providers and recipients of goods and services. Because resources were limited, members of the African American mutual-aid network developed a complex system for exchanging goods and services. When members of the network had exhausted their available resources, they sought other sources to ensure that the basic needs of African American families were met. Individuals were accorded status based on their willingness to assist others. Further, the possession of resources that one refused to give to others was negatively sanctioned. As Harriette McAdoo so aptly stated, in her research on African American mothers and kinship networks, one of the benefits African American family members once associated with money and material possessions was the ability to share them with each other.[26] For this gesture, African American families and other members of the African American community bestowed status and esteem. Conversely, negative sanctions were imposed on individuals who refused to share resources that were needed or in demand. These values were so deeply inculcated during the socialization process that, no matter how limited one's resources were, each member of the network felt compelled to share. Stack's contribution in this regard is invaluable, as she revealed examples of mutual sharing even in light of meager resources of both recipients and providers.[27]

Three factors contributed to the ongoing functioning of African American mutual-aid networks. They are the recognition of a commonality of interests, a uniqueness of history, and the lack of available alternatives.

## THE GOVERNMENT: AN INSTITUTIONAL ALTERNATIVE

In response to the demands of the 1960s social revolution, the federal government intervened and became involved in developing, expanding, monitoring, and funding social services. African Americans and other economically disadvantaged groups demanded that the government supplement existing resources partly because of the dwindling resources available to informal social-support systems and to the families themselves. In addition, the civil rights movement, which served as the conduit for these demands, received mass support from advantaged groups, who linked their dissatisfaction with America's military involvement in Vietnam with the ongoing demands for social and economic equity espoused by African American men and women. Moreover, the growing sophistication of the mass media informed large numbers of African American families of their relative impoverishment. In fact, the concepts of "cultural deprivation," "underprivileged," and "disadvantaged" permeated all layers of society and were believed to accurately describe African American families and their members.

Thus, the government was constrained to make reparations, which were felt to be immediate, intense, and overdue. All costs were to be borne by the government. Representative agencies were to be established and expanded to provide myriad goods and services to African American and poor families. With the formulation of this plan, there was little reason to believe the outcome would not be positive. Further, the initial investment by the government appeared to be sufficient and infinite enough to permanently reduce the burden that families, friends, the church, and other members of the African American mutual-aid network had assumed.

Services provided by formal social agencies included financial assistance, child care, educational and job training programs, housing subsidies, and nutrition programs. A description of these programs, including patterns of utilization and monetary expenditures over the 20-year period from 1960 to 1980, is presented in chapter 4. In retrospect, there are many indications that the government's expanded role in social-service delivery was politically motivated, void of deliberate planning, and in dire need of time-specific, attainable goals. Evidence to support this position is found in the manner in which programs were developed, expanded, and amended. For approximately 20 years, social services and legislation were created, amended, and later rescinded with a great degree of frequency. A prime example of the government's uncertainty in the area of social policy is apparent by examining the "unemployed parent program." In 1961 the "unemployed parent program" was enacted. This act extended the AFDC program to a child with an unemployed parent. Earlier legislation had defined "dependent child" as a child under age 16 deprived of parental support by reason of a parent's death, continued absence from the home, or physical or mental incapacity. In 1967 the "unemployed parent program" was amended and became the "unemployed father program"; families in need as a result of the unemployment of the father of at least one of the children became eligible for AFDC. In 1979 the "unemployed father program" was amended and once again became the "unemployed parent program." This change was mandated when the Supreme Court ruled it was unconstitutional to make AFDC payments available to unemployed families with an unemployed father, but not to families with an unemployed mother. The development and administration of social programs was characterized by trial and error.

Efforts to gauge the effectiveness of social welfare programs were unmethodical and fragmentary. Although evaluation and research were highly integrated into nearly all social programs, there was little consensus among policy makers, practitioners, or researchers regarding how to operationally define "success," "effectiveness," and "cost efficient"—concepts that, in theory, were to determine the fate of social programs and their recipients. Equally problematic was the construction of research designs that could control the effects of a multiplicity of programs on individuals with diverse backgrounds. Because of the inconclusiveness of the findings of numerous social-service studies and for the sake of political expediency, the government continued this hit-and-miss approach to the delivery of social service to African American and poor families.

It should be noted that not all African American families used social-service programs directly; yet it is fair to say that most African American men, women, and children were affected by their existence. However, the government's systematic neglect of African American families, its subtle and sometimes overt refusal to provide essential social services, and its previous failure to ensure the physical safety of African Americans had created a collective sense of distrust of government agents and agencies. For many African Americans, their only contact with government representatives had been a police officer or agent of the Internal Revenue Service. Both were perceived as unsympathetic, hostile, and formidable. Before African American families could fully use diverse social services sponsored by a government viewed as uncaring and oppressive, African Americans had to analyze the costs, rewards, and projected outcomes. In effect, the costs and rewards of using informal social-support systems versus formal social-support systems had to be carefully assessed.

According to Emerson and other social-exchange theorists, certain factors influence people to maintain or dissolve relationships.[28] Based on this model, rewards minus costs equal outcome. Accordingly, people tend to remain in relationships if their rewards are satisfactory and there are no available alternatives. Conversely, relationships are likely to be terminated when a person perceives the rewards to be meager and an alternative relationship is available. Of equal importance are the costs that individuals incur in a relationship. During the 1960s and 1970s, the rewards from mutual-aid networks were decreasing. As cited earlier, African American families, as members of mutual-aid networks, incurred both monetary and latent costs. The strain of urban living, with high rates of unemployment and underemployment, made it difficult for members of the mutual-aid network to continue to aid others without depleting the resources of their own families. In order to be a member of the mutual-aid network, African American families were expected to participate in church activities and to come to the aid of other members of the network. Although these conditions had become antithetical to urban living and the American way of life, both the Black Church and the mutual-aid network were important to African American families. On the other hand the government, with its amorphous and enigmatic nature, appeared to be a service provider without any discernible costs but with definite rewards. Besides, civil rights leaders and other social activists established that the United States, which included the government, had long been a beneficiary of African American labor and taxes. So it was the government, with its indebtedness to African American families, that had an obligation to discharge. This perception of the government as the recipient and African American families as the provider was consistent with the belief that reparations were needed for the social injustices African Americans had experienced in America. This rationale helped African American families make the transition from the almost exclusive use of informal social-support systems to greater reliance on formal social-support systems.

## DECLINE OF MUTUAL-AID NETWORKS

Over the last two decades, government-sponsored social-service programs have dissipated the mutual-aid network and diminished its stabilizing influence on African American two-parent families. In reality, the government was expected to supplement rather than supplant the African American mutual-aid network. However, providing many of the fundamental goods and services formerly obtained through the mutual-aid network was taken over by government social-service agencies. If formal social-service agencies had been successful in enabling African American families and their members to become economically independent, the decline of informal social-support systems would not have had such a devastating effect on African American families. Despite modest advances African Americans made in the 1960s and 1970s, the overall socioeconomic status of African American families did not improve. The decline in mutual-aid networks, along with the federal government's ultraconservative posture in the 1980s, has left African American families in a precarious position. This reactionary posture has eventuated in the disallocation of federal moneys to social programs. Presently, the cyclical use of institutional and noninstitutional social-support systems, which has occurred in the larger society, now characterizes African American cultural patterns. Recently, the Black Church has begun to regain its authority. Once again, it is commonplace for Black Churches to provide food pantries, clothing, and open shelters; to distribute surplus commodities; and to serve as advocates for African American and poor families. However, what appears to be occurring at a slower pace is the revitalization of mutual-aid networks for African American two-parent families.

In light of this growing trend, there is a definite need for more effective approaches to bring about social and economic progress for African American families. It is a fact that deindustrialization is responsible for the presence of many permanently displaced African American workers. Occupational displacement of African American male and female workers reduces the resources that were once available to exchange with members of their informal social-support system. In effect, the supply cannot realistically meet the demands that many economically disadvantaged families have for obtaining basic necessities. Clearly, this is likely to be an important factor in determining the number of significant others that individuals have, as many of these others are likely to make up an individual's informal social-support system. Thus, it is understandable that Wilhelmina Manns's study revealed that a correlation exists between a person's number of significant others and the individual's social class and that those who occupy a lower income status have more significant others than their middle-class counterparts.[29] While these structural changes necessitate greater involvement from the government to assist in providing these essential goods and services, historically there is a surfeit of evidence that government involvement, like any other relationship, is not without its share of costs.

## NOTES

1. Carrie Allen McCray, "The Black Woman and Family Roles," in *The Black Woman*, ed. La Frances Rodgers-Rose (Beverly Hills, Calif.: Sage Publications, 1982), p. 71.

2. David J. Rothman, *The Discovery of the Asylum* (Boston: Little, Brown & Company, 1971).

3. Charles Zastrow, *Introduction to Social Welfare Institutions: Social Problems, Services and Current Issues* (Homewood, Ill.: Dorsey Press, 1982), p. 19.

4. Niara Sudarkasa, "Interpreting the African Heritage in Afro-American Family Organization," in *Black Families*, ed. Harriette Pipes McAdoo (Beverly Hills, Calif.: Sage Publications, 1981), p. 46.

5. John Hope Franklin, *From Slavery to Freedom: A History of American Negroes* (New York: Alfred A. Knopf, 1948), pp. 132–156.

6. Mary Francis Berry and John Blassingame, *Long Memory: The Black Experience in America* (New York: Oxford University Press, 1982), p. 74.

7. Andrew Billingsley and Jeanne M. Giovannoni, *Children of the Storm: Black Children and American Child Welfare* (New York: Harcourt, Brace, Jovanovich, 1972), p. 46.

8. Herbert Gutman, *The Black Family in Slavery and Freedom, 1750–1925* (New York: Pantheon, 1976), pp. 498–500.

9. Lambert Maguire, *Understanding Social Networks* (Beverly Hills, Calif.: Sage Publications, 1983), p. 51.

10. Ibid.

11. E. Pattison et al., "A Psychosocial Kinship Model for Family Therapy," *American Journal of Psychiatry* 132 (1975): 1246–1251; and Christopher Tolsdorf, "Social Networks, Support and Coping: An Exploratory Study," *Family Process* 15 (1976): 407–417.

12. Maguire, *Understanding Social Networks*, pp. 52–54.

13. Gerald Gurin, Joseph Veroff, and Sheila Feld, *Americans View Their Mental Health* (New York: Basic Books, 1960), pp. 364–371.

14. United States Bureau of the Census, *America's Black Population, 1970–1982: A Statistical View.* Series P-10/POP 83-1 (Washington, D.C.: U.S. Government Printing Office, 1983), p. 16.

15. Harriette Pipes McAdoo, "Black Mothers and the Extended Family Support Network," in *The Black Woman,* ed. La Frances Rodgers-Rose (Beverly Hills, Calif.: Sage Publications, 1980), pp. 136–141.

16. Andrew Billingsley, *Black Families in White America* (Englewood Cliffs, N.J.: Prentice-Hall, 1968).

17. W.E.B. Du Bois, "The Function of the Negro Church," in *The Black Church in America,* ed. Hart M. Nelsen, Raytha L. Yokley, and Anne K. Nelsen (New York: Basic Books, 1971), pp. 77–81.

18. Robert Hill, *The Strengths of Black Families* (New York: Emerson Hall, 1972); and Robert Hill, "The Black Family: Building on Strengths," in *On the Road to Economic Freedom: An Agenda for Black Progress,* ed. Robert L. Woodson (Washington, D.C.: National Center for Neighborhood Enterprise, 1987), pp. 71–92.

19. John W. Blassingame, *The Slave Community* (New York: Oxford University Press, 1972), p. 74.

20. Theressa Hoover, "Black Women and the Churches: Triple Jeopardy," in *Sexist Religion and Women in the Church,* ed. Alice Hageman (New York: Association Press, 1974), pp. 63–76.

21. Carol Stack, *All Our Kin: Strategies for Survival in a Black Community* (New York: Harper & Row, 1974), p. 28.

22. Maguire, *Understanding Social Networks,* pp. 51–55.

23. Alvin Ward Goulder, "The Norm of Reciprocity: A Preliminary Statement," *American Sociological Review* 25 (1960): 161–178.

24. Melville Herskovits, *The Myth of the Negro Past* (Boston: Beacon, 1970), pp. 182–184; Blassingame, *The Slave Community,* p. 41; and Sudarkasa, "Interpreting the African Heritage," p. 45.

25. Sudarkasa, "Interpreting the African Heritage," p. 44–46.

26. Harriette Pipes Mcadoo, "Black Mothers and the Extended Family Support Network," pp. 125–126.

27. Stack, *All Our Kin,* p. 38.

28. Richard M. Emerson, "Power-Dependence Relations," *American Sociological Review* 27 (1962): 31–41.

29. Wilhelmina Manns, "Supportive Roles of Significant Others in African American Families," in *Black Families,* 3rd ed., ed. Harriette Pipes McAdoo (Thousand Oaks, Calif.: Sage Publications, 1997), pp. 198–213.

# CHAPTER 4

# The Era of Liberal Social Policy

The decades of the 1960s and 1970s bear a striking resemblance to the Depression era of the 1930s. Some have argued that the radical change in social policy initiated by Franklin D. Roosevelt set the tone and direction of the sweeping social and economic programs introduced by John F. Kennedy and expanded by Lyndon B. Johnson.[1] Certainly African Americans' demands for civil rights and the recognition that federal initiatives were essential to securing social equality were as evident in the Johnson and Kennedy administrations as in FDR's. During the 1960s the revolutionary position of the federal government in planning, developing, and monitoring social programs to facilitate self-reliance and economic independence for African American and poor families was more pronounced than in the Roosevelt administration. This transition, beginning in the pre-Roosevelt era, from conservative to liberal, to quasi conservative, and again to liberal social policy, reflects the cyclical form that social policy took. In the latter case, liberal social policy in the 1960s and 1970s, while innovative in approach, closely paralleled the New Deal in fundamental assumptions regarding poverty. In both cases, federal intervention was to be temporary and of such magnitude as to bring about a permanent change in the circumstances of disadvantaged Americans. The major difference was the composition of the poor, for whom federal programs were geared. In the Depression years, social services were designed to meet the needs of the "new" poor, composed largely of whites, as opposed to the 1960s when these programs were targeted to the "old" poor, in which African Americans were overrepresented. Clouded in the sociological lexicon, African Americans were defined as victims of slavery and racial inequities that had created structures and patterns of functioning, which, if not corrected, would continue to manifest social anomalies.

It was not that African American families were unfamiliar with poverty and its concomitants. What was new was the increased visibility of the debilitating conditions that African American and poor families were encountering. The social revolution made all Americans aware of the plight of African American families. And rioting, looting, and other civil disturbances forced the majority of Americans, irrespective of race or ethnic background, to experience social problems associated with poverty and social inequality. Essentially, the devastating consequences of occupying an economically depressed status, characteristic of an inordinate number of African American families, left the confines of the African American community and became a societal rather than an African American problem. Until this point in history, few white families had been directly affected by the socioeconomic status of African American families. But with mass demonstrations and an upsurge of urban violence, a number of Americans began to seek solutions to the lower status of African American families.

Philosophical tenets stressing frugality, productivity, and social rewards commensurate with hard work remained an integral part of the formulation of liberal social policy. It was firmly believed that the cycle of poverty could be broken with global federal assistance. Necessarily, policymakers envisioned social programs that would enable African Americans and the nation's poor to rise from poverty and lead constructive and productive lives. By providing services to meet social, educational, and economic needs and enacting legislation to eliminate racial barriers, the Johnson administration believed it was ensuring that African American families, as a collective, would be rescued from material deprivation. Never before in the history of the country had an effort of this magnitude been undertaken. But an investment of this nature was projected to bring a return. Although conservatives argued against federal intervention, not everyone opposed to liberal social policy questioned the ability of the government's plan to produce desired results. Some of the most adamant opponents expressed concerns over the size of budgetary allocations to the proposed social programs. Further, they warned of the disastrous effects to the free enterprise system. Adding to this argument, others articulated the history of immigrant groups who had come to this country penniless and had risen to phenomenal economic wealth on their own merits. Despite the overwhelming dissatisfaction of political conservatives, the federal government put in force social programs and civil rights legislation that had long been sought by African American families and their members.

One of the most notable changes was the administrative centralization of social programs. In the years preceding Johnson's War on Poverty, assistance to the poor was almost exclusively handled by state governments. Allowing states to administer their own welfare programs, establishing eligibility and benefit amounts without monitoring, often led to overt discrimination against African American families needing assistance. Granted the use of unlimited discretion, many states had such ambivalent and, oftentimes, negative attitudes toward the poor, in which African American families were overrepresented, that they held dollar amounts on AFDC payments to extremely low levels. For example, in 1940 Mississippi had only 104 families on the ADC rolls. Surprisingly, this occurred five years after the program was enacted.[2] Little had changed by 1981, when Mississippi had the lowest welfare payments in the country, $96 a month for a typical welfare family of three, while Wisconsin paid $473 a month for a family of the same size.[3] There is a great disparity in the 4 percent per capita income, which the Mississippi legislature allocated to welfare assistance, versus matching amounts paid by Wisconsin, which at the time was 24 percent of the per capita income. This does not take into account other regional disparities in welfare payments or the methods used by states, prior to the centralization of social welfare programs, to disqualify prospective recipients. One of the most important factors that contributed to the civil rights protests and the subsequent reformulation of social and economic policies was the frustration voiced by African Americans regarding exclusionary practices of societal institutions and social welfare programs.

Despite the trend toward centralization of social welfare programs, renewed efforts to decentralize social-service delivery and to lessen the federal government's involvement in the delivery of social services became evident during the Nixon administration. Numerous decentralized block grants, such as the Comprehensive Employment Training Act (CETA), Community Development Block Grants (CDBGs), and Title XX, were enacted under the Nixon administration. The purpose of such programs was to transfer more responsibility for the provision of social welfare services to the states. Therefore, job training programs were made available through CETA, cities were permitted to establish priorities for social services through CDBGs, and Title XX gave states more responsibility for social services while limiting the federal government's role in the delivery of social welfare programs. However, while President Nixon was committed to correcting mistakes of the Great Society programs, many of his proposals for reform conformed to liberalism. For example, Nixon proposed, albeit unsuccessfully, a Family Assistance Program, which would have replaced the Aid to Families with Dependent Children program. The Family Assistance Program would have provided a guaranteed minimum cash income to every family with children that needed it. The passage of the Supplementary Security Income (SSI) legislation, establishing a uniform national minimum cash income to the aged, blind, and disabled, occurred under this administration. The food stamp program was also expanded under the Nixon administration.[4]

The Nixon administration, with its propensity for conservatism, has been characterized negatively by some.[5] However, because of the compromising nature of the administration in its relationship with Congress and its overwhelming uncertainty in the arena of social policy, the Nixon administration's involvement in domestic social policy was amorphous at best.

A close examination of social welfare programs developed and expanded by the federal government during the 1960s and 1970s reveals that while efficacy and design are questionable, few areas reflecting the social and economic needs of African American and poor families were left untouched. Basically, the development of social and economic programs had a snowball effect. As programs were implemented, new ones were created. And as social programs increased, so did federal expenditures. Of the large number of social welfare programs in which the federal government played a critical role, the major ones were AFDC; food stamps; Medicaid; child development centers; nutrition programs; job training, Work Incentive (WIN) programs, Job Corps, and CETA; and subsidized housing. Many of these core programs spread further into related services and served as the basis for the continuous evolution of other social welfare programs.

Before scrutinizing the extent to which African American families utilized social programs, we must examine utilization rates from another perspective, which is purely political. From this vantage point, utilization patterns of African American families was one basis that was used to justify liberal social policy. The question asked and answered most frequently, particularly by advocates, was, How many? How many African Americans were participants in CETA? How many minorities received educational grants? How many African Americans were recipients of housing subsidies? Not only did advocates of liberal social policy raise the question of how many, they also provided the public with the answers. Unfortunately, the numbers game they played tended to obscure the disadvantages and the emergence of social problems that needed to be addressed.

Success or failure of social policy should be based on retention and permanence, not merely on utilization. The fact that the number of African Americans deriving benefits from social programs increased dramatically should not have led policy makers to infer that the status of African American families had significantly improved.

Toward the end of the 1970s, political conservatives became involved in a numbers game of their own. They began to look at service utilization in terms that triggered strong public emotions. The conservatives' answer to How many? differed significantly from that of proponents of social and economic programs. Blaming the failing economy, high rates of unemployment, and huge federal deficits on out-of-control government spending for social programs, they concluded that far too many federal dollars had been allocated to social welfare programs without achieving the desired results. However, for them, the question, How many? was applied to a different set of variables, such as, How many African American families continue to have incomes below the poverty level? How many African American families are female headed? How many African American children are born out of wedlock? To these questions of How many? the answers were decidedly different. For both political persuasions, the full implication of the last 20 years was submerged by a myopic view of social policy.

In order to discern the overall impact of social and economic programs on African American families, it is essential to examine the extent to which African American families became the recipients of newly sponsored government social services. It should be noted that patterns of service utilization alone are not sufficient to explain the relationship between social and economic programs and the stability of African American nuclear families. But statistical data reflecting rates of service utilization, in conjunction with program design and administration, are all factors that have contributed significantly to the disintegration of African American nuclear families. Theories that attribute the decline of African American two-parent families to a changing economy and the decreasing African American male labor market participation rate, without examining the relationship between social policy and these occurrences, are ignoring the fact that an efficient, well-designed, and well-monitored service-delivery system would have recognized these societal changes and implemented social and economic programs to avert the crisis that now confronts African American families.

Trendline data for many of these social and economic programs is difficult at best to obtain. In some cases generic data on patterns of service utilization have not consistently been aggregated on the basis of recipient characteristics. When participants' characteristics have been reported, gender frequently has taken precedence over race. Until the late 1960s and into the 1970s, many social programs reported "race" using the term "minorities," which was all too often a catchall for African Americans, Hispanics, and other nonwhite racial and ethnic groups. In other instances, when data are available on the race of social-program participants, definitional changes in obtaining data and other modifications in the instruments used to capture the data make reliability and comparability unlikely. However, since the mid-1970s there appears to be more consistency in reporting data. Still, it is too early to determine if statistical data on participant characteristics will be gathered uniformly and maintained at a central repository. Collecting, reporting, and compiling data on social and economic programs is politically determined. This became fairly ob-vious with the Reagan administration and its new thrust for decentrali-zation. This posture has not only reduced program administration to a local level, it also deemphasized the central reporting and maintenance of social-service data.

## SOCIAL WELFARE PROGRAMS

### Eligibility

Determining criteria for entitlements has more of a bearing on utiliza-tion of social welfare services than any other factor, with perhaps the exception of the fair administration of program guidelines. During the era of liberal social policy, eligibility requirements were substantially altered, thereby extending entitlements to a broader range of African American and poor families. Providing social welfare services to larger numbers of persons, and monitoring to ensure that policies were followed, enlarged the pool of social welfare beneficiaries. Even though the FDR administra-tion developed federal-funded and federal-state-funded social welfare programs, states continued to maintain a tremendous degree of latitude in determining eligibility. The government's renewed involvement in so-cial welfare programs brought about changes in the role of the states in governing social-service delivery. The decision to institute centralization was based to some degree on African Americans' claims of discriminatory policies and practices at regional and local levels of government, marking a distinct departure on the part of the federal government. Prior to the 1930s, between 1940 and 1960, and in the early 1970s, states' rights or federalism was enmeshed in federal-state relations. It would be pure na-ïveté to believe that the issue of differential access to social welfare pro-grams had not been voiced by African Americans in the past. In the Depression years, when African Americans were confronted with social and economic pressures unparalleled by those of other groups, letters were sent to FDR by African American men and women and African American leaders who relentlessly stressed their inability to obtain relief throughout the country. The influence of race on states' welfare practices, including the administration of relief programs, did not go unheeded by Roosevelt. Yet he conceded that his priority was one of accommodation to political constituents to obtain support for the passage of social pro-grams. Thus, he felt the need to relegate racial issues in favor of what he deemed political exigency. Roosevelt's sentiments clearly indicated the priorities of his administration when he succinctly stated, "First things come first, and I can't alienate certain votes I need for measures that are more important at the moment by pushing any measures that would entail a fight."[6] In so doing, Roosevelt obtained the votes necessary to pass his emergency relief programs and the Social Security Act, leaving African

Americans with the formidable task of extracting economic and social support as best they could. This pattern continued for African American families until the next era of liberal social policy.

Until the 1960s, social welfare programs, particularly ADC and low-income public housing, continued to narrowly define eligibility with the intent of maintaining exclusivity, thus preventing African American families from becoming recipients of various social services. Despite practices to curtail beneficiaries, expenditures climbed at a dramatic rate. As the country's elderly benefited from Social Security, company pensions, and federally financed low-rent public housing, a shift occurred in the composition of the poor. Between 1950 and 1960, the number of elderly recipients decreased from 50 to 37 percent of the public assistance population. Conversely, the ADC program increased to approximately 3 million recipients by 1960.[7]

In the 1960s the extension of entitlements to a vast array of African American and poor families was instituted on three levels. First, major policy changes were initiated in ADC eligibility requirements. Second, the development of new social programs like Medicaid, Medicare, and job training programs subsumed under the 1964 Economic Opportunity Act omitted restrictions for entitlements, which characterized earlier social welfare programs. Third, over a 20-year period successive amendments to social welfare programs tended to expand instead of constrict eligibility to individuals and families. Moreover, states' discretion over eligibility was curtailed legislatively and informally through political persuasion.

From this point forward, eligibility for social welfare programs was established, encompassing larger numbers of individuals and families. By extending eligibility to a vast number of economically disadvantaged families, the government unknowingly facilitated demands from other groups voicing the need for government intercession on their behalf. Observers of the evolution of liberal social policy have subsequently argued that these new contenders for social power—women, elderly, handicapped, and other minorities—diffused efforts initiated by African Americans and minimized gains made available during the earlier stages of social welfare expansion.[8] With demands from diverse groups for social justice, eligibility criteria became unusually broad.

After introducing numerous social and economic programs and legislation designed to respond to the needs and interests of African American families, the government and public assumed a wait-and-see posture.

## ANTIPOVERTY PROGRAMS

### Aid to Families with Dependent Children

One of the most controversial of all public assistance programs is AFDC. By 1980, one of every five African Americans received AFDC. Since its inception in 1935 (originally called ADC, later called AFDC in 1950), this program has continued to represent the largest cash outlay by the federal government. In 1980, nearly $11 billion was spent on the AFDC program.[9] Between 1960 and 1980, AFDC was subjected to numerous eligibility and administrational changes. More commonly known as "welfare," AFDC has been stereotypically viewed as a parasitic program for African American women, their mates, and children. Persistent inaccuracies have resulted in the proliferation of myths about AFDC recipients.[10] Some of the more popular misconceptions include: most AFDC recipients are African American, have large families, and consist of able-bodied individuals who are not willing to work. Since efforts to dispel these myths have been restricted to academic circles, the general public continues to hold negative attitudes toward government assistance and recipients. Expanding AFDC to include unemployed parents, particularly fathers (AFDC-UP), fostered the belief that men too lazy to secure employment were benefiting directly from public assistance.

Regarding the AFDC program, public outcry rose to a level commensurate with the number of recipients. The number of AFDC families rose from 1.3 million in 1967 to 3.2 million in 1979. This increase over a 12-year period represents a 162 percent and 165 percent increase for white and African American families, respectively. What is surprising is that these increases exceeded the percentage increase of white and African American female-headed families with children, which rose 90 and 108 percent, respectively. Despite the drastic increase in the number of families receiving AFDC, the composition of these families in the caseloads remained fairly stable. In 1979 white families comprised 52 percent of the AFDC recipients, down from 53 percent in 1967. African Americans represented the same proportion of the AFDC caseload, 44 percent, in 1967 and 1979. Currently, approximately 3.9 million families receive AFDC. In general, the average family receives welfare benefits from 18 to 24 months. Of this number, 900,000 have been on the program for more than five years.[11] Ten percent have received benefits for 10 years or longer.[12] Another indicator of the level of service utilization is the rate at which families return to AFDC and other public assistance caseloads. However, reliable data reflecting a national pattern of repeated social welfare service use is not available.

### Work Incentive Programs

An adjunct to public assistance, Work Incentive (WIN) programs were created in 1967. By design these programs mandated that recipients be referred by the states for either gainful employment or vocational training. Some exclusions that exempted individuals are as follows: (1) under age 16, (2) ill or incapacitated or attending school, and (3) those who needed to be continually present in the home because of the illness or incapacity of another member of the household. Thus, female heads of households with dependent children, who are recipients of AFDC, are permitted to claim exemption due to the latter stipulation, which excludes women with children under six years of age. By 1971, WIN policies became even more stringent, as all AFDC current and prospective recipients were required to register for a manpower training program or seek employment. Failure to comply with this mandate could mean the loss of benefits.[13]

In 1976, the total number of WIN registrants was 1,740,085; 928,519 (53.4 percent) were white, 705,054 (40.5 percent) were African American, and the remaining 106,512 (6.1 percent) included American Indians, Hispanic Americans, and other minorities. By 1983, WIN guidelines had once again undergone modification. New federalism resulted in states having the option of providing WIN, or other forms of employment-oriented programs, in an effort to reduce welfare rolls. At this time, in the 34 regular WIN states, a total of 1,325,879 participants were registered. Of this number 581,606 (43.9 percent) were white, 418,915 (31.6 percent) were African American, 227,716 (17.2 percent) were Hispanic, and the remaining 97,642 (7.4 percent) were American Indian, Alaskan Native, Asian and Pacific Islander, and other minorities. Comparing these two categorizations of the racial and ethnic characteristics of program participants for 1976 and 1983 illustrates that observable changes occurred in data collection, reporting, and compiling.

The enactment of the Manpower Development and Training Act (MDTA) in 1962, along with the passage of the 1964 Economic Opportunity Act and the Emergency Employment Act, represents the development of contemporary federal manpower programs. Principally the goal of such programs was to assist the young urban poor, included in which are African American youth, in acquiring and refining marketable job skills.[14]

Another employment and job training program established under the Nixon administration to enable African American and white underclass families to acquire economic independence was the CETA program. Distinguished by various Title numbers, these programs offered manpower training and public jobs to disadvantaged youth and adults. In 1976 and 1981, the cumulative totals remained under 3 million participants, 2.5 and 2.9 million, respectively. During this time the percentage of white participants declined from over 50 percent in 1976 to 45 percent in 1981, while the proportion of African American CETA participants, over this period, increased from 29 percent in 1976 to 37 percent in 1981.[15]

An interest in creating job opportunities for low-income families was also indicated by the Carter administration, as was the belief that income-support programs should be consolidated into one system. In 1977 President Jimmy Carter presented the Program for Better Jobs and Income. Essentially, this program, while exempting the aged, blind, disabled, and single parents with children under seven, required the principal wage earner in each family seeking public assistance to participate in a five-week program to secure a job. If a job could not be found, then a public-sector job would be made available. Ultimately the wage earner was to obtain a private-sector job. In addition this proposal contained a provision that individuals who did not generate sufficient incomes could receive a direct cash benefit or an expanded earned-income tax credit. Accordingly, the principal wage earner would be able to keep $3,800 of earned income, after which federal cash benefits would be reduced 50 cents for each dollar. The earned-income tax credit was designed to encourage private-sector employment by providing income tax credits on annual earnings in the labor market. This portion of the plan was to be administered by the Internal Revenue Service. However, Carter's welfare proposals, focusing largely on increasing private-sector employment for poor families, failed to receive congressional support. In general, the Carter administration's propensity for liberalism was thwarted by a mood of conservatism that had begun to engulf the country.[16]

Opponents of social welfare programs did not look favorably upon policies that prevented recipients from engaging in employment or activities that would not rapidly lead to a job. This sentiment increased when large numbers of women sought employment in the labor market. At this time the expression of compassion and empathic understanding for women remaining in the home to care for children rapidly diminished. There was even less tolerance for women who remained in the home because they were recipients of social welfare services.

To give women with children an opportunity to acquire and refine marketable job skills, as well as to mediate the concerns of those who saw public assistance as a means of avoiding employment, child-care centers proliferated. The relationship between WIN, CETA, and other employment-oriented programs and government-funded child-care centers became obvious. Each program was designed to enable single-parent heads of households, typically women, to ultimately secure and retain employment. Following the Depression and post-World War II period, as the number of women workers in industry began to decline, and prior to 1975, when federal and state governments increased funds to day-care centers under Title XX of the Social Security Act, public financial support for child-care services had dwindled considerably. The timing of the government's influx of funds to day-care centers cannot be taken lightly. Although practitioners argued for mechanisms that would support women willing and eager to acquire job skills and secure employment, the visibility of married and unmarried female workers with children was sufficient evidence that given adequate child care women could become productive outside the home. In 1974, one year before the revitalization of child-care centers, 30 percent of women with children under the age of 3 were in the labor force, and 33 percent of married women with children between the ages of 6 to 17 were working outside the home. Added to this number, 67 percent of female single parents with school-age children were employed, and 54 percent of these women had children under the age of 6.[17] Suffice it to say, the federal government's decision to provide day care for recipients of AFDC was lauded on many fronts.

### Food Stamps

Like many other antipoverty programs, the food stamp program, established in 1939 and ended in 1943, was reinstituted in 1961 during the Johnson administration. Under the auspices of the U.S. Department of Agriculture, food stamps are purchased by eligible persons for a portion of their face value or received without payment based on family size and income, and are used for the purchase of food products in grocery stores.[18] In 1980, one of every four African Americans was a recipient of food stamps. The number of food stamp recipients rose from 400,000 in 1965 to 21.6 million in 1983. Examining households that received food stamps for one year, we find that in 1982, 7.2 million households received food stamps. A racial breakdown reveals that 4.6 million were white and 2.3 million were African American. Generally food stamps are available to recipients of public assistance to supplement their income and ensure an adequate diet. A concern of critics is the use of food stamps for the purchase of commodities that have been deemed frivolous. As a consequence, government policies specify the nature of expenditures that can be made using food stamps. Despite the stipulation that payment cannot be made using food stamps for nonfood items, the myth that recipients of food stamps purchase alcohol and expensive cars has been slow to fade.

Another concern has been the selling of food stamps illegally in exchange for money. For the most part, the use of food stamps continued to be a denigrating endeavor, as they were distributed in many states in the same fashion as surplus commodities. In both instances, recipients were compelled to wait in extremely long lines in and outside social-service offices to obtain food stamps. Despite the inconvenience, the exigency of this transfer program resulted in a high rate of utilization. Federal expenditures for food stamps increased from $600 million in 1970 to an estimated $8.7 billion in 1980.[19] Newer methods of distribution were later introduced as electronic cards were designed to purchase food and they began to be delivered by the U.S. Postal Service.

In conjunction with the food-stamp program, the federal government made financial assistance available to state governments willing to provide matching dollars for other nutrition programs. Supplementary food programs such as school lunches and dairy and other nutritional food products have been made available to eligible women and children in programs such as the Women, Infants, and Children (WIC) program.

A look at the school lunch program for one year reveals that a large number of African American and white families have relied on these supplementary programs to augment their diets. For example, in 1982 a total of 5.6 million households received free school lunches; 3.5 million were white and 1.9 million were African American. As with other social welfare programs, tremendous furor has been generated over nutrition programs. Many believe that financial assistance and food stamps are more than ample to meet the needs of welfare families. For some, ancillary food programs support the contention that recipients of public assistance are incapable of money management. Arguing for the continuation of food programs by citing high incidents of infant mortality and deaths related to poor nutrition, common among African Americans and the poor, proponents have experienced some success in retaining these programs. Although nutrition programs are not offered by all states, monetary allocations have continued to escalate for them.

### Medicaid

Both Medicaid and Medicare were enacted in 1965 as Title XIX of the Social Security Act. Medicaid defrays medical and health costs primarily for individuals receiving public assistance, while Medicare is designed specifically for the elderly, paying some portion of their health care costs. Originally, Medicaid legislation encouraged states to provide coverage to all self-supporting individuals whose low incomes made medical expenses unaffordable. However, since this condition was not mandatory and states vary on their definition of "medical indigence," only recipients of public assistance were assured coverage.[20] With the exception of Arizona, all states provided for basic health care services for eligible low-income persons.[21]

Critics have argued that Medicaid is dangerously close to socialized medicine and is in part responsible for escalating health-care costs. Statistical data on racial and ethnic characteristics of Medicaid recipients, like other social-service data, was minimally reliable until fiscal year 1980. Prior to 1980, states reported data on recipient characteristics in a dichotomized form using two categories, "white, non-Hispanic" and "unknown," for all nonwhites who received Medicaid services. On the basis of this typology, data reflect that in 1975, the first year for which such data are available, there were 8,384,300 (42 percent) whites and 11,936,069 (58 percent) unknowns, or minorities who were recipients of Medicaid. However, by 1983 the proportion of minorities receiving Medicaid had decreased to 44 percent and the number of white recipients had increased to 55.8 percent. Specifically, a breakdown of recipients reveals Medicaid was received by the following in 1983: 11,129,942 whites (not Hispanic origin) or 55.8 percent, 7,215,640 African Americans or 36.2 percent, and 1,590,400 other minorities or 8 percent. The percentage of Medicaid payments made to minorities also declined between 1975 and 1983. In 1975 whites received $7.5 billion or 61 percent, compared to $4.7 billion for minorities or 39 percent. Corresponding figures for 1983 indicate that $11 billion or 70.4 percent in Medicaid payments went to whites and $9.6 billion or 29.8 percent went to minorities. Total Medicaid payments received by African Americans for the year was $8 billion or 25 percent.[22] Healthcare services due to Medicaid have had a demonstrable impact on attenuating disease and reducing infant mortality for African American and poor families. Today one of every four African Americans is enrolled in Medicaid, which accounts somewhat for the fact that African Americans have experienced a dramatic reduction in heart disease and have prevented serious health problems through medical screening and early diagnosis and treatment over the last 20 years.

In spite of the availability of Medicaid, most African American families have benefited little from this government-sponsored program. Because most African American men and women comprise the working poor, who do not qualify for government-subsidized medical care, they are more likely to forego necessary health-care services or to incur enormous hospital and medical expenses when medical care is an imperative. Johnson says that the working poor can manage adequately until a medical emergency arises. At that point, the medically indigent can be confronted with a financial disaster that is difficult to overcome.[23]

Recognizing the importance of health services to families who do not qualify for cash welfare programs, which automatically entitle them to Medicaid, approximately 29 states include families in their definitions of the medically needy. Medicaid benefits are extended to families whose incomes do not meet welfare requirements or whose medical expenses reduce their incomes to medical needy levels.[24]

### Subsidized Housing

In 1983, 54.7 percent of all African American families were renters compared to 32.7 percent of white families in the United States.[25] Hence, available and affordable rental units are extremely important to African American families. During the riots in the 1960s, African Americans drew attention to substandard and overcrowded housing, which characterized their communities. The term "ghetto," which defined the physical and psychological limitations imposed on inhabitants of metropolitan areas, generally on the periphery of the inner city, became synonymous with absentee slum landlords, dilapidated housing, and overcrowding.

However, concern about inadequate housing for the poor did not begin in the 1960s. The first federally sponsored housing program had its beginning in the New Deal era. In 1934 and 1937 the federal government passed the National Housing Act and the Housing Act, respectively. Just as social policy in general created public employment, pensions, and financial assistance for many who were economically disadvantaged, the housing program in the 1930s was beneficial not only to the poor but was also advantageous to the middle and upper classes. To say that the destitute did not benefit from the government's social policy in housing would not be completely true. Indirectly, African Americans and the poor were able to obtain suitable housing through the trickle-down effect. When middle-class families became upwardly mobile and migrated to suburban areas, their homes were placed on the market for working-class families to occupy.[26] In addition to ensuring loans to stimulate the housing market and to allay the fears of individuals faced with loan defaults, the Wagner-Steagall Housing Act of 1937 created the United States Housing Authority (USHA). Through the USHA loans were made available for the construction of low-income dwellings.[27] Equally important, the housing act enabled states to provide low-rent public housing to the needy.[28]

Unsurprisingly, African American families did not benefit much from these new housing measures. Because the FDR administration espoused government decentralization, local government officials mediated social programs in their own geographic areas. In effect, racial discrimination made it difficult for African Americans to receive the benefits of social welfare programs, including adequate low-cost housing. As late as 1944, seven years after the passage of the Housing Act, 83,000 of the 92,476 housing units in which African Americans resided were totally segregated or had quotas limiting African American occupancy.[29] Moreover, in Buffalo, New York, where 76 percent of the city's 5,343 dwelling units remained unoccupied, government officials refused to permit the temporary use of these units by African Americans.[30] In contrast to this period, a resurgence of federal funding of housing along with the enactment of fair housing legislation in the 1960s and 1970s produced gains in housing ownership and improvements in overall living conditions for some African American families.

One of the oldest and widely used programs under the aegis of the U.S. Department of Housing and Urban Development (HUD) continues to be low-rent public housing. Because a disproportionate number of African American families are renters, as opposed to homeowners, the availability of public housing is essential. However, despite increases in the occupancy rates of public housing, the proportion of these units occupied by African American families has decreased. In 1972, African American families occupied 49 percent and white families 43 percent of the occupied public housing units. Comparatively, in 1978, the proportion of low-rent public housing units occupied by African American families had declined to 47.1 percent and 38.4 percent for white families. Increases in occupancy that took place during this six-year span largely affected the Hispanic population. For this cultural group, public housing occupancy rose from 7 to 12.2 percent.[31]

Aside from the government's increased participation in the aforementioned social welfare services, other government-funded social and economic programs were provided to bring about parity in employment, education, and private enterprise, not to mention a myriad of social services to address the social and emotional needs of African Americans and poor families. The latter services generally took the form of community mental health centers, drug abuse programs, delinquency prevention projects, and so on. While many of these and related programs attempted to transform poor African American and white families into viable social and economic units, African American working- and middle-class families sought policies to further enhance their status. Other than grants and loans for education, housing, and business ownership, many of these families were unable to derive immediate benefits from the expansion of social welfare services, as their incomes precluded entitlement.

Meeting the needs of the growing African American middle class required substantially more than increased monetary expenditures in social welfare programs. What African American middle-class families also expected was a change in discriminatory practices in education, employment, and housing. For instance, in 1960 and 1970 the proportion of African Americans employed in managerial and professional occupations was 7 and 10 percent, respectively.[32] Finding inequities in the labor market, middle-class African Americans challenged the federal government to enact legislation and empower government agencies with enforcement capacity to effect social justice. Hence, affirmative action laws, by design, were to bring about parity in institutions that had historically excluded African Americans.

## AFFIRMATIVE ACTION

### Employment

Resistance to affirmative action programs was undoubtedly greater in this area of social policy than in any other. Still, the government, under demands from African American leaders, the African American student movement, and coalitions of African Americans and white liberals took a giant step forward by mandating that African Americans be given equal access to employment and educational opportunities. To enforce affirmative action laws, various entities were established to issue legal sanctions for noncompliance. Both the public and private sectors were subjected to this legislative edict. To soften the blow, monetary incentives in various forms such as tax breaks were offered as inducements for adherence to affirmative actions laws. Evidence suggests that corporations implemented diverse policies to comply with federal initiatives. However, more often than not these measures were established reluctantly and resulted in a paucity of token jobs.[33] Some African Americans did benefit from affirmative action in employment. In this regard, Who? and How many? are pertinent. Hill indicates that African Americans were not the only ones to benefit from affirmative action legislation and policies. He states that between 1974 and 1977, 53 percent of all new jobs in the private sector went to white women. White males acquired 26 percent of new jobs, Hispanics 12 percent, and African Americans and Asians secured a mere 5 percent. Moreover, only 1 of every 1,000 jobs created between 1970 and 1983 went to African American males.[34]

In the corporate sector, executives found a catchall position for African Americans in human resources, which rarely led to promotion into higher-paying positions in other divisions within the company. In the main, trepidation regarding the loss of sizable government contracts was somewhat sufficient to evoke affirmative action policies from the most conservative corporate entities. The federal government, being the initiator of such policies, was one of the largest employers of African Americans. However, the government as a role model was nothing new. During the Depression, the percentage of African Americans in federal employment outnumbered the proportion in the population. This trend continues today, as African Americans and other minorities constitute one of every four federal workers.[35]

## ENTREPRENEURSHIP

In addition to the opportunities offered to African Americans in the labor force as a consequence of affirmative action, the government made numerous loans available to African Americans to establish, maintain, and expand businesses. Data on government loans to African American-owned small businesses are sparse. However, available data reflect that in 1970 a total of 15,100 loans were approved for small businesses; 6,300 (41 percent) went to persons of color and women-operated businesses, compared to 1980 when 31,700 loans were approved and 6,000 (19 percent) were for persons of color and women-owned businesses. By 1982 loans to small businesses were down to 15,400. In the same year, loans to persons of color and women-owned businesses had fallen substantially, to 5,900 or 13 percent, 28 percent below the level that existed more than two decades earlier.[36] The data indicate that considering the small percentage of businesses owned by persons of color and women, a relatively large proportion of these firms received loans from the federal government during the 1960s and 1970s. For instance, in 1977, of nearly 10 million industries, African American firms constituted only 231,000 or 2.3 percent. When the dollar value of these loans is considered, the proportion of actual dollars firms owned by persons of color and women received was far less than the percentage of total loans that were made to all small businesses. Specifically, in 1970 the value of total loans made to all small businesses was $710 million, of which $160 million (23 percent) went to small businesses operated by persons of color and women. By 1982, small businesses received loans in the amount of $2.5 billion dollars, and $238 million (13 percent) was received by firms owned by persons of color and women.

## Education

Barriers in educational institutions were also addressed. Although equal percentages of African Americans and whites were enrolled in school, in 1970 the median level (in years) of education for African Americans was 10.2 years, 12.0 for whites. An even greater disparity existed between the percentage of African American college graduates and their white counterparts.

Only 6 percent of African Americans had college degrees, compared to 17 percent of whites who had graduated from college in 1970.[37] Adding to this problem was the systematic exclusion of African Americans from predominantly white colleges and universities. Moreover, professional-school enrollment for African Americans was significantly less, thereby producing a negligible pool of African American lawyers and judges (1 percent), physicians and surgeons (2 percent), and teachers (8 percent). At this time actual African American enrollment figures for law and medical schools were as low as 3 percent. Almost 10 years later, in 1979, the enrollment of African Americans had risen to 4.2 and 5.7 percent in law and medical school, respectively. Furthermore, the percentage of African Americans majoring in business in 1969 and 1979 had increased from 5 to 8 percent.[38] Attributing low enrollments in white colleges and universities to limited financial resources and discriminatory practices, the federal government sought to alleviate both factors by appropriating moneys to make grants and loans available to African Americans and poor students. Furthermore, the federal government threatened to withdraw federal dollars from colleges and universities that failed to admit a reasonable number of African American students. This approach began to narrow the educational gap between African Americans and whites. Thus, the entrance of larger numbers of African Americans into predominantly white institutions of higher education was successfully accomplished. In 1980, 80 percent of all African Americans enrolled in colleges and universities were at these institutions.[39] With affirmative action in place, numerous social welfare programs, the 1964 Civil Rights Act, the 1965 Voting Rights

Act, the 1968 Fair Housing Act, and so forth, policymakers clearly envisioned that African American families would be strengthened through these social, economic, and political initiatives. At last it appeared that reparations were being made for past social inequities, which would permit, and even facilitate, African Americans joining mainstream America. As such, the prognosis for African American families was one of optimism.

### Community Mental Health Centers

It was not sufficient for the Johnson administration to seek solutions for curing the social and economic ills of African American families. The proclivity for holism surfaced in the expansion of mental health services to African American and low-income families. In 1963, when President Kennedy pushed for and succeeded in obtaining the passage of the Community Mental Health Centers Act, African American and poor families were designated target groups whose emotional status was considered as precarious as their financial one. In effect, this law, like similar laws enacted by states throughout the 1950s, shifted the care of the mentally ill from state hospitals to community facilities.[40] The trend toward deinstitutionalization, transferring responsibility to local community agencies for persons with mental disorders, was assigned to model cities organizations and various components within community action organizations. It came as no surprise that African American families were labeled as a high-risk group. The social and psychological indicators that mental health practitioners use to determine groups in need of mental health services—female-headed families, children living in female-headed families, and families subsisting on incomes below the poverty level—were descriptive of a larger proportion of African American than white families.[41] Added to the projected mental health needs of African American families was the high rate of institutionalization for African American men, women, and children. The population of mental institutions consisted of 21.7 percent African American males and 46.3 percent African American females in 1960, when African Americans comprised only 10.6 percent of the U.S. population.[42] In addition, differential U.S. mental hospital admission rates based on race for the year 1975, per 100,000 population, were as follows: for males, 214.2 for whites versus 444.5 for African Americans and other races, and for females, 111.2 for whites versus 212.0 for African Americans and other races.[43] Similarly, African Americans were overrepresented in correctional institutions. An estimate of the population of correctional institutions in 1960 reveals that African American males and African American females represented 55 percent and 11 percent, respectively. These and other factors were associated with poverty and defined as indicators of the need for mental health services.[44]

The expansion of community mental health services throughout the decade had a twofold goal of rehabilitation and prevention. By placing service delivery at the community level, the stigma and distrust of service providers was to be lessened. As a consequence, African American clients were to establish a greater degree of rapport and confidence in the therapist because facilities were in a familiar milieu. In addition, governing boards were formed with representatives of the community, who came to be known as "grassroots" persons, capable of proffering suggestions for treating African American families. Still, there was a larger number of African Americans who could not qualify for free mental health services because their incomes were slightly higher than the poverty index. The passage of Medicaid and Medicare extended mental health services to these individuals and families. Furthermore, the incorporation of a sliding fee scale and private insurance coverage of mental health services gradually made services available to all families with mental health needs.

In terms of the chronology of social policy, it would appear as if the enactment of Medicaid and Medicare and the earlier passage of the Community Mental Health Centers Act were a part of one great master plan. But there is little evidence to support this contention. Had there been strategic planning, the subsequent receptivity to and usage of community mental health centers by African Americans would have been substantially greater. Instead, African American families resisted such services and continued to view them with suspicion.

African American families' underutilization of community mental health centers was met with consternation and chagrin by both practitioners and policymakers. Few could understand African Americans' reluctance to voluntarily seek and continue participation in mental health services. After all, prevalence studies showed higher rates of schizophrenia among African American males and females, higher rates of institutionalization, and a preponderance of conditions indicating proneness to mental health disorders.[45] Given these projections, it is fairly obvious why practitioners expected African American families to be overrepresented in the utilization of community-based mental health services. In no way am I suggesting that African Americans did not utilize community mental health services, but their use of these services did not reach projected levels. Recognizing the goals of mental health policy, administrators convened meetings, seminars, and public forums to identify methods of increasing African Americans' utilization of services. Lefley and Bestman state that the National Institute of Mental Health's (NIMH) 1974 Mental Health Demographic Profile of community mental health centers revealed that policy recommendations were necessary to address underutilization by nonwhites.[46] Moreover, it was found that African Americans who had utilized community mental health centers had drop-out rates as high as

74 percent, which led researchers to conclude that drop-out rates are invariably higher for African American clients than for whites.[47]

In general, community mental health centers represent the major social-service program that was underutilized by African American families. When African American families did utilize these services, their use was frequently mandated by the courts, social welfare agencies, or some other entity with legal authorization to impose negative sanctions for failure to comply with their order.

## REASSESSMENT: A PRELUDE TO RETRENCHMENT

By the late 1960s, the federal government was firmly entrenched in establishing and expanding social programs. As gaps in service delivery were discovered, the government responded by either appropriating more dollars, amending legislation, or creating new programs. From the administration's perspective, unfair practices in social-service delivery by states and local governments were sure to be minimized by federal monitoring and enforcement agencies. During the late 1960s and the 1970s, a growing cadre of social conservatives began reassessing liberal social policies.

The emphasis on inculcating a strong work orientation, in exchange for social welfare services, paralleled vocal opposition to the expanded role of government in the delivery of social services. One of the gravest errors policymakers made was their attempt to mold African American families into a unit resembling white middle-class families, at the expense of jeopardizing vital African American formal and informal structures. The unique experiences of African Americans relative to economic deprivation and racial discrimination were responsible in part for the evolution of the structure and dynamics of family life, based on a complex informal exchange system. Although the mutual supportive network was unable to meet all the economic needs of African American families, it continued to provide invaluable social services. Further, it was not the government's responsibility to replace traditional African American formal and informal institutions. Instead, the government was expected to augment these social and economic systems. In the event that social and economic programs had succeeded in creating progress for African American men and women, disbanding these support structures would still have had a detrimental effect on African American families. Sufficient evidence exists in Jewish and Asian cultures to demonstrate that, although racial and ethnic minorities can achieve economic assimilation, socially they must maintain a strong sense of cultural unity. In fact, one of the ways in which racial and ethnic groups have acquired economic and political power is to retain traditional cultural institutions, which ensure unity, support, and a collective sense of responsibility. Using other successful racial and ethnic groups as a barometer, it is fairly safe to conclude that the structures necessary for African American upward mobility were weakened by liberal social policies. In effect, social programs that set out to improve the plight of African American families contributed to their instability.

Overall, Johnson's War on Poverty was a failure for the majority of African American families. The inability of African Americans to ascend into the mainstream and the steady decline of traditional social-support systems has exacerbated the problems already confronting African American families before the era of liberal social policy. Believing that the government had embarked upon a permanent position of ensuring parity— through affirmative action programs; the voting rights act; civil rights laws; affirmative action legislation; housing, educational and small business grants and loans; and social welfare programs—it was difficult for anyone to expect the rescission of liberal social policy.

Further, there was evidence to confirm the belief that African Americans were making significant gains. Government reports and studies showed positive gains for African Americans, which pointed to the success of social and economic programs. There was little indication that liberal social policy had brought about anything other than positive outcomes for African American families. Reports of the 1960s and 1970s were so convincing that the demands from other contenders for social and economic power became stronger. It was no coincidence that policymakers and program administrators generalized advances made by some African Americans to the African American population in general. Furthermore, social and economic factors tended to perpetuate these efforts. First, during the 1960s and 1970s, numerous jobs had been created, not simply for African Americans but for whites as well. These were subject to elimination if social and economic programs were deemed ineffective. Second, after 200 years of being economically disadvantaged, 20 years of government assistance was too soon to determine success or failure. Third, political reasons precluded objectivity in evaluating social programs and their impact on African American families. Most of these reasons were easily translated into numbers in the form of constituents and, in election years, votes. Suffice it to say, policymakers considered it unwise to acknowledge that social programs, as designed, were incapable of solving the problems of African American families. And identifying problems that these social programs had created for African American families would have been even more disastrous. It became evident during the era of liberal social policy that this "either-or" approach to the formulation and implementation of social policy rendered social and economic programs virtually ineffective. When social policy is more accurately viewed as a continuum, it is not "either-or," rather it is "more-or-less."

While civil rights organizations and federal authorities sought to un-
cover service gaps and inconsistencies in the provision of social and economic programs, countercurrents became more pronounced. Critics
argued that expenditures for social programs were rising at an alarming
rate and were too exorbitant for the taxpayer to bear. According to Guzzardi, federal grants-in-aid to states for transfer payments exceeded the
growth of inflation. He states, "For over two decades federal grants grew
after inflation at an average annual rate of 10 percent; in fiscal 1978 they
hit a high of 17.3 percent of federal outlays. Further, he adds that in 1981
federal grants were around $95 billion, or 14.5 percent of federal
outlays."[48]

In order for social programs to be effective, they must be subjected to
critical evaluation and redesign without the fear that opponents will
charge total failure. In the main, social policy should be perceived as a
process that leads to a well-designed, well-implemented, and well-
evaluated plan.

Finally, in 1980 the federal government began to reassess its carte
blanche approach to social policy. Under pressure from various groups,
the government had to justify escalating expenditures for social programs.
This took place as governmental agencies identified social and economic
gains, which were touted as indicators of benefits that African American
families were deriving from social programs. However, African American
families were experiencing other "gains," which surprisingly were overlooked. And by the 1990s the recognition that these social policies, with
their illusion of making significant changes in the institutional structure
of the social, economic, and political system, had contributed to the destabilization of African American families was met with an antagonistic
posture in that subsequent administrations assigned culpability to the
families. It was at this point that social policies had gone full circle. They
had become firmly enmeshed in a conservative posture in which administrations were determined to transfer the responsibility for the failures of
these poorly designed and inconsistently applied social policies and in-
frequently enforced civil rights legislation to African American families
and their members.

## NOTES

1. Robert McElvaine, *The Great Depression: America, 1929–1941* (New York:
Times Books, 1984), pp. 188, 334–336.

2. Ibid., p. 309.

3. Walter Guzzardi Jr., "Who Will Care for the Poor?" *Fortune*, February 1982,
pp. 34–42.

4. Beulah Roberts Compton, *Introduction to Social Welfare and Social Work*
(Homewood, Ill.: Dorsey Press, 1980), p. 537.

5. Alphonso Pinkney, *The Myth of Black Progress* (New York: Cambridge University Press, 1984), p. 168.

6. McElvaine, *The Great Depression*, pp. 188–189.

7. June Axinn and Herman Levin, *Social Welfare* (New York: Dodd, Mead and Company, 1975).

8. James E. Blackwell, "Persistence and Change in Intergroup Relations: The Crisis upon Us," *Social Problems* 29 (1982): 325–346.

9. Charles Zastrow, *Introduction of Social Welfare Institutions: Social Problems, Services and Current Issues* (Homewood, Ill.: Dorsey Press, 1982), p. 105.

10. Wayne Johnson, *The Social Services: An Introduction* (Itasca, Ill.: F. E. Peacock Publishers, 1982), pp. 57–59.

11. Muriel Feshbach, "Dynamics in the AFDC Caseload, 1967–Present" (Washington, D.C.: Department of Health and Human Services, 1982), unpublished report.

12. U.S. Department of Health, Education, and Welfare, *Findings of the 1973 AFDC Study: Part 1* (Washington, D.C.: National Center for Social Statistics, 1974).

13. U.S. Department of Labor, *WIN Handbook*, No. 318 (Washington, D.C.: U.S. Government Printing Office, 1984), I-l.

14. Compton, *Introduction to Social Welfare*, pp. 543–545.

15. "Employment and Training Reporter: 1982 Employment and Training Report to the President: Selected Tables" (Washington, D.C.: Bureau of National Affairs, August 23, 1982, p. 64.

16. Compton, *Introduction to Social Welfare*; and Zastrow, *Introduction to Social Welfare Institutions*, pp. 520–521.

17. Therese W. Landsburgh, "Child Welfare: Day Care of Children," *Encyclopedia of Social Work*, 17th ed. (Washington, D.C.: National Association of Social Workers, 1977), p. 138.

18. Johnson, *The Social Services*, pp. 62–63.

19. "Still More Billions for Food Stamps," *U.S. News and World Report*, May 1980, p. 7.

20. Zastrow, *Introduction to Social Welfare Institutions*, pp. 103–104.

21. Johnson, *The Social Services*, p. 151.

22. U.S. Department of Health and Human Services, "Statistical Report on Medical Care: Recipients, Payments, and Services," Health Care Financing Administration, unpublished report, 1984.

23. Johnson, *The Social Services*, p. 60.

24. U.S. Social Security Administration, "Aid to Families with Dependent Children," *Social Security Bulletin, Annual Statistical Supplement* (Washington, D.C., Department of Health and Human Services, 1982).

25. U.S. Bureau of the Census, *Statistical Abstract of the United States: National Data Book and Guide to Sources* (Washington, D.C.: U.S. Government Printing Office, 1984).

26. Johnson, *The Social Services*, pp. 397–399.

27. McElvaine, *The Great Depression*, p. 303.

28. Chauncey A. Alexander and David N. Weber, "Social Welfare: Historical Dates," *Encyclopedia of Social Work*, 17th ed. (Washington, D.C.: National Association of Social Workers), pp. 1497–1503.

29. William L. Evans, *Race, Fear and Housing in a Typical American Community* (New York: National Urban League, 1946).

30. Ibid.

31. *1979 Statistical Yearbook*, United States Department of Housing and Urban Development, Superintendent of Documents (Washington, D.C.: U.S. Government Printing Office, 1979), p. 206.

32. U.S. Bureau of the Census, *The Social and Economic Status of the Black Population: An Historical View, 1790–1978*. Series P-23, No. 80 (Washington, D.C.: U.S. Government Printing Office, 1979), p. 74.

33. Theodore Cross, *The Black Power Imperative* (New York: Faulkner Books, 1984), pp. 808–809.

34. Robert Hill, "What's Ahead for Blacks?" *Ebony*, January 1980, 27–36; "America's Underclass, Broken Lives: A Nation Apart," *U.S. News and World Report*, 17 March 1986, p. 20.

35. Milton Coleman, "Reagan's 'Rising Tide' Is Sinking Blacks," *National Leader*, February 1984, p. 1.

36. U.S. Bureau of the Census, *Statistical Abstract of the United States*.

37. U.S. Bureau of the Census, *America's Black Population: 1970 to 1982, A Statistical View*. Special Publication, P-10/POP 83-1 (Washington, D.C.: U.S. Government Printing Office, 1983), p. 16.

38. William L. Taylor, "Access to Economic Opportunity: Lessons Since Brown," in *Minority Report: What Has Happened to Blacks, Hispanics, American Indians and Other Minorities in the Eighties?* ed. Leslie W. Dunbar (New York: Pantheon Books, 1984), p. 31.

39. Taylor, "Access to Economic Opportunity," p. 31.

40. Morton Kramer and Nolan Zane, "Projected Needs for Mental Health Services," in *The Pluralistic Society: A Community Mental Health Perspective*, ed. Stanley Sue and Thom Moore (New York: Human Sciences Press, 1984), p. 55.

41. Ibid., p. 57.

42. Ibid., p. 54.

43. Harriett P. Lefley and Evalina W. Bestman, "Community Mental Health and Minorities: A Multi-Ethnic Approach," in *The Pluralistic Society: A Community Mental Health Perspective*, ed. Stanley Sue and Thom Moore (New York: Human Sciences Press, 1984), p. 118.

44. Leo Levy and Louis Rowitz, *The Ecology of Mental Disorders* (New York: Behavioral Publications, 1973).

45. Kramer and Zane, "Projected Needs for Mental Health Services"; and Lefley and Bestman, "Community Mental Health and Minorities," p. 118.

46. Lefley and Bestman, "Community Mental Health and Minorities," p. 141.

47. George H. Wolkon et al., "Ethnicity and Social Class in the Delivery of Services: Analysis of a Child Guidance Clinic," *American Journal of Public Health* 64 (1974): 709–712.

48. Guzzardi, "Who Will Care for the Poor?"

# CHAPTER 5

# The Impact of Social and Economic Gains on African American Families

There has been considerable debate over the extent to which gains were made by African American families and their members between 1960 and 1980. These advances apparently correspond with the social programs implemented during this period. What remains as a point of contention is which and how many African American families and their members made advances over the 20-year period. A related area of uncertainty is assessing the magnitude of social and economic progress for African American families. Increasingly, there appears to be some consensus that the social and economic progress that occurred was differentially experienced by African American families and their members. Undoubtedly, disparities in upward mobility for African American families were related to social class. Furthermore, there were differences in the rate of progress among members of African American families as well. In this case, differential progress was based on gender. That is, not all African American families or their members experienced mobility as a consequence of innovative social policies. To the contrary, many African American families remained static, while others descended into poverty. Of the latter group, African American families whose lifestyles have become deeply entrenched in poverty are said to be among a growing permanent underclass.[1] This alone is evidence that liberal social policies enacted over a 20-year period did not have the same positive effect on all African American families.

Considering the gains that were made by African Americans during the 1960s and 1970s, it becomes obvious that social class played a critical role. At that time, African Americans with middle-class status were able to solidify their positions and continue their ascent on the social and economic ladder.

There is little consensus among scholars as to which indicators should be used in defining the African American middle class.[2] Though some agree that income is an important determinant of stratification among African Americans, there is considerable disagreement about what range constitutes various social-class levels. Thus, the income range for African American middle-class families is found to vary from $15,000 to $30,000 annually. However, Robert Hill, a sociologist, states that in 1970 when the U.S. Bureau of Labor Statistics intermediate level was set at $10,664, 24 percent of all African American families were "economically middle class." And by 1979, the percentage of African American middle-class families (those with incomes over $20,517) had risen to 26 percent.[3] Not only did the majority of African American middle-class families remain stable during this period, their numbers also increased.

For the most part, African American middle-class families were in a better position to benefit from massive liberal social policies in the 1960s and 1970s. Basically, educational grants and loans, affirmative action, and civil rights legislation served to reduce the rigidity and exclusivity that had characterized traditional institutions. Thus, social policies enabled members of African American middle-class families to access educational, political, economic, and legal systems. Prior to the 1960s and 1970s, the same institutions had either prevented the entrance of African Americans or had established conditions that resulted in inequitable treatment for African Americans once they were granted entrée. One reason African American middle-class families benefited more than other African American families is that they were already successfully participating in the same institutions on a microcultural level. In other words, before the 1960s, many African Americans in this stratum attended institutions of higher education, held professional positions, established and owned businesses, and were buying rather than renting their homes. Therefore, they had already acquired pertinent information about how to gain admission and function effectively in salient social systems. The primary difference was that the institutions in which they participated were generally African American controlled. However, their almost total participation in predominantly African American institutions was generally not by choice. Instead, the exclusive nature of African American institutions was due to racial segregation and was therefore imposed by the larger society. However, liberal social policy of the 1960s and 1970s eliminated the barriers that had kept African Americans from participating in institutions previously available only to whites. African Americans already actively involved in African American institutions were able to participate with greater facility in social systems within mainstream America. What was required was simply to generalize knowledge acquired in African

American institutions to those that were predominantly white. Hence, members of African American middle-class families experienced a great deal of success in these institutions. In all, they made the transition from African American institutions to white ones with greater ease than did African Americans who were members of working-class and lower-income families.

This is not to suggest that only African American middle-class families benefited from social policies enacted during this era. On the contrary, empirical evidence shows that gains were experienced by working-class African American families as well.[4] However, advances made by lower-income African American families were miniscule compared to those in the working and middle classes. Because of a number of adverse social and economic events that occurred during the era of liberal social policy, the overall effects of these gains are somewhat lessened and obscured. For example, lower-income families might have made greater gains as a result of liberal social policy if old-line industries had not begun to decline. In addition, an economy marked by inflation and recession during this period had a negative effect on all Americans, particularly the disproportionate number of African American families at the lower end of the social and economic ladder. In fact, three recessions occurred between 1960 and 1980. According to Hill, the recessions of 1969–1971, 1974–1975, and 1980 proved to be devastating to the African American community.[5] Despite these occurrences, had liberal social policy been effective, there was sufficient time to implement programs to assuage the catastrophic effects of the occupational displacement caused by massive industry shutdowns and layoffs. Clearly, lower-income African American families were adversely affected as the economy began to change from highly industrialized to service oriented. One major reason is that African American males were overrepresented in the skilled and semiskilled occupations. In essence, an inordinate number of African American males were employed in industrial jobs as factory workers.

Most of the occupational advances experienced by African American males took place between 1940 and 1960. It was during this period that the proportion of African American men working in operative (skilled and semiskilled) occupations rose from 13 percent in 1940 to 23 percent in 1960, with an additional increase to 26 percent in 1970. By 1970, a higher proportion of African American men (one-fourth) was employed in operative occupations than in any other major occupational classification.[6]

In some cases, African American men working in these occupations were members of working-class and middle-class families. As a consequence, the occupational displacement of the 1970s tended to lower their social class, causing many stable African American families to experience downward mobility.

Social class is not the only barometer for measuring differential social and economic gains for African American families. Other observable distinctions in advances made by African American families occurred among their members. As cited earlier, these differences in progress were also gender related. For example, disparities can be found in occupational gains for African American men and women. Between 1960 and 1980, occupational upgrading occurred with greater frequency for African American women than for African American men. Moreover, African American females made substantially greater gains in education than did African American males.[7] It is plausible that African American women who experienced occupational upgrading did so in large measure because certain white-collar professions were available to them, but there were no parallel positions for African American males to occupy. For the most part, African American women who moved into white-collar professions were placed in low-paying jobs in clerical and sales positions.[8] A corollary can be found between African American middle-class families and African American females. As stated earlier, the African American middle class had a historical precedent for successful maneuvering in salient institutions, albeit African American. Similarly African American females have generally been enrolled in institutions of higher education in greater proportions than African American males. Consequently, familiarity with colleges and universities and the availability of a larger number of female role models and mentors who had matriculated in these institutions provided a decided advantage for African American females. Unquestionably, these factors placed African American females, rather than African American males, in a favorable position, particularly in light of the new external institutional support provided in the form of government educational grants, loans, and affirmative action legislation. Thus, African American females were not only able to sustain educational gains but were also able to expand educational attainment into areas that had been restricted to both African Americans and women. Some may even argue that the feminist movement, which focused on the inequitable access and treatment of women in general, may have had some residual effect on occupational and educational advances made by African American women. In all, African American women made advances between 1960 and 1980 that were unparalleled by African American males. These differences have had a direct impact on the structure and dynamics of African American families. What follows is a closer examination of the specific gains made by African American families and their members in education, occupation, business and home ownership, life expectancy, and so forth. These changes are discussed as they occurred from 1960 to 1980. Then the impact of these gains during the first 20-year period, 1960–1980, as well as the adverse effects of these policies on African American families during this era will be discussed. Moreover, conservative and reactionary social policies introduced in the 1980s that firmly entrenched institutional forms of racial, gender, and class inequality will be explored, along with their devastating effects on African American families.

## GAINS: PROGRESS FOR AFRICAN AMERICAN MALES AND FEMALES, 1960 TO 1980

### Educational Attainment

Contrary to popular belief, there has never been a major disparity in the overall educational attainment for African American men and women. Admittedly, African American women have had slightly higher rates of educational achievement but, across the board, these differences have not been significant. Where substantial differences in educational attainment for African American men and women have existed, they have been found at the collegiate level; historically, more African American females than males have attended college. Various theories claim to explain African American families' decisions, in the years preceding 1960, to send their daughters to college in numbers that greatly exceeded that of their sons. One of the most intriguing, and perhaps more valid, notions is that African American females in the 1940s and 1950s had but two occupational choices. They could either become teachers or domestics. The former occupation was available to African American females upon whom college diplomas were conferred. Those without credentials were relegated to the status of domestic. Given these rather extreme occupational choices, African American families opted to educate their daughters to ensure their chances for a professional career.[9] Conversely, African American males could enter a variety of occupations. They had opportunities to become skilled or semiskilled laborers or to work in the agricultural or service industries. Although these positions did not have the relatively high status associated with teaching and other female-dominated professions, the income, considered by most to be satisfactory, was sufficient to enable the African American husband to be the primary breadwinner in most African American families. Thus, while most African American families had two wage earners, African American men generally had higher incomes than their wives.[10]

What emerged from the differential rates of matriculation for African American females versus African American males in institutions of higher education was an African American middle-class family that was in some respects the antithesis of the white middle-class model. In these families, African American males, like their white counterparts, made the greater economic contribution to the family income. However, the two families diverge from this point. In the African American family, frequently the wife, and not her spouse, had a higher-status occupation. Therefore, many

African American middle-class families evolved in which high income and occupational status were not possessed solely by the male, as in white families, but were shared by the African American husband and wife.

Speaking strictly of educational attainment, in most African American marriages the wife is more educated than her spouse. It is estimated that in the past, 55 percent of African American female college graduates were married to men whose educational achievement was less than theirs.[11]

The phenomenon of disproportionate numbers of African American females vis-à-vis African American males enrolled in and graduating from college continued over these two decades. An overview of college educational attainment for African American men and women reveals that in 1956 approximately 62.4 percent of all African American college graduates were women. This ratio of African American college graduates was maintained until the latter part of the 1960s. It was not until the 1970s that African American men began to narrow this educational margin.[12]

Looking at statistics, we come to a clearer understanding of the gains made by African American men and women in the area of education. In 1960, the median years of school completed was 7.7 for African American males and 8.6 for African American females. By 1975, the impact of the Supreme Court's ruling in *Brown v. Board of Education* and the government's affirmative action edict began to significantly alter low levels of educational achievement for the entire African American population. At this time, the median years of school completed rose to 10.7 and 11.1 for African American males and females, respectively. As further evidence of the effect of liberal social policy on educational attainment, African American males reached parity with African American females by 1980, when the median years of education for both sexes was 12 years.[13]

College enrollment statistics also began to reflect an unprecedented growth. The increase in the number of African Americans enrolled in colleges, especially in predominantly white institutions, was heralded as an indicator of the success of affirmative action. However, when closely examined, those increases reveal that while the number of African Americans enrolled in colleges and universities had risen, the actual percentage of African American males in these institutions was gradually declining. Thus, African American females, not African American males, made major gains in attending institutions of higher learning during the 1960s and 1970s. In 1960, of the 134,000 African Americans enrolled in college, 48 percent were African American males and 51 percent were African American females. Over the next 20 years, there was a steady decline in African American male enrollment. Simultaneously, African American females' college enrollment increased dramatically. By 1980, 688,000 African Americans were enrolled in college. Of this number only 278,000 or 40 percent were African American males and 410,000 or 60 percent were African American females.[14] Twenty years later in 2000, these percentages had changed, as there was continuous decline in African American male presence in institutions of higher education—over 2 million African Americans were enrolled in colleges and universities, of which 62 percent were females and 38 percent were males.

African American males not only decreased in numbers on college campuses, they also had a higher rate of attrition, which meant a lower rate of graduation, than African American females. Basically, there are three degree levels—baccalaureate, doctorate, and professional—in which African American women made gains. Between 1976 and 1981, African American women experienced the following percentage increases in these degrees: baccalaureate, 8 percent increase; doctorate, 29 percent increase; and professional, 71 percent. The only area in which a decrease occurred for African American women was in the master's degree, which declined by 12 percent. Still, this decline is less than half that of African American males, who experienced a decrease of 21 percent at the master's degree level. In essence, African American males did not fare as well as African American females at any degree level. Degrees for African American males declined in all four degree areas, the bachelor's, master's, doctor's, and professional levels.[15]

However, as a group, African Americans made unprecedented gains at the collegiate level. There were observable increases in African American enrollment in professional schools, especially in medical and law schools. African American enrollment in law schools rose from 3 percent in 1969 to 4.2 percent in 1979. Likewise, African American enrollment in medical schools escalated from 2.7 percent in 1968 to 5.7 percent in 1980. The significance of this change is evident, as there were 3,000 African Americans enrolled in medical school in 1974, during a time when there were only 6,000 African American physicians in the entire country.[16]

In spite of disparities in educational achievement for African American men and women, African Americans as a cultural group made major strides in education during this era. Comparative statistics reflect that whites had a median of 10.9 years of schooling compared to 8 years for African Americans in 1960. Two decades later, in 1980, the educational gap had been significantly bridged, as African Americans were almost approaching parity with whites. At this time, African Americans had a median of 12 years of education compared to 12.5 years for whites.[17] However, the increase in the number of African American female college graduates along with the constant decline in African American male college graduates during this 20-year period continues to impact on the structure of African American middle-class families.

## Occupational Mobility

There is a direct correlation between education and occupation in contemporary American society. Although there is a definite relationship between education and income for whites, inconsistencies in earnings based on race and gender result in the association being tenuous for African Americans.[18] Affirmative action is often cited as having granted African Americans access to occupational areas that had been closed or severely restricted to African American men and women before the 1960s.

Major occupational changes did occur between 1960 and 1980. During this period, African Americans made significant advances, moving from service and semiskilled occupational groupings to white-collar jobs. Only 16 percent of all employed African Americans were working in white-collar jobs in 1960, compared to 47 percent of employed whites. By 1980 the percentage of African Americans in white-collar occupations had risen to 36.6 percent. Comparably, the proportion of whites in white-collar occupations had increased to 53.9 percent.[19] Nevertheless, two factors should be taken into consideration in interpreting these data. First, the mere fact that African Americans are categorized, for census purposes, in white-collar positions does not mean that they have white-collar incomes.[20] As such, positions that are most likely to be considered white collar tend to be low paying or entry level. For example, the percentage of African American women working in clerical and sales jobs increased from 1 percent in 1940 to 9 percent in 1960. Additional increases occurred as this proportion climbed to 21 percent by 1970, and later reached 34 percent in 1980. Decreases in the proportion of African American women domestics also took place from 1940, when 60 percent were employed in household service work, compared to 1970, when the proportion had dropped to 15 percent.[21] Moreover, the greatest percentage decrease in African American female domestics occurred over the 10-year period from 1960 to 1970. Still, when all service occupations are included, such as nursing aides, attendants, cooks, and so on, the proportion of African American women in service-related occupations in 1980 was more than one-fourth (29 percent or 1.5 million).

Second, occupational segregation remained egregious, as the homogenization of workers in high-status and high-income positions was maintained. Gains by African Americans moving into professional occupations did not take on the magnitude of other occupational shifts for African Americans over the 20-year period, and the progress was still modest.[22] Again, African American women were more successful in moving into the ranks of professional occupations than were African American men. African American women showed a percentage gain, moving from 10 percent in 1970 to 11 percent in 1980. African American males' advancement into professional occupations was even less as their numbers increased from 5 percent in 1970 to 5.5 percent in 1980. Gains made by many African American men and women were in occupations traditionally held by women, such as teaching, nursing, and social work. To a degree, both African American men and women, particularly the latter, made some inroads into professional occupations in which they had been highly inconspicuous two decades earlier.

## ECONOMIC GAINS

### Income

In looking at an overall picture of African American progress in the area of income, it is inaccurate to categorically describe what occurred as gains or losses. Primarily, what took place was that one segment of the African American population registered gains in earnings while other segments of the African American population continued to lag behind whites. Positive increases in income were experienced by African American two-parent families. In addition, African American females increased their earnings at a rate that exceeded that of African American males. During this period, African American females began to significantly reduce the income differential that had existed between themselves and African American males.

Income for African American two-parent families climbed 6.9 percent from 1971 to 1981, which reflected an increase from $18,370 to $19,620 in constant dollars. The figures for white families were $25,130 in 1971 to $25,470 in 1981. Even in the most optimal situation, when intact African American families are compared with white husband-wife families, African American families have an income of only 77 percent of the income of white families. Nonetheless, some African American families did move into the middle class. Those who did accomplish this significant feat are highly visible, which leads to the regrettable misconception that the majority of African American families fared as well. Spratlen states that the rather conspicuous signs of affluence among African American families belie this overwhelming evidence that racial inequality has continued to significantly affect the economic status of African American families. To illustrate, he points to figures that indicate that the number of African American families earning $25,000 or more per year, having increased between 1970 and 1978 from 49,280 to 79,404, remains small relative to white families with similar income. Spratlen further argues that 29.5 percent of all white families versus 13.4 percent of all African American families make up this income group, which earns $25,000 or more annually. Thus he concludes there is an "inequality gap of nearly one white family in three versus one African American family in seven."[23]

Income figures for African American families in general are even more alarming when they are considered in total. African American families actually suffered a decline in income, relative to that of white families. In 1971 African American families had a median income of $14,460, which was 60 percent of the median, $23,970, of white families. By 1981, the ratio of African American family to white family income was 56 percent. One explanation for the decrease in income is the decline in the number of African American married-couple families. These families dropped from 74 percent in 1960, to 68 percent in 1970, down to 55 percent in 1982.[24] This decline continued and by 2000, 48 percent of African American families were married-couple families, which represented less than one-half of all African American families. However, an increase in the ratio of African American family income compared to that of white families between 1990 and 2000 is attributed in part to the economic growth that occurred during the 1990s, which was quite advantageous for African American married-couple families, as it was this family structure that was essentially needed for African American middle-class status.

One other income-related phenomenon that took place during the 1960s and 1970s was the differential increase in the income of African American family members based on gender. Certainly, the differential rate of advancement for African American females versus African American males in education and occupational areas helped African American women to close the income gap that had existed between African American males and females. In 1962 African American women's median income was 61.1 percent of the median income of African American men. At that time, African American women's median income was $6,975, compared to $11,414 for African American men. By 1982 African American women's median income had risen to $12,577, or 75.3 percent of the African American male's median income, which had reached $16,710. By contrast, white females in general continue to earn considerably less than white males. While white females did make advances in terms of income, they did so minimally. In 1962 white females earned a mere 59.8 percent of the median income of white males. Specifically, the median income for white women was $11,430 and $19,127 for white males. Twenty years later in 1982, there had been little change, with white women earning $13,847, 62.3 percent of the white males' median income of $22,232.[25]

### African American Entrepreneurship

African American business ownership has a definite impact on African American families. In many instances, African American–owned and operated establishments have been and continue to be sole proprietorships operated by African American family members. Moreover, African American businesses, like the majority of all small businesses in this country, provide jobs and serve as an economic resource in the community where they operate. Accordingly, there is a direct correlation between the economic solvency and status of African American families and African American business ownership.

Figuratively, African American–owned businesses, particularly those firms operated as sole proprietorships, grew between 1969 and 1980. Data reveal that African American entrepreneurship rose from 163,073 African American–owned firms in 1969 to 231,000 in 1980.[26] Gross receipts increased during this same period from $4.5 billion to $9.5 billion. This growth represents a 42 percent increase in African American–owned firms and a 111 percent increase in gross receipts. Despite this unprecedented growth, African American–owned businesses accounted for only 2.3 percent of all firms in 1980. Interestingly, this represents an overall decrease in the percentage of all businesses that were African American owned in the United States. Earlier figures reveal that in 1969 African American–owned businesses accounted for 2.6 percent. Thus, it is fairly evident that African Americans were not alone in taking advantage of government loans and other economic development programs, which aided in the establishment and successful operation of small businesses during this era.

### Home Ownership

Home ownership is an area in which African American families demonstrated enormous growth over this 20-year period. It was during the late 1960s and throughout the 1970s that African American families made significant gains in their transition from renter to homeowner status. In 1980, approximately 49 percent of all African American families owned their homes, compared to 38 percent in 1969. However, the rate of home ownership for African American families consistently lagged behind that of whites, with the latter owning 67 percent of the houses they occupied in 1980. Much of the disparity between the rate of home ownership for African American and white families can be attributed to higher income levels and the reluctance on the part of financial institutions to lend money to African American families for the purchase of property. The growth in home ownership for African American families that occurred during this period is a function of increased salaries and governmental programs, both legal and economic, that promoted home ownership among African American families and other racial and ethnic groups.[27] It is important to note that while these gains were made, African Americans still had not reached the rate of home ownership that characterized white families 100 years ago. The earliest available data on housing patterns show that in 1890 white families owned 51 percent of the housing units they occupied.

### Life Expectancy

African American family members also made notable gains in life expectancy over the last 20 years. Like whites, African Americans can attribute these increases to several factors. First, there has been a dramatic improvement in the affordability and availability of health care. Next, a marked decline in infant mortality, although twice the rate of whites, has affected life expectancy. Finally, a decrease in maternal mortality rates has had a positive effect on life expectancy.[28] Statistics bear out the fact that gains made by African Americans in life expectancy were greater than those for whites. Still, whites have a life expectancy at birth that exceeds that of both African American males and females. In 1981, life expectancy averaged 66 years for African American males and 75 years for African American females, doubling the life expectancy averages of the earlier decades of the century. Comparatively, life expectancy for whites in 1981 averaged 71 years for males and 79 years for females.[29]

Furthermore, a disparity in life expectancy for African American males and females at all ages continued. These differences in life expectancy for African American men and women have had a significant influence on the structure of African American families. The fact that African American females live an average of nine years longer than African American males has numerous implications for African American family structure. For example, African American women are likely to become single heads of families at some point in the family cycle. While this also holds true for white women, African American women are more likely to assume headship due to widowhood at a younger age.

Other factors that contribute to disparities in life expectancy for African American men and women are homicide and suicide rates, which are higher for African American men than African American women.

## OTHER "GAINS"

Aside from advances made by African American families in the areas of education, occupation, income, business development, home ownership, and life expectancy, increases in other social and economic spheres affected African American families immensely. Many of these changes were more subtle in nature. Some of the more conspicuous problems were frequently ignored, and for obvious reasons. One principal reason these "gains" were not emphasized, or even acknowledged, was the belief that opponents, having maligned social and economic programs, would point to liberal social policy as the culprit. Using this rationale, it was reasoned that critics would demand the total elimination of social and economic programs. Had there been a precedent for evaluating and correcting ineffective public policies without placing all social and economic programs in jeopardy, in all likelihood social welfare advocates would have been less reluctant to identify problems and programs that were adversely affecting African American families. This dilemma led to the growth of problems that, left uncorrected, began to have a devastating impact on the stability of various African American family structures.

It was not until the 1980s that attention began to focus on these other "gains." When policymakers did turn their attention to these social and economic problems, it was exactly for the reason proponents of social welfare programs had projected—to eliminate liberal social policy. What follows is an examination of "gains" that have been equated with the retrogression of African American families in America.

### Civilian Labor-Force Participation

Given that one of the chief purposes of liberal social policy was to enable African American families and their members to become economically independent by increasing African Americans' participation in the economic sector, it is imperative that we examine the extent to which African American family members became active in the civilian labor force. This, in conjunction with income, is an important indicator of the overall impact of social and economic programs on the status of African American families.

An historical overview reveals that following the Depression the African American labor force continued to increase, albeit more slowly than the white labor force. From the mid-1950s until 1965, a new pattern began to emerge, as the African American labor force began to grow at a rate that exceeded that of whites. Over the next 10-year period, both the African American and white labor forces grew at essentially the same rate. In 1982, approximately 11 million African Americans were in the civilian labor force, accounting for nearly 10 percent of the total civilian labor force; this figure represents an increase of 2.7 million persons over 1972, or a 31 percent increase.[30]

Historically, African Americans have had a higher civilian labor-force participation rate than whites. One explanation for the greater proportion of African Americans in the labor force is that more African American women were gainfully employed. However, with larger numbers of white women entering the labor force in the 1970s, this disparity began to gradually disappear. The numbers of African American and white workers began to coincide around 1970, when both groups had a 57 percent labor-force participation rate.[31]

Two factors apposite to any assessment of the civilian labor-force participation rate of African American family members are age and gender. While African American women made positive advances by increasing their numbers in the civilian labor market, the opposite was true for African American men. Instead of increasing their participation in the labor force, the percentage of African American males outside the civilian labor force climbed steadily over these two decades.

In looking at African American women's labor-force participation rate, it becomes clear that the percentage of African American women in the labor force under 65 continued to increase. In effect, the proportion of African American women in the labor force rose from 48 percent in 1960 to 54 percent in 1982. Conversely, the proportion of African American men in the labor force declined from 83 percent in 1960 to 70 percent in 1982.[32] Here the "gain" is recorded as an increase in the percentage of African American men outside the labor force, many of whom have permanently given up looking for employment. Some researchers argue that this precipitous decline in the African American male civilian labor-force participation rate is highly correlated with the growth in the number of maritally disrupted African American families.[33] Consistent with this notion is the argument that African American males who are no longer actively participating in the civilian labor force lack one of the most essential prerequisites for marriage—a job.

The importance of age when examining African American labor-force participation rates becomes clear when a total picture of employment and unemployment trends is examined.

### Employment

The ever-changing economy and industry shifts created high rates of unemployment for African American family members at various times over the 20-year period. Variability in the rate of African American male and female unemployment has, unquestionably, influenced the stability of African American families. Beginning with a double-digit unemployment rate for African American persons of 10.2 percent in 1960, the rate of unemployment for African American men and women reached its highest since World War II when it peaked at 18.9 percent in 1982. Throughout the 1960s and 1970s, the unemployment rate for African Americans continued to be double that for whites, which was 4.9 percent in 1960 and 8.6 percent in 1982.

Youthful members of African American families also felt the effects of a depressed economy, as the rate of unemployment for African American teenagers climbed to 48 percent in 1982, exceeding that of white teens (20.4 percent) by more than 100 percent. Differential rates of African American teenage unemployment were also discernable by gender. In the same year, African American male teens' unemployment rate was 48.9 percent compared to 47.1 percent for their female counterparts.[34] The fact that unusually high rates of African American unemployment prevailed for the better part of two decades points to the fact that various social and economic programs had not adequately provided African American men, women, and youth with the necessary job skills or financial solvency to thwart the effects of an economic downturn. Thus, for African American families, downward economic spirals continued to be cataclysmic, as their ranks among the unemployed swelled. These increases led to still other "gains."

## Poverty Rate

The proportion of African American families with incomes below the poverty level fluctuated throughout the 20-year period from 1960 to 1980. In 1960 approximately 1.9 million, 48.1 percent, of all African American families had incomes below the poverty level. Declines in this figure became evident as the percentage of African American families in poverty dropped to a low of 27.1 percent in 1975. However, in spite of government intervention in social-service delivery up to this point, the proportion of African American poor families began a gradual surge upward. By 1980, the percentage of African American families in poverty had increased to 27.6 percent.[35] An equally striking occurrence was the increase in the number of these families consisting solely of women and children.

## Female-Maintained Families and Their Children

In the 1980s the dramatic growth in the number of African American families maintained by women generated much debate. In general, female-headed families were the fastest-growing segment of the poor population. One reason African American female-maintained families, like their white counterparts, have attracted considerable attention is due to concomitant problems associated with female headship. A major concern of these families is financial. In 1982, the growing proportion of African American families headed by women accounted for 70 percent of all African American poor families in this country. In 1960, only 22 percent of African American families were headed by women; this figure had risen to 46 percent by 1982.[36] Further, it was projected that if these trends continued, the number of families headed by African American women was expected to reach 59 percent by the year 1990.[37] While the percentage of African American females who maintain families did increase, it had not reached these projections, even by the twenty-first century, as is discussed in chapter 10.

The strain encountered by African American families maintained by women is not solely financial in nature. Studies reveal that female heads of families are more likely to be victims of physical and mental illness than their married counterparts.[38] Clearly, African American women who maintain families are not the only family members who experience the ill effects of a family structure in which no male is present. African American children in families headed by women are also faced with poverty and related social anomalies. The fact that the poverty rate among African American children was rapidly growing is an understatement. In fact, in

1982 the poverty rate for all African American children under the age of 18 was higher than at any time since 1967.[39]

More specifically, the percentage of African American children living with one parent increased sharply, from 25 percent in 1960 to 49 percent in 1982. Although the proportion of white children living with one parent more than doubled, from 7 percent in 1970 to 17 percent in 1982, only 42 percent of all African American children were living in two-parent families in 1982, compared to 81 percent of all white children.[40]

Growth in the number of African American women maintaining families is largely a function of still other increases. A rise in the divorce rate, a low remarriage rate for African American women, and an increase in the number of births occurring to African American unwed mothers are correlated with the disproportionate number of African American female single-parent families.

### Marital Disruptions: Separations and Divorces

One of the most dramatic influences on the structure of African American families was the increase in the number of marriages disrupted by separation and divorce.

Until 1980 separations outnumbered divorces for African American men and women. In 1960, of all African American males and females between 25 and 54 years of age who had ever married, 8.2 percent and 12.4 percent, respectively, were separated; in 1980, 10.4 percent of African American males and 18.7 percent of African American females of the same group were separated. A significant increase in the divorce ratio for African American men and women took place between 1960 and 1982. Defined as the number of divorced persons per married persons, the ratio of divorced African American males reached 151 per 1,000 in 1980, compared to 45 per 1,000 in 1960. The divorce ratio for African American females rose from 78 per 1,000 in 1960 to 257 per every 1,000 married persons in 1980. While the divorce ratios for white males and females also showed an unprecedented growth during this same period, the divorce ratios for African American men and women more than doubled the rates for their white counterparts. More specifically, the divorce ratio for white men was 27 per 1,000 in 1960 and 74 per 1,000 in 1980. White women had a considerably higher divorce ratio of 38 per 1,000 in 1960, compared to 110 for every 1,000 in 1980. In short, over two decades the number of divorces grew at a rate of 300 percent for white couples and 400 percent for African American men and women.[41]

### Out-of-Wedlock Births

There was a steady rise in the percentage of births to unwed mothers among African American and white females since 1960. Figures reflecting the number of out-of-wedlock births should be interpreted with the knowledge that they are computed based on the number of births to married women. Thus, as the percentage of births to African American married women has declined, the proportion of births to African American unmarried women has risen. In 1960, the percent of births to African American (21.6) and white (2.3) unmarried women was appreciably less than in 1982, when 55 percent of all births to African American women occurred out of wedlock, compared to white women, whose out-of-wedlock birth rate had risen to 11 percent.[42] As cited earlier, a related causal factor in the growth of African American families with female heads can be attributed to the growing number of African American women with children who never marry. One major factor that accounts for the disproportionate number of out-of-wedlock births among African American women is that, between 1960 and 1980, the rates of adolescent marriages dropped 45 percent for African American teens. By contrast, marriages for white teens declined only 4 percent during the same period.[43] The limited availability of employment for males and the poor-quality education that results in males who are not acquiring marketable job skills that enable them to make a meaningful contribution to the family income is yet another explanation for the growth in female-maintained families.

### Suicides

At the end of two decades, African Americans experienced a relatively new phenomenon. During the 20-year period, the rise in suicides for African American women was negligible. But for African American men and African American male youth the suicide rate had shown a definite increase. The suicide rates for African American males, up from 8 per 100,000 in 1960 to 10.8 per 100,000 persons in 1980, continued to be less than one-half the rate of suicides for white males (18 per 100,000 in 1970 to 20.2 per 100,000 persons in 1980).[44]

It is interesting to note that age is a salient factor in differential suicide rates for African American and white men. Suicides for white males tend to take place in greater numbers in the 65 and over age range. On the other hand, the highest rate of suicides among African American males occurs between the ages of 25 through 34.[45] While suicides have a profound impact upon family structure and dynamics, irrespective of the age, race, or ethnic background of the suicide victim, the fact that African American males tend to commit suicide at younger ages is likely to have a profound impact on the structure of African American families. For example, individuals in this age group fall within the pool of males eligible for marriage as well as those who are married and in the early stages of the family life cycle. Thus, in addition to creating female-headed families, African American males who commit suicide are more likely to leave dependent children.

Given that suicide is likely to be an indication of an individual's perception of self-worth, and that our society measures self-worth, particularly for males, on the basis of one's socioeconomic status and the acquisition of material objects and status symbols, it seems reasonable to assume that white males nearing the end of their professional careers might question their usefulness and ability to make valuable contributions. Resultant frustration may lead to suicide. Likewise, a growing number of young African American men, unable to attain societal goals and conform to the traditional definition of men as providers and protectors, also commit suicide. In both cases, the actual age is not as much an issue as is being socially consigned to a position of helplessness and forced unemployment. The obvious question is, What effect did liberal social policy have on the increased rate of suicides among African American males? It appears paradoxical that the percentage of African American male suicides would increase during a period when innovative social programs were created to enhance social and economic opportunities for African American family members. However, high rates of unemployment, a low civilian participation rate, and the acceptance of a value orientation that equates individual self-worth with one's ability to produce and consume create a better understanding of why increasing numbers of young African American males experience the same lack of purpose as do white males approaching the age of retirement. There is little doubt that visible gains made by some African American family members overshadowed the overall lack of progress by others.

### Crime

The rise in the proportion of crime affecting African American families became an issue of great concern. An increase in the number of African American males as victims of homicides took place between 1960 and 1980. Becoming a homicide victim is highly correlated with race, gender, and age. Data reveal that African American men are the most likely victims of homicide. Between 1960 and 1980 the rate of homicides for white males (3.6 per 100,000) more than doubled.

Furthermore, in 1960, the homicide rate for African American males was 36.7 per 100,000. In 1980 African American men had the highest homicide rate (60 per 100,000), followed by African American women (13 per 100,000), white men (10 per 100,000) and white women (3 per 100,000). As can be seen, the homicide rate for African American males exceeded the rates for white males, African American females, and white females combined. Again, the implications for African American families are serious. For example, African American males were most likely to be victims of homicide between the ages of 15 to 24. This not only creates a female-maintained household due to death, but another one resulting from incarceration.[46] Typically, this occurs because the majority of African American male homicides are perpetrated by other African American males. Thus, dual female-maintained families are generally the end result of African American male homicides. According to some, this gives further credence to the idea that African American males began to experience mounting frustration and anger, which increasingly became manifested as displaced aggression, when goals and expectations set at the beginning of the turbulent 1960s failed to come to fruition.

## UNDERSTANDING THE GAINS AND "GAINS"

### Liberal Social Policy: Mission and Assumptions

It is fairly evident that not all segments of the African American population experienced social and economic gains similarly. Moreover, race, age, gender, and social class were important determinants of the level of advances made by African American families and their members. How social policy of the 1960s and 1970s contributed to the success of some and the failure of others is of paramount importance. To understand this phenomenon, we must examine the tenets and underlying assumptions associated with liberal social policy.

First was the assumption that, in order for African American families to become viable economic units, they must become an integral part of mainstream America. A second and related condition for remedying the social and economic ills of African American families was embodied in the notion that African American families should strive for and be transformed into the idealized nuclear family. Underlying each of these expectations was the belief that extant African American families were in need of change in terms of their structure and dynamics. Because of this conceptualization of African American families, academicians and policymakers set forth theories characterizing African American families using the culture of poverty and matriarchal and criminal subculture paradigms.[47] To this end, African American families were categorized similarly and without delineation based on regionalism, education, occupation, or income. In the main, there was little recognition that a form of stratification existed among African American families. Nor was there an understanding that there were structurally functional systems operating in the African American community, which, if tampered with, could have negative consequences for African American families.

A significant amount of emphasis was placed on the need for integration of African Americans in social institutions. Support for the internalization of mainstream values and norms abounded from both the academic and nonacademic communities.[48] Furthermore, it was held that if African Americans and whites were placed in the same social and economic milieus, whites would become more tolerant and sensitive to the needs of African Americans. African Americans, too, were expected to acquire norms, values, and other benefits from this association. Hence, liberal social policy was based on a thesis that defined African American families as culturally deprived and socially inadequate. And given that Moynihan, in his work *Family and Nation,* found the growth in African American underclass families as vindication for his earlier analysis and projections, it becomes questionable whether the real issue of blaming African American families for their economically depressed status and other concomitants of poverty will ever be properly addressed by policymakers.[49] From its onset, liberal social policy was fraught with problems that emanated from the failure to adequately assess and integrate the strengths of African American families into social and economic programs.[50] The end result has been an illusion of assimilation and a decline in systems (e.g., mutual-aid networks and African American institutions) that had previously ensured the survival of salient African American family structures.

In trying to understand the impact of liberal social policy, which resulted in some African American families experiencing greater social and economic gains than others, it is useful to distinguish the underclass from more advantaged African American families. The latter group, composed largely of working- and middle-class families, was among those for whom social and economic gains occurred with greater frequency.[51] African American underclass families were not as successful.

According to Miller, the underclass consists of those persons and families who experience continuous unemployment and whose incomes tend to fall below the poverty level as established by the U.S. government. Miller categorizes families with incomes exceeding the poverty line as working class or middle class.[52] The ensuing emphasis on submerging African American family values, which were diametrically opposed to those of the general society, began to occur as African Americans were permitted access to various social, economic, and legal systems.[53] Before the formulation of liberal social policy, there was convergence on the part of African American and white families regarding some societal values.[54] However, since African American families' means of attaining these goals were restricted, their goals were also more narrowly defined, inasmuch as the goals that African American family members sought to attain, being within the realm of realism, were not as broad as those of their white counterparts. In other words, a African American male child, unlike his white counterpart, may have aspired to become a president of a African American–owned business rather than a chief executive officer of a major corporation.

Differential access to opportunity structures caused by economic and racial discrimination has affected the level of goal setting by African American middle-class family members and is responsible for the greater divergence in the goals of African American underclass families and other families in society. To be sure, working-class and middle-class African American families are more likely to predispose successive generations to becoming successful.[55] Because of massive governmental intervention, resources that African American working- and middle-class families possessed were enhanced by liberal social policies.

Though differential gains can be isolated by social class, emergent conditions arose in which the social position of African American families became irrelevant to the overall debilitating effects of liberal social policy on their structure.

African American families, in assuming values inherent in the dominant culture, began establishing goals and expectations consistent with this orientation.[56] Seeking and gaining admission into predominantly white institutions, African American families began to anticipate outcomes commensurate with their own social, psychological, and economic investments. In other words, African American men and women assumed that new social programs and legislation would effectively de-emphasize race as a criterion for success. The increase in the scope and magnitude of social and economic programs seemed ample proof that "race" was losing its significance in determining an individual's life chances in our society. Mass media reports corroborated this perception that affirmative action programs, the 1964 Civil Rights Act, the voting rights act, and so forth were augmenting economic development programs and assuring African American families equal opportunity for upward mobility. Had liberal social policy been effectual, the extent to which an ethnic group became integrated in a majority culture would be purely academic. That this did not occur makes this an issue that warrants consideration. An assessment of African American progress over the last 20 years suggests that African American families and their members became only partially assimilated and experienced modest positive gains. Subscribing to the values of the society at large is useful, to the extent that individuals can reasonably establish and attain goals that represent those of the larger society. For African Americans, other ethnic minorities, and women, this has not held true. Although African American family members can now establish goals broader than those they were limited to before liberal social policy, in no way are these goals parallel to those that can be reasonably established, pursued, and attained by members of white families, particularly white males. Some social scientists cite examples of racial and ethnic minorities who were able to achieve economic wealth and political power by maintaining interdependent family units that engage in mutual cooperation, thereby consolidating their resources.[57] However, autonomy on an individual and familial level is a norm stressed as both important and essential for adequate functioning in Western culture.[58]

In sum, economic independence and growth did not become a reality for many African American families. For the most part, the growth that occurred did little to promote ongoing economic independence for African American families and their members. As the government began to withdraw fiscal responsibility for various social and economic programs, it became clear that advances made by African American families were tenuous and temporary. Much of the growth that African American families had experienced in 20 years was predicated on government involvement and restrictive participation. This has been true in virtually all social and economic areas. Positive gains made by African American families were difficult to sustain without continued government support. Anderson's discussion of the proprietary versus participatory nature of African American enterprise is a poignant illustration of the continued marginal and dependent status of African Americans in general and African American families in particular. In assessing African American entrepreneurship, he posits that

Participatory Black entrepreneurship means that Blacks simply share or participate in the execution of a firm's policy. Where Black proprietary entrepreneurship exists, Blacks decide or make the policies. Between 1960 and 1980, most of the civil rights legislation and affirmative action policies aimed toward giving Blacks the opportunity to function within the business mainstream of the society have been only participatory in effect.[59]

Although Anderson focuses on African American enterprise, his analysis is equally applicable to the relationship of African American families to American institutions in general. Needless to say, although greater numbers of African American families are participating more fully in a larger number of social institutions, neither their participation nor the economic benefits are equal to that of white families. A chief reason for the peripheral relationship between African American family members and social and economic systems can be found in the consignment of African Americans to positions, job sectors, and organizational units that are of low to moderate esteem and status. The increasing proportion of African Americans participating in institutions creates the myth that great gains were made by African American families. However, aside from the inordinate number of entry-level positions that they have assumed, African Americans who make up professional and managerial ranks are generally located in enclaves. This form of neosegregation operates in a fashion quite similar to de facto housing segregation. In the latter case, there is generally evidence that African American families reside in virtually all geographical areas within a given city; yet, closer observation shows that while this may be true, African Americans tend to be concentrated in certain census blocks or subareas within any designated region. Therefore, African American families tend to be isolated from and have limited contact with white families who, while living in the same community, are separated by physical and social distance. As this relates to institutional gains of African American family members, a number of examples of this phenomenon can be found. In the corporate sector, African Americans tended to be isolated in human resources; in government, African Americans became concentrated in community development and human-services departments; and within academia, the largest percentage of African Americans were employed in Black Studies departments. The end result was that African Americans secured positions within traditional institutions, yet remained outside of the mainstream. Thus, as C. Eric Lincoln posits, African Americans need to not only be in the place but in the process.[60] The skills acquired and personal and professional contacts obtained through these positions seldom have intra- or interinstitutional generalizability. That is, these positions are likely to lead to lateral rather than vertical mobility for African Americans.

What appeared to be conformity to liberal social policy was in many instances institutional resistance. Employing African Americans in positions of limited utilitarian value did more to promote dependence than economic independence. Rather than fostering economic independence, liberal social policy created a level of dependence that has been relatively unknown to African American families. Clearly, the hopes and aspirations for many African American men, women, and children were dashed. For others, they were realized only in part.

The adverse consequences of liberal social policy for African American families have been inestimable. It cannot be denied that liberal social policy has had sociopsychological implications. The replacement of a value system that emphasized personal qualities and collective responsibility with one that was more object oriented, focused on the acquisition of goods, social isolation, and independence, combined with unfulfilled expectations, has left many African American families with feelings of frustration, consternation, and confusion.

### Idealized Nuclear Family

The ultimate goal of liberal social policy was the transformation of African American families into self-sufficient economic units akin to the ideal nuclear-family model. Along with the nuclear-family model came traditional male and female role expectations. These role expectations defined men as the sole breadwinners and assigned women to an affective role, whose primary responsibilities were domestic. During the development and expansion of social and economic programs, it appeared as though

African American families who wished to embrace this model would be able to do so. Aside from the fact that economic progress for African American families did not become a reality as projected, the resurgence of the women's movement in the 1970s brought about the evolution of new gender role definitions. As larger numbers of white women became financially independent because of their increased labor-force participation, they challenged traditional definitions that relegated wives to positions subordinate to their husbands. Simultaneously, white middle-class families based on the ideal nuclear family model began to dissolve as marital disruptions throughout the general population increased. This role confusion had an equally devastating effect on African American families who had yet to attain the white middle-class nuclear model. Faced with high rates of African American male unemployment and underemployment, failure of African American businesses to thrive, a differential rate of progress for African American families, disparate social and economic gains for African American males and females, and continued institutional isolation, African American families began to undergo strain brought on by these and other inexorable social and economic pressures.

### A Challenge to African American Family Stability

There is little doubt that the disintegration of African American nuclear and extended families is related to liberal social policy. Attendant problems facing African American families, such as poverty, low civilian workforce participation rates for African American males, and the like, are also indicators that becoming a viable member of our society is far from a reality for many African American men, women, and children.

It was assumed that African American families interested in upward mobility needed only to follow social prescriptions, which encompassed taking advantage of various social and economic programs and accepting a value system considered more amenable to success in an urban post-industrial society. However, liberal social policy was not equipped to efficiently and effectively address the needs of displaced workers, to challenge institutional recalcitrance, and to cure an economy plagued by inflation and recession, thus creating feelings of inadequacy and hopelessness among African American families and their members. In addition, racial inequities became more covert but continued to have a counteractive effect on liberal social and economic programs. Clearly, institutions that obeyed the letter rather than the spirit of civil rights legislation gave rise to what became popularly known as institutional racial discrimination. However, the effects of this surreptitious form of discrimination on African Americans and other ethnic minorities, with its uncertain and elusive nature, are undoubtedly detrimental to the psychological well-being of African American families.

Thus we conclude that structural factors as well as liberal social policy, with its mission and underlying assumptions requiring a social and economic metamorphosis, failed to bring African American families to a position of financial well-being. This failure has contributed significantly to the high rate at which African American nuclear and extended families dissolved over the 20-year period.

Liberal social policy notwithstanding, African American families in general were not prepared to take full advantage of the social and economic programs for which they were the designated beneficiaries. Having been systematically excluded from societal institutions, African American families lacked critical information necessary for accessing social institutions and making optimum use of the myriad social programs available. Therefore, many African Americans were without critical information necessary to make adequate decisions that affected the academic and professional careers of adult and child family members. According to Naisbitt, in an industrial society the strategic resource is capital. But in our new society, as Daniel Bell first pointed out, the strategic resource is information. Not the only resource, but the most important. With information as the strategic resource, access to the economic system is much easier.[61]

Considering the limited knowledge African American families possessed of the complex social, political, and economic systems, the gains made by African American families are commendable. Undoubtedly, much of this can be attributed to the high achievement and work orientations of African American families.[62] It should also be noted that African American women have been compelled to participate in the civilian labor force due to racial disparities in income and economic opportunities faced by African American men, which has historically prevented the inclusion of African American women, wives and mothers, in the cult of domesticity.[63] In general, there were far too many factors that militated against positive gains for an inordinate number of African American families.

In the main, African American families' assimilation was social psychological rather than economic. Thus, they adopted the norms and values of mainstream American society but continued to be permitted limited access to economic opportunities. The illusion of African Americans having made monumental gains and the myth that social institutions have become sufficiently malleable to ensure equity for African Americans are responsible, in part, for the trend to rescind liberal social policy that emerged in the 1980s.

## NOTES

1. Douglas G. Glasgow, *The Black Underclass* (San Francisco: Jossey-Bass, 1980), p. 3.

2. Alphonso Pinkney, *The Myth of Black Progress* (New York: Cambridge University Press, 1984), pp. 99–103.

3. Robert Hill, *Economic Policies and Black Progress: Myths and Realities* (Washington, D.C.: National Urban League, 1981), pp. 39–43.

4. Robert Hill, *The Strengths of Black Families* (New York: Emerson Hall, 1972), pp. 28–32.

5. Hill, *Economic Policies and Black Progress,* pp. 15–17.

6. U.S. Bureau of the Census, *The Social and Economic Status of the Black Population in the United States: An Historical View, 1790–1978,* Series P-23, No. 80 (Washington, D.C.: U.S. Government Printing Office, 1979), p. 62.

7. K. Sue Jewell. "The Changing Character of Black Families: The Effects of Differential Social and Economic Gains," *Journal of Social and Behavioral Sciences* 33 (1988): 143–154.

8. U.S. Bureau of the Census, *The Social and Economic Status of the Black Population in the United States,* p. 62.

9. K. Sue Jewell, *From Mammy to Miss America and Beyond: Cultural Images and the Shaping of U.S. Social Policy* (London: Routledge, 1993), p. 171.

10. Hill, *The Strengths of Black Families,* pp. 11–15; and Jewell, "The Changing Character of Black Families."

11. Graham Spanier and Paul Glick, "Mate Selection Differentials between Blacks and Whites in the United States," *Social Forces* 58 (March 1980): 707–725.

12. U.S. Bureau of the Census, *Statistical Abstract of the United States, National Data Book and Guide to Sources* (Washington, D.C.: U.S. Government Printing Office, 1984).

13. Ibid.

14. Ibid.

15. Ibid.

16. William L. Taylor, "Access to Economic Opportunity: Lessons Since Brown," in *Minority Report: What Has Happened to Blacks, Hispanics, American Indians and Other Minorities in the Eighties?* ed. Leslie W. Dunbar (New York: Pantheon Books, 1984), pp. 31–32.

17. U.S. Bureau of the Census, *America's Black Population: 1970 to 1982, A Statistical View.* Special Publication, P-10/POP-83-1 (Washington, D.C.: U.S, Government Printing Office, 1983), p. 16.

18. Cayton S. Drake, "The Social and Economic Status of the Negro in the United States," in *The Negro American,* ed. Talcott Parsons and Kenneth B. Clark (Boston: Beacon, 1965), pp. 16–20.

19. Gai Berlage and William Egelman, *Experience with Sociology* (Reading, Mass.: Addison-Wesley, 1983).

20. Hill, *The Strengths of Black Families,* pp. 11–12: and Hill, *Economic Policies and Black Progress,* p. 41.

21. U.S. Bureau of the Census, *The Social and Economic Status of the Black Population,* p. 62.

22. Pinkney, *The Myth of Black Progress,* pp. 86–87.

23. Thaddeus H. Spratlen, "The Continuing Factor of Black Economic Inequity in the United States," *Western Journal of Black Studies* 6 (summer 1982): 73–88.

24. U.S. Bureau of the Census, *The Social and Economic Status of the Black Population,* p. 103; U.S. Bureau of the Census, *America's Black Population: 1970 to 1982. A Statistical View.* Special Publication, P-10/POP 83-1 (Washington, D.C.: U.S. Government Printing Office, 1983), pp. 18–19.

25. K. Sue Jewell, "The Changing Character of Black Families."

26. U.S. Bureau of the Census, "Current Population Reports," United States Department of Labor (unpublished report), 1984.

27. U.S. Bureau of the Census, *The Social and Economic Status of the Black Population*, p. 126.

28. Ibid., p. 117.

29. U.S. Bureau of the Census, *America's Black Population*, p. 18.

30. U.S. Bureau of the Census, *America's Black Population*, p. 9.

31. U.S. Bureau of the Census, *The Social and Economic Status of the Black Population*, p. 60.

32. U.S. Bureau of the Census, *America's Black Population*.

33. Tom Joe and Peter Yu, *The "Flip" Side of Black Families Headed by Women: The Economic Status of Black Men* (Washington, D.C.: Center for the Study of Social Policy, 1984).

34. U.S. Bureau of the Census, *America's Black Population*, p. 9.

35. U.S. Bureau of the Census. "Current Population Reports."

36. Joe and Yu, *The "Flip" Side of Black Families Headed by Women*.

37. Joe and Yu, *The "Flip" Side of Black Families Headed by Women*; and Pinkney, *The Myth of Black Progress*.

38. Lois M. Verbrugge, "Marital Status and Health," *Journal of Marriage and the Family* 41 (May 1979): 267–285.

39. Marian Wright Edelman, "The Sea Is So Wide and My Boat Is So Small: Problems Facing Black Children Today," in *Black Children*, ed. Harriet McAdoo and John McAdoo (Beverly Hills, Calif.: Sage Publications, 1985), pp. 72–82.

40. U.S. Bureau of the Census, *The Social and Economic Status of the Black Population*, p. 101; and U.S. Bureau of the Census, *America's Black Population*, p. 18.

41. U.S. Bureau of the Census, *Statistical Abstract of the United States*.

42. Ibid.

43. Louise Meriwether, "Teenage Pregnancy," *Essence*, April 1984, p. 96.

44. U.S. Bureau of the Census, *Statistical Abstract of the United States*.

45. Walter Leavy. "Is the Black Male an Endangered Species?" *Ebony*, June 1983, pp. 41–46.

46. Ibid.

47. E. Franklin Frazier, *The Negro Family in the United States* (Chicago: University of Chicago Press, 1939); Daniel P. Moynihan, *The Negro Family: The Case for National Action* (Washington, D.C.: U.S. Government Printing Office, 1965); Lee Rainwater, *Family Design* (Chicago: AVC, 1965), pp. 308–309; Hyman Rodman, "Family and Social Pathology in the Ghetto" *Science* 161 (1968): 756–762; and Marvin E. Wolfgang, *The Culture of Youth* (Washington, D.C.: U.S. Government Printing Office, 1967).

48. Elliot Leibow, *Tally's Corner* (Boston: Little, Brown, 1966); and Moynihan, *The Negro Family*, pp. 3–8.

49. Daniel P. Moynihan, *Family and Nation* (New York: Harcourt Brace Jovanovich, 1987), pp. 134–135.

50. Robert Hill, "The Black Family: Building on Strengths," in *The Road to Economic Freedom: An Agenda for Black Progress*, ed. Robert L. Woodson (Washington, D.C.: National Center for Neighborhood Enterprise, 1987), pp. 71–88.

51. Pinkney, *The Myth of Black Progress*, pp. 99–114.

52. Seymour Michael Miller, "The American Lower Classes: A Typological Approach," in *Blue Collar World*, ed. Arthur B. Shostak and William Gomberg (Englewood Cliffs, N.J.: Prentice-Hall, 1964).

53. Wade A. Boykin, "The Academic Performance of Afro-American Children," in *Achievement and Achievement Motives*, ed. Janet T. Spence (San Francisco: W. H. Freeman and Co., 1983), p. 328.

54. Wade A. Boykin and Forrest D. Toms, "Black Child Socialization: A Conceptual Framework," in *Black Children*, ed. Harriette McAdoo and John McAdoo (Beverly Hills, Calif.: Sage Publications, 1985), pp. 33–51; John H. Scanzoni, *The Black Family in Modern Society: Patterns of Stability and Security* (Chicago: University of Chicago Press, 1977); John H. Scanzoni, "Black Parental Values and Expectations of Children's Occupational and Educational Success: Theoretical Implications," in *Black Children*, ed. Harriette McAdoo and John McAdoo (Beverly Hills, Calif.: Sage Publications, 1985), pp. 113–122.

55. Scanzoni, *The Black Family in Modern Society*, p. 153.

56. Boykin and Toms, "Black Child Socialization," pp. 33–51.

57. Thomas Sowell, *The Economics and Politics of Race* (New York: William Morrow and Co., 1983).

58. Talcott Parsons and Robert F. Bales, *Family, Socialization and the Interaction Process* (Glencoe, Ill.: Free Press, 1955), pp. 10–11.

59. Talmadge Anderson, "Black Entrepreneurship and Concepts Toward Economic Coexistence," *Western Journal of Black Studies* 6 (summer 1982): 80–88.

60. C. Eric Lincoln, "Black Studies and Cultural Continuity," *Black Scholar* 10 (October 1978): 12–18.

61. John Naisbitt, *Megatrends: Ten Directions Transforming Our Lives* (New York: Warner Books, 1982), p. 15.

62. Hill, *The Strengths of Black Families*, pp. 1–4; Bart Landry, *Black Working Wives: Pioneers of the American Family Revolution* (Los Angeles: University of California Press, 2000): pp. 56–81.

63. Landry, *Black Working Wives: Pioneers of the American Family Revolution*, p. 82.

# CHAPTER 6

# Expectations versus Realization

## SOCIAL WELFARE: A MARRIAGE DISINCENTIVE?

Disagreement over the effects of liberal social policy on African American families can be seen in its most dramatic form in the area of social welfare recipiency. Controversy, which centers on the causal relationship between social and economic programs and African American family stability, invariably finds its locus in the analysis of transfer payments provided by government-sponsored social welfare programs. Although considerable attention has focused on the advantages and disadvantages of social welfare programs on the structure of African American families, a tremendous amount of inconclusiveness and uncertainty remains. Because the urban African American welfare recipient is highly visible, and because the percentage of African Americans who received welfare in 1980, 37 percent, exceeded the 12 percent of the U.S population comprised of African Americans in that year, inordinate attention is drawn to this segment of the population. The inability to establish a correlation between the receipt of welfare benefits and African American familial instability is generally ignored by those outside academic circles. Thus, policymakers take unswerving positions on whether welfare causes African American family instability. In so doing, they use studies that substantiate their arguments as evidence in support of social-policy decisions. Unlike studies that rely on census data, welfare benefits, and other secondary data sources, primary research, in which data has been gathered from questionnaires administered to welfare recipients, has yielded findings that indicate that there is no correlation between African American women's receipt of wel-

fare and marital breakups.[1] Using this method, the only correlation between welfare recipiency and African American women's marital status
is that African American women who receive welfare have lower remarriage rates. However, the extent to which this factor alone contributes to
lower remarriage rates for African American women who receive welfare
is questionable. Other factors, such as imbalanced male-female sex ratios
and African American male unemployment and underemployment, are
also likely to play a significant role in the relatively low rate of remarriage
for African American women. After all, lower-income African American
females who receive welfare benefits are not alone in having low rates of
remarriage. Rather, African American women across all socioeconomic
levels tend to remarry at a rate lower than their white counterparts.[2]

## THE ECONOMIC MOTIVATION ARGUMENT

One reason for conflicting findings of studies that sought to measure
the relationship between welfare recipiency among African American females and marital disruption is that the primary unit of analysis is economically based. Using the normative paradigm, where economics is
thought to be a primary determinant of marital stability, economic feasi-
bility in determining marital disruption is likely to result in findings that
reveal either no relationship or a spurious one when African American
families are studied. Not that there is no economic basis for marital disruption, but that other factors aside from economic ones are likely to be
a greater determinant of marital breakups among African American men
and women.[3] Even in the general population, Mott and Moore challenge
the importance of economic factors in determining marital disruption.
They assert that marriages are not economically determined, and, as a
consequence, neither are dissolutions. Again, this is not to imply that economic solvency does not play a role in marital stability, only that marriages are not likely to be dissolved simply because they are economically
weak. However, evidence suggests that welfare recipiency is a significant
factor in marital disruptions among lower-income white women.[4] In such
cases, it is plausible that economic factors, while not being the sole determinant of marital stability among white couples, may be more important
to white females than to African American females. Thus, it is not surprising that studies reveal white females generally experience status ele-
vation through marriage.[5] Further, it has been empirically verified that
African American women, while earning less than African American men,
do not have as great a salary differential as do white men and women.
Moreover, in many marriages African American women may have education equal to or greater than their spouses. And in occupational areas
African American women may have a higher-status position, either in a
service or high-tech industry. Thus, although economic factors are likely

to be more important in determining marital stability among whites, their value is greatly diminished for African American married couples. Those who expect to find logical explanations for marital disruptions among African American welfare recipients by using an economic incentive model are likely to continue to meet with disappointment.

Does this mean that welfare recipiency positively affects marriages for lower-income African American families? To the contrary, social welfare programs by design and administration have had a debilitating effect on African American families. The fact that welfare places African American men, women, and children in a position of ignominy is difficult to disprove. Moreover, following marital disruption, African American female heads of households and their charges all too frequently become immersed in a vicious cycle of poverty and welfare recipiency, the latter of which can only be escaped temporarily. One of the most unfortunate consequences of the current social welfare system is its inability to enable recipients to become socially and economically independent. Some social scientists rely on statistics on the relatively short duration of welfare recipiency of African American families to refute arguments that the U.S. welfare system produces chronicity for families with incomes below the poverty level, but they overlook the fact that far too many African American families subsist in a state that narrowly exceeds the poverty line, which qualifies one for welfare. Furthermore, the welfare recipient's anxiety and relentless struggle associated with the cyclical pattern of rising and falling in and out of the social welfare system is clearly a position not to be coveted. Coupled with being African American and female, occupying the status of a welfare recipient does little to enhance the already double negative status held by African American women. In addition to economic barriers, African American women who receive welfare must overcome their psychologically and sociologically inferior statuses that may prevent upward mobility because of both intra- and interpersonal factors. In many cases, the obstacles, including welfare recipiency, that African American female heads of households are forced to overcome are insurmountable in the absence of considerable support from external sources.

Because welfare programs have been basically ineffective in improving the standard of living of lower-income African American families, there are few options available to elevate the status of African American poor families.

## A SOCIAL-PSYCHOLOGICAL EXPLANATION

In the past, support from mutual-aid networks had a stabilizing effect on African American two-parent families. Because of an increase in demand for assistance from informal social-support systems, a decrease in resources (due largely to high rates of African American unemployment), and an economically depressed economy, the support that informal self-help groups now make available to African American families maintained by women is not likely to be sufficient to permanently alter the family's economic status. Thus, the tenuous nature of the member's resources, those of the mutual-aid network or kinship network, and societal proscriptions severely limit the extent to which informal helping systems can assist families, whether intact or maritally disrupted.

Still other problems produced by the social welfare system negatively affect African American families that are recipients. A welfare system that provides services to two-parent families, yet has as its primary recipients the mother and children, is divisive in nature. The extent to which social welfare programs are detrimental to intact families is related to their policies and practices, which exclude males in African American two-parent families. Hopkins, in his study of the treatment of African American males by social-service agencies, cites the manner in which administrators and practitioners relegate fathers to a position of unimportance.[6] As Hopkins asserts, African American fathers whose families are recipients of welfare are seldom asked for input into decisions that will affect their family. The fact that needed goods and services are provided by government-supported agencies is not justification for a paternalistic approach to social-service delivery. Given that the African American father's perception of his self-worth and competency in relation to his family is a determinant of marital stability, social-service agencies can influence family stability by the way they relate to the father. Thus, social-psychological attributes are greater predictors of marital outcome among African American families than are economic ones. Specifically, Hampton found that the husband's "self-satisfaction, efficacy, and sense of trust-hostility or the degree to which he feels that he is competent in handling his own destiny" are factors that determine whether the marriage will be sustained or disrupted.[7]

Because separation is a common form of marital dissolution among lower-income African American families, social welfare programs should be designed to relate to absent as well as resident fathers, particularly when reconciliation is possible. Accordingly, social welfare programs should incorporate marriage, family, and employment counseling into their services for adult family members. The tendency to overlook and dismiss African American fathers is one of the obvious ways that social welfare services disrupt African American families. The most common image social welfare agencies maintain of African American fathers and husbands is directly related to the African American male's inability to provide financially for his family. Despite the reason for the family's need for welfare—whether due to layoff, disability, or unemployment—the perception of the irresponsible, lazy, nonproductive African American male influences the service-delivery process. The fact that underclass African

American families occupy a position of economic dependency generally means that powerlessness is experienced by both mothers and fathers. When social welfare agencies become the chief provider of services, they tend to assume an authoritarian posture relative to recipient families. The provision of social welfare services by service providers who perceive themselves as the ultimate authority on matters pertaining to the family's well-being contradicts the societal definition of masculinity, and the African American male's role is usurped. Thus, social welfare programs, not wives, push the African American father and husband out of the family. Furthermore, the African American father, forced out because of his inability to provide financially, is then defined as a liability rather than an asset by social agencies. In view of these circumstances, it is understandable how social agencies can foster discordant relationships in families who receive welfare.

The fact that African American fathers love their children and are sensitive to their needs is an attitude that, as Hopkins indicates, is rarely given serious consideration by service providers in social welfare agencies. He adds that the seed of the self-fulfilling prophecy is sown as African American fathers are perceived as being of marginal utility and are ignored. The end result is the emasculation of African American fathers by a social welfare system that is impervious to the holistic needs of African American underclass families. Hence, the exclusion of African American fathers serves to facilitate their departure.

This gives rise to the image, and stereotypic view, of the female-headed African American underclass family, whose absent father is synonymous with African American male irresponsibility.

To the extent that social welfare programs are correlated with female headship, this phenomenon is more likely to be related to the familial disruptiveness caused by the policies and practices of receiving social welfare. Thus, marital disruption caused by social welfare programs is largely related to the extent to which the African American father's role is undermined by social-service agencies. Moreover, social welfare policy affects the economic stability of intact African American families when occupationally displaced fathers are not successfully retrained and equipped with skills that will enable them to regain or exceed their earlier occupational and economic status. This being the case, efforts to correct social welfare programs should focus on programmatic and policy changes that will provide planning and programming for all family members.

## STATUS OF THE POSTDIVORCE AFRICAN AMERICAN FEMALE-HEADED FAMILY

It is highly unlikely that African American lower-income females are unaware of statistics that reveal that post–divorce women and their children are more likely to experience such disruptions as a drastic decline in their standard of living, adolescent pregnancies, high school dropouts, drug abuse, delinquency, crime, and mental and physical illness than are members of two-parent families.[8] Yet, marital disruption continues to escalate among African American couples.

Unlike African American women, white women generally remain in a postdivorce status for a period of five years. After remarrying, a white female's second spouse is more likely to not only increase her divorced standard of living but to provide an income that exceeds that of her previous marriage.[9]

While it is easy to focus attention on the effects of marital dissolution on underclass African American female-headed families because of the multiplicity of problems they face, marital disruption has consequences damaging to African American families at all socioeconomic levels. Furthermore, marital disruptions occur at a faster rate among college-educated African American females than among African American females in the general population. Corroborating this statistic, Robert Hill found that in 1980 female-headed households were increasing 10 times faster among college-educated African American women than for African American females who had not completed high school.[10] While there is reason to concede that women in the middle and upper classes have greater resources available for accessing social institutions, abundant evidence supports the contention that female-headed families, irrespective of socioeconomic level, have a plethora of problems to overcome. In addition to problems in the labor market, which are related to discriminatory practices and limited opportunities in educational institutions for African American children, still other problems arise because of society's differential treatment of individuals based on race, gender, and class. What this means is that female-headed families cannot function at the same level as male-headed or two-parent families, irrespective of income. However, the basis for the lower-level functioning of female-headed families in general, and African American–maintained families in particular, is not inherent in the structure. Rather, two-parent families are able to optimize their capacity to function because of the presence of the male. For instance, males are guaranteed higher earnings and greater opportunities for promotion and are better able to devote a larger percentage of their careers to work than are mothers with children. The expectation that husbands perform instrumental roles and become the families' chief breadwinners contributes significantly to the preferential treatment of men in the labor market. Since men are treated more favorably, two-parent families derive economic rewards from the male's presence. In effect, these benefits enable two-parent families to function at levels higher than families whose structural arrangements differ from the nuclear type.

Because race and gender also differentially affect income and societal treatment, it is understandable that African American female-headed families, even under optimum conditions where the African American female's income is moderate to high, are likely to have a reduced level of functioning compared to two-parent families. Moreover, because it is highly improbable that a male will be present in the household, because of relatively low remarriage rates, problems faced by the African American female-headed family are likely to persist. Thus, for African American women who experience marital disruption, the real conflict between expectations and realization centers on the fact that the expectation of marital stability is all too often incongruent with the reality of marital dissolution. And in many instances where intact African American families receive welfare, marital disruption, the inability of couples to reconcile, and low remarriage rates could be favorably affected by an effective social-service delivery system. Hence, marital disruption is not likely, as economic motivation theorists suggest, to be a function of the African American female's expectations that her postdivorce standard of living will be improved.

### Remarriage: Private versus Public Transfer Payments

Postdivorce African American females are unlikely to receive compassion or understanding as an institutional response for their economic destitution. The position of the Los Angeles Court of Domestic Relations, which to a large extent is reflective of courts throughout the country, is that following divorce, women who wish to increase their resources have but two choices. In substance, they can either receive public assistance or remarry. Additional support for remarriage as a solution to poverty among female heads of households is provided by the men and women who make up the New Right.[11] The difference between the proponents of this conservative persuasion and the American judicial system is that the former, while supporting marriage as a viable strategy for economically depressed females who maintain families, also seeks the total elimination of welfare. This lack of sensitivity to the economic problems of divorced women is inexorable when one considers that race, age, and number of children affect a woman's ability to remarry.

While there is evidence to support the notion that second marriages, for many women, appear to be more economically motivated than first marriages, compelling women to rely on remarriage as a primary method of elevating their economic status is hardly a viable alternative. And when race is a variable, the chances of remarriage improving the African American female's standard of living is diminished due to an imbalanced sex ratio and unemployment and underemployment among African American males. Duncan and Hoffman, in their study of the economic consequences of marital dissolution, discovered that in their sample after a five-year period of divorce, new husbands of remarried African American women earned significantly less compared to those of white women. They concluded that women who remain divorced were less likely to attract men with high incomes.[12] Thus, the belief that remarriage is a viable alternative to the economic insolvency that typifies the divorced female who heads a family is untenable. The sex ratio makes it even more difficult for African American females to remarry, given the relatively small pool of African American men eligible for marriage.

Limiting the alternatives for greater economic independence for female single parents to choosing between public assistance or remarriage is tantamount to accepting and reinforcing female dependence. That is, females are expected to be unable to adequately provide for their families without depending on external sources of support. This concept supports the differential treatment of women in the labor market, which is translated (among other things) into pay inequities and the underrepresentation of women in mid- and high-level positions where greater economic rewards can be secured. Clearly, the assumption here is that because women are not perceived as the primary source of financial support for their families, there is no justification for paying them wages comparable to those of males with equal qualifications and job responsibilities. Along this line of reasoning, it is the male, not the female, irrespective of her marital status, who is primarily responsible for meeting the financial needs of the family. Therefore, following divorce, females are expected to remain dependent and to transfer their dependency from their former spouses to either the public welfare system or a new spouse. The real irony is that during the era of liberal social policy, social and economic programs were developed to reduce female dependency by fostering the acquisition of skills, particularly for women who were heads of households, yet the judicial and public welfare systems offered little support.[13]

The paradox is that American society expects female single parents to be financially independent, yet the American judicial system, one of the most important of American institutions, does little to assuage institutional or individual dependency. For African American underclass women, the extent to which the courts and other societal institutions were truly interested in promoting economic independence for female heads of households is even more questionable.[14] Moreover, marital status affects child-support payments, as divorced and separated women and widows are more likely to receive child-support payments than are never-married women.[15] It is little wonder that single mothers, including African American women who head families, experience dire economic conditions. Furthermore, the inordinate number of lower-income African American families that terminate marriages by separation rather than divorce, along with an increase in the percentage of African American families headed by never-married women, means that many African American women are in the two categories where absent fathers are least likely to fulfill their financial obligations for child support.[16] Equally alarming is the finding that one year after divorce only 50 percent of divorced fathers pay child support.[17] Based on the modest child support the courts award to women in general and African American women in particular, in conjunction with the laxity with which nonresident fathers comply with child-support awards, the institutional response that perceives welfare or remarriage as a feasible alternative to the plight of female single parents is damaging to female-maintained families.

This idea that female heads of families should receive either public or private transfer payments rather than contribute significantly to their own families conflicted with the societal value of individual autonomy. While efforts were being undertaken to enable African American men and women to develop skills that would promote more independence, counterefforts were encouraging female economic dependence. These double messages served to confound and thwart economic stability for African American families.

## THE NEVER-MARRIED AFRICAN AMERICAN WOMAN

The African American woman whose marriage is dissolved is not alone in experiencing conflict between expectations and realizations caused by marital status. There is a growing number of African American women who are joining the pool of never marrieds. Included in this segment of the African American population are increased numbers of female-maintained families with children. In addition, there is a definite growth in the number of African American women with college degrees who do not marry. Though these women are at opposite ends of the spectrum, theories that have been set forth to explain African American singlehood, with or without children, are similar in nature. The notion has been advanced, in the case of the underclass African American female with children born out of wedlock, as well as the better-educated, more financially independent African American woman, that the paucity of eligible African American males accounts for their inability to enter into a marital union. As such, the chances of their remaining single tend to increase rather than diminish with age. Here the conflict over expectations versus realization is related to the propensity for individuals to marry at some point in their lives, since African Americans, like their white counterparts, continue to value marriage as an institution.

The never-married African American woman with children is not a new phenomenon, yet the proportion of single African American women with children who do not marry began increasing in the 1960s. Many attribute the growing number of African American single women to a shortage of African American males, but at the beginning of the era of liberal social policy African American males and females envisioned a society in which African Americans would assume traditional gender role positions as husbands and wives. However, liberal social policy was unable to create significant occupational advances for African American males, which would have enabled them to earn substantially larger incomes and to have a greater degree of security in the marketplace. Replacing discriminatory practices with those that lead to greater job retention and promotions would have reduced the proportion of single African American females.

One consequence of the industrial displacement of African American males, many of whom have become chronically unemployed, is manifested in retreatist behavior. Having given up hope of becoming gainfully employed, and frustrated with their inability to find permanent employment, many of these once-eligible marriage partners have withdrawn from the labor market entirely. Having done so, they are represented among others within society who, like themselves, have given up the American Dream. They have adopted a lifestyle that by most standards is its antithesis. Thus, for some underclass African American males whose labor is only temporarily in demand, drug abuse, alcoholism, and mental illness are the collective responses of alienation caused by the overwhelming lack of opportunities for participation in mainstream institutions. Other self-destructive behaviors, such as homicides, are more spontaneous in nature but also reflect cultural disaffection and the lack of control over one's destiny. These forms of apathy and aggression, while undoubtedly a reaction to thwarted goals and aspirations, tend to seriously attenuate the number of African American males eligible for marriage.

## AFRICAN AMERICAN TWO-PARENT FAMILIES

Not all African American families are maritally disrupted. Approximately 55 percent of African American families were intact in 1980; however this percentage began to decrease and represented less than the majority of African American families in the twenty-first century, which will be discussed in chapter 10. However, such families are to be commended, as they are able to remain intact against extraordinary odds. These families, like other families, irrespective of structural arrangement, share the same expectations for familial stability and social and economic progress. When one considers that some African American families remained intact, recorded gains throughout the 1960s and 1970s, and continued to demonstrate upward mobility in the 1980s, there is little doubt that these families accomplished an extraordinary feat. Certainly, such families can provide invaluable insight into establishing strategies that ensure the sustenance and viability of the African American family as a unit. Specifically, they are likely to possess critical information on the use of social-support systems, the ability to establish and reformulate goals, and the capacity to synthesize important cultural values inherent in the larger society with those within the African American community. All too frequently, structures, particularly those within the African American community, that manage to survive and progress seldom receive the attention essential for providing clues to their survival. To this end, a number of questions can be raised for which answers are definitely needed.

## NOTES

1. Stephen Bahr, "The Effects of Welfare on Marital Stability and Remarriage," *Journal of Marriage and the Family* 41 (August 1979): 557; William A. Darity Jr., and Samuel L. Myers Jr., "Does Welfare Dependency Cause Female Headship? The Case of the Black Family," *Journal of Marriage and the Family* 46 (November 1984): 766–767.

2. Greg J. Duncan and Saul D. Hoffman, "A Reconsideration of the Economic Consequences of Marital Disruption," *Demography* 22 (November 1985): 493–495.

3. Frank L. Mott and Sylvia F. Moore, "The Causes of Marital Disruption among Young American Women: An Interdisciplinary Perspective," *Journal of Marriage and the Family* 41 (May 1979): 363–364.

4. Bahr, "The Effects of Welfare," p. 557.

5. Duncan and Hoffman, "A Reconsideration."

6. Thomas J. Hopkins, "The Role of Community Agencies as Viewed by Black Fathers," *Journal of Orthopsychiatry* 42 (1972): 508–516.

7. Robert L. Hampton, "Institutional Decimation, Marital Exchange, and Disruption in Black Families," *Western Journal of Black Studies* 4 (summer 1980): 134–135.

8. Lenore Weitzman, "The Economics of Divorce: Social and Economic Consequences of Property, Alimony and Child Support Awards," *UCLA Law Review* 28 (1981): 1228; and Lois M. Verbrugge, "Marital Status and Health," *Journal of Marriage and the Family* 41 (May 1979): 267–283.

9. Christopher Jencks, "Divorced Mothers, Unite!" *Psychology Today* 16 (November, 1982): 73.

10. Barbara Ehrenreich and Karin Stallard, "The Nouveau Poor," *Ms.* 11 (August 1982): 222.

11. Weitzman, "The Economics of Divorce" and Ehrenreich and Stallard, "The Nouveau Poor," p. 223.

12. Duncan and Hoffman, "A Reconsideration."

13. U.S. Bureau of the Census, *Statistical Abstract of the United States: National Data Book and Guide to Sources,* 106th ed. (Washington, D.C.: U.S. Government Printing Office, 1986), p. 286.

14. Ibid.

15. Ehrenreich and Stallard, "The Nouveau Poor," p. 219.

16. Jencks, "Divorced Mothers, Unite!" p. 74.

17. Jencks, "Divorced Mothers, Unite!" p. 74; and Ehrenreich and Stallard, "The Nouveau Poor," p. 219.

# CHAPTER 7

# The 1980s: A Period of Social Conservatism and Social Reawakening

The "patient's" vital signs were rapidly deteriorating, blood pressure was rising, temperature climbing, and pulse throbbing. Eventually, the overall system was in a state of disequilibrium.

Code Blue was called.* Attendants and other experts rushed in and confirmed the "patient's" declining status. Initially prognosis was uncertain, yet there was room for hope. Later, it was thought that with emergency treatment and artificial life-support systems, the "patient's" condition would improve markedly. Although the "patient" would be in a total state of dependency, experts believed that the use of life-support systems would allow time for monitoring, stabilization, and experimentation with new treatments, designed to bring about an improved level of functioning. Barring complications, recovery seemed likely.

A sigh of relief could be heard from those concerned. Now that chances for survival appeared good, a series of questions were posed to the experts. Will the "patient" survive? How long will it take for full recovery? Will the level of functioning remain at the pretrauma level, improve, or decrease? What will be the monetary costs for treatment? The answers to these and similar questions remained ambiguous and inconclusive. A wait-and-see attitude prevailed.

With the passage of time and the application of numerous modalities of treatment, the "patient" continued to remain in a state of dependency. The prolonged use of artificial life-support systems became a point of contention, as dependency resulted in rising costs. Earlier considerations, once liberal, became conservative as the experts' prognosis for improved functioning was grim. Since continued dependency on artificial means failed to result in independent functioning, hope begun to fade. At this time, concern for the emotional and monetary costs to others began to take precedence over earlier considerations for the "patient." The question now posed to the experts was, "Should we pull the plug?"

[*Code Blue means human life is at risk and immediate intervention is necessary.]

## A CASE OF SOCIAL TRAUMA: SHOULD WE PULL THE PLUG?

This scenario, more commonly applied to patients undergoing medical crises, is equally applicable to individuals experiencing social trauma. Taking place on a grand scale in the 1960s, the "patient" represents the inordinate number of poor and African American families; the "experts," the policymakers; and the "concerned," the more economically advantaged and socially informed American men, women, and students.

Underlying the massive change in social policy in the 1960s and 1970s was the belief, held by civil rights activists and others concerned with the plight of the poor, that economically disadvantaged groups were faced with social and economic exigencies requiring emergency measures. This trauma was manifested in its most dramatic and volatile forms by social movements, urban violence, and student protests. The new social and economic programs were considered temporary measures to allow for stabilization and ultimately to enable poor and African American families to function better by increasing their participation in the mainstream United States. Moreover, these efforts were considered social and economic remedies to make up for the past injustices to African Americans. Accordingly, the "recovery" hoped for was a level of functioning for African American families that, according to African American scholars, had been destroyed by slavery. Thus, subsidized housing, liberalized public assistance, child-care development centers, Medicaid, food stamps, job-training programs, affirmative action, and so on were intended to promote economic independence for poor and African American families.

Unfortunately, complications set in as inflation grew, established industries declined, and a multiplicity of social and economic programs failed to curb social isolation for poor and African American families throughout society. After monitoring the progress of poor and African American families for more than a decade and assessing the mounting costs for government-supported programs, the country entered into a period of reassessment. Many American taxpayers were disenchanted with the depressed economy and believed that social policies were benefiting poor and African American families at the expense of the majority. Policymakers who represented the taxpayers began to raise questions regarding the costs and utility of such efforts. It was then concluded that dependence in this state appeared permanent, probability for improvement was slim, and that social and economic life supports should be removed. Because they were dependent and powerless, the approximately 5.3 million poor families in America in 1980, 1.7 million of whom were African American, had little input into this decision. Irrefutably, the artificial measures had not enabled social-policy experts to identify viable methods for effecting financial independence for poor and African American families. In the case of medical emergencies, when life-support systems are withdrawn, some patients survive, while others do not. How well poor and African American families in America would survive in the absence of formal social-support systems became an issue of much heated debate. On one side were advocates who indicated that formal social-support systems had not been maintained long enough. Critics argued that poor and African American families had had sufficient opportunities to benefit from these measures, which their constituents were no longer willing to pay for. What began to surface from this conservative persuasion was the prevailing attitude that poor and African American families had not demonstrated the will to live. Hence, the onus for survival was transferred from the government to its dependents: poor and African American families.

### Reassessment and Retrenchment

The social and economic climate of the late 1970s and the 1980s indicated that poor and African American families were unlikely to progress beyond a level of social and economic dependency.

Emphasis on needs began to shift from the economically disadvantaged to problems encountered by other members of society. Increasingly, attention was focused on majority families, especially those with middle-class status. The change in government policy in the 1980s was due to many of the same social and economic factors that had adversely affected African American families. High rates of unemployment, escalating crime rates, growing out-of-wedlock births, and an increase in marital disruptions were among the many problems that made policymakers reexamine governmental expenditures. However, these problems, while critical, were not exclusively responsible for the mood of conservatism that engulfed the country in the 1980s. Of paramount importance was the public's declining confidence in the government's ability to stabilize the economy, maintain a lower debt ceiling, and assure employment for numbers of displaced workers.

Understandably, the focus of attention was placed on government spending. When the country's economic woes were blamed on runaway government spending, domestic programs came under vicious attack. This not only set the stage for a careful reexamination of social and economic programs but for a reassessment of the status of the recipients of such programs. The outcome of such analyses was to restore the economy and American families' confidence in it.

Ushered in on a platform of social reform, the Reagan administration began to reformulate social policy. In so doing, conservatives highlighted negative conditions facing poor families in general and African American families in particular. By attributing these problems to liberal social policy, rather than to regulations, administrative policies, and preexisting conditions that mitigated the effectiveness of liberal social policy, social conservatives proposed the rescission of social and economic programs.

While the Reagan administration claimed to be following a public mandate to make major changes in social policy, liberals maintained that support for these undertakings was not as prevalent as suggested.[1] Naisbitt asserts that while 43 million people voted for Ronald Reagan, 42 million voted against him.[2] For this reason, some have questioned the level of public support for these major changes in social policy. Nevertheless, the Reagan administration was not influenced by admonitions from individuals opposed to this reactionary form of social policy. What followed were proposals for and the eventual implementation of budgetary cuts to existing social and economic programs. Aside from advocating that civil rights legislation, such as affirmative action and the 1965 Voting Rights Act, be rescinded, the Reagan administration invoked the furor of its political adversaries by espousing the complete decentralization of government, known as "New Federalism." The establishment of new governmental priorities, designed to end what was labeled as reverse discrimination and economic injustices to majority families, resulted in the reformulation of a plethora of social policies. What began as a period of reassessment made the 1980s a decade of retrenchment.

### Reformulation of Social Policy

The Reagan administration's agenda encompassed massive, and what some refer to as radical, reform. Efforts to bring government spending under control for the purpose of balancing the federal budget were expressed as the fundamental basis for making drastic cuts in domestic programs. Supported by welfare revisionists, a return to true conservatism was imminent as the withdrawal of government involvement in social welfare programs was proposed and quickly implemented in 1981. The new set of government policies placed defense as a top priority and relegated social welfare programs.[3] Just as liberal policymakers had found an abundance of academic support for their inventive programs, conservatives from the academy came to the aid of welfare revisionists by advancing theories and postulates that discounted the effectiveness of liberal social policy. Traditionalists were among the growing list of scholars claiming that the number of families in poverty was substantially lower than reports would indicate. By relying on a new set of criteria for measuring poverty, which entailed counting all welfare benefits, cash and noncash, as income, one such report indicated that the number of persons in poverty had been overestimated by 4 million in 1976.[4] Lending even more support for abandoning social welfare programs, other scholars, such as Roger Freeman, were convinced that changes proposed by the Reagan administration would cause distress only to those who, as Freeman states, were getting too much in the first place anyway.[5] Among the various programs affected by these new conservative social policies were Aid to Families with Dependent Children, Medicaid, educational grants, federal subsidized housing, food stamps, and affirmative action. Left virtually unaltered were Social Security, Medicare, and veterans' benefits.[6]

Other changes became apparent as the decade progressed. The Reagan administration, after a second electoral victory, resumed its program of government decentralization of and disengagement from social services. Legislation intended to buttress a return to community and private responsibility was proposed and in some cases enacted. For example, the Reagan administration supported bills that enforced paternal responsibility for child support. Such measures proposed the withholding of overdue payments through seizure of federal and state tax refunds and reducing welfare benefits for women who remarry by expecting stepfathers to provide financial support for stepchildren. The ultimate aim of these laws was to relieve the government of its financial responsibility in this area.

The abrupt rescission of various programs on which African American families had become dependent revealed the extent to which progress had truly taken place. As conservative social policies began to unfold, it became apparent that many African American families who appeared to have escaped to the middle class had done so only peripherally. For them, ascent was merely temporary.

## SOCIAL POLICY REFORMULATED

### New Federalism

New Federalism was designed to return to the states the power and authority to make critical decisions regarding the establishment of priorities and the administration of social welfare services. Delegating additional responsibility to state government for the delivery of social services was proposed to give states more latitude in policy formulation and the dispensation of funds. Specifically, New Federalism entailed the federal government taking over Medicaid costs, while the states assumed responsibility for food stamps, AFDC, and other welfare programs. Considerable disagreement took place over the capacity of state governments to run social programs efficiently and fairly. At this point, glaring differences were apparent in the percentage of government funds that states allocate for social welfare services to the poor. Because states do not uniformly treat social services as a priority, the effects of New Federalism can result in minuscule benefits to African American and poor families solely on the basis of geographic residence.

### From Collective to Private Responsibility

The conservative policy initiated by the Reagan administration, intended to absolve the federal government of its responsibility for social welfare programs, involved more than the transference of authority for welfare programs to the states. Included in this attempt to reduce the federal government's commitment to social welfare programs was an effort to ensure that the private sector assumed a greater share of the responsibility. The argument conservatives advanced to substantiate this move was that the expanded role of government had served to reduce charitable contributions to private organizations.[7] It was suggested that the private sector's enormous resources had remained untapped over the two preceding decades and that the sheer magnitude of resources needed to care and provide for the poor had to be provided in part by others, particularly the private sector. To effect this transition, proposals entailed tax breaks and various incentives, such as collapsing CETA and transforming this job training effort to Private Industry Councils throughout the country. Support for this program, which reassigned the government's function of social-service delivery to the private sector, came from the trickle-down theory. The government held that by easing regulations and providing corporations with incentives and financial opportunities for expansion, the private sector would respond by creating jobs, thereby reducing unemployment and poverty. In this same vein, the federal government encouraged and supported the introduction of what proved to be unsuccessful legislation to lower the minimum wage. Arguing that a lower minimum wage would result in numerous jobs for youth (rather than their exploitation, as opponents of this bill argued), the Reagan administration remained undaunted and determined to effect this controversial change in social policy.

The shift from collective to private responsibility included more than a greater role for the private sector. Volunteerism was promoted as a moral obligation and an avenue that had been underutilized over the 20-year period during which the government was predominant in the provision of social welfare services.[8] Government reports indicated the extent to which volunteers were already an integral part of social-service delivery systems, especially those geared to children in child-development centers and the aged in area agencies for the aging. According to these same government sources, evidence indicated that innumerable volunteers were available representing untapped resources, which, if utilized, would reduce government expenditures. This approach to social-service delivery, in which communities were expected to shoulder more responsibility for their own members, was further evidence that the country had gone full circle, from neighbors helping neighbors to institutional responsibility and back to self-help.

### Workfare Mandated

Based on the philosophical tenets that welfare recipients are inherently lazy and lack any real incentives to work, workfare programs took on greater importance. The 1981 Omnibus Budget Reconciliation Act, which shifted welfare responsibility to the states, offered three optional programs from which the states could select: Community Work Experience (workfare), Work Supplementation, and the Work Incentive Demonstration Project. A year later the government transferred even greater responsibility for social-service delivery by having states assume the administration of employment programs.[9]

The purpose of such programs was to reduce welfare caseloads. Moreover, workfare was the government's attempt to inculcate welfare recipients with acceptable work habits and to convince the general public that an economic exchange system was still in place. The government's stance was designed to allay the concerns of those who shared the welfare revisionist's conviction that welfare recipients should work in exchange for benefits, irrespective of the nature of the work in which they were engaged.

To further heighten the already punitive stance of neoconservatives regarding social welfare reform, the U.S. Senate on June 17, 1988, overwhelmingly voted to approve a bill that its supporters labeled the first federally mandated work program for able-bodied welfare recipients. Upon becoming law, the Family Support Act, including JOBS, the Jobs Opportunities and Basic Skills Training Program, required states to provide education, training, and jobs for able-bodied adults on welfare, except those with children under three. Further, this legislation increased child-support payments by requiring states to withhold wages of absent parents and required that the parent or guardian work a minimum of 16 hours each week in community service in exchange for welfare benefits.[10]

### Other Policy Changes and Their Outcomes

Following the Reagan administration's first year of leadership, considerable changes in social policy had already begun to take place. In addition to cutting millions of dollars from the federal budget for social welfare programs, eligibility requirements had reduced the number of welfare recipients. Efforts were being made to lower expenditures for still other social programs, but the political resistance and opposition voiced by liberals prevented them. For example, controversy erupted when federal government nutritionists proposed that pickle relish and catsup be classified as vegetables, a proposal that was later rejected. Still, cuts in federal funds allocated to the National School Lunch and National School Breakfasts programs were made.[11]

The fact that not all domestic programs underwent budgetary cuts raised questions regarding the federal government's partiality for various segments of the population. The most vocal and ardent foes of welfare revisionists were quick to point to the government's protectionist attitude toward middle-class Americans, who were the beneficiaries of social programs that remained virtually untouched. These groups of individuals whose benefit levels were not reduced were beneficiaries of Social Security, veteran's benefits, and Medicare. When objections were made to budgetary cuts that affected the poor but not the middle class, the government's retort was that the truly needy among the poor would also be provided for. Thus, safeguards were provided, which theoretically guaranteed that families who could demonstrate, using revamped means tests, that they were destitute would be eligible for and receive federal assistance. Those exempted from benefit reductions were protected by what Reagan termed a "safety net."

Policy changes were not limited to social welfare programs alone. As cited earlier, civil rights legislation was subjected to a complete reappraisal. Both affirmative action plans and the voting rights acts of 1965 and 1968 underwent reassessment. The number of litigations for affirmative action and voting rights violations greatly diminished during Reagan's term in office.[12] Moreover, companies with federal contracts that were mandated to report their affirmative action contracts were no longer compelled to adhere to this stipulation unless their contract met the new fiscal criterion: The minimum was raised from $50,000 to $1 million. Thus, companies receiving federal contracts under the $1 million amount were exempt from submitting affirmative action plans. Other firms were notified that their affirmative action plans would be reviewed only every five years.[13]

This radical shift in social policy from liberal to conservative did far more than reduce moneys to social and economic programs. It established a new social climate with a growing intolerance for conditions facing African American and poor families in the United States. In making monumental changes in social policy, the federal government insisted that middle-class families had been ignored and had become the caretakers of African American and poor families for 20 years. Using this rationale, the government decided that greater benefits would be realized by all if the following occurred: the federal government placed greater emphasis on and appropriated more dollars for defense, budgetary cuts in social welfare programs were made, and the government deregulated industry and implemented tax incentives for big business to boost the economy.

The federal government moved rapidly toward attaining its goals. By cutting the food stamp and AFDC programs, welfare recipients with earnings were among the poor to feel the impact of these initiatives, which were supposed to balance the budget and restore economic and moral stability to the country. Levitan and Johnson assert that these budgetary cuts raised marginal taxes substantially, which meant that many African American families who constitute the working poor were no longer eligible for any form of welfare assistance. These policy changes caused the disposable income of the average AFDC family with earnings to fall in every state in 1982. In addition, this created the very work disincentives that conservatives had attributed to liberal social policy. Thus, in 12 states a nonworking AFDC parent with two children was better off financially than a working non-AFDC parent in comparable circumstances.[14] In 1981 budgetary cuts in social programs had removed nearly 500,000 families from the social welfare rolls.[15] Moreover, Joe and Rogers assert that the Reagan administration failed to replace work incentives to the working poor, in spite of the fact that this group displayed the "self-supporting" behavior that the administration was interested in promoting.[16] While these were some of the more immediate effects of the implementation of conservative social policy, continued efforts in this direction resulted in even more changes.

Advocates of liberal social policy expressed considerable dissatisfaction over policy goals and objectives that they considered grossly insensitive to the needs of African American and poor families. Nevertheless, the federal government did not halt its effort. Rather, the administration continued working to bring reactionary policy to fruition. After four years of conservative policy, the federal government claimed that the economy had made a phenomenal recovery. The social and economic policies to which the Reagan administration referred, also known as "Reaganomics," generally impressed conservatives and repulsed liberals. Reaganomics could be defined as a strategy to return the country to economic stability and to return government to the people; the latter goal was to be achieved by giving responsibility for social programs to the states, the private sector, and the community. However, for many African American families, Reaganomics symbolized a return to the pre-1960s era, when civil liberties could not be taken for granted. The "good old days" the welfare revisionists so frequently lamented were ones that civil rights activists and advocates of liberal social policy had directed tremendous effort to change.

African Americans, instrumental in the social revolution that precipitated liberal social policy, perceived these revisionists policies as more than mere attempts to shore up the economy. In general, the Reagan administration was considered an ally to the rich and an adversary to poor and African American families. Although other groups demanded that power and wealth be redistributed, African American families, with the exception of those few who belonged to politically conservative interest groups, were appalled by the measures taken by welfare revisionists. In the main, African American intellectuals believed that the welfare revisionists' attempts to extend policy recommendations—from cutting the federal budget for social programs to attacking affirmative action, the voting rights act, and educational grants and loans—would have a definite impact on African American families across all socioeconomic classes. Even the more conservative element among African Americans, generally represented by African American businessmen, expressed dissatisfaction over the government's proposal to reduce support for federal guaranteed loans to small businesses.

African American families' disillusionment was largely rooted in the negative assumptions that underscored conservative social policy. The social-inadequacy theory of African American family life, once used by liberals as the basis for the social and economic programs of the 1960s, was now used by conservatives to explain the necessity for eradicating social and economic programs. African American families, they believed, had been receiving undeserved benefits from social and economic programs. They also believed that the disproportionate number of African American families receiving welfare had other alternatives for producing and consuming than relying on the federal government for support. The prevailing image was one of welfare recipients as able-bodied individuals whose abuse and fraudulent behavior at the taxpayer's expense would no longer be tolerated. To be fair, the image of welfare being synonymous with African American families was not peculiar to any one political persuasion. However, the notion that somehow there was a parasitic relationship between African American families, in all strata, and the government was novel.

This stereotype of African American families, created by the development of social programs and civil rights legislation, made some people feel that the government was solicitous and unduly generous toward all African American families in America. People also believed that African American families were benefiting at the expense of white families, and that the rewards African American families received were more than commensurate with their efforts.

In many respects, this nondiscriminative perception of African American families set in motion a slow but gradual rekindling of racial unity and activism among middle-class African American and intellectuals, the significance of which cannot be understated, as African Americans who were active participants in the civil rights movement once again began to recognize their commonality of interests with African American families in the underclass. Heretofore, social activism among African Americans had reached the predictable lull that characterizes social revolutions, as they peak and recede in a cyclical fashion.[17] The contention was that African American families were prospering at a rate that surpassed that of the average American family because it was believed that opportunities were being made available to African American families in inequitable proportions; this attitude led the Reagan administration to emphasize the need to restore institutions to their pre-1960s state. In so doing, they argued, African Americans would no longer receive preferential treatment at the expense of other cultural groups. The implication was that African Americans were receiving benefits to which they were not entitled. Because of the contention that many undeserving African American families were receiving government goods and services, while other families were going wanting, the administration became preoccupied with ensuring that the work ethic become the focal point of all social programs, particularly social welfare services. The assumption of policy revisionists was that liberal social policy had given rise to social and economic programs with built-in work disincentives.[18]

The trend toward lowering the federal budget by reducing the federal government's involvement in social welfare programs continued throughout Reagan's first term and was reemphasized when he resumed office for a second term. Between 1980 and 1985, the Reagan administration took credit for economic growth and a reduction in the overall rate of unemployment. The economic upturn, frequently mentioned by administration officials, was labeled by Reagan as a sign that the country was experiencing an economic recovery. The withdrawal of government support for social welfare programs and the laxity of monitoring and enforcing civil rights legislation were considered—along with other policy modifications, including tax inducements to big business—as having contributed to the improved economic conditions during Reagan's first term in office. Given their high degree of success, the welfare revisionists continued to move forward with similar policy goals in the second term of the Reagan administration. Depending on one's political persuasion, the Reagan administration's social-policy initiatives can be categorized as conservative or radically conservative.

It became increasingly clear following Reagan's election to a second term of office that the country had become polarized. Disavowing the administration's claim of an economic recovery, African Americans offered little support for Reagan in the 1984 national election.

Although many argued that the general public remained reticent and ambivalent regarding conservative social policy, the tenor of feelings and attitudes regarding African American and poor families in 1984 had changed little from those of 1980. In fact, the undercurrent of dissatisfaction with government's expanded role in providing social programs was more firmly rooted in 1984. It was no longer considered socially unacceptable to voice disapproval for the continued inability of African American and poor families to rise out of poverty. The continued economically depressed status of African American and poor families and attendant problems were considered further evidence of moral turpitude. Moreover, the public's increased awareness of intergenerational poverty, interpreted by culture-of-poverty theorists as inspired by a deviant value system and lifestyle, provided ample justification for eliminating welfare programs, which were perceived as exacerbating the cyclical nature of poverty and dependency. The media was unrelenting in its portrayal of poor African American families as morally corrupt, which lent further credence to welfare revisionists' position that African American underclass families were contributing to the annihilation of traditional American cultural values. Embraced by a growing cadre of supporters who had combined religious beliefs and political action and were calling themselves the Moral Majority, the Reagan administration vigorously pursued the mission of improving the economy by offering economic incentives to industry to boost the free enterprise system. At the same time, efforts were made to safeguard against what was believed to be the further moral decline of society by removing social welfare programs that were considered work disincentives for poor families. In this context, equity and social justice were felt by conservatives to be lacking. Where violations of civil rights were said to occur, conservatives argued that the nonpoor were the victims rather than the poor. Old arguments that stressed the frugality of poor immigrant families who had successfully ascended from poverty resurfaced. Along this line of reasoning, George Gilder, in analyzing social welfare programs and the lack of parity between African American families and their white counterparts, suggested that the triumvirate that was the basis for economic mobility for other ethnic groups was lacking among African American families. According to Gilder, those elements "family, work and faith," were all but decimated by liberal social and economic programs.[19] Adding more support for conservative ideologues was Lawrence Mead's analysis of liberal social policy, in which he concluded that the permissive nature of social welfare programs, whereby the government failed to set up conditions for reciprocal exchange, had resulted in irresponsibility among the poor and an overall deterioration in their moral character.[20] These and similar expositions by Charles Murray and others were myopic and failed to capture the crucial elements that contributed to the failure of liberal social and economic programs to radically alter the despicable conditions facing African American and poor families in America.[21] In general, they have chosen to ignore the fact that liberal social policy was ill equipped to alter societal institutions, making them permanently amenable to affording African American families opportunities for social and economic progress. Clearly, intellectuals of this genre have had a profound impact on the proliferation of conservative social welfare policy during the 1980s. Despite Reagan's campaign promise to balance the budget within two years by making drastic cuts in social and economic programs, the country's debt grew uncontrollably. The federal budget deficit soared from $74 billion in 1980 to an unprecedented $221 billion in 1986.[22]

A major occurrence that raised serious questions regarding the government's future role in social-service delivery was the passage of the Gramm-Rudman-Hollings plan in December 1985. This law, more popularly known as Gramm-Rudman, was designed to gradually eliminate the federal deficit, which in 1985 exceeded $200 billion, by imposing mandatory spending cuts in domestic programs. Considerable disagreement existed over the constitutionality of this law, which invoked an automatic formula for mandatory cuts in domestic programs in the event that the administration failed to enact voluntary reductions in federal spending. There was also genuine concern over the effects of this legislation on social welfare programs. On the one hand, social welfare advocates wondered how these programs would fare under this edict. Alternatively, ardent supporters of conservative welfare policy voiced reservations and trepidation over the potential of Gramm-Rudman to make deep cuts in the defense budget. One pivotal issue centered on whether the government's reluctance to raise taxes would lead to drastic cuts in budgetary allocations to social welfare programs. The fact that these programs had already been subjected to earlier budgetary cuts and policies that had reduced the level of benefits and beneficiaries generated suspicion that Gramm-Rudman's effect on social welfare programs would be ominous and far reaching. Under the terms of Gramm-Rudman, the federal government was compelled to make budget cuts to reach a zero deficit by 1991. To eliminate the $200 billion federal deficit, a reduction of $144 billion was projected by 1987. Further, an additional $36 billion budget cut a year was deemed necessary to achieve a zero deficit by 1991. Given the Reagan administration's conservative policy and disaffection for social welfare programs, liberals believed that the programs that would be voluntarily cut to prevent the invoking of automatic reductions would be social welfare programs. The provision that liberals found objectionable—and which the U.S. Supreme Court ruled unconstitutional, citing that it violated the constitutional requirement that the executive and legislative powers of government be kept separate—stipulated that if Congress and the president could not reach a consensus on how to trim the budget, automatic cuts would occur that would either reduce or eliminate many federal programs. Still, the court's ruling does not allay doubts over policymakers' sensitivity toward the poor during an era of conservativism.[23] Further evidence of the Reagan administration's social-policy failures (and of the failure of their assurances of an economic recovery) was the 1987 stock market crash. On Monday, October 19, 1987, stock values plum-

meted, causing a worldwide economic panic. Furthermore, many economists believe that the 1987 Wall Street crash had negative economic
consequences exceeding those of the 1929 crash.[24]

In sum, social policy throughout the first half of the decade of the 1980s
continued to reflect social conservatism. What is striking about social neoconservatism is the redefining of the victims of social injustice. In this
sense, neoconservatism replaces African American and poor families as
victims of social inequities with majority families. Moreover, the perpe-
trators also change places. Accordingly, African Americans and not society are blamed for the lack of parity between African American and white
families in America. Hence, social policy formulated with a conservative
undergirding operates on a zero-sum basis, whereby equity for African
American families is thought to result in social inequities for majority
families.

### Social Conservatism and the African American Community

It is not always easy to separate the effects of one phenomenon from
another. In many respects, a number of years that yield repeated obser-
vations are necessary to isolate the impact of social, political, and economic events on major institutions. Another salient factor in determining
the effects of social phenomena on various societal systems is the fact that
the effects of preexisting phenomena cannot always be successfully controlled. In this case, where do the effects of liberal social policy end and
the impact of conservative public policy begin? The answers to this and
related questions are not clear-cut, particularly in the case of conservative
social policy, since it is still in the process of being formulated. As conservative social policy takes on new dimensions, brought on by policymakers, current and future events, and political opposition, it is
impossible to predict with a high degree of reliability the overall impact
of the new wave of conservatism. It is difficult to accurately gauge the
total array of factors that may militate against a continuation or escalation
of conservative social policy. However, it is clear that the formulation of
conservative social policy is responsible for some discernible changes that
have begun to occur in African American families. Moreover, changes in
the structure and dynamics of other institutions and patterns of interaction are becoming increasingly apparent within the African American
community.

### Revitalization of Mutual-Aid Networks

The welfare revisionists' insistence that communities assume more responsibility for social-service delivery when authority is transferred from
the federal government to state and local governments, the private sector,

and volunteers is coming to fruition. The increased participation of these segments of the population is not solely due to the demands of social conservatives. Greater involvement of these entities has occurred out of necessity, rather than being directly related to a strong sense of moral responsibility. After all, the values in our society place heavy emphasis on social isolation and familial autonomy, and they continue to govern the lives of economically advantaged families in this country.

In general, there is sufficient evidence that community self-help is on the rise. The interesting issue, however, is who is helping whom. As one looks closely at the growing rate of networking throughout society, it is increasingly the case that most of these efforts take place in the inner city. Local church groups and other organizations that are centrally located and easily accessible to the poor (who lack the money to afford transportation) are in the vanguard of self-help efforts. Moreover, civic and neighborhood associations have been the prime sponsors of numerous social services to the poor. That is not to say that individuals residing on the periphery of and outside major metropolitan areas do not contribute to less-advantaged families. In fact, there has been a conscious effort to donate foodstuffs and other essentials not only to poor families in the United States but to those living abroad as well. The growing concern about and consciousness for alleviating U.S. and world hunger arose from famine relief efforts for Ethiopia, largely promoted by well-known entertainers.

The stimulus for African American families to revitalize mutual-aid networks has not been limited to radical changes in social welfare policy alone. While the increase in African American unemployment has necessitated a resurgence of community self-help, the increasing percentage of African American families headed by women due to separation, divorce, and out-of-wedlock births has also been an impetus for the resurgence of mutual-aid networks. As stated earlier, African American women have historically been in the vanguard of self-help groups. Moreover, the vital functions of child care and the exchange of goods and services that mutual-aid networks perform are particularly critical to African American female single parents, of which there are a growing number. Thus, mutual-aid networks must provide basic goods and services to individuals who, because of new policy guidelines, no longer qualify for public assistance, as well as those whose earnings have been diminished by loss of employment and marital breakups. The fact that many African American families have become downwardly mobile because of inordinate rates of marital disruption, the lack of marketable job skills, and unemployment places an added burden on mutual-aid networks. For example, the fact that African American female heads of households experience a greater need for financial support from informal support systems than their married counterparts underscores specific needs brought about because of the male's absence.[25]

Structural arrangement is the basis for the middle-class status of many African American families; hence, familial structure is to a great extent a determinant of economic status in the African American community.[26] Still, it should be noted that the higher economic status of African American married-couple families is socially determined and is not inherent in the structure itself. Given that the high rate of unemployment and underemployment for African American males requires both the husband and wife to be employed outside the home, combined with the fact that males have a higher earning potential than females, it is understandable that these families had a median income of $20,586 in 1983 compared to the median income of $14,506 for all African American families in the same year. The importance of male presence in reducing the need for financial support from informal support systems cannot be overstated. According to James McGhee, even in African American married-couple families where the wife was not in the paid labor force the median income in 1983 was $16,348, approximately twice that of female-headed households, whose median income was $7,999. In the case of the latter group, the median income was less than one-third that of married-couple families with both the husband and wife in the paid labor force.[27] This is not to suggest that African American middle-income families do not receive financial support from mutual-aid networks, only that the nature of support tends to be emotional rather than monetary.

Though they continue to provide essential services to African American families, mutual-aid networks in the African American community are faced with a problem of supply and demand, which makes the adequate provision of goods and services difficult at best. The greater demand for African American families to give to each other, following what appeared to be substantial growth in the number of African American middle-class families, makes even more vivid the fragility and transitory nature of the nouveau African American middle-class family.

### The Black Church

Because of the traditional role of the church in providing and coordinating goods and services to African American families, the Black Church has assumed its primary function as overseer and mediator of the increasing number of self-help activities. There is a certain degree of irony associated with the increased visibility of the Black Church. For example, during the 1960s and 1970s, the enhancement of Black Churches and other African American institutions vital to the functioning of African American families and the total African American community could have had a profound impact on African American family stability.[28] Instead, the government's method of formulating and implementing social and economic programs ignored African American institutions, including the Black Church. However, the reactionary posture of welfare revisionists—which extols traditional institutions, values, and norms and attempts to restore to societal institutions a high level of authority for reestablishing social order and moral responsibility—has enhanced the position of the Black Church. Consequently, the Black Church began to reaffirm its mission to economic development of the African American community through myriad entrepreneurial initiatives.[29] The government's social conservatism is not the sole reason that the Black Church as well as other religious organizations are resuming an honored position. As social anomalies related to the family continue to escalate, without any apparent methods for prevention or control, the Black Church with its moral obligation is expected to provide answers.

Moreover, cutbacks in federal spending that reduce monetary support for social services, such as community mental health services, result in the church assuming greater responsibility for pastoral counseling. Because African American families are faced with the debilitating effects of high rates of unemployment, economic hardships, marital breakups, and a demoralizing social welfare system, the Black Church has an extremely important role to play. In many respects, Black Churches must not only address these problems using their own resources but must identify other sources to address the myriad needs of African American families. Black Churches function as the dispenser and coordinator of resources, a difficult role to play, not only because of limited resources but also due to the still impersonal nature of an urban environment. It is obvious that mutual-aid networks consisting of consanguine as well as fictive kin are antithetical to the value orientation, which became pervasive over the last 20 years, that prescribes personal and familial autonomy as an ideal characteristic for American families. One conclusion that can be drawn from the move from liberal to conservative social policy is that the African American family, among other African American institutions, must assume the formidable task of addressing problems caused by the social and economic programs that created unattainable expectations and aspirations. Conservative social policy of the 1980s has compounded the already egregious conditions facing African American families by indiscriminately reducing federal expenditures for social programs, further dashing the hopes and dreams of African American families who have yet to gain entrance or permanence in mainstream America. In addition, conservative policy has created disillusionment for those African American families whose middle-class status is not only predicated on a married-couple family with both husband and wife in the paid labor force but for whom economic status is based on civilian labor force participation of one or both spouses in government service.

### Status of African American Families in the 1980s

The African American family, like the white family, had already begun to undergo significant change when social conservatives began exploring ways to implement deep domestic budget cuts, which would move the federal government away from social-service delivery. Interestingly, welfare revisionists maintained that policies that were being enacted were for the express purpose of reversing the debilitating effects of liberal social policy. Since the implementation of conservative social policy, a number of changes have taken place. For example, in 1980, 8 million or 34 percent of American African Americans were in poverty. By 1985 the proportion of African Americans with incomes below the poverty level was still at 34 percent. Moreover, the jobless rate among African American males was still double that of white males—13.1 percent in 1985.[30] So while the Reagan administration assumed credit for bringing about an economic recovery and lowering the rate of unemployment, these improvements did not affect African American families similarly.

By all indications, African American families, particularly those who constitute the underclass, felt the greatest impact of the illusion of acculturation and mainstream society participation brought on by liberal social policy. Furthermore, the rescission of these policies has worsened the status of many African American families. However, renewed efforts are underway to identify strategies from within the African American community that will enable African American families to effectively solve social and economic problems caused by liberal social policy and further exacerbated by a new breed of policymakers with a predilection for conservatism. The continual plunging of African American families into poverty as a result of radical changes in social policy substantiates the extent to which upward mobility and enhanced economic status were ephemeral for an overwhelming number of African American families. What occurred when liberal social policy was succeeded by social conservatism is akin to big business lending its support to a small but struggling business, exploring methods to remain viable. In such cases, when a larger enterprise contractually agrees to provide the failing business with the basic necessities and adds to these fundamentals an abundance of other resources, such as equipment, facilities, supplies, and contacts, eventually the small business begins to thrive. In addition, the small business establishes long-term goals and reaches a level of economic solvency. However, while the small enterprise is progressing, it has not acquired sufficient resources to sustain its growth independent of the larger corporate concern. Let's assume that big business decides that maintaining the contract is no longer in its own interest. Therefore, at the end of the contract, big business decides not to renew the agreement and withdraws the abundance of support. In such a case, it is highly probable that the small business is worse off because of the relationship. In fact, the small business is likely to have become dependent on the larger company, operating at a level far exceeding that at which it functioned before entering into the contractual relationship. Thus, when the contract is abruptly terminated the small business suffers immensely because it does not possess the resources or the capacity to sustain operations at this higher level. And in many cases, the smaller business folds. This raises the question of whether the smaller business would have failed without the added support. The answer is, not necessarily so. First, the larger enterprise could have shared its expertise, which would have assisted the smaller business in developing its own capabilities, which would enable the small business to operate independently. Second, the smaller business could have elected to consolidate with similar companies. The range of options that a fledgling business could pursue are too numerous to explore. However, when a struggling business enters into a contractual agreement with a big business, it should do so recognizing that while such an arrangement appears palatable, the risks of such a relationship are in direct proportion to the rewards.

In many respects, this is what happened to African American families and their members due to the radical shift from liberal to conservative social policy. To suggest that liberal social policy during the 1960s and 1970s created real opportunities for African Americans to gain access to, and compete in, an open market ignores the fact that African Americans' participation in traditional institutions was based on legislative edict, in the form of affirmative action, grants and loans for financing education and African American–owned businesses, and the like. At the beginning of the 1980s, when the federal government began to "pull the rug" from under African American families by withdrawing social and economic programs upon which they had become dependent, the overall effects were pernicious.

Previous experience indicates that economic instability is accompanied by increased levels of nuclear family stability.[31] In times of economic crisis, families generally become more unified and consolidate their resources. Clearly, the current economic recession and inflation, unlike before, did not reduce the number of marital breakups for African American families. Given the systematic high rates of unemployment for African American men and women and the growing number of African American families who are becoming members of the impoverished class, the standard of living for African American families has not improved substantially. In addition, the dire economic exigency that African American families face has not been a unifying force in keeping families together. The same appears to hold true for white families as well.

Although it may be premature to assess the overall impact of social conservativism on the disintegration of African American married-couple families, conservative social policy unequivocally must shoulder responsibility for the growing number of men, women, and children who are without a familial structure. In effect, cuts to federal programs have increased the number of individuals in our society who are categorized as the homeless. According to recent studies conducted on this population, the homeless represent people who for the most part have exhausted both kinship and mutual-aid networks. Afterward, with limited or no financial resources, the homeless find themselves outside any familial structure. The trend toward deinstitutionalization, which began over 20 years ago, left many individuals, who otherwise would receive institutional support, without an adequate support system. Added to this situation is the welfare revisionists' determination to make even deeper cuts in institutional and community-based programs. Though social conservatives tend to minimize the pervasiveness of this phenomenon, figures for the homeless range from 192,000 to 2.2 million. Many of these individuals were previously members of some type of family arrangement.[32]

More than halfway into the decade of the 1980s, the African American family continued to be confronted with severe economic and social problems. For the most part, this return to true conservatism, while failing to halt the decline of African American married-couple families, has resulted in an increase of individuals without families and in other social anomalies, all of which are associated with the economic destitution and hopelessness that confront a growing number of African American under-class families. However, one aspect of conservative social policy that should not be overlooked is the fact that although not by intent, it has unveiled the myth that the advantages of liberal social policy outweigh the disadvantages. On the other hand, liberal social policy did have definite advantages for some African American families. In fact, one can even argue that some African American families made advances that are sure to fortify their positions in the middle class. Still, gains made by an inordinate number of African American families were temporary. The rescission of liberal social policy indicates that, though the short-term effects of social and economic programs may have had some positive consequences, the long-range effects of liberal social policy must be measured, interpreted, and presented with extreme caution.

Liberal social policy has had devastating consequences for African American families, and the conservatism of the 1980s did not bring about a diminution of these problems but has shifted the government's attention away from the status of African American families. The responsibility for identifying strategies to solve the problems confronting African American men, women, and children rests almost exclusively on the shoulders of African American families, particularly those African American families whose middle-class status is more solidly based, either due to intergenerational economic advantage or the nature of their occupational marketability.

## NOTES

1. "Reagan's Polarized America," *Newsweek,* 5 April 1982, p. 17.

2. John Naisbitt, *Megatrends: Ten New Directions Transforming Our Lives* (New York: Warner Books, 1982), p. 103.

3. Floyd W. Hayes, "The Political Economy, Reaganomics, and Blacks," *Western Journal of Black Studies* 6 (1982): 90.

4. Martin Anderson, *Welfare* (Stanford, Calif.: Hoover Press, 1978), p. 163; and "Report of the Department of Health and Human Services before the Subcommittee on Public Assistance and Unemployment Compensation" (June 23, 1982), unpublished report, p. 2.

5. "Life Below the Poverty Line," *Newsweek,* 5 April 1982, p. 25.

6. "Reagan's Polarized America," *Newsweek,* 5 April 1982, pp. 17–18.

7. Sar A. Levitan and Clifford M. Johnson, *Beyond the Safety Net: Reviving the Promise of Opportunity in America* (Cambridge, Mass.: Ballinger Publishing Company, 1984), pp. 74–80.

8. Levitan and Johnson, *Beyond the Safety Net;* and "Report of the Department of Health and Human Services," p. 2.

9. "Employment and Training Reporter: 1982 Employment and Training Report to the President: Selected Tables" (Washington, D.C.: Bureau of National Affairs, August 23, 1982), p. 64.

10. "Senate, 93–3, Votes Welfare Revision Mandating Work," *New York Times,* 17 June 1988, p. A-1.

11. Jan Yoon, "Republican Plan for Children Too Hard to Swallow," *Yale Herald, Inc.,* 1995.

12. Tom Joe and Cheryl Rogers, *By the Few for the Few: The Reagan Welfare Legacy* (Lexington, Mass.: Lexington Books, 1986); and Nicholas Laham, *The Reagan Presidency and the Politics of Race: Pursuit of Colorblind Justice and Limited Government* (Westport, Conn.: Praeger, 1998).

13. Laham, *The Reagan Presidency;* and Dona Cooper Hamilton and Charles V. Hamilton, *The Dual Agenda: Race and Social Welfare Policies of Civil Rights Organizations* (New York: Columbia University Press, 1997), p. 233.

14. Levitan and Johnson, *Beyond the Safety Net,* p. 43.

15. Joe and Rogers, *By the Few for the Few.*

16. Ibid., p. 116.

17. James W. Vander Zanden, *Sociology: A Systematic Approach* (New York: Ronald Press Company, 1970), pp. 319–320.

18. Levitan and Johnson, *Beyond the Safety Net,* pp. 47–51.

19. George Gilder, *Wealth and Poverty* (New York: Basic Books, 1981), p. 68.

20. Lawrence Mead, *Beyond Entitlement* (New York: Free Press, 1986), p. 1.

21. Charles Murray, *Losing Ground: American Social Policy, 1950–1980* (New York: Basic Books, 1984).

22. Bill Barol, "The Eighties Are Over," *Newsweek,* 4 January 1988, p. 44–45.

23. "One Giant Step for Washington," *U.S. News and World Report,* 23 December 1985, pp. 18–19; and "Court to Congress: You Cut Budget," *USA Today,* 8 July 1986, p. 1.

24. Barol, "The Eighties Are Over," p. 44.

25. Harriette Pipes McAdoo, "Black Mothers and the Extended Family Support Network," in *The Black Woman*, ed. La Frances Rodgers-Rose (Beverly Hills, Calif.: Sage Publications, 1982), pp. 137–138.

26. James D. McGhee, "The Black Family Today and Tomorrow," in *The State of Black America* (New York: National Urban League, 1985), p. 4.

27. McGhee, "The Black Family," p. 4.

28. Bill Alexander, "The Black Church and Community Empowerment," in *On the Road to Economic Freedom: An Agenda for Black Progress*, ed. Robert L. Woodson (Washington, D.C.: National Center for Neighborhood Enterprise, 1987), pp. 45–69.

29. Alexander, "The Black Church and Community Empowerment," p. 51.

30. David Swinton, "Economic Status of Blacks, 1985," in *The State of Black America* (New York: National Urban League, 1986), p. 14.

31. Robert McElvaine. *The Great Depression: America, 1929–1941*. New York: Times Books, 1984.

32. Dee Roth et al., *Homelessness in Ohio: A Study of People in Need* (Columbus: Ohio Department of Mental Health, 1985), p. 1.

# CHAPTER 8

# A Reaffirmation of Institutional Exclusivity: Removing the Façade

More than 15 years have passed since I first examined the phenomenal feat performed by the African American family: namely, its survival for more than 300 years in spite of horrific social, economic, political, physical, and ideological assaults. The very fact that the family, the most salient institution in any social system, within the African American community has continued to exist, remain constructive, functional, optimistic, and determined to participate in, and derive benefits from, a society that has designed myriad methods to preclude its inclusion is astounding. I do not believe that I can overemphasize the overt and covert institutional and individual attacks that have been, and continue to be, waged against the African American family and its members. These systematic forms of oppression to which the African American family has been subjected include slavery, black codes, the convict lease system, tenant farming, sharecropping, de jure and de facto segregation, lynching, race riots, sexual assaults, and inaccessible and unresponsive macrocultural institutions, as well as cultural humiliation and devaluation supported by the mainstream media's historical perpetuation of stereotypical imagery and information, and virtually every societal institution in America.

Clearly these policies, laws, and practices have been implemented to— or at best have served to—exploit, control, and exclude African American families from participating fully in societal institutions. Moreover, those who mediate societal resources, and their functionaries who represent their interests, have utilized every system of power at their disposal to ensure that African American families are denied their inalienable rights as citizens of the United States. The most precious of these rights is the right to life, which African American families and their members, unlike their white counterparts, have never been afforded the opportunity to take for granted. Given the experiences of African American men, women, and children in America they cannot realistically look to law enforcement and others within the legal system to ensure their safety. Historically, African American families have had innumerable reminders, which continue to be manifested with the commencement of the twenty-first century, that the legal system designed to guarantee their personal safety all too often poses one of the greatest threats to the physical survival of the African American family and its members.

What is amazing is that over the past 15 years numerous policies, practices, and laws have been enacted that have had a significant impact on the African American family. In many ways the effects of these policies have resulted in stagnation for many African American families, while others that had registered gains during the 1960s and 1970s and began to experience retrogression during the 1980s were not able to recover in the 1990s from the recision of liberal social policies and economic downturns. Despite the unrealized economic opportunities during the conservative era of the 1980s, African American families regained hope when the 1990s ushered in a new Democratic administration, under the presidency of William Jefferson Clinton, more popularly known as Bill Clinton. This renewed confidence and optimism in the Democratic Party under the new leadership was expressed and felt by many African American families throughout the United States. One reason for African American families' belief that they would receive support in eliminating social, economic, and political barriers strengthened during the Reagan-Bush administrations was because the Democratic Party has served as a symbol of opportunity for African American families. This belief was also due to their comfortableness with Bill Clinton based on what appeared to be his familiarity with and appreciation for African American culture in the form of its music, its food, its verve, and its people.

African American families continued to remain hopeful throughout the two Clinton administrations that Clinton would implement policies and support the passage of legislation that would significantly diminish historical and contemporary racial discrimination in American institutions. However, their needs and concerns as an important special-interest group were seldom realized. In fact, by the end of the Clinton administration it became increasingly evident that the policies and laws that were implemented and enacted during this administration had done little to reduce the racial tensions and animosity directed toward African American families and their members by whites who controlled their awareness of, access to, and availability of economic opportunities. These opportunities included such things as mortgage loans for houses; matriculation to and graduation from institutions of higher education; quality public education; equal opportunity employment, pay equity, and promotions; quality health care; and an impartial and judicious legal system. Instead, African American families, much to their chagrin, could identify countless policies and practices that represented enormous challenges to the stability and the survival of African American families and their members. In effect, the 1993 Anti-Crime Bill signed by Bill Clinton placed 100,000 police officers on the streets, officers who were untrained in racial and cultural awareness and sensitivity, and expanded the list of federal crimes defined as capital crimes. The bill offered little in the form of crime prevention or diversionary programs as a costly alternative to imprisonment that would reduce the likelihood that young first-time offenders and petty drug violators would become entrenched in a system of prisonization by their confinement with experienced repeat offenders.

The increase in African American males imprisoned during the 1990s was unprecedented, due in part to the privatization of prisons, whereby private ownership focused on the needs to ensure profitability in keeping with the tenets of the free enterprise system. Accordingly, the contractual relationship with the state had implicit expectations that privately owned prisons would undoubtedly benefit from being filled to capacity as opposed to having empty beds. By 2000, facilities that were privately operated incarcerated 87,369 inmates.[1] Another factor that led to the increased incarceration of African American males was the long-standing practice of differential sentencing that became increasingly applied to mandatory minimum drug sentencing for the possession and sale of crack versus powder cocaine. In spite of myriad accounts of serious criminal offenders being released to make room for petty drug offenders, most of whom were African American and Latino, this practice of incarcerating African American and Latino males, and increasingly African American females, continued. This occurred even though studies revealed that individuals use and sell drugs almost in proportion to their presence in the population. Therefore, despite the reality that more white males were using and selling crack cocaine and powder cocaine, more African American males were being the target of this new federal policy, and once again being victimized by a biased legal system. In effect, the war on drugs even today entails drug sweeps in which petty drug dealers are arrested. These dealers are overrepresented among members of impoverished African American families, an institution whose poverty has been deliberately reproduced in substandard housing, poor nutrition, and the lack of quality health care due to failed and inadequate urban schools ill equipped to provide the most basic skills necessary for young African American male and female students to succeed. They are not able to overcome the next hurdle, which is an inequitable economic system whose employers rely on queues to fill jobs, even those in the lowest level of their organizational sectors. Placing African Americans in the lowest queues and maintaining stereotypes regarding African American workers have proven to be major obstacles for African Americans seeking labor-force participation, even when they are in possession of superior qualifications, work experience, and academic credentials.

Other conditions of Clinton's anti-crime bill included a three strikes and you're out sentencing policy, whereby individuals convicted of three felonies at the federal level were automatically sentenced to life imprisonment. In addition, the Clinton administration assumed a punitive stance regarding juveniles who commit federal crimes, in that this anti-crime bill authorized the criminal prosecution of juveniles as adults in the federal court system. This provision of the 1993 anti-crime bill contributed to the increase in incarceration rates for African American and Latino young males, largely due to the harsh and severe sentencing of judges relative to African Americans charged with and convicted of criminal offenses. This same law, inarguably, influenced a plethora of similar get-tough-on-juveniles or zero-tolerance policies for juveniles convicted of criminal offenses at the state and local levels of government. Such policies began to emanate from state legislatures at an alarming rate throughout the remainder of the decade. Regrettably Clinton's anti-crime bill, which thrust numerous African American males, youth, and young adults in prison and under the supervision of the criminal justice system, fails to recognize the multiplicity of actions and inactions on the part of teachers, staff, and administrators in urban schools who create and maintain hostile learning environments or at the very least those that are alien, unfriendly, and culturally debasing and negating to African American students and their culture. Ostensibly, many local urban school systems also began implementing zero-tolerance policies for students accused of engaging in behaviors labeled as dangerous and intolerable. Consequently, due to the salience of race in applying discipline within urban schools in the United States, the brunt of such policies has been felt by African American students, especially African American males, as these authorities, like their counterparts in decision-making positions in all major societal institutions, tend to vilify them. Whether in employment or the political or educational systems, and in every phase of the criminal justice system from detainment to sentencing, the privileged and their agents use race as the basis for unfairness, malevolence, and arbitrariness relative to their treatment of African American males, females, and children. Many contend that those who are placed in positions to mediate societal resources systematically attempt to make the African American male the object of devaluation, subjugation, and fear. In so doing, they are accepting the privilege-controlled mainstream media's purveyal of African American males as aggressive, dangerous brutes, who in a society in which white superiority and patriarchy are pronounced represent the greatest threat to the existing unequal distribution of power and wealth. Consequently, in the 1980s, 1990s, and the twenty-first century traditional methods have been utilized and resurrected in conjunction with new strategies and social policies to ensure the continuation of the existing control of wealth and power of the privileged. Moreover, the wealthy used the 1980s, influencing social policies, to expand their control over societal resources, significantly widening the gap between the wealthy and those who are impoverished. Furthermore, the privileged made tremendous strides in the 1990s, expanding their monopoly on domestic and global resources and establishing a race and class caste system that basically guarantees that the privileged and poor classes will reproduce themselves, and provides those born into poverty with virtually no legitimate avenues out of poverty. And because a disproportionate number of African American families are poor, the policies, laws, and practices that have led to the construction of this untenable social structure since the 1980s have necessitated that African American families and the entire African American community make diverse and innovative adaptations for the sole purpose of survival.

Clearly, Clinton's anti-crime policy has helped to solidify the prison-industrial complex, which merely replaced the Reconstruction-era convict-lease system that had as its forerunner the institution of slavery. In addition to the economic exploitation of African American males and their families, who are placed at a great disadvantage by the enforced absence of their male members by the prison-industrial complex, many insist that this system of rampant incarceration of African American males is designed to remind African American families that in spite of their activism, aspirations, and anticipations through their civil rights struggles and achievements of the 1960s and 1970s that the 1980s and 1990s reestablished for them the existence of race-specific behavioral norms and spatial parameters that represent rigid boundaries necessary to regulate and contain them. Even so, when African American families and their members refrain from overstepping these boundaries, this is no guarantee that the privileged and their representatives will not abandon their predatory behavior against the African American family that has become their undeniable prey. The brutal assaults, both institutional and individual, on African American men and women that have been brought to the national attention of American citizens and many abroad provide ample evidence that African American families and their members are under siege.[2] The fact that the most egregious attacks against African American men, women, and youth have produced rage in the African American community but little collective expression of disgust or outrage from the majority of white Americans, not even white clerics, offers little encouragement to African American families and the African American community. The silence of the white majority and their religious leaders gives tacit support for these innumerable acts of aggression often by the state against African American men, women, and youth. The willingness of the white masses to take a public stand against environmental issues, gun control, abortion, and so forth, yet to view videotapes of brutal police beatings and to read of murders of innocent African American men and women without a demand for the end of such brutal and inhumane treatment reveals the powerful and effective impact of socializing agents, particularly the mass media, that have created an in-group orientation. Accordingly, the social distance that is maintained and the silence, indifference, and insensitivity demonstrated by whites, who comprise a majority in America, when African Americans are undoubtedly subjected to brutality and even bestiality reaffirms the significance of race in America and refutes the existence of a color-blind society. In their discussion of the societal need to end racial disparities in hiring, housing, and the acquisition of major purchases like automobiles and to eliminate racial profiling, Julianne Malveaux and Clifford Alexander in the video *True Colors* state that until whites become as outraged as African Americans these practices will continue.[3]

Still other challenges emanated from the macroculture designed to instill fear in African American families and their members and to remind them they were not entitled to the civilities and liberties that are the birthright of their white counterparts. Racial profiling and police brutality, while not new experiences to African American men, women, and children, continued into the twenty-first century and received substantiation and verification through well-designed covert studies and privately owned and photographed camcorders that provided visual documentation, respectively.

Racial profiling—the practice of stopping, questioning, detaining, and even arresting African Americans engaged in what are typically considered daily mundane activities such as driving, walking, flying, standing, and so forth—transcends social class. Historically, there have been numerous incidents of racial profiling and police brutality against African Americans. However, typically, police departments, highway patrol, and other law enforcement agencies either vehemently denied these occurrences or concluded through their self-investigations of their own officers that their conduct was justified for any number of reasons. For example, the state of New Jersey had long been suspected of differentially stopping and ticketing African American motorists, a practice more commonly known as driving while black, on the New Jersey Turnpike. This practice was recognized at least 25 years ago by African Americans. Therefore, African American motorists traveling on the New Jersey Turnpike were often forewarned that there was a high probability that they would be stopped and ticketed for no legitimate reason. Nevertheless, there was no empirical evidence to support these experiences that were unjust, culturally humiliating, and financially costly to African American families and their members. Such unwarranted stops, along with the verbal and even physical aggressions of law enforcement officers directed toward African American drivers and entire families travelling together, are twentieth- and twenty-first-century methods of law enforcement agents and agencies perpetrated against African Americans to instill fear, docility, frustration, hopelessness, and ultimately subordination. When studies began to confirm that a disproportionate number of African Americans were being oppressed through racial profiling in its variable forms and abuses, legislation, H.R. 1443, was introduced by Representative John Conyers (D-MI) in the hope of attenuating this practice.[4] While this bill passed in the House on March 24, 1998, it was defeated in the Senate. Several law enforcement agencies reported their intention to train law enforcement officers to refrain from this practice of using race as the sole determining factor when stopping, detaining, questioning, harassing, and ticketing and arresting African American men, women, and youth. This legislation if passed would have uncertain consequences as it would have required, at least in the case of racial profiling while driving, or driving while black, that the law enforcement officer record the race of the driver that was stopped, ticketed, and so forth.[5] Ultimately, data collected nationally from such traffic stops would have been used to study this problem more thoroughly. This legislation has still not become a federal law, but in cities where it has been implemented its usefulness is questionable, as it requires honesty and integrity on the part of law enforcement officers. This is a definite contradiction for officers engaged in the unlawful practice of racial profiling. Expecting such officers to record valid information regarding the race and ethnicity of individuals who have been the victims of racial profiling is akin to asking them to indict themselves, as law enforcement officers responsible for enforcing laws, as agents of the state who have violated the law by engaging in this illegal practice. Obviously, to ensure the validity of demographic information collected and recorded on drivers that are stopped by law enforcement officers would require an independent research firm to investigate and verify or deny the accuracy of the racial and ethnic characteristics of drivers that law enforcement officers have recorded.

African American men are not the only members of the African American community who have been targeted for racial profiling. It is also the case that African American women have consistently been the victims of this illegal practice. One instance in which African American women are systematically detained and subjected to unlawful and humiliating physical searches and other denigrating physical and verbal abuses is when encountering the U.S. Customs Service upon returning to the United States after traveling abroad. Throughout the last decade, an inordinate number of African American women have been required to submit to strip searches, X-rays, ultrasounds when they are pregnant, and even on some occasions required to take laxatives, under the guise that they are drug smugglers. This practice was acknowledged by the director of the U.S. Customs Service as being inconsistent with data that reveal that African American women are the least likely individuals to be engaged in trafficking drugs by bringing them into the country. In fact, white women and males are more likely than African American women to be involved in illegally transporting drugs into the United States. However, this practice because of its prevalence resulted in a class action lawsuit filed in Chicago, Illinois, on behalf of approximately 1,300 African American women.[6] It is also important to note that racial profiling can and does transcend social-class lines, as there are many middle- and upper-middle-class African American women, including lawyers and doctors, who are plaintiffs in this litigation.

Police brutality against African Americans is also a long-standing practice of law enforcement officers and has been disproportionately targeted at African American males. Typically, it has been and continues to be perpetrated against lower-income African American males who have limited resources to legally challenge these practices where they are the victims of physical abuse, not to mention the psychological damages inflicted on individuals who are the victims of diverse forms of excessive force, which commonly are ruled justifiable by law enforcement agencies at all levels of government.

The 1980s ushered in the first major case of police brutality that was irrefutable due to the availability of a relatively new technology known as video camcorders. The case of Rodney King received national attention, as a videotape recorded by a private citizen allowed the world to view an African American man, offering no resistance, being severely beaten by police officers in Los Angeles, California. Earlier beatings and excessive force used by law enforcement officers against African American men, women, and children were denied or justified by police agents who conducted their own investigations of such allegations. Before the recording of police brutality on videotape, victims had to rely on witnesses whose accounts of these beatings were contradicted by police officers, as were the accounts of events provided by the victims of police brutality. However, unlike eyewitnesses, videotaped police brutality provided incontrovertible evidence of the excessive use of force, captured on video camcorders. A few of these cases did gain notoriety and were purveyed internationally by many news agencies.

Despite the fact that police brutality has been recorded on videotape, police investigations continued all too often to deny that excessive force was used. In some cases police officers and investigators would claim that the videotape did not contain the entire encounter, and that the earlier aggressive actions of the victim were not recorded. In still other cases, juries comprised largely of whites have been biased and refused to convict a police officer of excessive force even when there was a preponderance of evidence confirming that this behavior occurred.[7] In cases where predominantly white biased juries find the police officers not guilty of excessive force, acquittals frequently serve as the precipitating factor for civil disobedience in the forms of violence and riots on the part of African American citizenry who find such decisions ominous and unconscionable. Such jury decisions represent the further victimization of individuals and their families who have been the target of police brutality as well as the continuous collective victimization and disregard for the entire African American community. Clearly these decisions represent behavioral retentions from slavery, in which enslaved people of African descent had no rights in disputes with whites that members of the white community were obligated or even expected to recognize. In fact, throughout American history, white Americans for the most part have been reinforced for supporting aggressive conduct exhibited by other whites directed against African Americans. By contrast whites have been punished or at the very least rewards have been withheld for siding with or collaborating with African Americans against members of their own race. In effect whites have been socialized to embrace a zero sum game relative to whites and African Americans, in that a win for African Americans in interactions with whites is considered a loss for white Americans. These recurrent incidents in which internal affairs departments of law enforcement agencies and biased jury decisions find law enforcement officers not guilty of egregious and well-substantiated cases of police brutality deepen the racial chasm between African Americans and white Americans. In fact, these outcomes are generally the norm rather than the exception and give credence to the absolute absence of civil liberties and human rights for enslaved African Americans and subsequent disenfranchisement, after Emancipation, through apartheid policies, practices, and laws that continue to reinforce attitudinally and behaviorally that those imbued with the authority to govern American institutions are permitted and expected to use different standards of conduct in their relationships with African Americans. This is not to ignore or minimize the importance of individual whites who take a public stand against such abuses of justice, but the absence of a collective will or conscience among whites simply perpetuates such inhumane conduct.

The more common occurrence, in which no videotape is made, is even more difficult to prove even when the individual is maimed or murdered. This is due in part to the highly reputed "code of silence" that police officers maintain, offering cover-ups for each other as well as entire law enforcement agencies engaging in such practices. Nevertheless, while the code of silence may be difficult to penetrate, and although other obstacles stand in the way of verifying police brutality, more recent cases of brutality in which an African American man is handcuffed, subdued, and restrained by some other methods or lying prone on the ground have occurred. There is no believable explanation that police officers can provide to justify brutal whippings, punches, kicking, and choke holds, oftentimes delivered sequentially by virtually every police officer present or on the scene. The fact that in some cases police officers, while not actively engaged in the use of excessive force, will stand by idly and not intervene or attempt to stop this form of police misconduct should make them complicit in these cases of unwarranted police aggression. This raises serious questions about the character and moral and emotional makeup of police officers when such occurrences take place. For instance, are police officers conditioned or taught to conform at all costs by supporting their fellow officers even when they engage in inappropriate and illegal behavior? In addition, are they rewarded for exhibiting blind loyalty and punished informally or formally for not supporting their peers, while on duty?

Many of the civil rights that African Americans obtained in the 1960s and 1970s were miniscule gains relative to the economic system. Affirmative action, fair housing legislation, welfare reform, and Small Business Administration programs such as 8a were insufficient to even begin to diminish the major racial disparities that existed between the wealth of African American families and whites. These programs also included governmental set-asides ensuring that African Americans and other protected groups receive a greater proportion of government contracts that had earlier been almost exclusively acquired by white-owned companies with a tradition of wealth, resources, and important governmental personal and professional contracts and that were integral partners in old boy networks that guaranteed their ability to compete for and secure government contracts. These Great Society programs merely scratched the surface in terms of eliminating gross economic inequality between African American families and their white counterparts. Efforts were well underway in the late 1970s and into the 1980s and 1990s, including anti–affirmative action U.S. Supreme Court rulings and state-initiated and -supported movements. In California in 1998, Proposition 209 received voter support to end state funding of governmental agencies and their contractors that used race as the basis for awarding contracts and for admission into state-supported institutions of higher education. The challenges to legislation and policies that were designed to redress a long history of injustices within the economic system and every mainstream institution in the United States have either been rescinded, nebulously redefined, or unenforced. And although the 1980s ushered in a period of ultraconservatism and in some dimensions was even reactionary, there were ongoing efforts to supplant liberal social policies with the preexisting legislation, policies, and laws with white privilege, which has been and continues to be the most prevalent form of affirmative action. This latter form of preferential treatment is institutionalized within the United States and grants goods and services to white Americans based largely on race rather than merit. That is not to suggest that merit is not a consideration in determining access to and acquisition of American cultural goals, but that race is a primary determinant of an individual's access to education and experiences that enable individuals and families to garner qualifications, including credentials that are considered meritorious. Hence, whites are more likely to be exposed to popular and high culture; have more resources to enjoy recreational activities, travel, and acceptance as members into exclusive clubs and organizations that afford greater economic opportunities; and reside in neighborhoods where schools provide a quality education. Whites are better able to afford private schools that offer even more enhanced educational and cultural experiences, including social networking; to own and operate successful businesses; to secure high-status and high-income positions; and, equally important, to be inculcated with a value orientation that attributes an exaggerated sense of self-worth to the privileged and devalues African Americans and members of the lower classes who are outside of the exclusivity of privileged families and their members.

The 1990s are best characterized by the continuation of traditional forms of economic exploitation and the exclusion of African American families but are also known for the introduction of innovative economic practices that created even greater debt dependency and deficit spending for African American and other economically disadvantaged families and their members. These financial institutions introduced new methods of acquiring the already systematically produced limited resources of African American families. Many of these economic practices can be subsumed under the rubric of predatory lending. Essentially, check cashing and cash or payroll advance offices along with the infamous rent-to-own stores began overtaking the inner-city landscape throughout most metropolitan cities. Despite criticisms and opposition from African American politicians, community activists, and academicians, these establishments became firmly rooted in communities highly populated by African Americans and people of color throughout the country. Recognizing that financially strapped members of urban areas were generally barely surviving from paycheck to paycheck, and that many were without checking accounts in established banking institutions, check cashing and cash advance financial organizations were able to derive substantial profits by providing financial services that were generally unavailable to economically strained families and their members. Check cashing establishments, also known as fringe banking organizations, provide people an invaluable service as they cash payroll checks, welfare checks, income tax checks, and so forth for those without banking accounts at local banks. Many banks refuse to cash checks for individuals who are not regular customers, in that they have no established checking or savings account at their financial institution. It is also the case that many banks will not permit individuals to open a checking account if they have had a history of writing checks for which there were insufficient funds, even if those checks were later paid by the individual who wrote the check. Therefore, many who are impoverished or earn near poverty level incomes have been forced to utilize check cashing establishments, whose practice it is to charge exorbitant rates to cash checks for individuals who have few if any other means of cashing checks.

Another practice that also expanded the innumerable approaches of financial institutions to erode the meager resources of African American families and reduce the likelihood that they will ever acquire financial solvency are cash or payroll advance businesses. These businesses provide small, short-term loans for an unusually high fee. Generally, such businesses, located in areas highly populated with lower-income African American families, will give individuals loans or cash advances, upon receiving a postdated check, usually for a maximum of two weeks. Because many workers are paid biweekly or every two weeks the extent of the loan is usually for a period of two weeks, upon which the loan plus an exorbitant interest rate must be paid. The interest rate is included in the postdated check that the recipient of the cash advance or loan writes to the business that makes the loan available to the individual. Such establishments provide other financial services as well, such as money orders and often sell lottery tickets. Clearly, owners of these establishments recognize that low-income and low-skilled individuals have limited options available to generate large sums of cash. Consequently, playing the lottery for many in low-income areas provides hope that they will win, and in so doing improve their standard of living or in many cases simply allow the individual or family to pay delinquent bills, purchase needed medications, or have disconnected utility services restored. One of the reasons this game of chance is so omnipresent in impoverished communities is because of, not simply the prevalence of unskilled and low-skilled workers, but also because of the area in which these families reside, which provides limited access to employment, full time and part time, which all too frequently is located in suburban areas and other geographical locations on the periphery of the city, where mass transportation provides limited or no service. Given that many inner-city residents rely considerably and some exclusively on mass transportation to access markets, most of which are outside their communities, there are few available alternatives for securing employment, not to mention supplementing the family's income. Hence, businesses that offer high-interest payroll advances, check cashing for high fees, and lottery games provide the most residentially contained form of comprehensive economic exploitation of African American families with restricted incomes that exists today. It is also important to note that the African American elderly, many of whom have incomes below the poverty level, are also viable economic prey for these businesses. What is more disconcerting is that government does little in terms of formulating policies that will increase benefits to the elderly and provide income supports and meaningful training and educational opportunities to families in urban areas to make predatory lenders unnecessary. Quite the contrary. The government has not deemed such organizations to be illegal, and states actually benefit financially from state-supported lottery games that, unlike reliable government-subsidized housing, increased Social Security benefits, and a universal health-care plan, offer little more than a ray of hope for African American low-income families to escape a subsistence standard of living.

The 1968 Fair Housing Act continues to offer little relief for African American families who seek to purchase and refinance houses. The covert and insidious practices of realtors and financial institutions resulted in only 46.3 percent of African Americans owning their homes compared to 72.4 percent of whites who owned their homes in 2000.[8] Studies conducted in the 1990s and replicated in the first years of the twenty-first century continued to reveal significant racial disparities in financial institutions that made loans available to African Americans versus white potential home buyers. Consequently, home ownership for African Americans had decreased from 49 percent in 1980, while the number of whites owning their homes had increased from 67 percent in 1980. Moreover, studies also showed that African Americans were required to pay higher interest rates than their white counterparts. It was also startling and disconcerting to learn that upward social mobility for African American families, even those deemed credit worthy, only increased rather than diminished the likelihood that they would experience housing discrimination when attempting to purchase a house compared to similarly situated white families.[9] It has always been the hope, and often the belief, of African American families that upward social and economic mobility would eliminate racial discrimination. However, this expectation is not empirically supported by studies that have examined the experiences of African American, white, and Hispanic home buyers. These alarming findings give credence to the need for renewed pressure to be placed on the U.S. Department of Housing and Urban Development (HUD) as well as the executive branch of government to issue an executive order or edict to disavow such prevalent practices and to provide severe penalties for businesses that continue to violate the rights of African American home buyers.

The 1990s also brought forth the verification of another revelation that had long been believed to exist by African Americans, but for which no genuine irrefutable evidence existed. Specifically, in the area of purchasing insurance, several court cases revealed that African Americans had been the victims of economic exploitation by insurance companies, some of whom were considered reputable and well established. The outcomes of these cases demonstrated that African American families and their members were frequently illegally denied insurance and often charged higher rates for insurance policies than their white counterparts. Several of these lawsuits represented class action litigation, offering varied awards and settlements. Nevertheless, the 1990s brought forth indisputable evidence that African Americans' standard of living and purchasing power was yet another economic condition reduced by the policies and practices of specific companies within the insurance industry. To many, this finding by the courts was not surprising, in that the insurance industry was among three major industries that had historically denied services to African Americans, which led to the emergence of the old African American middle class.[10] It was this class within the African American community that provided the goods and services needed by African American families and their members that were not provided by white-owned businesses. In addition to the insurance industry, the other two businesses that gave rise to the old African American middle class were the beauty and funeral industries. Therefore, it is not surprising that while contemporary insurance agencies may sell insurance to African American families, their unwillingness to live up to these contractual arrangements, manifested in these court decisions should not come as a complete surprise. There are numerous cases in which African Americans have paid insurance premiums yet have not been paid benefits when filing claims. And in yet other cases insurance companies continue, as in the past, to refuse insurance coverage or charge higher rates to African Americans than their white counterparts.

In the area of education, African Americans during the decade of the 1990s and into the twenty-first century have not experienced any significant advances relative to academic achievement at the precollegiate or collegiate levels. In fact, nationally African Americans constitute 50 percent of all school dropouts. It is also the case that the number of African Americans who matriculate to college after completing high school has decreased. Further, African American males matriculating to institutions of higher education have a higher attrition rate than African American female students. Moreover, during the 1990s there was a substantial decline in enrollment in two-year community colleges, the avenue to ascend from poverty for many African American students as well as other students reared in impoverished families. Equally important, in spite of the fact that 79 percent of African Americans 25 years and older graduate from high school, serious questions are raised regarding the quality of education that they have received and the usefulness of the skills they have acquired to prepare them for the labor force today. Much has been written on the poor quality of urban education in the United States.[11] Recognizing that the majority of African American families reside in urban areas and send their children to urban schools, it is a common belief that African American youth are not being equipped with the skills and knowledge necessary to qualify for jobs in the labor force today. While there are a plethora of factors that contribute to the underdevelopment of human capital among African American youth, many frequently cited problems associated with urban education include inadequate funding of public schools; the poor quality of facilities and equipment; incompetent teachers; teachers who enter the classroom with stereotypes and low expectations of African American students and their ability to learn; teachers' and administrators' lack of awareness of, and appreciation for, African American culture and African Americans' contributions to the United States and the world; distorted and culturally nonrepresentative curricula; insufficient presence of African American teachers and administrators in urban schools; and standardized tests that are culturally biased, including proficiency tests that reduce African American teachers' presence in the classroom and reduce the number of African American students who are eligible to graduate. It is also a commonly expressed criticism that the urban school does not provide an African American student-friendly or African American parent-friendly educational environment. Ostensibly, the latter affects the extent to which African American parental involvement occurs in urban schools, a factor that is inarguably essential for student scholastic achievement.[12]

It is also the case that African American families have experienced overwhelming setbacks with companies leaving urban communities for handsome tax abatements in suburban communities and lower wage labor abroad. Accordingly, these policies have created a spatial mismatch, leaving many African American families and their members without access to jobs. Adding to this problem, a major jolt was felt when the Clinton administration signed into law the 1996 Welfare Reform Act, known as the Personal Responsibility Work Opportunity Reconciliation Act. Throughout the decade of the 1990s states had been permitted to experiment with diverse welfare programs. Most were developed to reduce welfare rolls based on the premise that welfare programs and the existing U.S. social welfare system was too lenient and benevolent with welfare recipients, namely women and children. It was further argued that if welfare recipients were required to work, limit their family size, and allowed to receive social welfare benefits for a limited time that many would be forced off the welfare rolls, leaving more money for the states to spend on other more "important" and less controversial programs. Ignoring the fact that schools and other societal institutions had in many cases already perpetuated or reproduced impoverished families, that the average welfare family usually consisted only of a mother and two children, and that the average time families received welfare was twenty-three months, states went forward in introducing new programs that were based on at least one of the foregoing misnomers regarding welfare recipiency. In any case, by 1996 these independently state-supported experiments became accepted and advanced as one federally sponsored piece of legislation. Many supporters of liberal social policy exclaimed their dismay at the welfare reform act that replaced categorical grants with block grants to the states, allowing them more latitude to decide how these monies for poor families were to be spent. The punitive criteria contained in the 1996 Welfare Reform Act, while permitting states to exempt certain categories of individuals, established a broad policy of workfare, time limits, and so forth that would substantially reduce the welfare rolls, rather than poverty and near-poverty rates. What many liberal policymakers found more disturbing was that the 1996 Welfare Reform Act eliminated the already modest monthly cash allotment to impoverished families after two consecutive years of recipiency. In addition, stringent regulations required work on the part of adult guardians, as defined by the state, and a total of five years of welfare recipiency over a family's lifetime. The act also required that a minor parent live with a responsible adult in order to receive welfare. The criticisms of this act were limitless by proponents of liberal social policy, impoverished families, community activists, and many academicians who recognized that there was little change in the legislation that enabled poor families to rise out of poverty, only to be removed from the welfare rolls. The fact that many were surprised by this punitive approach toward families receiving social welfare benefits was astounding, as the Clinton administration had been straightforward in announcing its intention to make radical changes in the existing social welfare policy that had been implemented during the era of liberal social policy. In fact, Clinton campaigned on the promise that he would end welfare as we know it. The words themselves do not imply that he planned on making the U.S. social welfare system a viable one that would provide the necessary educational, training, income, in-kind services, and family assistance programs that would give families engulfed in a cycle of poverty viable methods to ameliorate their social and economic conditions. In effect, what has become clear from this legislation and other policies that were formulated and instituted by the Clinton administration is that there are few political allies for African American families and that symbols do change. Given that symbols are objects, ideas, and things with shared meanings should not be interpreted to mean that these symbols are static and do not undergo change. The fact that Clinton labeled himself as a centrist and did not promise to represent the interests of African Americans during his campaign or in his administration should not have been ignored because of his membership in the Democratic Party. While it is understandable that to a collective of African Americans who all too often are ignored, disrespected, and the objects of overt and covert forms of discrimination and daily micro-aggressions (e.g., elevator doors are not held open, older white women clutch their purses in the presence of African American men, cashiers wait on a white customer although an

African American customer was next in line, judges and school teachers scowl toward African Americans in their respective milieus, etc.), simply because a candidate for an elected office and later an elected official smiles at African Americans, appears comfortable in their presence, plays the saxophone, and plays music that is enjoyed by many African Americans should not disavow the politician's stated intentions or any other actions that may suggest that the candidate is committed to addressing issues facing African American families and their members. Many African American families' dismay and chagrin regarding policies that were formulated and implemented during the Clinton administration occurred largely because symbolism overshadowed sensibility.

The beginning of the twenty-first century is best characterized as a whirlwind of discontent and disenfranchisement for African Americans, according to numerous politicians and civil rights activists. In the 2000 presidential campaign, with candidates Al Gore, of the Democratic Party, and George W. Bush, the Republican presidential nominee, many within the African American community expressed disbelief that thousands of African American votes were disqualified, or inaccurately marked and numerous other voting irregularities at the polls were identified, particularly in the state of Florida, a state in which Jeb Bush, George W. Bush's brother and son of former President George Bush, was governor. Other election irregularities cited by the U.S. Civil Rights Commission chaired by Mary Frances Berry included road blocks, preventing African Americans and other voters access to the polls; falsely registering African American voters as felons in the state of Florida, which prohibited them from voting; language difficulties in that foreigners who were naturalized citizens were not assisted in reading the voting ballots; and so forth. The highly disputed election was finally determined by the U.S. Supreme Court, with a disproportionate number of its members having been appointed by Republican presidents. Essentially, they ruled that the election results would stand, giving Al Gore the popular vote but assuring a victory for George W. Bush, who had won the electoral vote. Many within the African American community refused to recognize the legitimacy of the Bush presidency and chose to refer to George W. Bush as the president select instead of the president elect. Accordingly, there were a plethora of African Americans who firmly believe that the discounting and disqualification of thousands of African American votes was tantamount to a monumental violation of the 1965 Voting Rights Act. The cloud that these anomalies cast over the Bush administration did not significantly alter the African American community's perception or expectations of George W. Bush, as he received only a modicum of support, 9 percent of the vote, from African American voters.

Bush's domestic policies during his first years in office were merely extensions of those implemented by the Clinton administration, with the exception that he was able to get congressional support for school vouchers, allowing parents of children attending public schools and receiving failing grades to be sent to alternative schools that their parents believe will result in higher levels of scholastic achievement. These alternative schools may be Christian or private; therefore, there are those who argue that the voucher system is a violation of the constitution that mandates that public tax dollars not be used to fund religious organizations. Typically, there is a split along partisan lines, in that Democrats argue that these monies are of greater benefit to parents who can benefit from vouchers because they can be used to supplement the parent's own monetary resources to send their children to private or parochial schools that provide a better quality of education. Because the vouchers alone are not always sufficient to cover the tuition and other costs of private or parochial education many Democrats believe that working-class and lower-income families' children are not likely to derive any real benefits from this policy. Conversely, Republicans provide unwavering support for the voucher system, which is beneficial to their historically more affluent constituency. Bush's educational policy, "No Child Left Behind," requires more innovation among school systems to produce proficiency in math and reading for the third to the eighth grades. And the increased use of proficiency tests is required to measure the success of these state-devised educational initiatives, which the Bush administration plans to reward monetarily.

Finally, the Bush administration spent a considerable amount of effort attempting to encourage churches to provide fundamental social services through the Faith Based Initiative, which was initially proposed by the Clinton administration. The Black Church has been slow to embrace this policy, as some argue it could weaken the financial independence of one of the most important and influential institutions that provides spiritual, economic, educational, and political guidance for African American families and the entire African American community. Regarding other policies advanced by the Bush administration, emphasis has been placed on strengthening marriage through counseling, increasing the number of hours welfare recipients are required to work, and providing financial awards to states that lower their out-of-wedlock birthrates and abortion rates, all stipulations of the original 1996 Welfare Reform Act.

It is unquestionably clear that the 1990s and the twenty-first century have not produced policies, laws, and practices that have significantly improved the life chances and standards of living of African American families. Rather, the converse actually was experienced by many African American families, who became more firmly entrenched in low-paying, monotonous, and menial jobs in the secondary labor force, high rates of joblessness, continued underemployment and unemployment, even during the 1990s economic boom, poor-quality education, relegation to an inferior dual health-care delivery system, systematic racially based injustices in the legal system, an inadequate educational system, and an exclusionary and unrewarding economic system.

The fact that considerable evidence exists that reveals that racial discrimination in all major American societal institutions can be observed and measured suggests a complete indifference to the attitudes and behaviors that undergird policies, laws, and practices that are responsible for maintaining African Americans in a subordinate and oppressed status on the part of policymakers, the privileged who control this country, including its institutions and large organizations that continue to violate the civil rights of African Americans in spite of evidence confirming this systematic practice. Whether the George W. Bush administration issues any executive orders or signs into law any meaningful and significant legislation to lessen the institutional and individual forms of discrimination experienced by African American families remains to be seen. Clearly, African American families in general would welcome such efforts but have not indicated that they expect such policies and actions to be forthcoming. The earlier stages of his administration demonstrate a continuation of the policies of the 1990s, and little else for African American families that is novel or needed. Much of his administration's attention has been placed on the war on terrorism due to the loss of lives that occurred on September 11, 2001, when four airplanes were hijacked, two of which were flown into the World Trade Center, one flown into the Pentagon, and one crashed in a field in Pennsylvania and was believed to have been targeted for the destruction of another major building. Hence, there has been little effort directed toward establishing a domestic agenda, but emphasis has been placed on domestic security.

However, it has become apparent that the 1990s, in which a president who was self-identified as a centrist, made no real promises to address African American issues during his campaign, and implemented few policies during his presidency to enable African Americans to enjoy the civil rights to which they are entitled, only exacerbated challenges for African American families. In fact, the incidence of racial disparities in many American institutions increased during the Clinton administration, particularly in the criminal justice and welfare systems. Regrettably, the symbolism of the Democratic Party, which Clinton represented, was interpreted by African Americans as optimism and hope that some of the liberal social policies of the 1960s and 1970s would be reintroduced, expanded, and enforced. Contrary to their expectations, many of the policies that were forthcoming in the Clinton administration did little to increase their inclusion in American institutions or to remove identifiable barriers, but led to the further attenuation of their rights to enjoy the wealth and power and concomitant benefits to which numerous African American families aspired, and for which many who had pulled themselves up by their bootstraps and overcome seemingly insurmountable obstacles were qualified.

## NOTES

1. Allen J. Beck and Paige M. Harrison. "Prisoners in 2000." U.S. Department of Justice, August 2001.

2. Donna Franklin, *Ensuring Inequality: The Structural Transformation of the African-American Family* (New York: Oxford University Press, 1997), pp. 153–181.

3. *True Colors*, Northbrook, Ill.: Coronet/MTI Film and Video, 1993.

4. Kenneth Meeks, *Driving While Black: What to Do if You Are a Victim of Racial Profiling* (New York: Broadway Books, 2000), pp. 17–18.

5. Ibid.

6. Katti Gray, "Take a Stand: Flying While Black," *Essence*, February 2001.

7. Jill Nelson, "Introduction," in *Police Brutality*, ed. Jill Nelson (New York: W. W. Norton & Company, 2000), pp. 9–13.

8. U.S. Census Bureau, "The State of the Nation's Housing 2000."

9. Jodi Nirode and Stephanie Brenowitz, "A Dream Denied: Even with High Incomes, Blacks Face a Tough Time Getting Home Mortgages," *Columbus Dispatch*, 3 June 2001, pp. A1, A9.

10. Bart Landry, *The New Black Middle Class* (Berkeley: University of California Press, 1987).

11. Jonathan Kozol, *Savage Inequalities: Children in America's Schools* (New York: Crown Publishers, 1991); Beverly Daniel Tatum, *Why Are All the Black Kids Sitting Together in the Cafeteria?* (New York: Basic Books, 1997); and Janice E. Hale, *Learning While Black: Creating Educational Excellence for African American Children* (Baltimore: Johns Hopkins University Press, 2001).

12. Jawanza Kunjufu, *Countering the Conspiracy to Destroy Black Boys* (Chicago: African American Images, 1995), p. 43; and Louis E. Jenkins, "The Black Family and Academic Achievement," in *Black Students: Psychological Issues and Academic Achievement*, ed. Gordon LaVern Berry and Joy Keiko Asamen (Newbury Park, Calif.: Sage Publications, 1989), pp. 138–152.

# CHAPTER 9

# The 1990s: The Decade of Demystification

The beginning of the 1990s was not significantly different from the latter years of the 1980s in that African American families had still not realized the American Dream, nor had they achieved any real semblance of this societal ideal. To say that the 1990s were marked as a decade of shattered myths regarding African American families would be an understatement. Many truths were revealed that had resulted in unrealistic expectations and the acceptance of various aspects of a European American philosophical and behavioral paradigm defining what factors, conditions, and attributes were necessary for success for African American families living and functioning in America and within its major societal institutions. For example, African American families had been informed that the more rapidly their families assimilated and the more likely that their family structure and dynamics, including values, norms, and belief systems conformed to those of white middle-class families, the more readily they would be accepted and embraced by whites and permitted to achieve the cultural goals inherent in the American Dream (i.e., diplomas, jobs, houses, cars, luxury clothing, and so forth). However, it became apparent, during this decade, to many African American families across all socioeconomic lines, that the American Dream would be elusive and a carrot that would always be dangled before them irrespective of the culturally prescribed criteria that was espoused by the privileged through their controlled instruments, namely middle-class white Americans and their invaluable appendage, the mainstream media. That is, it became increasingly evident that even when African Americans acquired the highest and most prestigious credentials and tremendous wealth they would still not be granted the most basic and fundamental civil rights due any citizen of the United States. For example, they would continue to be considered suspicious persons if they were in predominantly white neighborhoods, their mere presence on city streets at night would engender fear and avoidance behavior on the part of whites, they would be bypassed by taxis in major metropolitan cities even when dressed in the most fashionable attire, and they remained the victims of racial profiling simply by driving expensive luxury cars, as law enforcement officers used the excuse that they believed that these vehicles were unaffordable by African Americans; hence, detainment was necessary to ask questions as to whether these cars were acquired through theft.

The decade of the 1990s debunked myths that had placed the responsibility for upward mobility and for obtaining the privileges and standards of living that white families take for granted squarely on the African American family and its members. It also dashed hopes and aspirations of many African American families but invigorated and reaffirmed the commitment of others to transmit and proliferate information to African American children that they had been inculcated with myths and blatant falsehoods by those who control societal institutions and mediated information for the privileged (i.e., teachers, ministers, employers, politicians, judges, social workers, television, books, magazines, newspapers, and so forth) that if they played by the rules and conformed to middle-class white American values, norms, and beliefs, they too would enjoy the benefits and privileges experienced by white middle- and upper-class families. Obviously, there were African American families, academicians, ministers, activists, and others who had already exposed this mythology, which had been perpetuated by the mainstream media and gatekeepers or functionaries, assigned to maintain the status quo and to ensure that institutional policies and practices of all major social systems were designed and functioning to ensure that all social classes were reproduced, retaining their composition based on race and ethnicity.

It is fair to say that the revelation of these myths that had been systematically imbued into African American families and their members by the white middle class with whom most African Americans had contact were as startling as was the stark reality that the true basis for lynchings, exposed by Ida B. Wells-Barnett in the *Free Speech* in 1892, was not because of sexual assaults of African American men on white women.[1] Unquestionably, this revelation that the inordinate number of African American men who were being lynched, contrary to popular belief, occurred because they posed a threat—usually to the economic order or because of their unwillingness to accept a subordinate status; therefore, they challenged Southern laws, policies, and convention—was unprecedented. Thus, Ida B. Wells-Barnett learned through her close associates, that their refusal to close their business, which represented competition for a nearby white-owned business, ended in their deaths by lynching. Prior to this discovery, Ida B. Wells-Barnett and myriad others, including some African Americans, had been convinced through ideological hegemony purveyed by the mainstream media and the informal perpetuation of myths that the lynching of African American men was a result of their unrestrained sexual desires that culminated in sexual assaults against white women.

The explosion of a multiplicity of myths in the 1990s regarding the intergenerational socially, economically, and politically depressed conditions and status of African American families has served two important functions. First, African American families now recognize that for the most part obstacles to achieving equal opportunity and other inalienable civil rights are not simply a function of individual, familial, or cultural limitations. Moreover, the dispelling of these myths attributing the slow rate of African American family progress to anomalies within cultural value orientations and norms within the African American family—especially the mother, who like in other families is the primary socializing agent—is significant, as it indicates how impenetrable these structurally erected barriers are in the absence of an accurate explanation for their existence. Secondly, and equally important, the destruction of myths during the 1990s regarding the limited progress and even retrogression of some African American families is significant to the academic community as it challenges and negates theories advanced by both liberal and conservative academicians. These academicians have typically attributed the failure of African American families to function effectively to unsound and empirically unverified theories that proffered untruths and partial truths, in that symptoms of institutional inequality were incorrectly identified as major factors contributing to the limited progress of African American families (i.e., joblessness, unemployment rate, school drop-out rate, female-maintained families, crime, etc.). It is even more unfortunate that several African American academicians have erroneously advanced theories explaining the intergenerational nature of poverty and the social and economic problems and institutional transformations of African American families to these existing paradigms, with slight modifications. Frequently, African American academicians have been deemed as acclaimed because they have been under the tutelage as students of highly regarded social scientists; therefore by association they too have built their careers on misguided theories like their mentors. These are academicians who read criticisms or explanations of a theory or phenomenon and lump or place all such works that are critical of the same theory or phenomenon together, rather than determining if different factors are identified as evidence to support or refute a theory or argument. For example, in the first edition of *Survival of the Black Family*, I attributed many problems facing African American families to the failure of liberal social policies to provide the necessary training for African American workers displaced by deindustrialization and their failure to ensure that when civil rights violations in the areas of education, employment, and housing occur that litigation, arbitration, and other remedies were realistic and affordable to African American families and their members who were victims of discrimination. The failure of affirmative action to make meaningful and significant differences in the life chances and social and economic gains of African American families is unacceptable and unjustifiable. The fact that there are and continue to be myriad examples of the African American families who have made only modest gains after the formulation and implementation of these policies and laws means that these efforts were insufficient to bring about meaningful changes in the lives of African American families and their members. Further, as I also stated, they have in many ways been responsible for altering important structures like multigenerational families, creating female-maintained families, and in states that require husband or male-absent homes, by reducing monthly cash assistance payments when there are two parents in the home. Because liberal social policies that were poorly conceived and difficult to enforce were implemented as well as laws such as the 1963 Equal Pay Act, the 1964 Civil Rights Act, the 1965 Voting Rights Act, the 1968 Fair Housing Act, and so forth, it does not mean they are not valuable and needed. Instead, these are glaring indicators that these policies and laws, along with many social policies of the 1960s and 1970s, are in need of revision and enforcement. In addition, agencies that have the capability to provide swift and severe penalties for civil rights violators must do so. However, to suggest that such criticism of liberal social policy meant that the policies were without any merit and should be eliminated, as has been proposed by opponents of liberal social policy like Charles Murray, Lawrence Mead, and George Gilder, to name a few, who argue that such policies are debasing and destructive to traditional American values that promote family, a strong work ethic, and moderate consumption, is absurd. Liberal social policies that are poorly conceived and implemented are a façade and another integral component of ideological hegemony used by those with wealth and power to regulate the poor, as Piven and Cloward so accurately described the U.S. social welfare system,[2] a system that was also expanded during the era of liberal social policy to quell the civil unrest in cities throughout the country, to meet the demands of African Americans for justice and equality. Those who genuinely devote their efforts toward improving conditions facing African American families, especially those who are severely economically disadvantaged, in terms of academic scholarship and community service, must not allow highly inaccurate analyses to deter their efforts, as there are already a sufficient number of externally imposed barriers to the survival and success of African American families in the United States.

What are the specific myths that were dispelled during the decade of the 1990s that had heretofore been considered major contributing factors or impediments to African American family survival and progress? Needless to say there were many theories that either individually or collectively were disseminated to explain the persistence of poverty among African American families and the social and economic problems that were persistent within the African American community. Many white Americans have argued that after the Great Society programs, known by many as liberal social policies, there is absolutely no excuse for African American families and their members to continue to occupy a marginal status in American society. Others point to liberal social policies and their continuation, especially affirmative action, as privileges denied to white Americans. Therefore, these critics state that African Americans have only themselves to blame for believing that African Americans have had policies and laws to guarantee their inclusion in societal institutions and laws that protect them from discrimination and that provide remedies for past racial discrimination. Still others argue that African American families lack the American values of hard work and family that are needed for maintaining two-parent families and acquiring the culturally prescribed goals of American society, especially wealth and the materialism and conspicuous consumption that it makes possible.

The myths are as follows:

1. African American families possess cultural values that are impediments to success in American institutions.
2. African American children have lower levels of academic achievement compared to white children because they are intellectually inferior due to biological deficiencies or because of cultural deprivation.
3. African American families are poor because they have a culture of poverty.
4. African Americans engage in more crime than other racial and ethnic groups because they are members of a criminal subculture.
5. African American families, like white families, have the same life chances and equal opportunities to achieve the American Dream, as they have equal access to American institutions because America is now a color-blind society.

These myths are not exhaustive but represent the most common beliefs that have been perpetuated from generation to generation and continue to be experienced over the last 30 years since the inception of liberal social policies and civil rights legislation. They are designed to explain the inability of African American families and their members to enjoy the same rights and privileges and their failure to take advantage of opportunities and to achieve cultural goals, thereby reaching a level of parity with white families. Collectively these myths ignore the continued existence of societal barriers such as race, class, and gender inequality and how the intersection of these systems of power prevents the majority of African American families from getting an opportunity to acquire even a semblance of the privileges and rights enjoyed by their white counterparts.

The most obvious question is what evidence is there to support the fact that these myths were shattered during the 1990s, leaving the harsh reality of institutional injustices and inequities that are based on race, gender, and social class that serve as forces to militate against upward mobility for the majority of African American families in the United States? Essentially, the issue is whether there are factual or empirical and ethnographic data that are responsible for exploding these erroneous but longstanding misconceptions regarding African American families and their members. Furthermore, who or what entities were integral to exploding the fallacious nature of these ideologies to African American families, the African American community, and in various mainstream milieus?

It should be understood that these myths regarding African American families and their ability to survive and progress in America have been dispelled through scientific research. This research includes diverse methodologies that have relied heavily on covert studies; statistical data maintained by various organizations that reveal disparate results based on race and ethnicity; and consensual validation among members of various social groups and white Americans, as well as African Americans whose light complexion and phenotype (i.e., lips, nose, hair texture, etc.) resulted in their passing or being accepted as white, making them privy to information regarding attitudes, beliefs, and behaviors of white individuals and mainstream institutional practices that provide advantages for whites and disadvantages for African Americans and other people of color, based on a racial hierarchy that is a mainstay in American society.

## MYTH #1: AFRICAN AMERICAN FAMILIES POSSESS CULTURAL VALUES THAT ARE IMPEDIMENTS TO SUCCESS IN AMERICAN SOCIETAL INSTITUTIONS

The belief that African American families adhere to some cultural value orientations that are contradictory to traditional American values that have been associated with those held by the white middle class is not totally untrue. However, to suggest that it is these values that are responsible for destabilizing African American families and thwarting the progress of their members is simply untrue. The specific values in question have been the values of an education, work, and moderate consumption. Clearly, many scholars who are exponents of the cultural relativism school identify these as values that African American families share with their white counterparts. It is also the case that these same academicians identify values that are unique to African American culture that conflict with mainstream values. However, there is a surfeit of evidence that these unique values that are common to many African American families are responsible for their survival and their ability to adapt to and overcome individual and institutional challenges and to continue to identify strategies to overcome innumerable racially constructed obstacles that are intrinsic to American social institutions. For example, African American families have historically valued cooperation, sharing, the family (including nuclear type, extended, augmented, and fictive members), spirituality, collectivism or elevating the interest of the group or family over that of the individual, and mutual dependence or interdependence of family and community members.[3] By contrast, according to the normative paradigm, family values should also consist of competition, rugged individualism, independence, and an isolated and a self-contained nuclear family. In sum, it has been argued that African American families' inability to acquire the culturally defined goals inherent in the American Dream result from their unwillingness to assimilate into American society and to undergo a complete process of acculturation, embracing and accepting these values of white middle-class families, since their emancipation from slavery and the elimination of de jure segregation. Those who believe that these values are critical to attaining the prescribed goals that are central to the American Dream label this the "bootstrap theory." Hence, they believe that individuals who are extremely independent, competitive, and live within a nuclear family will undoubtedly achieve success. Conversely, this theory holds that individuals who are unable to acquire the desired material possessions and societal privileges that are germane to the American Dream lack these important values and have themselves and their families to blame for their failure to transmit these values to their offspring. There is now a surfeit of evidence after the era of liberal social policy, in which affirmative action policies were implemented and Title VII of the 1964 Civil Rights Act was enacted, to refute the bootstrap theory. This evidence is quite compelling and credible as there are many African Americans whose families and themselves chose to adopt and strictly adhere to the bootstrap theory and to embrace all mainstream cultural values, thereby, theoretically, providing the blueprint for success for all Americans, irrespective of race or ethnicity. In many instances the individuals and families that had outcomes that repeatedly refute this theory were already members of the working and middle classes, therefore they did not have the financial constraints and concomitants of poverty as added barriers to overcome. This obviously gave them a slight advantage over those families who have the added burden of an economically depressed class status to overcome. Thus, for the vast majority of African American families who adopted these values and "played by the rules," they found that the American Dream, as experienced by white families, continued to be elusive. They were still unable to realize their potential, meaning they were unable to utilize the human capital or skills and abilities that they possessed to the same degree as their white counterparts. They found, in general, that the bootstrap theory had one major omission, which is race. In other words, this theory that has applicability to white families and their members does not apply to African Americans, although it is purported to have all of the characteristics of a good theory, according to Goode, as it explains, predicts, and controls relative to the phenomenon of success.[4] However, its applicability does not transcend racial and ethnic lines.

There are countless examples of those who were, because of liberal social policies, able to participate in mainstream institutions that prior to the 1960s and 1970s were reserved almost exclusively for white Americans. This is particularly true as affirmative action policies implemented by predominantly white institutions of higher education began opening their doors to more African American students in the late 1960s. However, although more African American students matriculated to predominantly white institutions of education, these campuses were not African American student–friendly. According to Jacqueline Fleming, Walter Allen, and others who studied this phenomenon, African American students attending these institutions often experienced alienation, isolation, and a culture that was exclusively white oriented relative to campus activities, traditions, and curriculum.[5] Moreover, there were seldom African American faculty with whom they could relate their classroom experiences of being ignored or the expectation that they, as the lone African American student, serve as a representative for the entire race when topics regarding African Americans in America were being discussed. They were also required to listen to, and not challenge, stereotypes and myths regarding social anomalies like delinquency, crime, substance abuse, drug trafficking, and the like that were frequently presented as phenomena that characterized the African American community, without the consideration of important qualifications like police and judicial discretion, social-class, residency (urban versus suburban), and other factors that alter the interpretation and meaning of statistical data that purportedly reflect conformity versus nonconformity to societal norms and laws. Equally important is that the sparse presence of African American faculty usually meant that there were fewer advisors who shared the research interests of African American students, particularly when these topics were related to African American experiences, institutions, and culture. Nevertheless, many African American students were able to persevere and graduate and to pursue careers and to do so adhering wholly to the highly championed values of rugged individualism, competition, and independence, all touted as prescriptions for success according to white middle-class values. In other cases, students were able to achieve their academic goals and their career goals by adhering to a combination of values, some representing both cultures. However, the latter requires compromises in that African American values are oftentimes adhered to within the context of the African American community, while mainstream values appear to be rewarded more within the larger society. Thus to some extent, two sets of values had to be learned and used within the appropriate milieu. However, it is the case that some African Americans seeking to become more fully integrated into societal institutions, to obtain culturally prescribed goals, did abandon many traditional African American values, especially whenever conflicts over values existed. For example, while it may not have been in the interest of the group (i.e., their families or community) to move to suburban communities or miles across the country, they often reluctantly left their families, taking valuable information and their ability to serve as a role model to locations designated by corporations and governmental agencies to expand their career opportunities. In some instances, they were able to rationalize such moves and to cognitively resolve these conflicts by believing that their individual success, affording them more monetary and material wealth, would be more beneficial to their families than their presence and participation. This generation, having gained a foothold in mainstream institutions, was also aware that declining promotions and refusing to acquire status symbols like homes in upscale suburban communities, luxury automobiles, sport utility vehicles (SUVs), and pedigreed pets would substantially limit their career opportunities, and in some cases significantly shorten their career ladders. In most cases, upwardly mobile African Americans hoped that their increased salaries and other perks associated with upper management and executive positions would enable their families and members of their communities to enjoy material possessions and the status and esteem with which they are associated, and in some small way that would make up for the harsh realities of racial discrimination and injustices that were a major part of their daily experiences.

It was also the case that African Americans were given to believe by those who controlled the positions and resources that they strove to achieve that there no longer existed racially based obstacles that would prevent them from acquiring these rewards, because of the enactment of affirmative action and civil rights legislation, as well as U.S. Supreme Court decisions that recognized the importance of race as a factor in admissions to higher education and in hiring and other liberal social policies. However, the use of race as a factor in admissions to institutions of higher education reappeared and was once again considered by the U.S. Supreme Court. The Court's decision to revisit the *Bakke* decision is discussed further in chapter 10.

Janice Hale describes the experiences of an African American lawyer who was educated at an Ivy League law school and was in the top of his class. He was then employed by a large prestigious law firm, upon graduation, but despite his distinguished career was denied a partnership in the firm. He filed a lawsuit charging racial discrimination against the law firm. In spite of the merits of his case he lost his lawsuit, proving much to his dismay and chagrin that it is not sufficient for African Americans to play by the rules, which include accepting a mainstream value system. There are other options: African Americans can reject traditional African American values when value conflicts occur and opt for white middle-class values or attempt to become bicultural, to the extent that that is possible. There are those who believe that the production of an African American elite serves an invaluable function, as those who have a monopoly on wealth and power in America consider them a vital component of the system of oppression, as they serve in the capacity as a buffer between the oppressor and the oppressed, fostering the illusion that all African Americans can overcome institutional barriers if they possess the exemplary qualities of the African American elite.[6] The paradox is that while some African Americans are able to surmount institutional barriers they are not interested or willing to adopt a value orientation and lifestyle of the white middle class. And this should not be a prerequisite for success, serving as the minimal requirements that are necessary to be tapped for initiation and quasi-inclusion in the white upper-middle and upper classes. African American families will probably continue to resist giving up their cultural identity to increase their opportunity to achieve those aspects of the American Dream that are available to them. It cannot be overemphasized, however, that embracing a mainstream value orientation does not guarantee this optimal level of success. However, the reality of a double consciousness is generally a realization for most African Americans if they are to function effectively in the larger society and within African American culture.[7] There are still other instances, which are the norm rather than the exception, in which African Americans have achieved enormous material success and economic wealth, yet are denied the opportunity to ascend the career ladder as high as their white counterparts. The glass ceiling is a phenomenon that has been the rage of the African American middle class. Again, as unfortunate as it may be, qualifications, work experience, and the adoption of white middle-class values, norms, and behaviors are not sufficient to overcome these firmly erected barriers to attain career success.[8] It is even more frustrating for those who have reached the pinnacle of success that includes high earnings and opulence in their surroundings, yet are still denied their civil rights and civilities that are generally assumed in social interaction and in day-to-day relationships in the communities in which they reside.[9] This is particularly true when they are victims of racial profiling as they drive expensive automobiles in the predominantly white neighborhoods in which they reside. It is also the case, because of the mainstream media's depiction of African American males as criminals and brutes, that African American males are likely be stopped and detained whenever a robbery or violent crime has occurred, even when they bear no resemblance to the suspect. Moreover, African Americans who have "made it" or are paragons of success still face embarrassment and insults, as reported by high-profile and nationally renowned African American members of the upper-middle class, as they are often mistaken for secretaries, janitors, and housekeepers rather than the professionals and businesspeople that they are. Indeed, upper-middle-class African Americans share a commonality with all African Americans as victims of what Daniel Georges-Abeyie calls "petit apartheid."[10] While he coined this phrase in the 1990s to describe daily insults that African Americans encounter in the criminal justice system, this phenomenon is also examined within the context of all American social institutions. Accordingly, these day-to-day subtle, but offensive, acts directed at African Americans have been labeled "micro-aggressions."[11] Micro-aggressions, along with more overt and blatant forms of aggression against African Americans, are intended, according to these theorists, to keep them docile or intractable and in a position of subordination relative to whites. Further, these micro-aggressions are also designed to intimidate African American families and their members and to instill fear in them, while transmitting the message that they are not entitled to and will not receive the same rights and privileges as whites. Former Virginia Governor L. Douglas Wilder describes how he was returning home at the Raleigh-Durham airport when he walked through the airport metal detector and the buzzer sounded. When he emptied his pockets and went through the metal detector again and it sounded, he realized that his suspenders may have activated the buzzer. When he told the white security man that he thought his suspenders set the alarm off, he was grabbed, pushed, and choked. Wilder filed a lawsuit against the airport, the airport security service, and the security guard. The lawsuit was settled for an undisclosed amount of money.[12] And for those academicians and others who believe that class is more important than race in determining one's life chances and opportunities, they should explain to the affluent and most wealthy African Americans why poor whites can hail a taxi and be driven to their destination, while African Americans who are among the most economically advantaged in America are denied access to the same simple but necessary service or mode of transportation.

## MYTH #2: AFRICAN AMERICAN CHILDREN HAVE LOWER LEVELS OF ACADEMIC ACHIEVEMENT COMPARED TO WHITE CHILDREN BECAUSE THEY ARE INTELLECTUALLY INFERIOR DUE TO BIOLOGICAL DEFICIENCIES OR BECAUSE OF CULTURAL DEPRIVATION

The explanations that are intended to explain why African American students have lower levels of scholastic achievement than their white counterparts are essentially one of two theories. One is a biological explanation advanced by biological and social scientists such as Jensen, Shockley, and Murray.[13] The other theory attributes African American children's lower levels of academic performance compared to white children to cultural deprivation.[14] These theorists are typically not controlling for social class, ignoring the small variability in grades and standardized test scores between middle-class African American students and white students. Instead they focus their analyses on African American families that are economically disadvantaged. These families are known to have inadequate resources to provide books, children's magazines, videotapes, educational toys, and cultural experiences such as trips to museums, movies, plays, concerts, and so forth. Clearly, these and similar activities aid in language proficiency, fine motor skills, and social and cognitive development necessary to perform well academically using instruments that measure a student's ability in subjects such as math, logic, language arts, and the like. In addition, experiencing various types of deprivation in terms of hunger, inadequate clothing, substandard housing, and limited monetary resources also lowers a student's attention span and interest in learning, as basic physiological needs are not being met that supercede cognitive needs or the acquisition of knowledge, which becomes secondary to the motivation and interest in meeting fundamental life-sustaining needs. Obviously, children from more economically advantaged families have the necessary resources and experiences that facilitate higher levels of performance in terms of scholastic achievement. However, although these concomitants of poverty exist in the families of impoverished children they can be overcome through student-centered teaching styles and educational environments that have the capacity to provide support, reinforcement, and opportunities that ensure that students have resources and experiences that otherwise would not be available to those whose families occupy a lower socioeconomic status.

The biological theory that maintains African Americans' innate inferiority simultaneously portends white intellectual superiority. In fact, the basis for explaining institutional arrangements in the United States is attributed to the intellectual superiority of white males. Therefore, it is they who occupy the highest status and income positions. Thus, race and gender and class are the prerequisites for the superordinance of one group and the relative subordinance of others, as the former justify their career success on their greater ability to ensure the effectiveness and efficiency of all societal institutions and the optimal functioning of the entire social system.

The belief in the existence of groups of individuals who are members of a race that is biologically endowed with superior intellectual ability compared to other races has been negated through a preponderance of biological data, resulting from anthropological genetic research conducted in the 1990s. These scientific studies, conducted under the auspices of the Human Genome Project, reveal with a high degree of reliability that there are no real or sufficient genetic differences based on race that permit distinctions to be made among the traditional three theoretically established racial categories, the Mongoloid, Negroid, and Caucasoid races, according to Ian F. Lopes.[15] Consequently, it is a commonly held belief in the biological and medical sciences that "race" is a social, not scientific, concept.[16] Therefore, arguments that attempt to explain the scholastic performance of African American children based on their inherited intellectual inferiority must look to other more empirically verifiable social factors. It is absurd to cling to anachronistic forms of logic that have been refuted for the purpose of maintaining the existing unequal distribution of wealth and other societal resources. Because over the past 30 years there has been an explosion of information and mechanisms for disseminating information, larger segments of society are learning of scientific findings that were heretofore circulated primarily among the intelligentsia and privileged individuals who either privately or through corporate-sponsored research or foundations funded such studies.

It is understood by most that "race" is a social construction and as such is vague and ambiguous, making criteria that are designed to differentiate race unreliable indicators for categorizing individuals and groups of individuals in order to make broad and sweeping stereotypical judgments regarding their innate abilities, then arguing that these assessments are necessary to determine access to the valuable resources that exist within America and globally is unacceptable. In other words, relying on superficial features such as skin color and phenotype leads to considerable errors in placing individuals into racial categories, namely because of coerced sexual assaults against enslaved African women during slavery and the continuation of this practice after Emancipation. It is suggested that approximately 85 percent of African Americans are racially mixed with European ancestry. This in no way includes other racial mixtures, including American Indians, whose presence preceded that of Europeans in America and who married and established strong bonds with many people of African descent prior to slavery, during slavery, and after Emancipation.

Regarding the second theory that has been used, often by liberal social scientists and policymakers, that African American students experience relatively lower levels of achievement compared to white students because a greater proportion of African American students are from economically disadvantaged homes, including those who have attended Head Start and similar preschool, not to mention those from working-class and middle-class families, and therefore their lack of academic preparedness upon attending school affects their scholastic achievement throughout their entire academic career. Many studies find that African

American children enter school at essentially the same levels as do their white counterparts. However, by the end of the first year African American students start to lag behind white students. Moreover, this achievement gap continues to widen, so that by the 12th grade, the gap is wider than the gap that existed in the 1st grade. In addition, by the 4th grade many African American students dislike school and feel a sense of hopelessness.[17] Studies have revealed several important factors that have been found to contribute immensely to the lower levels of academic achievement among African American students compared to white students. These factors include lower levels of funds that are allocated to fund urban public schools where most African American children are educated, school policies formulated and implemented by school boards, large classroom sizes, outdated textbooks and equipment, and teachers who enter classrooms with stereotypes regarding the intellectual ability of African American students and therefore have lower expectations of them and give them less attention and other school resources.[18] The fact is that 69 percent of African American students attend public schools where at least one-half of the student body is comprised of students of color, while the majority of white students attend schools that are 80 percent or more white.[19] This is problematic, in that urban schools where the overwhelming majority of African American students are educated are funded at much lower levels than those schools that educate white students. In fact it is an understatement to say that urban schools receive inadequate levels of funding, especially compared to the funds that are made available per capita for students attending suburban, private, and parochial schools. Relying on property taxes in inner-city communities where property is not highly valuated and therefore produces a relatively low tax base from which to fund public schools is a well-known and accepted occurrence that has lowered the level of education for African American children throughout the United States. The manifestations of low levels of funding for public schools can be seen in many of the aforestated conditions as well as in inadequate plumbing, poor heating, unsafe walls and ceilings, and antiquated wiring that does not have the capacity to accommodate the installation of computers and computer laboratories, which are necessities rather than luxuries, to ensure that students acquire computer literacy that will increase their matriculation to technical schools, colleges, and universities. Moreover, increased technological knowledge of information systems ultimately increases students' marketability in a labor force that has a great demand for individuals proficient in this field.

One cannot discuss scholastic achievement in any meaningful way without considering the influence of educational policies on academic achievement, student absenteeism, and attrition rates. Oftentimes school boards, unfamiliar with the culture of students for which they are developing policies, establish policies that are counterproductive to the values, belief systems, norms, and day-to-day experiences of students attending urban schools. In addition, some school policies are differentially applied based on the student's race and gender. This is particularly true when policies offer rigid and inflexible forms of discipline for various rule infractions. It is no secret that the zero-tolerance policy, in-school detentions, and expulsions are characterized by arbitrariness when applied to African American students compared to white students. This is generally the case when disciplinary action is used on African American male students as opposed to white male students.

Generally, the zero-tolerance policy is used for behaviors that include physical aggression or the threat of violence. For example, fighting usually results in suspensions and expulsions. However, there is no need for zero tolerance, as it denies students the right to due process, which is theoretically a right to which adults are entitled. If a school policy requires that any student involved in a physical altercation be suspended, then whether a hearing is held to gather factual information is irrelevant because the discipline is mandatory and ignores mitigating circumstances in many cases. In far too many cases, African American students, according to the reports of educational associations, are disciplined disproportionately compared to white students, and the punishment that they receive is relatively more harsh and severe for violating the same school rules as white students.

This punitive trajectory on which African American students are placed is reflected in annual reports for schools in given school districts. Despite the recurrent nature of in-school differential discipline based on race this practice continues. Unquestionably, such arbitrariness contributes to high levels of absenteeism, truancy, a higher school dropout rate, and an overall disaffection for education and learning. Together these factors contribute to lower levels of academic achievement among African American youth in general, and African American males in particular. Clearly, the alienation and frustration that these youth experience has an impact on their academic performance but also on their overall negative evaluation of the entire educational experience provided by urban schools with public dollars, including those of their parents and family members.

It is also alarming to learn that the experience of African American young female students in public schools also fails to provide adequate rewards and enhance learning. In a 1992 study conducted by The American Association of University Women the findings revealed that girls, irrespective of their race, tend to be ignored more than boys by the teacher and that texts that were used contained male images five times more often than female images, affording male students more opportunities to identify with the character in the text, which tends to increase their interest in the subject matter. The study also indicated that male students were more capable of becoming proficient in math and science than female students.

However, it was also found that African American girls were not only ignored by teachers but were rebuffed by them as well.[20] Hence, African American female students, based on the findings of this study, were subjected to petit apartheid or micro-aggressions at an early age from teachers, which means there are few opportunities to insulate or protect African American children in the classroom from this type of petit apartheid or others, such as the mislabeling of African American children as ADHD, slow learner, or educable mentally retarded; their misplacement in lower-ability groups; and inappropriate tracking. The resegregation of African American children in the classroom using ability groups and tracking are also issues addressed by Beverly Daniel Tatum.[21]

Educators, social scientists, and policymakers must continue to address methods of transforming conventional classrooms into African American friendly and not hostile learning environments by rewarding African American children; providing culturally relevant and accurate curricula; utilizing teaching styles that promote greater student participation and facilitate the acquisition of knowledge; employing methods of evaluation that more accurately measure students' knowledge, abilities, and aptitudes; and eliminating teacher and administrative stereotypes that result in treatment that is insensitive and discipline that is harsh and arbitrarily applied based on the student's race and gender.

There is definitely the need to increase teachers' awareness of preconceived ideas and stereotypes that they possess regarding African American students. A major impediment to learning for African American children is attributed to teacher stereotyping. Many teachers enter the classroom with the belief that African American children have learning difficulties that are a result of either biological or cultural deficits. According to the Conditioned Failure Model, teachers' stereotypes of African American children result in their having low expectations of an African American student's ability to learn, and that by communicating this to African American students in myriad ways teachers plant the seed of the self-fulfilling prophecy. As such, many African American students fulfill this prophecy with low levels of academic achievement.[22] The Conditioned Failure Model also contends that when an African American student demonstrates the ability to learn and perform well on tests, teachers attribute these positive academic outcomes to luck or some other external factor over which the student has no control, rather than complimenting and rewarding these students for their abilities and scholastic achievement.

## MYTH #3: AFRICAN AMERICAN FAMILIES ARE POOR BECAUSE THEY HAVE A CULTURE OF POVERTY

Some theorists discount the importance of quality schools, health-care delivery systems, suitable and affordable housing, adequate food and clothing, and so forth but attribute the existence of a disproportionate number of economically disadvantaged African American families to the belief that they value a culture of poverty. Moreover, these theorists argue that African American poor families develop a lifestyle in which they accept poverty with its concomitants such as substandard housing, poor health, drug abuse, alcoholism, crime, low levels of academic achievement, high infant and maternal mortality rates, teenage pregnancy, lower life expectancy, and so forth as a way of life. This theory advanced by Oscar Lewis is among the most ludicrous that has ever been advanced to explain why a disproportionate number of African American families become engulfed in a cyclical form of intergenerational poverty.[23] One of the major fallacies of this theory is that it implies that African American families who are poor occupy this economically disadvantaged position on their own volition. To suggest that human beings, particularly those who conform to the definition of family, would deliberately choose a life replete with pain that greatly reduces their quality of life and increases their mortality rate ignores the fact that human beings, like other living organisms, have built-in mechanisms to sustain themselves. In addition, it defies sound logic to believe that poor families would opt for poor-quality education; inadequate, incompetent, and limited legal representation; and economic exploitation through low-paying, monotonous, menial jobs and substandard housing, not to mention the plethora of stereotypes and stigmas that are glaring indicators that they are poor, lazy, and characterized by moral turpitude. These symbols of poverty that stigmatize African American poor families are far more visible than those that inform the country that whites are impoverished. In fact, because of the pervasiveness of stereotypes regarding African American families in general, and those that are economically disadvantaged in particular, most Americans are unaware that the majority of poor people in the United States are white. This is true because of their low visibility, which is aided by the mainstream media. Moreover, their residency is yet another factor that limits the visibility of poor white families, as they tend to live in rural communities, small towns, and suburbs. By contrast, most poor African American families reside in urban centers where their poverty is egregious, as they are often stigmatized by low-income public housing or live in sections of the city that have been abandoned by industries and more affluent families. Moreover, African American families' inner-city communities can be readily identified by boarded-up buildings, vacant houses, pawn shops, liquor stores, ma-and-pa neighborhood stores that are proprietorships that are family owned and operated, thrift shop clothing stores, and their use of food stamp vouchers or electronic cards to purchase food. Still other symbols that stigmatize poor African American families are their inadequate transportation to markets, especially in areas where industries, with available jobs, exist in suburban communities; and the dismantling and disruption of families by child services agencies who agree that because impoverished families cannot provide for the basic needs of their children, they are defined as neglecting them. This determination permits the state temporary and permanent custody of children who are removed from their homes. Because of persistent poverty, a disproportionate number of African American children comprise out-of-home placements or foster care.[24]

Finally, the African American poor single mother is also a victim of the contemporary cultural label of the welfare queen. This contemporary cultural image, which symbolizes African American women who maintain their households and are recipients of social welfare services, is no more than a synthesis of the mammy and Jezebel images. Accordingly, she is purveyed by the media as obese and neglectful of her children. However, she is also believed to be preoccupied with sex as is the case of the Jezebel image and therefore she is defined as sexually reckless and promiscuous and erroneously she is believed to have many children. It is further incorrectly assumed that her perceived promiscuity is evident in the belief that she continues to have more children to increase her welfare benefits, which obviates her participation in the labor market. These demoralizing myths have no empirical validity, as African American women who are heads of households and recipients of social welfare services have an average of two children and usually do not bear more children while they are receiving welfare benefits, which is generally for 23 months.

The premise that African American families who are poor lack a strong work ethic and are lazy simply ignores the historically high levels of labor market participation by African Americans who head families in the United States. Moreover, such a tenet fails to recognize the significance of race on the part of industries that underwent economic restructuring by relocating to suburban communities and to foreign countries. In exchange for moving industries to suburban communities generous tax abatements were offered by local governments, aware of the number of jobs that would be created and the number of new families that would be attracted to their areas, which meant greater infusions of dollars. Clearly, corporations considered relocating industries to the South and to foreign countries where labor costs are lower a feasible option. It is the case that in making these decisions to relocate, corporations were fully aware of the impact of these decisions on urban residents upon whom their corporations had depended for growth and development. Occupational displacement should have been more of a concern of corporate executives and shareholders rather than profit margins and maintaining an inequitable distribution of the corporate wealth, with executives and shareholders receiving incomes and assets that far exceeded those of the average worker. In effect, earning high salaries and benefits that are incomprehensible to the average worker are taken for granted by corporate executives in the United States, who are insensitive and indifferent to the fact that their inordinate share of corporate earnings are a result of the economic exploitation of entry-level workers and employees with near-poverty salaries, as well as higher-income professional employees. In the case of the latter they are usually blinded by the fact that they are not considerably more financially well off than lower-level workers, and that the higher standard of living that they enjoy is not because of their salaries but due more to the higher levels of credit made available to them and to their indebtedness to mortgage companies, financial institutions for cars, and credit cards.

It must be recognized that institutional racial discrimination is as much a factor in corporate flight during the 1980s, 1990s, and even today as white flight that occurred in the 1970s when white families fled to the suburbs to prevent their children from attending racially desegregated schools. Corporations who flee urban areas are well aware of the fact that they will be reducing their workforce and significantly eliminating jobs held by African Americans and other people of color. While economic restructuring and deindustrialization is real, it cannot be examined apart from the significance of race in corporate policies to relocate away from urban centers. After all, there are other measures and available alternatives that corporations could pursue to reduce their costs, including reducing the earnings of management. It is also the case that while deindustrialization has played a role in creating joblessness for African American family members, particularly heads of households, this economic condition alone is not responsible for severely reducing the presence of African American workers in these industries. Accordingly, Steinberg states that regarding working-class African American workers, they have historically been denied blue-collar jobs.[25] Therefore, we should consider the significance yet not overemphasize the phenomenon known as a spatial mismatch. Moreover, Hacker states that even if these industries had remained in urban communities, the number of African Americans that they employ would not be proportionate to their availability in the workforce, because of racial discrimination. Accordingly, Hacker indicates that too many African American workers are perceived as detrimental to business by corporations, as their white workforce and customers are not comfortable with African American employees when they are too visible in these companies.[26] This should come as little surprise, as social scientists have found that the same holds true for predominantly white communities in that the fear factor begins to set in when the proportion of African Americans in the community reaches approximately one-third of the population. Thus, it appears that a similar rule is in effect in the workplace as well as other institutions and organizations such as schools. There is no reason to believe that the same principle does not affect African American presence in elected offices as well as in churches throughout America.

African Americans have continued to be disproportionately affected by the failure of liberal social policies that require the government's intervention to retrain and rehire them and other occupationally displaced workers by intervening and creating living wage jobs repairing and restoring the rapidly deteriorating infrastructures of the United States. There is a definite need for roads, buildings, and bridges to be restored, repaired, and rebuilt. In addition, government subsidies to repair railways that would avert future derailments that have already been responsible for the loss of human life and costly damage to property are necessary to significantly reduce the surplus army of poor people who were once family members who made meaningful contributions to the financial well-being of their families. Unfortunately, the 1990s represented an even greater distancing of the federal government from intervention and assuming more responsibility to ensure that African American families and other economically disadvantaged families could increase their level of participation in societal institutions, including the labor market. In addition, the government, through its inaction in terms of formulating meaningful social policies to effect such a change and its role in the enactment of the 1996 Welfare Reform Act, embraced the culture of poverty theory and placed the responsibility for poverty disproportionately experienced by African American families and their members on African American families themselves.

## The 1996 Welfare Reform Act

The Clinton administration's 1996 Welfare Reform Act, known as the Personal Responsibility Work Opportunity Reconciliation Act, signed into law on August 22, 1996, was based largely on the tenets of the culture of poverty theory. The major premise of this theory was that families who were welfare recipients were avoiding work, as welfare was a work disincentive. The welfare reform act also found credibility in the assumption of the culture of poverty theory that poor families develop a lifestyle and culture centered on poverty and welfare recipiency. Accordingly, it was believed that teenage pregnancy resulted from adolescent females' beliefs that if they became pregnant and gave birth to children, they could receive welfare benefits, including in-kind services such as subsidized housing. In effect, this enabled them to move away from their parents' homes and establish independent living arrangements and obtain food stamps, Medicaid, and nutritional goods and services provided by WIC. Furthermore, this welfare reform act accepted the culture of poverty theory that poverty supported by welfare dependency is so highly valued that welfare dependency is also transmitted from one generation to the next because of the families' dependence on the government to meet their needs. Consequently, the 1996 Welfare Reform Act was designed to provide remedies for what was believed to be the pathologies that are described in the Culture of Poverty Theory.

The Johnson administration purportedly attributed the persistent poverty affecting a disproportionate number of African American families to slavery, de jure and de facto discrimination, and ongoing institutional racial discrimination, and therefore assumed that the government that supported these various forms of oppression had a responsibility to provide remedies to poverty and its concomitants including the existing exclusion of African Americans from societal institutions. Therefore, the Great Society programs that also evolved from liberal social policies, albeit poorly designed, were implemented. On the other hand, the Clinton administration, whose social policies were influenced by the tenets of the Culture of Poverty Theory, informed African Americans that they should not look to the state but to their own communities for solutions to their problems.[27]

Moreover, the Clinton administration took a punitive and rigid stance regarding welfare recipiency. In fact, one of Clinton's campaign promises was to "end welfare as we know it." Basically, the government was rescinding or at best significantly reducing its responsibility for providing for the basic necessities of families with children who were economically disadvantaged. Such a transformation in role of the government toward providing for the needs of families who were consumers but not producers would have been received with greater acceptance had it been enacted under a Republican administration. However, this and other legislation enacted by a Democratic administration left many in awe and others with the understanding that regulating the poor would occur through the use of other means, among them prisons and not placation. Moreover, this welfare reform act replaced categorical grants to the states with block grants that allowed states discretion in determining how these monies would be used to meet the needs of poor families.[28] This stipulation had already been instituted by many states that had already developed specific policies affecting the eligibility of poor families to receive social welfare services. For example, at the state level, time limits already had been placed on the length of recipiency and the right of the state to deny benefits to all children born after the mother and her children had begun to receive social welfare services, while another policy that had been instituted required grandparents to assume financial responsibility for grandchildren born to their teenage daughters, and so forth. In addition, this legislation contained federal guidelines the states were required to follow or risk losing federal funds. Accordingly states were expected to create jobs for the poor. Moreover, states had to establish paternity for children born out of wedlock. The new welfare reform law also compelled states to seek to vigorously collect child support from the nonresidential parent, which overwhelmingly was an absent father. Under this new welfare reform policy, states were permitted to deny cash assistance and other social welfare services to noncitizen, legal immigrant families. Furthermore, financial incentives were given to states that made substantial decreases in out-of-wedlock births and abortions. This new welfare reform policy, while allowing states a considerable amount of latitude in administering their own programs, mandated the following:

1. A two-year limit was placed on receiving the monthly cash allotment.
2. Welfare recipients were required to "work," as defined by the state, at least 20 hours each week.
3. A minor parent or unmarried welfare mother was required to attend school and to reside with an adult parent or guardian to receive public assistance.
4. Families could receive public assistance for only five years over their lifetime.
5. Low-income disabled children were to begin losing benefits, which were to be reduced over a six-year period.

## MYTH #4: AFRICAN AMERICANS ENGAGE IN MORE CRIME THAN OTHER RACIAL AND ETHNIC GROUPS BECAUSE THEY ARE MEMBERS OF A CRIMINAL SUBCULTURE

Criminal statistical data compiled by the Federal Bureau of Investigation known as the Uniform Crime Reports, which reflect only those crimes reported to law enforcement officers, and the National Crime Victimization Survey of the Bureau of Justice, in which respondents report their experiences as victims of crime, are not reliable indicators of crimes committed in the United States. For the most part, most crimes are not reported to law enforcement agencies because of the belief that nothing can be done once the crime is committed, and there are those who consider the crime to be relatively insignificant. These data represent a definite race and class bias, as those crimes that are likely to come to the attention of the police are usually dependent on their presence in certain communities and because police officers are usually assigned to lower-income urban communities rather than suburban areas. And since a disproportionate number of African American families reside in these communities, their family members, especially young African American males, are more likely to be targeted for arrest. Given police discretion that reveals a bias that is based on race and social class regarding the decision to detain, question, and arrest, it is understandable how young and older adult males in suburban communities are not monitored nor arrested at a rate consistent with that of lower-income African American residents, particularly young males, irrespective of their involvement in similar criminal activity.[29] In fact, even if their participation in certain crimes is disproportionately higher than that of lower-income inner-city African American males, suburbanites are still less likely to be arrested. Therefore, in view of biases in the assignment or placement of police officers, as well as racial and class biases that affect arrest rates, the accuracy of criminal activity in the United States based on data of reported crimes and those that are brought to the attention of law enforcement officers makes assessments regarding African Americans' greater involvement in crime questionable. In fact, whites are known to be overrepresented in the commission of certain crimes, such as white-collar crimes, corporate crimes, and organized crime, yet these are crimes that have low levels of detection and are significantly underreported. It is also the case that arrest rates for certain types of crimes such as drug-related offenses committed in low-income urban areas garner relatively high arrest rates for young African American males, as these are the kinds of crimes and neighborhoods that serve as the focus of law enforcement efforts.[30] Drug sweeps in these poor communities result in the imprisonment of petty drug dealers, while those trafficking in large quantities of drugs in office buildings, houses, and other relatively safe havens in urban and suburban communities are seldom the objects of these efforts, and arrest, conviction, and imprisonment tend to elude these individuals.

A study was conducted that reveals the importance of social class in influencing law enforcement officers' decisions to use differential enforcement decisions. The Roughnecks and the Saints were two high school-aged groups of males; the Roughnecks were from low-income families, while the Saints were members of middle-class families. Both groups engaged in the same behaviors, committing illegal and antisocial behavior such as reckless driving, overt cheating on examinations, and excessive drinking. Police officers labeled the Roughnecks as deviant, but did not assign any negative label to the Saints. The outcomes for each of these groups were decidedly different, as the Roughnecks, unlike the Saints, were punished for their illegal and socially inappropriate activities.[31]

It is also the case that social scientists, policymakers, and others who espouse the criminal subculture theory ignore the extent to which institutional racial discrimination eliminates legitimate opportunities for success in educational and economic systems for African American youth at very young ages, creating frustration and hopelessness and few legitimate opportunities to acquire the culturally prescribed goals that are overrepresented as material possessions that constitute to a large extent the highly pursued American Dream. It is also the case that the acquisition of highly visible and valuable material objects is equated with status and esteem and is essentially the determinant of an individual's worth in American society. It is little wonder why these material possessions are sought by many in America, in spite of the personal and sometimes professional risks associated with their acquisition. However, the requirement of the basic necessities of life is a difficult reality to meet for many in lower-income urban communities. And this fact, while difficult for many families to understand, is a fact of life for millions in the United States, where since 2000, 12 million children are in poverty, 5 million children go to bed hungry every night, and where 50 million Americans are without health insurance, which thrusts them into a capricious search for some semblance of quality health care.

It is also the case that the myth of African Americans constituting a criminal subculture is often used as the basis for the oppression of African American families and their members by law enforcement officers, in their efforts to justify racial profiling and police brutality against this segment of American society.

Clearly, race is one of the most important determinants of police discretion. It is cited by many social scientists, policymakers, and citizens as a major factor in racial profiling relative to stopping, detaining, and arresting a disproportionate number of African Americans, especially while driving. This practice, driving while black, gained a tremendous amount of publicity for the state of New Jersey during the 1990s. Specifically, the New Jersey Turnpike has had a reputation for over 25 years of engaging in racial profiling, which resulted in stopping and detaining a disproportionate number of African American drivers. Driving while black is a practice that occurs throughout the United States but is more prevalent in certain cities and states than in others.[32] It was during the 1990s that studies were conducted that provided empirical verification of this unlawful act on the New Jersey Turnpike and in other states in the country. It is also the case that the American Civil Liberties Union filed a class-action lawsuit against the Maryland State Police in 1993 for racial profiling of usually African American drivers along the I-95 corridor. Typically, African American male drivers are the victims of driving while black; however, law enforcement officers have not limited this illegal practice to African American males alone, as African American females are also victimized, intimidated, and subjected to this unjustifiable form of humiliation.[33] Unquestionably, driving while black, like other forms of racial profiling, is intended to have a specific effect on African Americans, the primary victims of this practice. Generally, after the harassment is over and the driver is permitted to leave, the law enforcement officers' mission has been accomplished in that they have misused their authority to displace anger and frustration associated with their own feelings of inadequacy. However, when each specific incident of driving while black, and its accompanying harassment, has ended, it is intended to leave the African American driver and passengers fearful of all law enforcement officers, because according to their own internal policies every law enforcement officer has the same discretion to and usually is permitted to engage in such conduct without reprisals. Dragan Milovanovic and Katheryn K. Russell concur in their discussion of petit apartheid, when they state that discriminatory and discretionary actions of police officers must be taken into account, including those that occur during the pre-arrest stage. Moreover, they indicate that put-downs, insults, indignities, actions that are belittling, or other micro-aggressions that police officers exhibit toward African Americans have "cumulative and interactional effects."[34]

### Bruce: The Bully Behind the Badge?

My own victimization, as a driver, by a law enforcement officer was absolutely unnerving. Regrettably, I was a victim of driving while black, which produced astonishing and disturbing facts regarding law enforcement officers, internal affairs departments, and this phenomenon.

Even more alarming than the incident itself was my firsthand experience with the difficulties associated with filing a complaint, as the staff of this law enforcement agency, the Franklin County Sheriff's Internal Affairs Department, closed ranks to protect an officer whom I alleged had violated my civil rights. The personnel and other officers in the internal affairs office did not know if my allegations were valid, nor did they initially make any effort to determine if this horrific incident had occurred. In fact, my initial efforts to report this occurrence were ignored and met with indifference and a collective refusal by office personnel to permit me to file a formal complaint. Though individuals are taught as children by various socializing agents that police officers are their friends, it became very clear through this experience why many African American families and their members perceive law enforcement officers not as friends but as foes.

In October 1999, I was driving home on the freeway from my office at the university. When I was within 10 minutes of my home, I suddenly noticed a sheriff's deputy riding on a motorcycle waving frantically at me, screaming and yelling. In addition, he appeared to be motioning for me to pull over to the side of the freeway. I was totally shocked as I was in the middle lane of the freeway and was aware that I was driving well within the speed limit. I was also puzzled and fearful because of the wild movements he was making with his hands and the scowl on his face that was accompanied by loud continuous yelling. I could not imagine what I had done to deserve this treatment and was also concerned about being made to pull over immediately in spite of the lanes of oncoming traffic that I had to cross to get to the berm, or side of the freeway. When I pulled over and stopped my car, the deputy disappeared briefly. When he returned he had another car with him that pulled over, both parking quite a distance in front of me. The sheriff's deputy parked his motorcycle in front of the car that had returned with him. The deputy walked past the car, without saying anything to the driver, and walked the distance to my car. The entire time he was approaching my car he was screaming and moving his hands frantically. I lowered my window, and he asked me, "What do you do when you see a funeral procession?" Still confused, I told him, "I pull over." He then told me that I had just pulled into a funeral procession. I then asked him to stop yelling at me. He said that he wouldn't because I had endangered his life. This statement left me even more perplexed, as I had no idea what he was talking about. I told him that I had not pulled into a funeral procession, and that he should stop yelling and screaming at me. He then asked for my driver's license, took it, and began walking toward the rear of my automobile. Before he walked away, I told him that I thought that I was being treated this way because I am an African American woman. He told me that was not true and pointed to the other car and said that the other driver had been stopped for the same reason. I had no idea who the driver of the other car was as the cars windows were tinted and it was parked a distance from me. The deputy said that he was going to call the local police department. He then proceeded to pace back and forth, walking by my car and in front and in back of it repeatedly for the next half-hour, as we waited for a local police officer to arrive. I had no idea what he was planning to do to me, as the anger he displayed was quite intense as indicated by his mannerisms and behavior. I began to wonder if he planned to pull me and drag me from my car, as I had just recently witnessed a law enforcement officer do to an African American woman on a videotape, played and replayed by various television newscasts. After nearly 20 minutes of waiting an older white male stepped out of the other stopped car and looked back at the deputy and me. He appeared unclear about what was occurring. He then reentered his car. Several minutes later, before the local police officer arrived, the deputy walked toward the driver of the other car and motioned for him to leave. This occurred without either of them having ever exchanged any words. When the local police officer arrived the two of them talked briefly. Then the deputy came to my car and told me that the police officer would handle this now. Before he walked away I asked him for his name. The deputy said that his name was Bruce. I then asked if the number on his helmet was his badge number and he replied yes. I then waited another 10 minutes before the local police officer came to my car. During this time, I did not know why I was still being detained or whether I was going to be arrested. The police officer walked to my car with a ticket or citation that he had just written. He asked me how I was doing and I explained to him how I had been yelled at and treated like a wild animal that was getting ready to attack. I also told the police officer that the deputy had accused me of interrupting a funeral procession and endangering his life. I told him that neither of these accusations was true. I also informed him that there had been a white male driver, with whom the deputy had never spoken, who was told to leave minutes before he arrived. I also asked the police officer why he had written me a ticket since he had not been there and had not seen anything. In addition, I asked him why the deputy did not issue me a citation himself because he had the authority to do so as I was not only in the city of Columbus, but also in

Franklin County. The police officer looked surprised upon hearing what had occurred and informed me that he was going to destroy the ticket. He drew a line through it and recommended that I report the deputy. He stated that I should contact the lieutenant of the motorcycle unit and report the deputy. The Columbus police officer told me the deputy's name was Bruce.

My several calls to the lieutenant were not returned. A day later I went to the Franklin County Sheriff's Internal Affairs Department to file a complaint. When I indicated that I would like to file a complaint I was told I should go home and call the office because no one was available to take my complaint. When I requested a complaint form, I was told that none could be located. Finally, I was given a complaint form, completed it, and submitted it to office personnel. However, after weeks had passed and I had not received any information regarding the status of my complaint, I made several calls to the office and was told by an investigator that my complaint had fallen through the cracks. I finally received a letter from the internal affairs office that stated that the deputy had been found guilty of violating a policy of the Franklin County Sheriff's Department. However, I was not informed of the policy that the deputy had violated nor was I told what disciplinary measures had been taken.

What was even more disturbing was that after I retained an attorney I learned that the findings of the investigation had concluded that the deputy's actions did give the appearance of racial discrimination. However, equally alarming was the fact that the investigative report revealed that the deputy had given me a false name and badge number. In effect, the name that he gave me—Bruce—and his badge number were both fabrications, and his real name was Kevin. When I learned of the deputy's real name I was also shocked because I had requested his surname from the office personnel in the internal affairs office and from the lieutenant who was conducting the investigation. No one would give me his last name. However, when I reflected on what had occurred I realized that while the deputy had given me a false name, I had inquired as to his surname to no avail, not realizing that his first name was not Bruce. No one in the internal affairs department would identify his last name, nor would they ever tell me that his name was not Bruce. This information did not even appear in the letter from the internal affairs department that informed me of the findings of their investigation.

My own experience of driving while black, along with accounts of other African Americans' experiences as victims of this form of racial profiling, prompted Representative John Conyers (D-MI) to propose a bill requiring the U.S. Justice Department to collect all law enforcement agencies' racial and ethnic data on all motorists who are stopped on the nation's highways, known as Traffic Stops Statistics Studies Act. This bill passed in the House but was defeated in the U.S. Senate in 1999.

My own experience with this phenomenon indicates the importance of such legislation, including a stipulation that federal monies be allocated to cover the costs of an independent research firm to monitor the accuracy of the data on the driver's race and ethnicity. In other words, each driver stopped by a law enforcement officer should have his or her race and ethnicity verified through an independent review. Otherwise, there is no reliable method for determining the accuracy of the information recorded in these incidents. Relying on fellow law enforcement officers to contradict the data recorded by another officer does not appear to be the most reliable method of verifying the race and ethnicity of drivers who are stopped. Moreover, those law enforcement officers willing to violate departmental policy and to disobey laws by targeting specific groups of people based on their race and ethnicity, which is a violation of their civil rights, cannot realistically be expected to accurately report the race and ethnicity of these drivers. Obviously, to do so would be to admit that they have engaged in acts that constitute departmental misconduct and that are in violation of the laws that they are sworn to uphold.

It should be noted that there is considerable resistance to laws at the federal and state levels that would mandate that law enforcement officers obtain information on the race and ethnicity of drivers they stop and detain. According to Nelson, in California, Governor Gray Davis vetoed SB78 in September 1999, which would have mandated the collection of racial and ethnic information on drivers in all traffic stops in that state.[35] Some states have voluntarily implemented the practice of having law enforcement officers record the race and ethnicity of drivers, while other states have opposed this practice.

An extremely important question brought up by driving while black and other types of racial profiling that has historically targeted African Americans is what the qualifications for being hired as a law enforcement officer are. It is extremely important to determine if law enforcement officers have intrapersonal and interpersonal characteristics that would interfere with their ability to be objective, impartial, and nonaggressive in relating to individuals from diverse cultural groups. This is particularly important because the mainstream media have historically used stereotypical imagery to depict African American families and their members. To a large extent, these cultural images have demeaned and devalued African American families and have systematically portrayed African American males as violent, aggressive, and brutes. The vilification of young African American males as irresponsible and as crooks and gangsters has the potential for influencing the beliefs and behaviors of those who must interact with them such as teachers, students from different cultures, police officers, lawyers, judges, and the like. Therefore, it is critical that a battery of tests to measure the extent to which prospective police officers are aware of their own attitudes, beliefs, and perceptions about

African Americans and members of various ethnic groups like Latinos be administered. In addition, cultural awareness and sensitivity training is imperative for police officers, both those who are recruits as well as veterans who have established careers with law enforcement agencies.

If such social-psychological instruments are being used then their reliability should be measured. If there are no such accurate instruments being employed during the initial interviews, then they should be designed or obtained and integrated into and heavily weighted during the pre-employment process to determine eligibility for employment in law enforcement departments. It is in the interests of African Americans and other communities of color not to be exposed to individuals who work in law enforcement yet are insensitive to their culture or possess individual characteristics that result in the inappropriate displacement of hostility and aggression due to their own personality and behavioral disorders.

In my own personal experience with the deputy that stopped and detained me while I was driving, the investigatory report contained several documents, including one that indicated that this deputy had received a written reprimand for leaving invalid telephone messages for his coworkers, informing them to call the coroner's office. In view of the deputy's answers to the internal affairs interview, citing that he was not expected to be an escort within this funeral procession as there was already an escort assigned and the funeral procession was too small to necessitate his involvement, along with his reasons for stopping and detaining me, which were that I had interfered with a funeral procession and that I had endangered his life, both of which were untrue, led me to ask my attorney, "Does this deputy have a preoccupation with death and a dislike for African Americans, whom he targets to reduce his stress and anxiety associated with this fear?"

In far too many instances, the aggression that is directed at African American families and their members is justified on the basis that there is a subculture of violence, particularly within low-income urban areas. However, the violence that is all too often directed toward African Americans is misinterpreted as emanating from the African American community as opposed to the real source, which is oftentimes a law enforcement officer who is projecting the existence of violence onto an entire population to justify aggression directed toward African American families and their members.

Richard Austin, in his analysis of racial profiling, discusses his own experiences when he and a friend were considered suspicious by police officers and subjected to verbal and physical taunts while walking. He asserts that one reason that African American males are criminalized, defiled, and targeted for racial profiling is because of the mainstream media's portrayal of them as drug dealers, absentee fathers, gang members, and high school dropouts.[36]

It may well be the case that the Clinton administration's 1993 anti-crime bill that placed 100,000 new police officers on the streets without adequate training in cultural diversity may have also contributed to this practice.

### Police Brutality

The prevalence of police brutality in the African American community is not new. It has existed and has represented a major challenge to African American families for decades. Many recognize the harsh reality that the excessive use of force directed primarily toward African American males engenders considerable fear and hopelessness on the part of African American mothers and fathers that their children's, especially their sons', lives are at risk by law enforcement officers. This fact continues to be a daunting reality, particularly in view of the serious nature of the cases that gained national and international attention during the decade of the 1990s.

The 1990s provided disturbing evidence that in spite of indisputable evidence captured on videotape and corroborated by eyewitnesses, police abuses of African American men, women, and youth occurs, in most cases, with impunity. While the excessive use of force against African Americans by law enforcement officers is considered a frequent occurrence throughout the country, the 1990s allowed the public to bear witness to the most blatant and excessive uses of force against African Americans captured through video recordings. While there were numerous cases of police brutality during the 1990s, some of the most notable to gain national attention included Amadou Diallo, the 22-year-old immigrant from Guinea, who in February 1990 was shot 41 times by police officers in the vestibule of his apartment after returning from getting something to eat. He was killed by four New York City police officers, who were each acquitted of charges including second-degree murder.[37] The African American community expressed amazement at the jury's verdict, recognizing that Diallo had done nothing wrong. He was reported to be a well-liked, hard-working young man without any history of criminal behavior. He did not represent a threat to anyone, not even the police officers who killed him, yet none of this had any bearing on the jury's decision.

Another highly visible case in the 1990s that involved the use of excessive force, again deadly force, by police officers occurred on December 28, 1998, when Tyiesha Miller, an 18-year-old African American female, sat unconscious in her broken-down car. She had a gun on her lap when she was shot 18 times and killed by police officers. In this case, it was her own family members who had called for help because of her impaired physical condition. The police officers in this case were also not indicted. However, they were later terminated from their jobs on the police force.

The case of Abner Louima, an American of Haitian descent, also registered shock and disbelief in the African American community and other communities of color when it was learned that he was severely beaten and sustained serious physical damages when he was sodomized by a police officer, Justin Volpe, using a broom handle in a New York precinct in Brooklyn. Two of the officers received a conviction, including Justin Volpe, who received a 30-year prison sentence. Ultimately Louima received a cash settlement of almost $9 million. His attorney, Johnnie Cochrane, reported that they considered this settlement to be an indication that this type of conduct was unacceptable and may prevent police officers from engaging in such actions in the future.[38]

Again, one is compelled to consider the ongoing incidents of violence that are directed against African American families and their members and question the validity of a subculture of violence existing among a segment within the African American community. One must also consider the extent to which violence is endemic to American society, and whether license is given to law enforcement officers to perpetrate aggression against African Americans as a means of social control and to remind them of their subordinate status and the social and physical boundaries that constrain them.

Given the frequency and severity of physical attacks perpetrated against African American families and their members, which represent practices that are institutionally sanctioned, there is sufficient evidence to support that "projection," a defense mechanism, is being used by those who control societal resources as well as those appointed as institutional gatekeepers, especially law enforcement and others within the legal system, whereby individuals perceive the qualities that they possess to be socially unacceptable and therefore attribute them to other individuals or a group of individuals. Hence, there is a culture of violence that characterizes those in power and others authorized to use any means necessary, including the excessive use of force to maintain the existing social order, with its unequal distribution of power based on race, sex, and class inequality.

### Imprisonment

The United States has the largest prison population of any country in the world, including similarly technologically developed countries. The prison population in the United States has reached 2 million adult males and females. African Americans, while constituting 13 percent of the population in the United States, make up 46.2 percent of the adult prison population while Latinos/as comprise 16.4 percent of the prison population and whites constitute 35.6 percent of those in prison.[39]

Some policymakers and social scientists argue that the disproportionate number of African American males who make up the adult prison population confirms their belief that African Americans are engaged in more criminal activity than their white counterparts, and that there is a sub-culture of violence in the African American community. However, such arguments fail to take into account the previously discussed role of race in arrests, convictions, and sentencing. Moreover, these arguments dis-avow the existence of the arbitrariness of a criminal justice system that is replete with overt and covert forms of institutional racism.

It is also important to acknowledge, when relying on rates of institu-tionalization, including prison statistics that reflect the racial makeup of these institutions, the precursors that lay the groundwork or increase the likelihood that individuals will be disproportionately present in environ-ments, like lower-income inner-city communities that serve as the primary repository for obtaining individuals to fill societal institutions like prisons, mental hospitals, and the like. After all, it is little wonder why such com-munities are more apt to have residents that are channeled into prisons and are under heavy surveillance, based on the assumption that they are more likely to be dangerous and engage in criminal activity, because they are stereotyped by the mainstream media, according to many theorists and researchers, and stigmatized by a plethora of labels, such as the un-deserving poor, the underclass, welfare dependent, and the homeless, as-signed to economically disadvantaged families and their members who are concentrated in these areas.[40] All of these labels are used to justify the scrutiny by law enforcement officers due to the perceived threat that in-dividuals and families, especially African American families and their members, are said to pose to society. It is, therefore, believed that those who live in the inner city, also known as ghettos, by virtue of the condi-tions of these areas find it virtually impossible to escape these physically and socially isolated and contained areas, except through avenues that lead to prisons, mental hospitals, and the military, one of the few sources of legitimate jobs available to economically disadvantaged males, espe-cially African American males, who face numerous institutional racial bar-riers to employment.

The influx of drugs into inner-city communities was also used to cor-roborate the existence of a subculture of violence. However, it is a widely accepted belief among social scientists that drug trafficking, like other forms of organized crime, is not controlled by poor inner-city residents or petty drug dealers. Many contend that the possession of considerable re-sources and the participation in illegal networks is largely responsible for the large quantities of illegal drugs that are deposited in inner-city neigh-borhoods, as well as more affluent suburban communities, throughout the country. Moreover, social scientists conclude, based on scientific research, that drug trafficking, like other forms of organized criminal activity, exists only because of the involvement of every branch of government, including law enforcement.[41] It is also the case that the majority of drug users are not African Americans but are white. Research, like that conducted annually since 1991 by the National Household Survey on Drug Abuse (NHSDA), revealed that in 1998 74.3 percent of drug users who had used drugs in the past 30 days were white compared to 15.4 percent who were African American and 10.3 percent who were Hispanic. In effect, these studies indicate that racial and ethnic groups use drugs roughly in proportion to their presence in the population.[42] The same is true for drug selling. Between 1991 and 1993, the same survey reported that of those who reported selling drugs, 82 percent were white and 16 percent were African American. However, when considering drug arrests the study found that between 1979 and 1998, there were markedly higher arrest rates for African American drug offenders compared to white drug offenders. It was also found that during this 20-year period the percentage of African Americans arrested for drug offenses increased, while the percentage of whites arrested for drug offenses decreased. The fact that drug enforcement is concentrated in large inner-city areas, along with racial profiling, has also contributed to the disproportionate drug arrests that are racially based. Moreover, Jeanette Covington confirms this practice of differential arrest rates for drug offenses, as she states that there are inherent biases in drug crack downs and drug sweeps that are usually carried out in inner-city African American communities, rather than suburban communities and other geographical areas that are predominantly comprised of whites. This is especially apparent in state courts among individuals who were convicted of drug felonies in 1998, as whites were less likely than African Americans to be sentenced to prison. Specifically, 33 percent of convicted whites received a prison sentence compared to 51 percent of African Americans.[43]

The federal drug sentencing laws that establish mandatory sentencing for the possession and trafficking of crack cocaine and powder cocaine enacted by Congress in 1986 and 1988 result in racial disparities in sentencing that also contribute to longer sentences given to African Americans, who in the 1990s were still incarcerated due to the disparities in these drug sentencing laws. Specifically, individuals convicted of the possession of five grams of crack cocaine receive a mandatory five-year prison sentence. By contrast, a person must be in possession of 500 grams of powder cocaine to receive the mandatory five-year prison term. The U.S. Sentencing Commission, aware of these sentencing disparities, estimated that the five grams of crack cocaine has a street value of approximately $500. And incarcerating a drug offender in a federal prison for five years at an annual cost of $23,000 per year results in an expense to taxpayers of $115,000. Thus, many have proposed that the most cost-effective approach would be drug treatment and related diversionary programs.

Despite demands and proposals from policymakers, social scientists, and community activists to reduce the mandatory penalties for the possession of crack cocaine, due in large measure to institutional racism

whereby young African American males in urban areas have been targeted for drug enforcement, Congress did not enact any legislation that
would reduce the penalties and lengthy sentences during the 1990s. While
such a sentencing policy is detrimental regarding its costs to taxpayers,
there are many academicians and others who believe that a prison-
industrial complex exists, whereby more affluent owners of private prisons through privatization programs and suppliers of goods and services
to prisons, as well as the government and corporations, benefit from the
low costs of prison labor, deriving profits and reducing costs for inmate-
generated products and services. In fact, some academicians refer to
prison labor as a new form of slavery, due to its exploitative nature. Another factor that has been attributed to the inordinate number of African
American males being incarcerated is the Clinton administration's 1993
anti-crime bill.

### 1993 Anti-Crime Legislation

The Clinton administration's punitive approach toward crime contributed immensely to the significant increase in the number of African American males who were imprisoned during the 1990s. Many scholars assert
that the crime bill catered to the needs of the white middle class, for whom
Clinton's centrists policies were designed. Many recognize that it is this
class from whom politicians and elected officials often seek approval and
votes, as they are often in a marginal position, which means that they can
be swayed to the Republican right or the Democratic left, depending on
the political candidate's agenda or platform. Because of the conservative
policies that emanated from the Clinton administration, there are those
who believe that theoretically it may be difficult to continue to see the
Democratic Party as left of the Republican Party. These individuals who
hold this opinion cite as one example of this assessment the Clinton administration's 1993 anti-crime bill.[44]

This legislation contained the following:

1. the authorization for the criminal prosecution of juveniles as adults
2. the three strikes you're out sentencing policy, whereby three felonies result in
   automatic life imprisonment
3. the death penalty authorization for an expanded list of federal crimes
4. 100,000 police officers to be hired
5. procedural reform for death row appeals
6. gun control, including a ban on assault weapons

The anti-crime legislation, as a bill, included crime prevention programs
that were excluded when it became a law. Thus, given the anti-crime

legislation, devoid of prevention and diversionary programs, and the existence of grand apartheid and petit apartheid in the criminal justice system, there is little doubt that the African American community is not a special-interest group that benefited from policies under the Clinton administration.

Positing another economic benefit that prisons serve, William Darity Jr. and Samuel L. Myers Jr. maintain that prisons are labor-market equilibrating devices, so that when there is a superfluous labor force there is an increase in the rates of imprisonment to drain off unwanted workers. By contrast, they state that labor-market shortages result in inmates being released by prisons in order to provide workers.[45]

The precedent for this type of economic exploitation of African Americans occurred during Reconstruction, known as the Convict-Lease System, in which African Americans, particularly men, who could not find employment were charged with vagrancy and jailed. Their former slaveholders would pay their bail. And when they were released from jail they were indebted to the farmer and had to work without pay to repay the farmer for putting up bail.[46] Hence, the criminal justice system has historically had a partnership with the economic system, where both benefited from and played a major role in the subordination, oppression, and economic exploitation of African Americans in the United States. Accordingly, the criminal justice system continues to undermine the stability and well-being of African American families. Thus the criminal justice system, from the pre-arrest to the incarceration stage, contributes enormously to the unavailability of African American males, contributing to the sex ratio imbalance, which inevitably leads to an increase in African American female–maintained families. And after their release from prison, the stigma associated with imprisonment, or being an ex-convict, further reduces the males' marketability, which precludes them from becoming gainfully employed, severely limits their role as a provider, and diminishes their ability to make any meaningful contributions to the family income.

Regarding the conservative nature of social policies that were formulated under the Clinton administration, there are those who believe that despite the opposition that Clinton received in Congress regarding many of his social policies, the Democratic Party and the Clinton administration were interested in appealing to the same constituency. They simultaneously distanced themselves from what Adolph Reed Jr. refers to as marginal constituencies such as civil libertarians, feminists, African Americans, other people of color, and so forth. Some academicians refer to this political persuasion once known as liberalism as "neoliberalism," "conservative democrats," or, according to Bill Clinton, "centrism."[47]

Thus, in general, the Clinton Administration and many of Clinton's Democratic supporters placed their emphasis on the needs, concerns, and interests of mainstream voters in America, which is synonymous with relatively well-off white males. Ultimately, the Clinton administration's policies continued to rescind gains or liberal social policies made in the 1960s and 1970s as it attempted to strengthen its relationship with its traditional social and political base, comprised of middle-class conservative whites, by focusing on economic policies that were designed to benefit and enhance their status.

### The Death Penalty

In 1976, the U.S. Supreme Court ruled that capital punishment was constitutional, reinstating the death penalty. This practice of the criminal justice system has continued to be devastating to African American families, as there are significant disparities in the rates at which African American males compared to white males are given capital sentences. Moreover, there is an abundance of evidence that race is a major factor in determining who will receive a capital sentence. According to U.S. Supreme Court Justice Harry A. Blackmun, "even under the most sophisticated death-penalty statutes, race continues to play a major role in determining who shall live and who shall die."[48]

Furthermore, there is considerable evidence that a disproportionate number of African American and Latino males receive capital sentences because of prejudices held by police officers, judges, prosecutors, and jurors. Amnesty International found that of the 500 prisoners executed between 1977 and 1998, 81.8 percent had been convicted of killing a white person. This was true in spite of the fact that African Americans and whites are victims of homicides in virtually equal amounts nationally.[49]

The races of offender and victim appear to be the overriding factor in capital cases, as an overwhelming number of death penalty sentences are given to African Americans when the victim is white. Thus, institutional racism is often cited for the racial disparities in capital sentences, as the finality of the death sentence is imposed on African American men, usually by whites, who systematically control and regulate their social environment to ensure that African Americans remain in a social position of subordination that existed prior to Reconstruction.[50] Furthermore, the racial disparities that result in a disproportionate number of African American males being given capital sentences is to instill fear in African American families and to perpetuate the image of African American males as individuals who belong to a criminal subculture, for whom members of the larger society should remain fearful. It is also the case that class is an important factor, as is race, in determining who is likely to receive a capital sentence. Thus, lower-income African American males are without adequate financial resources to afford private attorneys and are therefore appointed public defenders, many of whom demonstrate their incompetence in a number of ways. Studies reveal that serious errors are made in capital cases, and that these errors are not rare but are normative within the criminal justice system. In a landmark study conducted by James Liebman, a Columbia University law professor, all capital convictions (approximately 5,500 judicial decisions) and appeals between 1973 and 1995 were reviewed. The findings revealed that grave errors were made in these cases. This national study covered a 23-year period and revealed that major errors rather than minor technicalities occurred, resulting in the majority of convictions being overturned. Liebman identified the three most common errors that accounted for a total of 76 percent of all of the errors in these cases as the following:[51]

1. Blatantly incompetent defense lawyers accounted for 37 percent of the errors.
2. Prosecutorial misconduct, generally the suppression of evidence, constituted 19 percent of the errors.
3. Faulty instructions to jurors accounted for 20 percent of the errors.

Because of the serious and systematic nature of these reversible errors, and due to the irreversibility of the death penalty, where innocent men, primarily African Americans, are being put to death, many policymakers are calling for a moratorium on the death penalty until these systematic errors and biases can be eradicated. In chapter 10, a moratorium that was ordered in one state in the twenty-first century is discussed.

## MYTH #5: AFRICAN AMERICAN FAMILIES, LIKE WHITE FAMILIES, HAVE THE SAME LIFE CHANCES AND OPPORTUNITIES TO ACHIEVE THE AMERICAN DREAM, AS THEY HAVE EQUAL ACCESS TO AMERICAN INSTITUTIONS BECAUSE AMERICA IS NOW A COLOR-BLIND SOCIETY

Because of the modest success of liberal social policies in the 1960s and 1970s, the conservative and reactionary social policies of the 1980s, and the conservative social policies of the 1990s, numerous disparities in treatment and status continue to exist between African American families and white families. Nevertheless, the 1990s brought with them the myth that America had become a color-blind society, due in large measure to liberal social policies and laws enacted during the 1960s and 1970s. Such proclamations ignored the continued institutional policies and practices as well as individual aggressions perpetrated against African American families and their members. This myth was perhaps one of the easiest ones to dispel, and one that African Americans and members of other cultural groups committed to equality and justice discredited and negated by providing incontrovertible evidence and data from their various professions, businesses, and disciplines that there is absolutely no validity to the claim that America is a color-blind society.

Because of time and spatial limitations it is not possible to identify all or even most of the racially discriminatory practices that are institutionalized within every major societal institution in the United States. Accordingly, mainstream institutions systematically offer African American families and their members substandard and inferior treatment and services, while that which their white counterparts receive is far superior and of a higher quality.

The myth that America is a color-blind society in which all individuals have equal access to the same life chances is patently false and is clearly disproven by examining societal institutions. Four institutions will be briefly examined: the health-care system, the educational system, the economic system, and the legal system.

### Health Care Delivery System

The physical health of African American family members is critical to their individual and collective survival. While life expectancy of African American males and females has increased over the past 25 years, they are still disproportionately affected by many chronic health conditions and diseases. Specifically, hypertension, cardiovascular disease, cerebrovascular disease, cancer, diabetes, and HIV and AIDS have an adverse effect on African Americans and add to the financial and emotional strain that African American families must endure.

One reason for the disproportionately high morbidity and mortality rates due to these and other diseases that affect African Americans is the lack of available and affordable quality health care in urban areas where the majority of African American families reside. Studies also indicate that race is a major determinant in the actual medical care that African Americans receive. For example, in a study of more than 53,000 patients who had heart attacks, African American patients, unlike white patients, did not receive the same aggressive treatment. In this study African American patients who had heart attacks were less likely to be referred for diagnostic tests known as angiograms than white heart attack patients.[52] Moreover, in another study of patients receiving treatment in federal Veterans Administration hospitals, where medical care is expected to be more uniform, African American patients were less likely than white patients to receive more costly medical procedures like catheterization of the heart for blocked arteries. Finally, in a study of patients in hospitals in the United States, researchers found that only 47 percent of African American and poor patients were placed in intensive care units compared to 70 percent of white and poor Medicare patients.[53]

The Clinton administration attempted to address the problem of providing for the health care needs of all Americans, including the working class and lower-income class without either employer-sponsored health insurance programs or the ability to afford to pay the employees' share of the health insurance premium. The Clinton administration's proposal to implement a universal health-care plan was unsuccessful. In fact, Clinton promised a universal health care plan within the first 100 days after assuming the presidency during his campaign for the presidency. The failure of the Clinton administrations health care plan has been attributed to the complexity of his proposal and his inability to garner support from the necessary interests groups, particularly those in the health-care delivery system, who did not welcome any new restrictions on their "freedom to practice."[54]

Consequently, numerous Americans are without health insurance coverage and the private capability to pay for their own medical care. Clinton's proposed universal health-care plan was a necessity in the United States, where many communities both urban and rural are designated as "medically underserved." Today, the United States and the Republic of South Africa are the only remaining two technologically developed nations without a universal health-care plan.

## Educational System

While the educational system is extremely important to the survival and progress of families and their members, the fact is that African American students who largely attend urban schools rarely receive a quality education. The lower levels of funding that these public schools receive are because African American families have little control over their tax dollars. Because property taxes serve as the primary basis for funding public schools and the values of urban properties are not highly valuated, the lower tax base does not afford adequate funds for urban school students that are predominantly African American in many school districts. However, there are other sources of taxes and resources available to states that can be used to supplement the relatively low funds per capita for students in urban schools, yet African American families have no control and limited influence over the allocation of tax dollars and state's resources to ensure that urban schools are funded at levels comparable to suburban and private schools.

Another problem that contributes to the poor quality of education that African American children receive and their relatively lower levels of academic achievement is that African American families rarely have any meaningful influence over institutional policies that govern school administration, curriculum, textbooks, disciplinary policies, and the hiring and termination of teachers and administrators. Further, African American families have little influence over the various forms of creative re-production that are reflective of culture, like musicals, artwork, and fund-raisers. This is true even when the student body is predominantly comprised of students of color, largely African American and Latinos. Throughout the country, African American students attend schools that are comprised of 68 percent students of color. However, the majority of teachers and administrators, like principals and vice-principals, not to mention school boards, typically consist of whites. It is in the best interests of African American students to have teachers, administrators, and school board members who are in key decision-making positions be members of African American culture or acquainted with African American culture. Knowledge of African American culture should be acquired through college-level courses on African American culture, the African American family, and African American children and youth. It is important that teachers, administrators, and school board members accept the existence of African American culture with its own values, norms, and belief systems, as well as the contributions that people of African descent have made to the United States and to the world. It is extremely important to understand the day-to-day experiences of African Americans in the United States, as this will enable teachers, administrators, and school board members to become aware of the challenges that are daily occurrences for African American students, their parents, and members of their community that white counterparts are not likely to encounter or to relate to.

Efforts must be taken to increase the number of African American teachers in the classroom who serve as role models and mentors for African American students and who tend to have realistic expectations of their ability to perform well academically. One reason for the underrepresentation of African American teachers is due to their lower performance rates on teacher competency examinations. Clearly, these standardized tests continue to represent methods by which African Americans, whether students or teachers, are excluded from admission to various institutions because of their scores. Thus, it is important that other measures be used and standardized tests alone, with their built-in cultural and class biases, not be the sole or even primary determinant for inclusion or participation in various societal institutions and organizations.

Standardized tests, like IQ tests and the SAT, have been found to reflect cultural and class biases, rather than intellectual ability and accurate predictors of academic and career success. Studies reveal that the majority of the variance in standardized test scores can also be attributed to differential cultural experiences that give white middle- and upper-class students advantages, as their race and social and economic privileges afford them greater opportunities to become familiar with the kind of experiences that are conducive to enhancing their performance on the verbal portion and linear reasoning questions contained in these standardized tests. Further, in many private schools students are given several opportunities to take SAT tests repeatedly in lower grades, and are therefore more prepared to obtain competitive scores when these tests are administered to determine their eligibility for admission into institutions of higher education. Moreover, Claude Steele states that standardized tests measure only 18 percent of factors that predict freshman grades. Further, he asserts that standardized college entrance exams measure experiential knowledge, not innate ability.[55]

More African American representation is needed on urban school boards. However, despite the large number of African American candidates who campaign for these seats, they generally do not have the financial resources or the involvement in social and political networks that would enable them to win a seat on a school board. Therefore, policies continue to be established by white school board members for schools that have a disproportionate number of African American and Latino students. The results of these existing institutional arrangements are well known—in one word, "failure." Andrew Hacker has pointed out that even when schools appear to be administered by African Americans, they are still controlled by whites. Given the critical state of urban education, it is necessary to make reforms that include the greater inclusion of African American teachers, administrators, and parents in every aspect of the educational experience. Classroom management, for example, has not presented the same level of problems for African American teachers in classrooms comprised largely of African American students as those in which the teaching staff is predominantly white. Designing innovative policies is imperative, as traditional methods are highly ineffective.

The Atlanta Compromise is but one example of an educational policy initiative to afford African Americans a greater opportunity to establish policies and to govern schools that are predominantly comprised of African American students. Gary Orfield states that African Americans and whites agreed that African Americans would be given control over Atlanta's school board by agreeing not to pursue a metropolitan-wide desegregation case through the courts. While this arrangement did not become a model that was followed by school boards in the 1990s, perhaps the emergency states that many urban schools face in the twenty-first century, sometimes leading to the privatization of urban schools, will result in other school districts in the United States considering this and similar models.[56]

Another proposed social policy to increase African American representation may require legislation that would allow term-sharing, in which African Americans and whites can share a term on the school board by dividing the term in half. Otherwise, there is likely to be a continuation of the existing pattern of the underrepresentation of African American

school board members, since they rarely have the necessary financial resources nor, in many metropolitan areas, voter support form the majority
of voters, who are white, to wage a successful campaign and become
elected to the school board.

## The Economic System

The economic system in the 1990s can be examined from many perspectives, each of which clearly indicates that race is an important determining factor in the acquisition of goods and services and provides
unequivocal evidence that dispels the myth that America is a color-blind
society.

Whether focusing on the labor market, business ownership, home ownership, banking in terms of check cashing, borrowing money for major
purchases such as automobiles and houses, or obtaining material objects
such as stereo systems, televisions, household furniture, and the like, the
1990s economic boom notwithstanding, African American families continued to experience economic exploitation and institutional discrimination, both based on race. Diverse forms of economic exploitation were
systematically imposed by commercial banks, mortgage companies, and
insurance agencies. Because commercial banks began to reduce their presence in inner-city communities, many African American families, especially those in the working-class and lower-income class, were forced to
rely on fringe banking organizations that began replacing dwindling commercial banks in these communities. Fringe banking organizations include
rent-to-own stores, payroll advance and check-cashing businesses, high-
interest mortgage companies, pawnshops, and wire transfer companies.
These fringe banking firms tend to lend money at high subprime interest
rates for purchasing and refinancing homes and cars, charge astronomi-
cally high fees for payroll cash advances and to cash checks, and charge
exorbitant interest rates to customers without adequate or good credit
who need to finance the costs of household furnishings. Because these
customers in need of household goods have inadequate or poor credit
they are usually left with the option of renting household items at extremely high interest rates with the intention of buying them. While predatory lending is not a new practice, its prevalence and expansion in the
African American community and other communities of color occurred
during the 1990s.

Securing home mortgages from commercial banks during the 1990s continued to be difficult as numerous African American families deemed
credit worthy were denied mortgages, at rates that exceeded those of
white families, to purchase and refinance homes. Studies revealed systematic patterns of housing discrimination as inordinate numbers of African
American families seeking mortgages were denied the financing required

to purchase and refinance their homes. Equally disturbing were research findings that revealed that the higher the socioeconomic class, as indicated by income, the greater was the likelihood of African Americans being denied home loans throughout the United States. These denials to African Americans attempting to secure financing for mortgages to purchase and refinance homes substantially exceeded the denial rates faced by their similarly situated high-income white counterparts.[57] Clearly, in a color-blind society these occurrences would not take place. Moreover, such policies and practices violate the 1968 Fair Housing Act that prohibits racial discrimination in the area of housing in the United States. The continued practice of mortgage companies and commercial banks refusing to lend monies to African Americans to purchase and refinance homes is certainly indicative of institutional racial discrimination that is inextricably woven into the economic system. And the systematic nature of this practice further substantiates the extent to which African American families experienced the further erosion of social and economic gains obtained during the 1960s and 1970s, during the era of liberal social policy.

Regarding the economic boom that occurred during the Clinton administration, African Americans, whether high school graduates or college educated, continued to have shorter career ladders, as many were excluded from the labor market because of racial discrimination, while others encountered the glass ceiling, which limited any further opportunities for career mobility. There is also considerable evidence that an employer's refusal to hire African Americans is demonstrated by his or her use of queues, which is a system that places African Americans in the lowest queues to be hired after whites and others, based on race and ethnicity, who are given priority by employers and placed in higher queues. It has also been found that while employers are more likely to hire African American workers when there is a shortage of laborers, employers still retain racial stereotypes regarding African Americans, which obviously affects their ability to perform, the employer's assessment of their performance, and their career mobility.

President Clinton was clearly aware of the state of race relations in America and how racial discrimination impacts the lives of African Americans, as he established a Commission on Race and appointed John Hope Franklin, the renowned historian, to chair the commission and study the problem and to propose recommendations. Moreover, Clinton held town meetings in various American cities to discuss race relations; yet these institutional racially discriminatory practices did not diminish under his administration. Thus, it became increasingly clear that in order to increase the participation of African Americans in mainstream institutions, to increase their access to equal opportunities, and to reduce the probability that they would continue to be targets of civil and criminal injustices it would be necessary to introduce policies and executive orders and to support the enactment of legislation that would result in stricter enforcement of existing civil rights laws. In addition, the Clinton administration's policies should have ensured that affirmative action policies were effective and that alleged discrimination cases were brought to trial or mediation hearings more rapidly. In addition, an executive order, rather than another study of racial profiling, was needed to halt this practice or at least to significantly diminish its use.

Regarding affirmative action, in a February 1995 issue of *Newsweek*, the cover story claimed that affirmative action would be ended. Included in this issue, however, was a statement by President Bill Clinton relative to affirmative action, which was "mend it, don't end it." Some believe that this assertion was a façade for the quiet and subtle dismantling of affirmative action programs and the mechanisms they depend upon for their enforcement.[58]

What did become increasingly obvious during the 1990s was a growing anti–affirmative action movement. While there had always been critics of and court challenges to affirmative action, there had not been a collective movement to eliminate this policy. However, Ward Connerly, an African American businessman in the state of California, led a successful campaign that placed Proposition 209 on the ballot. Proposition 209 disallowed race to be used in admissions to institutions of higher education that were state supported and disallowed the use of race in the procurement of government contracts. This legislation was successful, as voters supported it on November 5, 1996. Consequently, race could no longer be the sole basis for matriculation to state colleges and universities, race-based scholarships at these institutions were prohibited, and race could not be used in hiring government workers or awarding government contracts.

The effects of Proposition 209 were significant, as African American student admissions to the freshmen class of UCLA in 1998 dropped 42.6 percent and 33 percent for Latinos. Overall, there was a 10 percent decrease in enrollment in students of color in 1998. Other universities like the University of Texas and the University of Washington enacted anti–affirmative action policies and they too experienced declines in the enrollment of students of color in the late 1990s. In fact, it was decided by the U.S. Court of Appeals in the *Hopwood v. Texas* case that race could not be considered a factor in law school admissions in March 1996. This decision also led to declines in admissions to the University of Texas law school. This race-neutral policy was also applied to all state-funded colleges and universities in Texas.

While these overall policies have generated considerable criticism for their failure to ameliorate conditions affecting many African American families, it is important to identify various policies formulated and implemented by the Clinton administration to address problems affecting lower-income people. While these policies were not race specific, they had the potential for improving conditions for African American families who are overrepresented in the lower-income class. In effect, the Clinton administration formulated and instituted empowerment zones and enterprise communities, a revised food stamp program, increased the earned income tax credit to assist economically disadvantaged families in the United States, and created a National Service Program for youth. These policies and programs were designed to increase jobs, goods, income, and scholarships to impoverished families and their members.

In 1993, the Clinton administration provided economic assistance to nine areas designated as Empowerment Zones and 95 communities designated as Enterprise Communities. These geographical locations were in both urban and rural areas. The purpose for infusing billions of dollars into these communities was to generate jobs in the country's most economically distressed areas. Monies were also to be used to finance community development projects to enhance the economic development of these severely economically depressed communities. Tax incentives were given to companies to hire residents within these zones, as well as providing employer tax credits for firms outside the zones that hired residents within the zones for specific targeted jobs.

In addition, the Clinton administration revised the food stamp program, raising food stamp benefits and increasing the number of families who are eligible to receive food stamps. They also introduced a policy that increased the amount of income that economically disadvantaged low-wage families could receive as a federal tax credit, through the earned income tax credit, which is made available to families upon filing their annual federal income tax returns.

Finally, the Clinton administration instituted a National Service Program that allowed young men and women to work for two years in community service, receiving minimum wages as well as a scholarship in the amount of $4,725 per year that they could apply toward their college or university expenses for a two-year period.[59]

These efforts on the part of the Clinton administration were certainly necessary but failed to address the institutional barriers that result in impoverished families, particularly African American poor families and their members confronted with the intersection of race, sex, and class inequality, being engulfed in a racial/class caste-like system that virtually ensures intergenerational poverty and the tenuous nature of middle-class status for African American families. In effect, the 1990s have firmly institutionalized social policies and practices that essentially guarantee that social classes will reproduce themselves. Basically, this meant that white upper-class families can be assured with a high degree of certainty that their monopoly of societal resources will continue along with the unequal distribution of wealth and power in America, which undergirds and perpetuates their privileged status.[60]

### The Legal System

I have already discussed many of the blatant forms of institutional racism that result in the political oppression of African American families and their members such as racial profiling, police brutality, and grand and petit apartheid that occurs from the pre-arrest to the incarceration stage. However, it is also important to examine the role of the judiciary itself as it relates to African Americans receiving justice and to determine what role institutional and individual racial biases play in civil as well as criminal cases. I have already pointed out how judge's instructions to juries in capital cases have been found to produce errors in convictions when a disproportionate number of the defendants are African American and Latino males. However, it is also the case that judges in civil cases make determinations on the basis of the race and class of the defendant. Accordingly, the 1990s produced a substantial body of evidence to dispel the myth that judges are objective and not racially biased in their decisions in civil cases. This knowledge became apparent due to the growth in prepaid legal insurance and its increased prevalence among working- and middle-class families. Prepaid legal insurance has allowed citizens to observe outcomes of civil cases when an attorney is present as a legal representative, compared to judicial decisions in similar cases when a defendant has no legal representation.

Prior to the affordability and widespread purchase of prepaid legal insurance most people in minor civil matters, especially in traffic cases, were unable to afford legal representation. Hence, they paid their moving violation, oftentimes even when they were innocent, believing that they would still be found guilty because the police officer's account of what occurred would be deemed more credible than their own account by the judge. Therefore, most drivers receiving citations decide to pay the ticket and avoid paying the ticket plus possible court costs if they opted for a hearing. In the 1990s it was increasingly common to see drivers charged with various traffic offenses appear before a judge, accompanied by an attorney. This is true because many prepaid insurance policies guarantee that the insured will have legal representation or an attorney to appear with him or her in court for charges involving moving violations. Because prepaid insurance requires a monthly premium it is still often unaffordable to those in the lower-income class. Obviously, this excludes a large number of African Americans, as they are overrepresented in the lower-income class. However, because of the institutional practice of racial profiling, it is African Americans who need to purchase such insurance policies to at least provide them with legal representation when they appear in court, either by choice or being summoned. It has become apparent that the outcomes of drivers with legal representation who appear in traffic court are often quite different than those who are without an attorney.

I first became aware of the differential judgments based on race, class, and legal representation, which in many cases are interrelated, when a friend was given a moving violation for exceeding the speed limit while driving a new car. My friend had recently purchased prepaid legal insurance and, believing the charge was false, decided to have a court hearing. An attorney did meet my friend in court, and the initial case was continued, which apparently is a common practice for those who request a hearing. However, we were both startled to learn that the judge had taken the liberty to reduce the speeding violation, which would have resulted in two points being placed on her driving record for a period of three years. That could have meant an increase in the insurance premium. Moreover, any attempt to change to another insurance company during this three-year period may have resulted in a higher insurance premium, as the preferred status, which affords drivers the lowest insurance rates, is not usually made available if a driver has a speeding ticket on record. And in some states, like the state of Ohio, all drivers must have automobile insurance. Failure to have automobile insurance, if it is discovered, results in an automatic 90-day suspension of the driver's license. In effect, the speeding violation was reduced to driving with a loud muffler, which carries no points. Therefore, after the fine was paid my friend's driving record remained clear. In yet another case, a driver was charged with failure to control and that charge was reduced to equipment failure. However, that defendant had entered a plea of not guilty, which was ignored along with documents from a state engineer that supported the plea. Moreover, the judge made the defendant pay the maximum court costs simply because judges are given this discretion. Thus, while the equipment failure resulted in no points, the case should have been dismissed had the judge considered the engineer's documented evidence, but the judge considered the police officer's opinion as more credible. This clearly indicates the arbitrariness of this system and the questionable ability of judges to render objective decisions in these civil matters.

This institutional practice of racial and class discrimination clearly indicates the necessity for studies to be conducted to determine the extent to which there is a systematic institutional practice and whether it, like many other practices in the legal system, is reflective of institutional racial and class discrimination.

There is definitely a need for judicial reform in both civil and criminal courts, as when judges render decisions they de-personify themselves, as the decision is the decision of the court, thereby personifying the court. However, when judges who are not appointed run for election and re-election they regain their personhood when their names appear on the ballots. It is clear that they are human beings who hold attitudes, beliefs, stereotypes, and biases that are likely to influence their decisions, as studies and experiential knowledge reveal.

However, when judicial decisions occur that reflect institutional race and class discrimination, a mockery is made of the ideals upon which America is founded, which guarantee liberty and justice for all. Systematic violations of these ideals result in hopelessness, frustration, and despair for African American families and their members, who by virtue of race and class are disadvantaged by societal institutions, including the legal system, while more economically advantaged families receive innumerable benefits and privileges from all societal institutions, including the legal system.

Clearly, these and other occurrences during the 1990s provide irrefutable evidence that race matters and that there is no validity to the claim that America is a color-blind society. However, for those who still accept this premise, the most compelling argument that can be given to support this claim is that if America is indeed a color-blind society, the institutional practices of racial discrimination prove that that there are three colors to which America is not blinded, and they are black, white, and brown.

## NOTES

1. Patricia A. Schechter, *Ida B. Wells-Barnett & American Reform: 1880–1930* (Chapel Hill: University of North Carolina Press, 2000), p. 18.

2. Frances Piven and Richard Cloward, *Regulating the Poor: The Functions of Public Welfare* (New York: Vintage, 1971), pp. 3–41.

3. Niara Sudarkasa, "African American Families and Family Values," in *Black Families*, ed. Harriette Pipes McAdoo (Thousand Oaks, Calif.: Sage Publications, 1997), pp. 30–38; A. Wade Boykin and Forrest D. Toms, "Black Child Socialization: A Conceptual Framework," in *Black Children: Social, Educational and Parental Environments*, ed. Harriette McAdoo and John McAdoo (Beverly Hills, Calif.: Sage Publications, 1985), pp. 39–47; and Andrew Billingsley, *Climbing Jacob's Ladder: The Enduring Legacies of African American Families* (New York: Simon & Schuster, 1992), p. 73.

4. Theodore Caplow, *Elementary Sociology* (Englewood Cliffs, N.J.: Prentice-Hall, 1971), pp. 41–43.

5. Jacqueline Fleming, *Blacks in College: A Comparative Study of Students' Success in Black and White Institutions* (San Francisco: Jossey-Bass, 1984); and Marcia L. Hall and Walter R. Allen, "Race Consciousness among African American College Students," in *Black Students: Psychological Issues and Academic Achievement*, ed. Gordon LaVern Berry and Joy Keiko Asamen (Newbury Park, Calif.: Sage Publications, 1989), pp. 174–176.

6. Stephen Steinberg, "Occupational Apartheid in America," in *Without Justice for All: The New Liberalism and Our Retreat from Racial Equality*, ed. Adolph Reed Jr. (Boulder, Colo.: Westview Press, 1999), p. 226.

7. W.E.B. Du Bois, *The Souls of Black Folks* (London: Longsman Green, 1965), p. 2.

8. Susan Toliver, *Black Families in Corporate America* (Thousand Oaks, Calif.: Sage Publications, 1998).

9. Ibid., p. 10; and Ella L. J. Edmondson Bell and Stella M. Nkomo, *Our Separate Ways: Black and White Women and the Struggle for Professional Identity* (Boston: Harvard Business School Press, 2001), pp. 159–173.

10. Daniel Georges-Abeyie, "Criminal Justice Processing of Non-White Minorities," in *Racism, Empiricism and Criminal Justice,* ed. Brian D. MacLean and Dragan Milovanovic (Vancouver: Collective Press, 1990), p. 12.

11. Dragan Milovanovic and Katheryn K. Russell, "Petit Apartheid," in *The U.S. Criminal Justice System: The Dark Figure of Racism,* ed. Dragan Milovanovic and Katheryn K. Russell (Durham, N.C.: Carolina Academic Press, 2001), pp. xix–xxi.

12. Hans J. Massaquoi, "The New Racism," *Ebony* 51, no. 10 (August 1996): 56–60.

13. Arthur R. Jensen. "How Much Can We Boost I.Q. and Scholastic Achievement?" *Harvard Educational Review* 39, no. 1 (1969): 123; and Richard J. Herrnstein and Charles Murray, *The Bell Curve* (New York: Free Press, 1994), pp. 269–316.

14. William Ryan, *Blaming the Victim* (New York: Vintage, 1971).

15. Douglas E. Crews and James R. Bindon, "Ethnicity as a Taxonomic Tool in Biomedical and Biosocial Research," *Introduction to Clinical Medicine: Medical Humanities Anthology* (2001): 353–359.

16. Jawanza Kunjufu, *Countering the Conspiracy to Destroy Black Boys* (Chicago: African American Images, 1995), pp. 31–56; and Beverly Daniel Tatum, *Why Are All the Black Kids Sitting Together in the Cafeteria?* (New York: Basic Books, 1997), pp. 62–65.

17. Wade A. Boykin and Brenda A. Allen, "Enhancing African American Children's Learning and Motivation: Evolution of the Verve and Movement Expressiveness Paradigms," in *African American Children, Youth, and Parenting,* ed. Reginald L. Jones (Hampton, Va.: Cobb and Henry Publishers, 1999), p. 116; Kunjufu, *Countering the Conspiracy;* and Stephen Samuel Smith, "Education and Struggle against Race, Class and Gender Inequality," in *Race, Class and Gender,* 2nd ed., ed. Margaret L. Andersen and Patricia Hill Collins (Belmont, Calif.: Wadsworth Press, 1995), pp. 289–304.

18. Jonathan Kozol, *Savage Inequalities: Children in America's Schools* (New York: Crown, 1991).

19. D. M. Cutler, E. S. Glaser, and J. L. Vigdor, "The Rise and Decline of the American Ghetto," *Journal of Political Economy* 107 (1999): 455; and Gary Orfield and Susan E. Eaton, *Dismantling Desegregation: The Quiet Reversal of Brown v. Board of Education* (New York: New Press, 1996).

20. American Association of University Women, cited in William Kornblum and Joseph Julian, *A Custom Edition of Social Problems,* 2nd ed. (Englewood Cliffs, N.J.: Prentice-Hall, 1998), p. 306.

21. Tatum, *Why Are All the Black Kids.*

22. Carolyn Bennett Murray and James S. Jackson, "The Conditioned Failure Model Revisited," in *African American Children, Youth, and Parenting,* ed. Reginald L. Jones (Hampton, Va: Cobb and Henry Publishers, 1999), p. 51.

23. Oscar Lewis, *The Study of Slum Cultures* (New York: Random House, 1968); and Charles Murray, *Losing Ground: American Social Policy, 1950–1980* (New York: Basic Books, 1984).

24. "Who Will Care When Parents Can't? A Study of Black Children in Foster Care," (Washington, D.C.: National Black Child Development Institute, 1989),

pp. 3–6.; and Dorothy Roberts, *Shattered Bonds: The Color of Child Welfare* (New York: Basic Books, 2002), p. vi.

25. Steinberg, "Occupational Apartheid in America," p. 20.

26. Andrew Hacker, *Two Nations: Black, White, Separate, Hostile, Unequal* (New York: Ballantine Books, 1995), p. 115.

27. Preston H. Smith, "Self-Help, Black Conservatives and the Reemergence of Black Privatism," in *Without Justice for All: The New Liberalism and Our Retreat from Racial Equality*, ed. Adolph Reed Jr. (Boulder, Colo.: Westview Press, 1999), p. 257.

28. Dona Cooper Hamilton and Charles V. Hamilton, *The Dual Agenda: Race and Social Welfare Policies of Civil Rights Organizations* (New York: Columbia University Press, 1997), p. 1; and Paul J. Quirk and Joseph Hinchcliffe, "Domestic Policy: The Trials of a Centrist Democrat," in *The Clinton Presidency First Appraisals*, ed. Colin Campbell and Bert A. Rockman (Chatham, N.J.: Chatham House Publishers, 1996), p. 280.

29. Coramae Richey Mann, *Unequal Justice: A Question of Color* (Bloomington: Indiana University Press, 1993).

30. Diana Kendall, *Sociology in Our Times*, 2nd ed. (Belmont, Calif.: Wadsworth Press, 2000), p. 179.

31. William Chambliss. "The Saints and the Roughnecks," *Society* 2 (1973): 24–31.

32. Kenneth Meeks, *Driving while Black: What To Do if You Are a Victim of Racial Profiling* (New York: Broadway Books, 2000), pp.13–18.

33. Ibid., pp. 21–34.

34. Milovanovic and Russell, "Petit Apartheid," pp. xix–xxi.

35. Jill Nelson, "Introduction," in *Police Brutality*, ed. Jill Nelson (New York: W. W. Norton and Co., 2000), p. 12.

36. Richard Austin, "Under the Veil of Suspicion: Organizing Resistance and Struggling for Liberation," in *Police Brutality*, ed. Jill Nelson (New York: W. W. Norton and Co., 2000), pp. 206–209.

37. Nelson, "Introduction," p. 10.

38. Ibid., pp.12–14; and Austin, "Under the Veil of Suspicion," p. 214.

39. Michael B. Katz, *Improving Poor People* (Princeton, N.J.: Princeton University Press, 1995), pp. 65–66.

40. Herbert Gans Jr., *The War against the Poor: The Underclass and Antipoverty Policy* (New York: Basic Books, 1995), pp. 59–73; and William A. Darity Jr. and Samuel L. Myers Jr. with Emmett D. Carson and William Sabol, *The Black Underclass: Critical Essays on Race and Unwantedness* (New York: Garland Publishing Co., 1994), pp. 13–40.

41. Kornblum and Julian, *Custom Edition*, p. 171.

42. Jeanette Covington, "Round Up the Usual Suspects: Racial Profiling and the War on Drugs," in *Petit Apartheid in the U.S. Criminal Justice System: The Dark Figure of Racism*, ed. Dragan Milovanovic and Katheryn K. Russell (Durham, N.C.: Carolina Academic Press, 2001), p. 33.

43. Ibid., pp. 31–32; and Matthew R. Durose and Patrick A. Langan, *Bureau of Justice Statistics, State Court Sentencing of Convicted Felons, 1998. Statistical Tables* (Washington, D.C.: U.S. Department of Justice, December 2001), Table 25.

44. Quirk and Hinchliffe, "Domestic Policy," p. 277.

45. Darity and Myers, *The Black Underclass*, pp. 54–55; and William Darity Jr. and Samuel L. Myers Jr., "The Impact of Labor Market Prospects on Incarceration

Rates" in *Prosperity For All?* ed. Robert Cherry and William Rodgers (New York: Russell Sage Foundation, 2000), p. 279.

46. Mary Frances Berry and John Blassingame, *Long Memory: The Black Experience in America* (New York: Oxford University Press, 1982).

47. Adolph Reed Jr., "New liberal Orthodoxy," in *Without Justice for All: The New Liberalism and Our Retreat from Racial Equality,* ed. Adolph Reed Jr. (Boulder, Colo.: Westview Press, 1999), p. 3; and Philip A. Klinkner, "Bill Clinton and the Politics of the New Liberalism," in *Without Justice for All: The New Liberalism and Our Retreat from Racial Equality,* ed. Adolph Reed Jr. (Boulder, Colo.: Westview Press, 1999), p. 12.

48. *Killing with Prejudice: Race and the Death Penalty in the U.S.A.* (New York: Amnesty International U.S.A., 1999), p. 1.

49. Ibid., p. 6.

50. Adalberto Aguire Jr. and David Baker, *Race, Racism and the Death Penalty in the United States* (Barren Springs, Mo.: Vende Vere Publishing Ltd., 1991), p. 40.

51. "Landmark Study Finds Capital Punishment System Fraught with Error." *Columbia (New York) News,* 16 June 2002, p. 1.

52. "Blacks Get Less Aggressive Heart Attack Care, Study Finds," *Columbus Dispatch,* 10 May 2001, p. 12A.

53. Sandra Blakeslee, "Poor and Black Patients Slighted Study Says," *New York Times,* 20 April 1994, p. B9.

54. Wilson K. Graham, "The Clinton Administration and Interest Groups," in *The Clinton Presidency First Appraisals,* ed. Colin Campbell and Bert A. Rockman (Chatham, N.J.: Chatham House Publishers, 1996), p. 226.

55. Claude M. Steele, "Expert Testimony in Defense of Affirmative Action," in *Sex, Race and Merit,* ed. Faye J. Crosby and Cheryl Van Deveer (Ann Arbor: University of Michigan Press, 2000), pp. 124–125.

56. Gary Orfield, *Desegregation of Black and Hispanic Students from 1968 to 1980* (Mass.: Joint Center for Urban Studies, 1982); and Gary Orfield, "America Lacks Equal Opportunity," *Los Angeles Times,* 26 December 1993, p. 5.

57. Jodi Nirode, "Paying a Steep Price: Blacks More Likely than Whites to Turn to High Cost Lenders," *Columbus Dispatch,* 4 June 2001, p. A5; and Jodi Nirode and Stephanie Brenowitz, "A Dream Denied: Even with High Incomes, Blacks Face a Tough Time Getting Home Mortgages," *Columbus Dispatch,* 3 June 2001, pp. A1, A9.

58. Steinberg, "Occupational Apartheid in America," p. 233.

59. Hamilton and Hamilton, *The Dual Agenda,* p. 237.

60. Andrew Hacker, *Money: Who Has How Much and Why?* (New York: Scribner's, 1997), pp. 10–11; and Mark Zepezauer and Arthur Naiman, *Take the Rich Off Welfare* (Tucson, Ariz.: Odonian Press, 1996).

# CHAPTER 10

# The Turbulent Twenty-First Century

The African American family's introduction to the twenty-first century was tumultuous. Many African American families, after the passage of the 1965 Voting Rights Act, considered political participation, in the form of voting, a right that had been won after a long and hard fight. The constant reminder from the Democratic Party during elections, especially presidential elections, was to get out and vote. Numerous organizations, groups, and community activists have encouraged African Americans to remain actively involved in the voting process. They have established and maintained voter registration drives through numerous events, always telling African Americans who are voting age of their obligation to vote because of the efforts of many within the African American community who engaged in various forms of protest and who made numerous sacrifices, including civil rights activists who died while seeking major voting reforms. Oftentimes, policies and procedures such as poll taxes, violence, the loss of employment, literacy tests, the grandfather clause, and so forth are cited as reasons that fostered the activism that seemingly ended racial discrimination at the polls. However, there has been growing skepticism with the policies and institutional forms of racial discrimination that have continued to persist in the United States in all systems, including the political system. While the numbers of congressional representatives have increased since the era of liberal social policy and the enactment of the 1965 Voting Rights Act, little has changed in terms of increasing the African American presence in the U.S. Senate. In addition, the increase in the number of African Americans involved in local government as state representatives and mayors, while showing an increase compared to the pre–civil rights movement, has not resulted in meaningful changes or improvements in the lives of an overwhelming majority of African American families. Nevertheless, there was 57 percent African American voter participation in the 2000 presidential election. Many were pleased with local election results, in that new African American mayors were elected and incumbent African American mayors regained their elected offices, bringing a tremendous amount of satisfaction to African American voters, who by virtue of their participation in elections reflect considerable optimism. This is true given that few African Americans are given real opportunities to wield power sufficient enough to determine who will be campaigning for major elected offices or even the vacant positions on school boards. Added to this fact is the reality that overall there is often little incentive for African Americans to vote for a slate that is generally selected by those with power and wealth who live outside of their communities. Also, numerous institutional constraints make it difficult for African American elected officials to eliminate institutional barriers that are responsible for the limited opportunities of most African American families and their members in the United States. Clearly, African American voters possess an enormous amount of hope, optimism, and patience as institutional racial discrimination continues to be a major factor in the social and economic and daily privileges simply in terms of civilities and civil rights that are the birthright of white families and their members.

The Al Gore–Joe Lieberman Democratic ticket versus the George W. Bush–Dick Cheney Republican candidates was predicted to be a rather close presidential race. However, as in the past since the Theodore Roosevelt administration, the Democratic Party felt confident that it had the support of African American voters. After all, Gore, who had been Bill Clinton's vice president, while not having the qualities that African Americans found some level of comfort with, did in fact represent the Democratic Party that many believed was more likely to stand for their interests than the George W. Bush–Dick Cheney Republican presidential ticket.

## THE CONTROVERSY—PRESIDENT ELECT OR PRESIDENT SELECT

The aftermath of the election, however, proved to be disastrous not only for Al Gore but also for African American voters, who were vehement about their voting rights being violated with numerous and diverse irregularities. What was even more disturbing to African American voters was that there were indications that a disproportionate number of these voting rights violations had occurred within the state of Florida, where Republican presidential candidate and Texas Governor George W. Bush's brother Jeb Bush served as governor. There was some amazement as it was that two brothers would ever be governors of major states, not to mention simultaneously. This fact alone suggested to many that there was a tremendous source of power and wealth possessed by the Bush family, specifically by former President George Bush, as well as a privileged inner circle to which the senior Bush had membership.

According to the election results Al Gore won the popular vote, while George W. Bush had a lead with the electoral votes, and the determining electoral votes from the state of Florida would decide which candidate would be the next president of the United States. Many television networks assessed exit poll surveys and announced that Al Gore would be the next president, despite the fact that he did not carry Arkansas, Bill Clinton's home state, or Tennessee, his own home state. However, it was later determined that this decision by the major networks was erroneous, as the day following the election George W. Bush was declared the winner of this presidential race. It was after this announcement that the Democratic Party and myriad African American voters, elderly voters, and Haitian-American voters made adamant complaints that the hole punch cards that were used for voting in Florida were confusing. Accordingly, many claimed that their intent was to vote for the Gore-Lieberman ticket but that they were not certain that the mechanism had correctly recorded their intentions. Other irregularities in the state of Florida included roadblocks by law enforcement officers, which many voters said dissuaded them from proceeding to the polls. Still others revealed that they had been denied the right to vote because they had been erroneously labeled as ex-felons, which denied them the right to vote in the state of Florida. Despite derailed efforts to manually recount votes that due to their construction may have been misread by the voting equipment, court challenges from the Democrats demanding that the manual hand count in specific Democratic areas be completed, and countercharges by Republicans that this method of vote recounting and relying on a consensus regarding whether a hole partially punched out was to be considered a vote for the Democratic candidate or the Republican candidate for president was unreliable, the matter was ultimately decided by the U.S. Supreme Court, which had in large measure been constituted by the Republican Reagan–Bush administrations. The Court rendered a decision that the vote recounting was not a reliable method of determining the voters' intentions and allowed the Florida state attorney general to accept the Florida Board of Elections' decision that George W. Bush had indeed won the state of Florida. Having done so, Bush had the necessary electoral votes to become the next president of the United States. In spite of the contentious nature of the election; the investigation by the U.S. Civil Rights Commission under the directorship of Mary Frances Berry, which confirmed irregularities in Florida and other states as well as charges by civil rights leaders; the belief of many voters and journalists that voting rights violations resulted in the disenfranchisement of thousands of African American votes because they were disqualified and not counted, George W. Bush became the 43rd president of the United States. Consequently, many within the African American community refused to acknowledge that George W. Bush was elected president through the established policies and procedures but rather was selected due to the intervention and decision of the U.S. Supreme Court. They labeled George W. Bush the president select and not elect. However, since Bush only received approximately 9 percent of the African American vote, there are those who believe that he was unaffected by these statements and the mass disaffection of African American voters with the process that left many believing that their voting in this election was an exercise in futility. Amid the dissatisfaction within the African American community with the outcome of this presidential election, many elected officials and organizations called for major election reform.

African American families were concerned over the election and the numerous irregularities at the polls, as they had not experienced significant advances during the 20-year period from 1980 to 2000. They were hopeful that Al Gore, if elected, would address some of the serious problems with which they were confronted. And Gore had included in his campaign agenda a pledge to end racial profiling, giving African American families even more reason to anticipate that he was willing to address this issue and other institutional policies and practices that were responsible for their lack of equal opportunity and inability to participate more fully in America.

## STATUS OF AFRICAN AMERICAN FAMILIES IN 2000

The structure of African American families underwent significant changes from 1980 to 2000. Noticeably, the number of African American two-parent families decreased from 55 percent in 1982 to 48 percent in 2000. Moreover, the increase in African American female-maintained families rose from 41 percent in 1982 to 44 percent in 2000. And the percent of African American male-headed families had doubled, rising from 4 percent in 1982 to 8 percent in 2000.[1]

Another startling occurrence was that the reasons for African American women maintaining their families had been attributed to families where the mother was divorced and those in which she had never married. The latter reason accounted primarily for the growth of female-maintained families, as 65 percent of African American females heading families were never married compared to 17 percent who were maintaining families as a result of divorce. Unquestionably, the challenges that African American females face when maintaining families are enormous considering the existence of salary structures based on race, sex, and class inequality. In addition, these same factors represent barriers in other institutions like the educational system, which frequently decreases the likelihood that African American female students will receive the skills necessary to compete for and secure employment opportunities that offer salaries that would enable them to provide for the economic needs of their families.

Considering education, in 2000, 79 percent of African Americans 25 years and older graduated from high school, compared to 83 percent of whites. Moreover, there was a slight increase in the number of African American females enrolled in college, as this percentage rose to 62 percent in 2000 compared to 60 percent in 1980, and a decline in the percentage of African American males enrolled in college, which decreased from 40 percent in 1980 to 38 percent in 2000. The percentage of African Americans graduating from college was 11.4 percent, compared to 18.6 percent for whites in 2000.

Regarding income, the African American female who maintains a family generated the lowest income compared to white males and females and African American males who headed families in 2000. Specifically, African American female-maintained families had a median income of $20,606 in 2000, compared to white females who maintained families, who had a median income of $30,417. In general, African American families' median income was $33,598, compared to $56,240, which was the median income for white families, and 59 percent of the income of white families. This represents a slight increase over the 20-year period when African American families earned 55 percent of the median income of white families. Examining other income data for African American families and their white counterparts reveals other significant differences, in that African American married couples earned a median income of $50,657 compared to white married couples, whose median income was $62,000, and African American males who maintained families and had a median income of $32,063, compared to white males who maintained families, whose median income was $41,352 in 2000.[2] In 2000 19.3 percent of African American families were in poverty compared to 5.4 percent of white families.

However, African American families maintained by females were also more likely to be in poverty than were other families. In fact, in 2000, 34.3 percent of African American females who maintained families were in poverty and 41 percent of these families with children under the age of 18 were in poverty in the same year. Comparatively, 17.8 percent of white females maintaining families were in poverty and 24.6 percent of these families with children under the age of 18 were poor.

Because of the increase in the number of African American female-maintained families, as well as those headed by African American males, the majority of African American children, 53 percent, live with one parent compared to 37 percent who live with two parents. Conversely, 21 percent of white children live with one parent and 75 percent live with two parents.

Labor-force participation rates continued to decline, and by 2000 African American males had a labor-force participation rate of 68.1 percent, compared to 74.3 percent for white males. On the other hand, African American women's labor-force participation rate was 63 percent, compared to 61 percent for white females.

There were some increases in the number of African Americans who held managerial and professional positions, as 21.7 percent of African American workers were in these positions in 2000, compared to 33.2 percent of white workers. Moreover, 21.7 percent of African American workers were in technical, sales, and administrative support positions compared to 30.3 percent of white workers. It was still the case that a large number, 22.6 percent, of African Americans were concentrated in service jobs, compared to 11.6 percent of whites. This represents a serious labor market problem, as the service occupations in which African American workers are generally hired are low-wage jobs with few benefits and increasingly are those abandoned by white workers who refuse to work in these positions. For example, many African American women work in food service as dietary aides and as nursing assistants, all jobs that generate low incomes, make it difficult to afford the basic necessities of life, and qualify some as the working poor.[3]

The unemployment rate for African Americans continued to be double that of whites despite the economic boom in the 1990s. In 2000, the unemployment rate for African Americans was 7.7 percent, compared to 3.4 percent for whites. However, this does not take into consideration the growing rate of joblessness for African Americans who have given up looking for employment and are permanently outside the labor market. African American teenagers continued to experience extremely high rates of unemployment, as 33 percent were unemployed in 2000, compared to 16 percent of white teenagers.

An African American male's life expectancy increased from 66 years in 1981 to 68 years in 2000. However, an African American female's life expectancy remained the same at 75 years.

The percentage of African Americans entrepreneurs increased over the 20-year period from 2.3 percent in 1977 to 4 percent in 2000. Further, 30 percent of the 50,420 loans that the Small Business Administration (SBA) made to small businesses went to businesses owned by people of color and women in 2000. In addition, of the $12.37 billion in loans that were made by the SBA to small businesses, $3.7 billion in loans went to businesses owned by people of color and women.[4]

Reports of declines in the numbers of African American and other families who were welfare recipients continued to be reported after the enactment of the 1996 Welfare Reform Act; however, stipulations that allow states exemptions and the newly established length of recipiency are affecting the extent to which real declines in participation and recipiency rates are likely to be permanent. Studies that examine the impact of these policy reforms after a ten-year period following the enactment of the 1996 Welfare Reform Act are expected to yield more reliable indicators of the impact of this policy. It should be noted that while welfare caseloads may be reduced, females entering the labor market are generally working in entry-level jobs with near-poverty incomes.

Clearly, the status of African American families who had not registered significant gains influenced African American families as they awaited the inception of a new presidential administration.

Once George W. Bush assumed the presidency, his administration began to propose policies that would have a significant economic impact on American citizens, particularly those who were wealthy. The Bush administration immediately proposed a tax cut, which was even criticized by some of its intended privileged beneficiaries as a tax cut in which only those in the top 5 percent of the country's population would receive 75 percent of the benefits. This tax bill was considered by many economists to be one that clearly favored and was extremely generous to the most wealthy families and individuals in America. Specifically, it was noted that the Bush administration's tax cut cut taxes for people in the lower 20 percent income group, with an average annual income of $8,600, by an average of $37, while simultaneously cutting taxes for individuals in the top 1 percent income group, with an average annual income of $915,000, by nearly $23,331 annually. The administration was successful in its efforts, when this tax bill became law as Congress provided legislative approval for Bush's tax cut for the wealthy and affluent by giving its support for his entire economic policy in March 2003.

The Bush administration also proposed a policy that was quick to draw considerable criticism, which was to allow workers to invest 2 percent of their wages in the stock market. This privatization plan was to be the focus of study for a panel that Bush constituted. The Bush administration justified this proposed policy stating that it would keep the Social Security trust fund solvent for many years, as the baby boomers retire.

It has been projected that the Social Security trust fund will remain solvent until 2038. Alternative policies that have been proposed in the past include tax increases and raising the retirement age, which is expected to reach 67 by 2037.

## FAITH-BASED INITIATIVES

Another policy that the Bush administration promoted but that received mixed support was the Faith-Based Initiative for churches in the United States. In February 2002, Bush invited approximately 200 religious leaders and clerics to a meeting to discuss his policy that would permit religious organizations the opportunity to compete for federal monies to accomplish their charitable goals. The monies, according to Bush's proposal, were existing federal monies, but restrictions would be raised that would permit government funds to be made available to faith-based organizations. Some religious groups had already been benefactors of such government dollars and welcomed the expansion of these federal funds to carry out their initiatives to support charitable causes. Some churches were skeptical, as they were unsure as to what federal guidelines would result that would allow them to provide charitable programs but prohibit their spiritual mission. Basically, they were informed that they could provide an array of social services, especially to economically disadvantaged families, such as food pantries, building housing for the poor and elderly, and after-school tutorial programs for children. However, they would not be permitted to distribute religious material nor could they require their clients to attend prayer meetings or to spread religious theology or doctrine. There have been many critics of Bush's Faith-Based Initiative who believe that it violates the principle, which many Americans value and upon which the government was established, of separation of church and state.

The Bush administration was still reveling in the success of its victory, announcing support for one other policy that was of critical importance to the African American community, namely racial profiling.

## RACIAL PROFILING/POLICE BRUTALITY REVISITED

In May 2001, Representative Eleanor Holmes Norton, Democrat, of Washington D.C., introduced a bill, the Racial Prohibition Act of 2001, cosponsored by Representative Carolyn Cheeks Kilpatrick of Detroit, Michigan, to withhold funding for road repairs from states that fail to record the race of drivers stopped by law enforcement officers. The significance of this policy rests in the fact that Congress was expected to allocate $250 billion to fund the repairing of bridges, roads, and freeways in 2002. This policy was an attempt similar to those previously made by Representative John Conyers, of Detroit, Michigan, who had proposed racial profiling legislation beginning in 1998.

The Bush administration, with Attorney General John Ashcroft, pledged their support to ending this practice of law enforcement officials targeting individuals on the basis of their race. Moreover, Bush instructed Ashcroft to collect data to study the problem. While Bush's response was favorable it did not acknowledge the plethora of data and studies that had been conducted and replicated and had already validated and substantiated the existence of this problem, which affects numerous African American families and their members throughout the country. Representative Norton's response to Bush's directive to Attorney General Ashcroft indicated that this measure had already been undertaken and that legislation and negative sanctions were now more appropriate.

It is undoubtedly a crucial issue that its recurrence is both frequent and serious and that this topic remains the focus of attention for many within the African American community, particularly African American families who are victimized and endangered by these systematic practices of racial profiling and police brutality. In effect they are often inextricably related, as detaining African Americans for unjustified reasons can and does lead to the act of police brutality. Therefore, it is imperative that racial profiling be eradicated as an ongoing practice by law enforcement officers.

An example of racial profiling that led to police brutality occurred on July 9, 2002, in Inglewood, California. This egregious case of police brutality was videotaped by an onlooker and demonstrates the severity of police brutality when directed toward African American males. In this situation, Donovan Jackson, a 16-year-old teenager, and his father stopped at a gas station. Donovan went into the gas station to pay for gas and purchased a bag of potato chips. Police officers who were driving in the area pulled into the gas station to inquire about Mr. Jackson's (the father) expired license plates. Donovan, unaware of what was occurring, left the gas station and approached his father's car. He was told by the officers talking to his father to drop the potato chips and to put his hands on the car, according to the *Los Angeles Times*.[5] It was at this point that Officer Jeremy Morse is shown on the videotape lifting a handcuffed Donovan Jackson, slamming his head onto the trunk of a car, and punching him in the face, according to the *Los Angeles Times*. The savage beating by Officer Morse, a three-year veteran, was so brutal and inexplicable that the Inglewood mayor called for the termination of the officer and insisted that he be charged with assault. Later, this incident continued to spark national attention as Mitchell Crooks, the 27-year-old white male who videotaped the beating of Donovan Jackson, was arrested on old charges of driving under the influence and petty theft. Upon his release, Crooks said that he feared for his life, as indicated in his screams when an undercover officer arrested him outside a television studio that had broadcast the videotape earlier. However, Crooks said he would not hesitate to videotape this situation if he had to do it over again. On July 29, 2003, a judge declared a mistrial in the police brutality case against Jeremy Morse because of a hung jury. A new trial date was scheduled because this jury, which included only one African American member, was deadlocked and failed to reach a verdict.

It should be noted that there were other incidents of African American males being brutally beaten by law enforcement officers within days of this occurrence, and like this case documented videotaped recordings substantiated police brutality that occurred when the victim was handcuffed and even on the ground.

Therefore, the serious nature of racial profiling and police brutality using African Americans as targets is a matter of such urgency that it should be resolved by the Justice Department and President George W. Bush, through policies that are supported by legislation and severe negative penalties for such blatant violations of African Americans civil rights and human rights. These policies should serve as deterrents for law enforcement officers who engage in this type of behavior and their coworkers who tacitly approve by ignoring it, covering it up, or conforming to what is reported to be a code of silence that unifies law enforcement officers and establishes an "us versus them" mindset, thereby guaranteeing protection for illegal behavior on the part of fellow law enforcement officers. These negative sanctions must extend to others who are employed in law enforcement offices, those who are responsible for ensuring that complainants are given an opportunity to file complaints and receive a fair and impartial investigation. Currently, the structure of law enforcement agencies, the conditioned camaraderie, and the informal practice of law enforcement officers providing unconditional support even when the rights of citizens are violated make it necessary for an executive order from the president of the United States to be forthcoming or for the executive branch to use its political power to facilitate the passage of legislation that will contribute to ending these policies and practices. Regarding racial profiling, it is simply not adequate to allow states to voluntarily implement policies to record the race and ethnicity of drivers who are detained. A federal policy that makes this compulsory is now the only mechanism that can safeguard the rights of African American families and their members who are the daily victims of this unbridled aggression.

## A MORATORIUM ON CAPITAL SENTENCES

Stating that serious flaws exist in capital sentencing and the entire legal and judicial system that result in capital punishment, Illinois Governor George Ryan placed a moratorium on capital punishment in 2000 after 13 inmates on death row were exonerated. Later, in 2003, Governor Ryan pardoned 3 other inmates who had received capital sentences and then commuted death sentences of 167 inmates to life without parole. These decisions received support as well as criticism. However, they were believed to be necessary, as Governor Ryan believed his actions were justified because of gross inadequacies and inequities in the death penalty system, which he characterized as arbitrary, capricious, and immoral.[6]

## BUSH'S EDUCATION POLICY

During the first 100 days of the Bush administration, President George W. Bush introduced his education policy proposal, No Child Left Behind.

It is an understatement to say that there was considerable interest in the nation's schools, namely urban public schools, which have long been under scrutiny and attack for numerous deficiencies that have basically left primarily African American children without adequate skills to be competitive and marketable given the demands and needs of the labor market in the twenty-first century. Accordingly, Bush attempted to formulate a policy that would address the deficiencies inherent in public education, primarily in urban schools, that would move the country in the direction of being on par with other school systems in similarly developed countries throughout the world. The Bush administration's plan has three components: to increase funding, accountability, and flexibility of the schools throughout the nation. Specifically, his educational policy makes funds available to states to address the problem of reading. This deficiency is evident in that 70 percent of students in urban communities, attending schools in high poverty areas, cannot read at their grade level. As such, states are to receive additional funding to design reading programs that improve reading proficiency among students in early elementary grades and for low-income preschool children. His proposal also increases funding to schools to improve math, science, and educational technology instruction for kindergarten through twelfth grade.

The Bush educational policy not only increases funds to schools throughout the country but also allows schools considerable freedom to design and implement methods and programs that are expected to improve reading and math. In addition, this policy requires accountability from schools, as they are given a high degree of latitude to use federal funds to ameliorate these programs and instruction. Accordingly, schools' success in improving reading and math performance would be assessed annually using tests to measure states' proficiency in these areas. In addition, the Bush administration's educational policy increases states' access to funding for the purpose of recruiting and hiring teachers who have the capability to effectively teach students.

One controversial component of the Bush educational policy is the voucher system, which has generally received support along partisan lines, with Republicans favoring this system while Democrats express opposition. Bush's educational policy allows parents and students the option of permitting students who are consistently receiving failing grades a choice of attending public or private schools, and providing federal dollars to fund these students' education at private schools. The reason this condition of the educational policy is contentious is because there are many who believe that tax dollars should be used to improve public education and not to pay for alternatives to public education. Further, many critics cite that when the parents' school preference is a parochial school there is no separation of church and state, as required by the Constitution. These taxpayers find it objectionable that their tax dollars are being used to fund Christian schools. Nevertheless, the Bush educational policy prevailed, including the voucher system, which received support in a U.S. Supreme Court decision affirming the constitutionality of the voucher system in 2002.

## A NATIONAL DISASTER

On September 11, 2001, the United States and its citizens experienced a horrific disaster of terrorism as four commercial passenger airliners were used to destroy America's symbols of wealth and power. Two of the airplanes carrying passengers were flown into the twin towers of the World Trade Center in New York City by those who commandeered them, using the planes as weapons to destroy two structures that were equated with America's tremendous wealth located in Manhattan, the financial capital of the United States. Not only were the passengers aboard these airliners killed, many working in the twin towers lost their lives as each of these buildings collapsed. A third commercial jet was flown into the Pentagon, and like the others led to the death of all its passengers and destruction of great magnitude to the Pentagon. The fourth plane crashed in a field in Shanksville, Pennsylvania, after what many believed was a struggle between several passengers and those who took control of the jet. In the end, nearly 3,000 people were killed in what has been called planned acts of terrorism. Those killed were of diverse cultures and included African American men, women, and children. As such many African American families, like other families in the United States and in various other parts of the world, were devastated by this occurrence.

The Bush administration responded by naming those responsible for these acts as members of al Qaeda cells, which were reported to exist in many countries, including America. The Bush administration identified Osama bin Laden, a Saudi Arabian in Afghanistan, as the leader of the Al Qaeda cells and declared a War on Terrorism, which included the bombing of Afghanistan.

Later Bush ordered the bombing of Iraq to end the government of Saddam Hussein, whom Bush accused of harboring weapons of mass destruction and being involved in terrorism associated with al Qaeda, which he charged was responsible for the attack on the United States on September 11, 2001. These military efforts were undertaken, according to Bush, to ensure the safety of Americans. This brought mixed support from many African American families, who hoped that future acts of terrorism would not occur but who were concerned that a disproportionate number of war casualties would be African Americans, as has been the case in previous wars. There were other African American families who also believed that domestic issues warranted new social policies to ensure the physical well-being of African American families experiencing numerous challenges in the United States. Thus, many African American families weight the importance of survival as well as safety. Clearly, these concerns mirror those described by Maslow in his hierarchy of human needs, where the greatest motivation or drive is toward satisfying physiological needs or survival and then safety needs.

These two military offensives have resulted in the expenditure of billions of dollars that some believe could have been channeled to domestic programs and services and to improve the overall economy, thereby providing direct benefits to African American families and others who are economically disadvantaged and struggling daily to survive.

The actions defined as terrorism were attributed in large measure to Arabs and those within the Muslim religion. Therefore, many citizens became suspicious of Arabs, Arab Americans, and Muslims, anticipating that they represented a future threat to America and its citizenry.

The Bush administration established the Office of Homeland Security, headed by former Pennsylvania governor Tom Ridge. The office's purpose is to prevent future acts of terrorism in America. New policies that were instituted by Homeland Security and other federal agencies included close security screenings of individuals entering government buildings, airports, bus stations, Amtrak stations, and so forth. Shortly after these new security measures were implemented, racial profiling was expanded to include not just African Americans but also Arab Americans and those who appeared by their dress to be of the Muslim religion. Despite objections and litigation, these civil rights violations have continued. However, the racial profiling of these new groups, although the result of a disaster of monumental proportion, finally gave credence to and provided corroboration for racial profiling, a practice that some journalists had called a myth and that had historically targeted African Americans.[7]

## THE USA PATRIOT ACT

The Bush administration then established far-sweeping measures to fight terrorism, which were implemented by the passage of the USA PATRIOT Act, also known as Providing Appropriate Tools Required to Intercept and Obstruct Terrorism.

Many of the provisions of this act gave the government expanded rights to conduct surveillance. The INS has broader authority to detain and interrogate immigrants suspected of terrorism. The act permits the collection of intelligence data through various means and provides for more methods to be made available for prosecution of those alleged to be involved in or planning acts of terrorism. Many civil libertarians viewed these provisions as a signal of the first step toward eroding or abrogating the civil rights of American citizens. Moreover, civil libertarians have warned that after the War on Terrorism is over that they fear that African Americans will be the most probable population targeted for civil rights violations, which would be justified by this law.

## OPERATION TIPS

The next policy that the Bush administration advanced, which was not approved, in an effort to prevent future terrorism was known as Operation TIPS, or Terrorism Information and Prevention System. This program, introduced in January 2002, was a reporting system created by the Department of Justice and various other federal agencies. Operation TIPS was to have provided various industry groups with a telephone hotline to report activities occurring in public areas that they believe to be terrorist related or have the potential to be terrorist in nature.

## THE WELFARE REFORM ACT

Another policy that the Bush administration proposed and that was later implemented was not new but instead represented an effort to provide additional welfare reforms to the Clinton administration's 1996 Welfare Reform Act, which required an extension as it was to expire on September 30, 2002.

The Bush administration's welfare policy entailed expanding the 30 hour work week to 40 hours for welfare recipients, 24 hours to be spent in actual employment while 16 hours could be devoted to job training, education, and family activities.

Moreover, the Bush administration wanted to address the importance of marriage, as had been the case in the existing 1996 Welfare Reform Act. In addition, the Bush administration proposed spending $300 million dollars to assist couples in resolving their problems prior to and during marriage. The rationale for continuing to promote marriage was based on the belief that strong marriages and stable families were in the best interests of children.

However, the Bush administration offered no real meaningful policies to address the systematic institutional racially discriminatory practices that affect the stability of African American families and their members. Therefore, it is necessary for African American families and other institutions within the African American community to develop strategies, methods, and time-specific goals that will at best minimize the institutional and individual assaults that its members encounter on a daily basis.

## THE FOSTER CARE SYSTEM

The 1996 Welfare Reform Act, in conjunction with policies that are inherent in institutionalized racism, has created an increased number of working poor families. The low-wage jobs in which the working poor are employed and the loss of benefits such as child care, health care, housing subsidies, and so forth have contributed to the disruption of these families by the child welfare system, an institution whose original mission was to facilitate the maintenance of intact families, and to an inability to provide for the basic needs of their children. In fact, the 1980 Child Welfare Act was designed to keep families together by reducing the duration of a child's stay in foster care and promoting the return of children to their homes. Plans were also expected to be made to explore all measures to keep children in their homes by providing services to children and families.[8]

In 2000, African American children comprised 42 percent of all children in foster care, yet they make up only 17 percent of children in the country. It is also the case that African American children are twice as likely to be separated from their parents and to remain in the custody of the state than their white counterparts.[9] The reason that such an inordinate number of African American children are in foster care, under the supervision of the state, is primarily because a disproportionate number of African American families are poor. And because being impoverished generally results in parents' inability to provide their children with the necessities of life, African American parents are more likely to be charged with child neglect. Furthermore, it is child neglect, not child abuse, that is the most common form of child maltreatment that results in children being separated from their parents and placed in the foster care system, sometimes lingering there indefinitely. Another reason for the substantially large number of African American children being removed from their homes is that the social-science literature is replete with studies and theoretical formulations that define African American parents and the socialization of their children as inappropriate, inadequate, and pathological.[10] These conclusions are based on differences in parenting and disciplinary styles of African American parents compared to white middle-class parents, who are believed to represent the ideal model for parenting children in America.[11] These racial stereotypes of African American families along with their impoverished status clearly affect the decisions of child welfare systems to remove African American children in such disproportionate numbers and place them in the foster care system. Dorothy Roberts provides a convincing argument that poverty, rather than children's parents, creates the situations that caseworkers associate with child neglect, such as serious health problems; poor nutrition; inadequate heating, electrical, and other services; and hazardous housing. She adds that it is the latter condition, poor housing, that is usually the primary factor that influences caseworkers to remove children from their families and to place them in foster care.[12] Given the fact that statistical data indicate that more families are being forced from the welfare rolls by the 1996 Welfare Reform Act, and thus join the ranks of the working poor, this increases the probability that more families will be disrupted by the child welfare system and their children removed and placed in foster care.

That there are numerous problems with the country's child welfare system is common knowledge. This system, receiving approximately $10 billion annually, has been found to allow children to remain in limbo without reuniting them with their families, not utilizing kinship networks sufficiently in the placement of children, prematurely terminating parental rights instead of seeking sufficient means of preserving parental rights, and maintaining high caseloads that are poorly managed, therefore precluding caseworkers from adequately meeting the needs of children placed in foster care.

A stark example of such an occurrence attracted national attention in April 2002, in Florida, when it was discovered that Rilya Wilson, a five-year-old African American girl, had been missing for over one year, while her caseworker reported her to be doing well in her foster care placement, based on her records of monthly visits that had not occurred. This case led to the identification of other service deficits, including other missing children and youth whom child welfare agencies hastily sought to locate. The case of the missing five-year-old, however, resulted in the juvenile justice system and Florida Governor Jeb Bush insisting on an assessment of the administration and policies of the child welfare system in that state. This case is yet another indication of how social systems establish and maintain policies that are contributing to the destabilization of African American families, even those families struggling and striving to meet the basic social and economic needs of their members. A society that is family oriented and child centered should formulate policies that would reduce the number of parents whose incomes and resources prevent them from meeting the needs of their families, including their youthful members. To do so would mean eliminating ineffective educational and training programs, providing living wages, increasing the availability of housing, other services such as government-sponsored child care, and a universal health-care plan that would significantly minimize the effects of poverty that result in families being charged with child neglect as well as reduce the parental role strain often associated with child abuse. Equally important is to provide in-service training to social workers and administrators in the child welfare system regarding African American family values, norms, and belief systems to ensure that their decision making is not influenced by racially biased information and inaccurate cultural images perpetuated by macrocultural institutions, including those purveyed by the mainstream media.

African American families were confronted with an unexpected event—the resurfacing of the question of the legitimacy of affirmative action for recruiting students in institutions of higher education became a national issue.

Clearly, this was not a new issue; as previously stated, anti–affirmative action legislation and policies had already been enacted in various states, such as California, Texas, and Florida, throughout the country. However, in 2003 the U.S. Supreme Court agreed to reconsider its earlier 1978 *Bakke* decision, in which they had ruled that race could be a factor in admissions decisions in institutions of higher education.

The newest anti–affirmative action lawsuit was filed by the Center for Individual Rights, on behalf of two white females, against the University of Michigan and the University of Michigan's law school. The plaintiffs claim that they were denied admission because of their race and that the University of Michigan's decision not to admit them constitutes reverse discrimination and therefore is a violation of their constitutional rights. Consequently, they believe that race should not be a factor in admission decisions in colleges and universities.[13]

Regrettably, this lawsuit fails to acknowledge that there are a multiplicity of nonacademic factors other than race—such as legacy (being related to an alumnus/alumna), athletic ability, state residency, being economically disadvantaged, and so forth—that the University of Michigan and other institutions of higher education consider in making admission decisions.

In fact, in the case of the University of Michigan there is a 150 point system, of which 110 points are for academic performance (i.e., G.P.A., S.A.T. scores, etc.), leaving only 40 points for nonacademic factors. The fact that race instead of any of these other factors is a point of contention is reflective of the extent to which race continues to be used and perceived as an acceptable basis, and effective means, for excluding African Americans from participating in significant mainstream institutions in America.

The Bush administration rallied to the support of this anti–affirmative action litigation when Bush filed a friend of the court brief in support of the plaintiffs, arguing that race should not be a factor in admission decisions made by institutions of higher education. In so doing, Bush took a definitive position that conflicts with interests of African American families and their members. The fact that affirmative action offers a miniscule remedy to the significant problem of persistent and substantial racial discrimination suggests that the Bush administration is not willing to concede that African Americans should have even a minute advantage that would grant them an opportunity for inclusion in colleges and universities throughout the United States. The fact that there remain relatively small percentages of African American students attending institutions of higher education requires more effective policies and not the elimination of minimal measures that increase the participation of limited numbers of African Americans. This action taken by Bush reflects the rigidity and entrenched resistance by those who are privileged, and their resolve to keep social structures firmly in place that will perpetuate the existing social order that keeps African American families and their members from acquiring the necessary resources, including skills and credentials, that will enable them to become viable competitors for culturally prescribed goals. Accordingly, they are maintained in a position of subordination and dependency that ensures that the American Dream continues to remain elusive to African American families.

In July 2003, the United States Supreme Court upheld the right of the University of Michigan Law School to use race as a factor in admissions—thereby recognizing the importance of providing and maintaining diversity in institutions of higher education—while the point system used by the University of Michigan's undergraduate school was ruled to be unconstitutional, as it was perceived as a quota system. However, the Court's decision concerning the University of Michigan Law School provides corroboration and legitimacy for the necessity of affirmative action and the benefits it provides to individuals, families, and institutions.[14]

## NOTES

1. U.S. Bureau of the Census, *Family and Nonfamily Household Type by Race and Hispanic Origin of Householder*, March 2000.

2. U.S. Bureau of the Census, *Type of Family, Black Families by Median and Mean Income: 1967 to 2001*, March 2001; and *White Non-Hispanic Families Median and Mean Income: 1987 to 2001*, March 2001.

3. U.S. Bureau of the Census, *Major Occupation Group of the Employed Civilian Population 16 Years and Over by Sex and Race and Hispanic Origin*, March 2000.

4. *Small Business Financing Hits Record High, Point of Beginning, 2000*, U.S. Small Business Administration, 2000.

5. "Officer Is Indicted in Beating That a Bystander Videotaped," *New York Times*, 18 July 2002, p. 18.

6. Dirk Johnson, "A Leap of Fate," *Newsweek*, 20 January 2003, p. 34.

7. George Will, "Will Wrongly Sees Need to Link Crime, Ethnicity," *Columbus Dispatch*, 19 April 2001, p. 12A.

8. *Who Will Care When Parents Can't?: A Study of Black Children in Foster Care*, (Washington, D.C.: National Black Child Development Institute, 1989), p. i; and Andrew Billingsley and Jeanne M. Giovannoni, *Children of the Storm: Black Children and American Child Welfare* (New York: Harcourt Brace Jovanovich, 1972), p. 97.

9. Dorothy Roberts, *Shattered Bonds: The Color of Child Welfare* (New York: Basic Books, 2002), p. viii.

10. Anderson J. Franklin, Nancy Boyd-Franklin, and Charlene V. Draper, "A Psychological and Educational Perspective on Black Parenting," in *Black Children: Social, Educational, and Parental Environments*, 2nd ed., ed. Harriette Pipes McAdoo (Thousand Oaks, Calif.: Sage Publications, 2002), p. 134; Daniel P. Moynihan, *The Negro Family: The Case for National Action* (Washington, D.C.: U.S. Government Printing Office, 1965); and Marie Ferguson Peters, "Historical Note: Parenting of

Young Children," in *Black Families*, 3rd ed., ed. Harriette Pipes McAdoo (Thousand Oaks, Calif.: Sage Publications, 1997), pp. 167–171.

11. Peters, "Historical Note," p. 173; Joan Aldous, "Wives' Employment Status and Lower-Class Men as Husbands-Fathers: Support for the Moynihan Thesis," *Journal of Marriage and the Family* 31, no. 3 (1969): 469–476; and Na'im Akbar, "Our Destiny: Authors of a Scientific Revolution," in *Black Children: Social, Educational and Parental Environments*, ed. Harriette McAdoo and John McAdoo (Beverly Hills, Calif.: Sage Publications, 1985), pp. 17–20.

12. Roberts, *Shattered Bonds*, p. 34.

13. Barbara Kantrowitz and Pat Wingert, "What's at Stake," *Newsweek*, 27 January 2003, pp. 31–37.

14. Evan Thomas and Stuart Taylor Jr., "Center Court," *Newsweek*, 7 July 2003, pp. 46–47.

# CHAPTER 11

# The Future of Social Policy and the African American Family

## LEARNING FROM SOCIAL-POLICY FAILURES

The formulation of liberal social policy, which led to the development of social and economic programs, is strongly related to the decline of African American two-parent families and extended familial structures. Nevertheless, some African American families, particularly those among the working and middle classes, were prosperous during the era of liberal social policy. In addition, some African American underclass families experienced upward mobility. For the most part, African American families already enjoying middle-class status before the 1960s continued to make gains in education and occupational areas. As a consequence, their socioeconomic status became more firmly entrenched and less susceptible to adverse changes in the economy. However, African American underclass families felt the brunt of industrial displacement, a downward economic spiral, and ineffective social and economic programs. Although modest gains were made, African American families across all social and economic levels have been adversely affected by liberal social policies and the overall impenetrability of societal institutions. What liberal social policy did was raise the hopes and aspirations of African American families to a level consistent with that of white middle-class families. What it did not do was improve social and economic conditions throughout society or among African American families so that the goals and objectives African American families shared with their white counterparts could be realized. In considering the positive and negative effects of liberal social policy, analysts ask the inevitable question (which has been systematically used as a rhetorical pawn by the major political parties), To what extent did social and economic programs sponsored and funded by the federal government lead to widespread economic dependency?

The most direct response for which empirical verification exists is that government dependency was created by the social and economic programs and legislation of the 1960s and 1970s. The paradox is that the very efforts designed to promote economic independence for African American families were, in many ways, responsible for government dependency for an inordinate number of African American families.

Typically, when one speaks of government dependency as a function of social and economic programs in the 1960s and 1970s, poor families that were recipients of various forms of public assistance come to mind. But government dependency occurred for other African American families, transcending socioeconomic levels. However, this is in no way intended to suggest that liberal social policy was totally ineffective, nor does it imply that all social and economic programs had negative outcomes. Even more important is the realization that the federal government does have and should continue to play a strategic role in developing, mediating, and enforcing social and economic programs.

Although some social and economic programs were detrimental to African American families, others could be deemed successful. It is difficult to evaluate the relative effectiveness of various social and economic programs developed and expanded during the 1960s and 1970s without examining other factors that affected their impact on African American families. If we remember that the civil rights movement was responsible for spurring the resurgence of the feminist movement and social activism by other members of society who, like African Americans, urged the redistribution of wealth and power, we can understand how social and economic programs initially designed to elevate the status of African American families became somewhat diluted. Though other groups, equally disenfranchised, were certainly warranted in seeking redress for past inequities, the concessions made through liberal social-policy initiatives did little more than amass a modicum of resources that were then divided among these contenders. The result was divisiveness, rather than unity, as African Americans, Hispanics, women, and others were made to compete for limited "set-aside" resources.

The way that contenders for economic and political power were forced to become social competitors is evident in the history of one significant piece of legislation enacted during the 1960s. Affirmative action, which received plaudits from supporters of liberal social policy, only superficially created benefits for African American families, while generating relatively more opportunities for whites in America.

Employment segmentation, the guise by which institutions responded to affirmative action by making job opportunities available to African

American men and women, yet positioning them in organizational sectors offering limited opportunities for advancement, has already been examined. In addition, the federal government assumed a significant role in hiring large numbers of African Americans, thereby serving as a role model to be emulated by others, especially those within the private domain. Another misconception regarding affirmative action is that it has been construed as having created substantial employment opportunities for African Americans within the private sector. As previously cited, Robert Hill's findings refute this contention.[1] Despite the financial incentives offered to employers in the private sector, the government has not been able to effectively persuade private industry to hire more African Americans. For example, a study conducted by the National Urban League revealed that "a majority of employers refused to hire African American youth even if their wages were subsidized."[2] Given the small percentage of African Americans working in private enterprise, particularly during the 1960s and 1970s when the government made such ventures financially attractive through tax credits and the like, there is little doubt that barriers still prevented economic independence for African American families. Government dependence caused by limited access to employment in private enterprise is not restricted to African Americans whose educational attainment is at the high-school level or below. African Americans with college degrees have also derived relatively few employment benefits from affirmative action programs. They too have had to rely quite heavily on the public sector for job opportunities. Martin Canory noted in 1970 that a majority of African American college graduates were employed in the public sector. And according to Andrew Hacker, public-sector jobs are still the primary source of employment for African American college graduates.[3]

It is also the case that jobs in the private sector generally offer more competitive salaries than do governmental positions; yet, it is difficult for African Americans to obtain private-sector positions as these employers frequently fill vacant positions through word-of-mouth in social networks. This informal method of recruitment reduces the effectiveness of affirmative action, as these networks that are used by private-sector employers, especially those for whom institutional racial discrimination is the norm, are not open to African Americans.[4]

Other social and economic programs, intended to enhance the status of African American families, also proved to be to their detriment. In terms of family structure, African American two-parent and extended families were seriously weakened during this period. Social welfare programs, such as AFDC, resulted in welfare benefits that were higher than earned income at the minimum wage and other essential in-kind social welfare services like health insurance, subsidized housing, food stamps and child care, thereby making near-poverty-level earned incomes disadvantageous.

Moreover, gearing programs toward mothers, who typically represent the primary recipient, does little more than create divisiveness between mothers and fathers in families receiving aid. Social welfare programs ignored adult males in the family by developing job training and other benefits primarily for women and their charges; by failing to consider the occupational needs of adult male family members, the programs were destined to fail and to injure the family in the process. Such programs are antithetical to maintaining two-parent families because they conflict with societal values, which require males to be the primary providers for their families. The failure of social and economic programs to include males was particularly detrimental to African American families because African American males already experienced high unemployment, caused by the decline of factory jobs when industries were permanently closed. Though some argue that a disproportionate percentage of African American families receiving welfare benefits are already maritally disrupted, they overlook the fact that a disproportionate percentage of lower-income African American women heading families are separated rather than divorced. When marriages have not been legally dissolved, appropriate measures conceivably may reunite the family. This is particularly likely when social welfare programs are purposely designed to enable families to attain this objective. Because a large number of lower-income African American families choose separation as the preferred means of marital dissolution, the importance of social programs that are capable of strengthening the family unit cannot be overemphasized. It was not until the enactment of the 1996 Welfare Reform Act that social services were incorporated into the social welfare system to strengthen marriages. This specific service became the focus of the George W. Bush administration's welfare reform initiatives. The Bush administration added this policy, which included increased funding to strengthen marriages, along with his other social-policy initiatives, which he stated would strengthen families and therefore be beneficial to children. In order for these families to reach a level of economic self-sufficiency, husbands and wives must acquire and enhance marketable job skills, after which employment opportunities must not be disproportionately located within the public sector. Anything short of a wide range of jobs available in both the public and private sectors only leads to the perpetuity of government dependency for African American families.

Still other programmatic, administrative, and social-psychological factors were associated with the negative impact of social welfare programs on African American two-parent families. Despite attempts to project positive images that social welfare services were acceptable and that African American families who were recipients of such services had an inalienable right to these entitlements, to make up for past social injustices, these programs continued to be cast in a negative light. While some of the stigma may have been assuaged due to the liberal nature of the era, social welfare services such as food stamps, AFDC, and other programs not provided to members of society at large were never free of public contempt. Perhaps this is one reason the receipt of social welfare services continues to be perceived as a temporary emergency measure. It is in this light that, in the past, welfare was more commonly referred to as "relief." Temporary Assistance for Needy Families (TANF) has only increased the stigma of receiving welfare by imposing work requirements and placing time limits on recipiency.

The dismantling of African American extended families has had both a philosophical and a social basis. In the latter case, housing subsidies, Social Security, pension benefits, and, equally important, an emphasis on independent living in our society have all contributed to the decline of African American extended families over the last 25 years. This decrease is significant when one considers the importance of families consolidating limited assets, whether in the form of financial, social, or psychological resources. In many cases it was found that many African American grandparents have adopted the mainstream value orientation of independence. And while they value their role as grandparents many prefer maintaining independent living arrangements, as opposed to living with their children and grandchildren in multifamily homes. However, it is also the case that 33 percent of the African American elderly population live in poverty, which suggests that there may be important benefits in terms of the consolidation of resources and providing elder care to relatives, particularly parents and grandparents as they age. One of the reasons for the reluctance to live in multigenerational families is that the larger society defines this type of family as an aberration or anomaly. However, because of the increasing number of African American female single parents, there is evidence that the resources of the grandmother are being depleted. This is especially true when the female single parent is an adolescent. In such cases the grandmother becomes the surrogate parent, assuming responsibility for socializing her grandchildren.[5] However, being defined as a member of the underclass or poor, according to Herbert Gans, is language that purposely labels individuals to devalue and stigmatize them and to define them as the undeserving poor. A dilemma is created in American society for those who are poor and who live in multigenerational family structures. Therefore, it may mean that some elderly grandparents may choose independent living arrangements, even when they are financially unable to afford the necessities of life, to avoid the dual stigmas of being labeled dependent and poor. In too many cases in which grandparents could derive a more comfortable standard of living and receive assistance, they strive to conform to the value of independence, causing some to forego meals and to reduce prescribed dosages of vital medications for serious and even life-threatening diseases in order to have some of the necessities of life. These are choices that are societally imposed based on a mainstream value orientation of middle-class white families, whose elderly parents and grandparents were paid higher wages and inherited resources or assets allowing them to derive benefits sufficient to sustain themselves in independent living arrangements. And when they cannot, there is no negative stigma related to being placed in a nursing home. Conversely, nursing home placement for African American elderly parents and relatives is highly devalued and viewed as unacceptable.

This concern regarding multigenerational families is one that does not affect many immigrants new to this country, as they have not been subjected to the same level of criticism, devaluation, and negative labeling as have African American families who do not conform to the family structure of the white middle class. Therefore, other ethnic groups entering the United States commonly pool their meager resources, establish multigenerational families, and engage in other forms of cooperative behavior until they have established a pattern of intergenerational affluence. Moreover, they do so without engendering the negative labels, stereotypes, and stigmas assigned to similarly situated African Americans.

Later, these same groups alter their family structure to form more independent family units, while maintaining strong kinship networks, whereas others prefer to continue residing in multifamily structures, especially when it is beneficial for elderly family members.

However, social and economic factors in the 1960s and 1970s resulted in the premature disruption of African American extended families. The support offered by extended families cannot be underestimated, particularly when such families contain an older adult relative. Given that in the majority of African American two-parent families both the husband and wife are employed outside the home, the extended family has offered relief in the form of child care, cooking and other domestic tasks, and emotional nurturance. The absence of this support frequently results in role strain and later in marital conflict. Although the African American extended family, an example of the most rudimentary form of strong kinship bonds, was altered, the viability of other kinds of kinship and informal support systems, which have also been the foundation for progress among African American families, were also challenged. Both extended families and kinship networks have been viewed by the larger society as impediments to upward mobility for African American families. However, as McAdoo states, these support systems are important to African American families.[6] Furthermore, she asserts that for African American families to experience intergenerational progress, they must continue to support others within their families. Extended family structures and other African American kinship support systems enable this type of intrafamilial sharing and mutual cooperation. Further, the absence of communal responsibility is likely to result in each new generation of African Americans starting anew, without the benefit of resources that tend to guarantee social advancement. Thus, liberal social policy contributed significantly to the alteration of a process that has contributed favorably to the success of other racial and ethnic minorities.

Conservative social policy, which has been largely responsible for the gradual resurfacing of extended families and other forms of kinship and mutual-aid networks, should not be viewed any more favorably than liberal social policy, which led to their decline. While the reemergence of these structures is fundamental to the progress of African American families, the dire economic conditions that engender the proliferation of these family arrangements militate against their effectiveness.[7] Social forces still make their functioning less than optimal. Inexorable problems confront African American families. As in the past, African American kinship networks, including extended families, must provide basic goods and services while meeting the growing needs of members. Since these structures have become inextricably infused into the broader society, African American families and self-help groups are now confronted with adapting to cultural values—which stress autonomy, competitiveness, individualism, and social isolation—once found primarily in the larger society and now a part of the African American cultural ethos. This has placed added strain on the African American extended family, kinship, and mutual-aid networks. By the 1980s, how well or poorly extant African American extended families and informal social-support systems would function was dependent upon their ability to reestablish and strengthen relations with more economically advantaged African American families, other racial and ethnic groups, and white families who were willing to provide opportunities that would lead to increased participation in the private sector. During the 1980s it was also important for helping networks in the African American community to look to the federal government for support to resolve social and economic crises facing African American families.

During the 1990s under the Clinton administration, especially the latter part of the decade, an economic boom occurred that had little impact on African American families.[8] It was also during this period that self-help from African American kinship networks, the Black Church, and other African American institutions was even more valuable as liberal social policies that had provided some benefits to African American families became further rescinded through a reprioritization of the Clinton administration's domestic agenda. For example, college financial aid—which before the 1980s had allowed more African Americans to attend institutions of higher education, thereby allowing them to experience upward mobility—was not restored in the 1990s, nor has it been increased in the twenty-first century. This continued reduction has decreased the number of students attending two-year and four-year colleges. In fact, the graduation rates from the two-year colleges have declined more greatly than the rates of graduation from four-year colleges and universities. This has presented a major problem for African American students, as two-year colleges once represented one of the most reliable avenues out of poverty for African American students and other students from economically disadvantaged families. However, major funding cuts in financial aid that occurred during the 1980s and were not increased over the next two decades have eliminated another legitimate avenue out of poverty for many students living in impoverished families.

Another social problem that continues to plague the country and African American families is the shortage of affordable housing. This condition has led to an increase in a new form of homelessness. For the first time, homelessness is not limited primarily to males but now includes an inordinate number of families headed by divorced and separated mothers and their children. Thus, single mothers and their families have helped to swell the numbers of individuals who must depend on homeless shelters, conferring upon them a stigma even greater than that which is associated with residing in low-income public housing projects. Certainly, this stigma does little to contribute to the development of self-esteem in children and to aid in their social and psychological development.

The overall effect of liberal social policy was to undermine African American two-parent and extended family structures as well as to foster a plethora of other problems. However, not all aspects of liberal social policy were destructive. To the contrary; several programs helped African American families. Had this not been the case, African American families and their members would not have achieved the social and economic gains presented earlier. The progress made by African American families is evidence that there are salvageable components of liberal social and economic programs, which, if adapted, can be utilized today to enable African American families to secure economic independence. The success of social and economic initiatives in the 1960s and 1970s tended to be limited to younger members of African American families. The initial advances made by African American families between 1960 and 1980 were in the areas of education (i.e., increase in high school graduation rates), infant and maternal mortality, life expectancy, and nutrition. The latter two are related to improved medical and health care, which suggests that Medicaid and Medicare have also had positive implications for the survival of African American families and their members. However, between 1990 and 2000 progress continued to be made by African American families in many areas except education. Other programs that played a critical role in African American family progress were Head Start, educational grants and loans, nutrition programs such as WIC, and the Job Corps. This is not to say that other programs and legislation have not resulted in success for some African American families in America.

Much of the progress that African American families made during the era of liberal social policy was conditional and nongeneric, and it was not sustained in the 1980s, 1990s, and early twenty-first century. Numerous reasons have been offered to explain the shortcomings of liberal social policy. Many believe that social and economic programs were too narrow in focus. Others maintain that they ended too soon. Still others attribute their lack of effectiveness to the small percentage of money allocated, relative to the total federal budget. Larger federal budgetary allocations were made to other departments and programs. Such social programs as Social Security, Medicare, unemployment compensation, and so forth have historically been deemed beneficial, as they are geared to nonwelfare, middle-income populations. Furthermore, critics of the social welfare system often contend that the Defense Department receives a substantially higher percentage of the federal budget, creating what Eisenhower called a military-industrial complex.

Still others place the blame for the inability of liberal social policy to eradicate or significantly reduce persistent poverty, which destabilizes a disproportionate number of African American families, on inefficient and insensitive state and local government administrations. While the list of problems that contributed to the failure of liberal social policy is long, there is growing consensus in many circles, and not simply among political conservatives, that many social policies implemented during the 1960s and 1970s did not produce the intended results of significantly attenuating persistent poverty, especially among African American families. And the extent to which some of these social-policy initiatives continue today has still not produced the desired outcomes.

Accordingly, Randall Robinson offers an assessment about one such policy, affirmative action, which while needed offers more opportunities to African American families and their members who are more economically advantaged than to those who have experienced persistent poverty and its horrific concomitants. He states, "It is again, not that affirmative action concepts are wrong-headed. They indeed are not. They should remain in place. But such programs are not solutions to our problems. They are palliatives that help people like me, who are poised to succeed when given half a chance . . . They do little for those Americans, disproportionately African American, who inherit grinding poverty, bad schools, unsafe neighborhoods, low expectations and overburdened mothers."[9]

This judgment, however, is not an indictment against liberal social policy as we have defined it, in which the government accepts its obligation to ensure that all citizens are guaranteed an equal opportunity to participate in societal institutions. What I am suggesting is that in order for social and economic programs to be truly effective and to meet desired goals and objectives, certain fundamental assumptions and policy directives must be integral to these goals and objectives. Ideally, social policy should be removed from the realm of partisan politics. To do otherwise confounds any attempt to address the needs of poor and African American families.

Clearly, the political nature of social policy lends itself to a cyclical process. Accordingly we move from individual to community responsibility and back. Further, when social policy relates to African American families, a greater degree of complexity surrounds its formulation and implementation. Much of this is due to the necessity for resolving both contemporary problems and historical ones. Because slavery and subsequent events had disenfranchised African American men, women, and children, liberal social policy was expected to provide remedies for past injustices as well as to ameliorate ongoing social and economic conditions. The fact that liberal social policy, as defined and formulated in the United States, has been ineffective in no way vindicates political conservatives who claim that social policy must not interfere with free-market forces. This argument in favor of the free market system, which requires minimal regulations and government interference, has generated a compelling body of contradictory literature that indicates that the government is quite involved in the free market system, and that many social policies that rely on tax dollars are far more beneficial to corporations and their wealthy shareholders than the general public realizes. To these theorists ADC means Aid to Dependent Corporations, which would not survive and thrive were it not for generous government subsidies. Substantial tax dollars, these theorists and researchers maintain, are used to finance corporations, allow them to write off billions of dollars to depreciate the value of equipment before it has worn out, provide billions of dollars in subsidies for wealthy ranchers to graze their herds at a nominal cost on public lands, allocate millions of dollars to mineral mining corporations that pay miniscule fees for leasing public lands, allocate millions of dollars that are used to subsidize advertising by corporations that export their food and wine products, and so forth.[10] In many cases, these federal dollars are used to subsidize projects that are corporate owned and operated, from which the average American family will derive little if any benefits. Profits from these federal monies given to large corporations are seldom passed on to the consumer. Regarding African American families, many of these corporations have not fairly and equitably integrated their workplaces but maintain the traditional institutional arrangements with white males holding 95 percent of executive positions in the United States, while African American men and women are relegated to lower-income positions. And those who have the qualifications for these senior executive positions are generally precluded from receiving promotions or appointments to these upper tier, decision-making positions. These institutional practices of racial and sex inequalities result in occupational segmentation in the private sector that creates a glass ceiling for African American workers. Marita Golden, Ella Bell, and Stella Nkomo, who examine the intersection of race and gender for upwardly mobile professional African American and white female workers, found that differential outcomes are experienced by each group of women. In effect, they contend that white female workers encounter a glass ceiling, whereas African American female employees are confronted with a concrete wall.[11] Ostensibly, Golden explains that a glass ceiling presents more reasons to be optimistic as it can be cracked, and those executives above the glass ceiling do know that there are individuals below their level who anticipate continued upward mobility. By contrast, she states that African American women are confronted with so many structural barriers that they can only hope to chip away at the concrete wall.

While a disproportionate percentage of African American two-parent families before the advent of liberal social policy remained intact, these families, although together in what approximated a nuclear family, did not enjoy the same material privileges as did their white counterparts. Neither liberal nor conservative social policy has successfully elevated large numbers of African American families to a solid position of financial comfort. In the case of the former, many problems evolved primarily because the nature, magnitude, and projected success of the federal government's involvement raised expectations among African American families that proved to be unattainable, given the realistic parameters of liberal social policy and ingrained systems designed to maintain the status quo. Moreover, liberalism created illusions of progress and gains that were only spuriously related to those achieved through open-market competition. Furthermore, liberal social policy dictated that certain cultural value systems be discarded so that African American families could be totally integrated in all spheres of society. A related requirement was that macrocultural systems and ideals replace microcultural ones, such as extended families, the Black Church, and mutual-aid networks. Finally, if liberal social policy had not operated from the social-inadequacy thesis, existing African American structures and their inherent dynamics would have been preserved, because they would have been perceived as having utility.

Liberal social policy did not have to take this course. Other avenues for the development and administration of social and economic programs would have worked better. More than any other factor, intransigence in the formulation of social policy is responsible for the extreme forms that social policy has taken. If social policy were not so highly politicized, a dialectic would not exist in which social policy becomes an either-or proposition. Moreover, if social policy is to be effective it must be supported by objective scientific investigation and should be developed on the basis of the strengths and not weaknesses of earlier efforts. Given the abundance of evidence regarding the outcome of various programs and government interventions, the impact of social policy is no longer capricious.

While I do not pretend to know all of the interrelationships between various programs, recipients, cultural backgrounds, and the like, a substantial quantity of data has been amassed and analyzed that can direct the formulation of an effective social policy. For example, few would disagree that various grants-in-aid to college-bound youth would enlarge the pool of college graduates, or that an ancillary service, such as child care, would facilitate skill acquisition or refinement for a mother who is a recipient of TANF, formerly AFDC. Moreover, affordable housing and a national health insurance plan are vital to the physical and mental health and economic well-being of African American families and their members. It would also be difficult to take issue with the beneficence of dual career planning, educational and training programs needed due to deindustrialization, and severe penalties for employers using queue systems.

While the most ardent proponent of conservative social policy would probably concede that these measures are in the interests of economically disadvantaged families, they do not necessarily see these policies as the government's responsibility. Economic policies that elicit mixed responses and considerable controversy are the efficaciousness of a living wage and guaranteed minimum incomes. Relying on scientific inquiry does little to provide answers, as the findings of research conducted in this area have yielded conflicting data. Nonetheless, there remain social problems, which have systematically confronted African American families, for which specific policy and programmatic direction is available. What is lacking is agreement over one fundamental social-policy issue. This concern is related to who is responsible for offering correctives for the plight of African American families. Social policy has differed significantly depending on the political climate. The answer to this question has in the past rarely been agreed on.

Whether liberals or conservatives are in a decision-making position, there has usually been either implicit or explicit agreement that the onus for the economically depressed status of African American families lies with African American families and not the government. Although both liberals and conservatives tend to deny that structural factors play a significant role in prolonging economic dependence for African American families, advocates of liberal social policy have been willing to permit the federal government to assume an integral role in ameliorating these conditions. While conservatives, like their liberal counterparts, blame African American families, conservative policymakers believe that, because the government is not to blame, it has no obligation to discharge. Therefore, conservatives expect African American families to find solutions to their own problems, rather than looking to the federal government for assistance. Ultimately, African American families get tossed from one side to the other. On the one hand, they are expected to look to a federal government that assumes a paternalistic posture. Later, when welfare revisionists enact a new set of policies, the approach becomes more punitive. In effect, what occurs relative to the push-pull cycle of social policy is a situation akin to the period following the Civil War. Essentially, in the Compromise of 1877, Rutherford B. Hayes promised to withdraw the federal troops, which had been sent to the South to ensure civil liberties for newly freed African Americans, in exchange for Southern Democratic support. At that time, the removal of federal troops resulted in losses for African American families both in terms of civil liberties and life.

The partisan nature of social policy has resulted in history repeating itself as the "troops," which are tantamount to the federal government's monitoring and enforcing civil rights for African Americans and other disenfranchised groups, are cyclically dispatched by liberals and with- drawn by conservatives. Hence, an unspoken compromise continues to affect the status of African American families with regard to social policy. It was during the 1990s that the centrist or neoliberal political persuasion, postmodern euphemisms for conservativism, effectively removed the guise that the Democratic Party truly supports liberal social policies. It is now more accepted that the Democratic Party of the last two decades expects African American families to accept responsibility for their own depressed social and economic conditions, attributed largely to slavery; segregation; institutional racial, sex, and class discrimination; as well as other forms of social oppression. Attributing the enactment of the social policies that have placed African American families in greater peril to conservative legislators during the 1980s and 1990s is unacceptable. And for the Democratic Party to hide under the pretense of innocence by at- tributing the enactment of these punitive and conservative policies to a Republican Congress and Senate is akin to saying that "the devil made me do it." Few African American families are so naïve as to accept this excuse for the implementation of social policies whose effects are racially based and whose costs, socially, politically, and economically, to African American families have been substantial.

## THE 1990s AND THE TWENTY-FIRST CENTURY

The 1990s and the new century firmly entrenched systems of power, such as race, class, and sex inequality, into American institutions, contrib- uting to the further destabilization of African American two-parent fam- ilies and increasing the likelihood that in the day-to-day experiences of African American female-maintained families they no longer encountered challenges but became struggling families with even fewer societal insti- tutions and resources available to meet their needs. In fact, African Amer- ican families, irrespective of their socioeconomic status, are more vulnerable to institutional assaults, some blatant while others are more subtle. It was also during this time period that it became clear that many of the social and economic gains that African Americans considered absolute were merely illusions and façades of equal opportunities and civil rights gains. One in particular that African American families believed represented a definite advancement was their right to vote. When elections, especially national elections, were soon to be held there would be an increase in activity in the African American community to register new voters and to provide assistance, including transportation for the elderly and for all registered voters within the African American community, to ensure that the civil rights activities in the 1950s, 1960s, and 1970s, including a multiplicity of forms of mass protests like sit-ins, marches, and lawsuits, along with the institutional resistance that resulted in beatings, disfigurement, and death, were not in vain. The hue and cry was and continues to be "Get out and vote, people died for the right to vote, so we owe it to them and to ourselves not to take this right for granted." However, after several local elections in which African Americans became concerned because elected officials were not living up to their promises to make meaningful social change for African American families and their members, in conjunction with the conservative policies that were cloaked under the banner of centrism that has indelibly etched a racial/class caste system into the fabric of American society, along with the cloud of impropriety of the 2000 presidential election, many African American families question the utility of their vote and the 1965 Voting Rights Act.

Because of the fact that policymakers, whether liberals or conservatives, tend to disagree on the role of the government in ameliorating conditions that have a historical basis in the economic exploitation of African Americans during slavery, in de jure and de facto segregation, and with conventional institutional policies and practices of racial inequality, African American families are not as uncertain as to the government's role in ensuring that they have greater access to wealth, power, and privileges to which they continue to be denied. In fact, the majority of African American families recognize that they are confronted with numerous challenges to their upward mobility that require some form of government intervention to overcome. Unfortunately, it is still the case that the remaining liberal social policies and laws that have not been further diluted have not ever been nor are they by design capable of eliminating or significantly diminishing the institutional barriers that thwart upward mobility and privileges for African American families across all socioeconomic classes. What is becoming increasingly clear is that far too many African American families comprise the poor and working poor classes, whose lack of resources will be transmitted to successive generations. And as McAdoo found, middle-class status for African American families is not being sustained, as future generations are increasingly losing the middle-class status that their parents worked relentlessly to attain.[12] It is also understood by many African American families that it is no longer simply African American lower-income families that are the targets of myriad forms of overt oppression, as all African American families have become prey for this form of cultural humiliation and civil rights violations. I am not suggesting, however, that African American poor families are not the victims of racial discrimination with the same level of frequency or severity as their middle-class and upper-middle-class counterparts, for such is not the case. African American lower-income families are more likely to have their members join the military as an alternative to being in the ranks of the unemployed or jobless, which makes them more likely to be candidates for wars and conflicts that are life threatening. African American poor families also provide the surplus laborers that are used as temporary and part-time employees who are not entitled to benefits like sick leave, vacation, and employer-sponsored health insurance, saving employers enormous labor costs. They also serve as targets for the war on drugs, which justifies the middle-income jobs of those employed to engage in drug enforcement. And even more regrettable is that it is the impoverished African American families whose members are prey for prisons, making them profitable for occupationally displaced rural and small-town residents and profiteers in the privatization of prisons. Moreover, this carefully crafted prison-industrial complex offers numerous economic benefits to the government, which receives virtually free labor for the production of goods and services by inmates, and to corporations, who employ what some now refer to as the new form of slavery or slave labor.

Because of the enormity of the problem now facing African American families, which has grown exponentially over the last 30 years, the strategies that are necessary to significantly alter these racially discriminatory institutional policies and practices must emanate from the African American community, with the family serving as its most critical agent of social change.

## TOWARD A VIABLE SOCIAL POLICY FOR AFRICAN AMERICAN FAMILIES: SOME CONSIDERATIONS

The social policies and institutional forms of race, gender, and class inequality have had a profoundly adverse affect on African American families during the past three decades. The 1980s, 1990s, and the early twenty-first century have effectively mitigated the most positive effects of liberal social policies, which were modest at best. In order for social policy to be effective, I believe that specific strategies and actions must be initiated by African American families and institutions within the African American community. African Americans must become fully committed to pursuing viable methods of halting the overt and covert assaults on African American families, their members, and institutions, and must do so with confidence and determination. We must recognize that many individuals who monopolize wealth and power in the United States and those to whom they delegate the responsibility to manage institutions that guarantee their power and privilege must not be allowed to use information and ideas to define what is acceptable and to determine how we should measure success. It is essential that African American families and their members, as well as those who control African American institutions, interpret our life experiences, goals, and expectations. It is also important that we become candid and critical of events, policies, and practices that are institutionally fraught with racial, sex, and class inequality. Simply because we have not been involved in most policy-making decisions in major societal institutions does not mean that we should allow those who formulate policies that affect our lives to devalue and disregard our contributions, abilities, and relentless efforts to achieve in spite of numerous obstacles that we encounter.

Accordingly, I have provided specific strategies that should serve as the preliminary endeavors of African American families and other institutions within the African American community to begin to restore and restabilize African American families, especially those that have begun to falter under the ideological, social, economic, and physical attacks that families and their members have sustained. The following proposed strategies are not exhaustive; rather, they represent a point of departure for regaining many of the traditional qualities and strengths that have been responsible for the survival and progress of African American families. Therefore, I believe that in order for social policy to be effective the following strategies and practices should be engaged.

1. Specific roles to be assumed by major institutions and segments of the population must be clearly delineated.

    The Black Church should initiate this process by organizing its clergy and religious leaders to meet with their white counterparts to address known inequities and to initially request that white clergy and religious leaders address these issues with their congregations. And for white clerics and religious leaders with access to a large public following, either through television, radio, or other forums they should be asked to take this first elementary but important step in publicly supporting practices that are fair and equitable. Moreover, they should also be requested to take a stand in opposition to the demeaning and dehumanizing practices of racial profiling and police brutality. The willingness of white clergy and religious leaders to deliver these views that are basic human rights issues will apprise African American families of the level of support that they can anticipate from mainstream churches and their parishioners, who are often placed in positions on a daily basis where they must make decisions that reflect fairness, equality, and justice that affect families and their members regardless of their race, class, or sex.

    Furthermore, other African American institutions, organizations, and associations should ask that their regional and national mainstream counterparts address the same issues in their newsletters, periodicals, and national meetings and conferences.

2. An understanding and agreement as to what constitutes success and failure for social and economic programs must be developed.

Each African American institution and organization must define success instead of allowing others outside the African American community to make this determination. Therefore, a baseline or barometer must be identified that constitutes success for African American families and their members. For example, annual goals should be established related to the number of tutorial programs, job fairs, college tours, new businesses, college scholarships, and college internships provided to African American students from businesses receiving African American patronage, or computers donated to local community centers and churches by companies who depend on African American consumer dollars. These goals should be established individually and collectively by local neighborhood associations, regionally and nationally by organizations such as the National Association for the Advancement of Colored People (NAACP), the National Urban League, Jack and Jill, and the Links, as well as sororities and fraternities that have local chapters, which should also be involved collaboratively with local neighborhood associations or organizations to set goals, define success, and annually determine whether these goals were met. They must also identify strategies to increase the likelihood that goals that are not attained within a designated time period will be met in the future. For example, it may require encouraging African American families to switch their patronage of one beverage company or sports shoe company to another. When this decision is made it should be aired on several syndicated radio talk shows, and where possible disseminated through other African American–oriented media or venues and by word of mouth.

3. Ground rules must be formulated that reflect clear-cut goals and objectives within a reasonably established time frame.

African American families must identify strategies to ensure accountability for their efforts, their time, and their money. While this strategy is of particular importance to elected officials who rely on African American voters to win and retain their elected offices, it also applies to any organization whose mission is to improve the lives of African Americans and to ensure equality and justice for African American families and their members. Therefore, in local, regional, and national campaigns African Americans should ask candidates for elected office what they hope to accomplish in office that will improve the standard of living and quality of life for African American families.

In addition, candidates should be asked to identify the venues or forums that they will use during their terms in office to identify these accomplishments and to identify impediments to achieving these goals. Regarding the publishing or dissemination of their accomplishments, elected officials who rely on support from African American voters should make their accomplishments known annually in periodicals, including newspapers and magazines that are widely available and accessible through affordable subscriptions or at no cost in public libraries. The electronic media are also venues, especially syndicated programs and local stations that provide an African American–oriented format. It is also critical to hear from elected officials for whom African American voters dis-proportionately constitute their constituency about what differences they think heading specific committees within government legislative bodies are likely to make for African American families, and about how their presence in office has made a difference or improved the lives of African American families. Con-versely, African American elected officials need to inform African American families what specific actions are needed from them and organizations and institutions with which they are affiliated to assist African American elected officials in making meaningful changes and influencing social policies that will enhance their lives and stabilize their families. The same expectations should be made known, and questions asked, to whites and other candidates for elected office who purport to represent the interests of African American fam-ilies and their members.

When candidates can demonstrate that they have made serious attempts to improve the lives of African American families and to live up to their campaign promises they should be rewarded with continued support. Those who fail to do so should not receive voter support from within the African American com-munity. African Americans must find those who will represent the interests of African American families and their members among those who are campaign-ing for office or write in the names of candidates in whom they have confidence. Continued voting for the lesser of two evils, just because African Americans rarely have the opportunity to influence the selection of candidates in most elections, is unacceptable. It is totally unconvincing to say that this type of election process and political participation is what many voting rights activists during the1950s and 1960s envisioned when they peacefully protested, yet were the objects of various forms of institutional resistance, including violence and death. Thus, the hue and cry in African American communities throughout the country, in rural, urban, and suburban areas must be for major reforms in voting and the election process. And given the outcome of the 2000 presidential elec-tion, with its myriad irregularities and disqualifications of large numbers of African American votes, election reform should be a priority of the political agenda of all candidates that profess to have the interests of African American families at heart, and especially for elected officials who depend on African American voters for their success at the polls.

The Black Church is another institution that should have a new set of ground rules established, along with goals and a time frame for achieving these goals. It is no longer acceptable, given the state of African American families, for any African American institution to ignore and deny the African American com-munity the use of human capital based on the same superficial qualities that are used in the larger society to deny equality and justice to African Americans.

Considerable emphasis is usually placed on unifying the African American community so that it can rally all of its forces including its strengths and abilities to continue to challenge racial injustices in the larger society. However, racial inequality is not the only form of injustice and inaccessibility to opportunities that African American families encounter in functioning in the larger society. African American families and their members are also the victims of institu-tional sex and class inequality on a systematic basis. In both instances being denied opportunities and being excluded from receiving resources or participating in policy-making positions are detrimental to African Americans' well-being as individuals, families, and the overall community. The workplace, however, is replete with sex discrimination that takes many forms, like pay inequality, denials of promotions, refusal to hire females, and even sexual harassment where usually the African American female is subjected to a work environment that expects sexual favors in exchange for employment, retaining a job, receiving pay increases, and promotions. In addition, African American women are frequently in work environments that permit sex-related verbal and physical conduct that makes it difficult for them to perform their duties. The pervasiveness of sexual harassment is not yet known; because of stereotypes of African American women as hypersexed individuals there are men in the workplace who have sexual fantasies regarding African American women, where there is no empirical basis, only stereotypes, to support these perceptions. These unrealistic fantasies have often led to sexual assaults that are responsible in large part for African American families sending their daughters to college to become schoolteachers in the early 1900s, as opposed to the other option, which was a domestic. These same expectations of African American female workers persist today and adversely affect their opportunities for career mobility. It is also the case that African American females are underemployed and experience occupational segmentation, whereby they are remanded to sectors of organizations that provide limited career opportunities and generate lower salaries for them. Again, while race plays a role in these institutional arrangements, sex discrimination does as well. Hence, the intersection of both race and sex discrimination simply exacerbate working conditions and career mobility.

The unfortunate consequence of sex discrimination is that it reduces the income that the African American mother has to contribute to the family income, as well as to the Black Church, as she is likely to be paid less than her male counterpart with similar qualifications and experience. When egregious forms of sex discrimination affect African American women, they should be able to corral the support of their family members as well as their church family, including their pastor. However, in far too many cases, African American women continue to be excluded from holding high-status, decision-making positions in their own churches simply because of their sex. The paradox here is real, as African American women have offered the predominant source of support for the development and growth of this extremely significant African American institution, as has been well documented by Evelyn Brooks Higginbotham. She provides vital information regarding the role of African American women in making the Black Church a major institution for self-help and an agent for social change.[13] While many Black Churches are encouraging and offering equal opportunities for women to assume roles as senior pastor and trustee board member, others are continuing to experience a cultural lag. However, it is no longer sufficient for church women to remain silent or to accept the premise that women should not assume the highest leadership role in the Black Church, as the pastor. Women should also be adequately represented on deacon boards and trustee boards and function in every capacity in the Black Church. The fact that this has not occurred does not negate the need for change; instead, it does mean that African American women must develop strategies to become more fully participatory in the church. To do otherwise is to concede that they have some shortcomings or deficits that preclude using their abilities and skills, which are needed throughout the Black Church and in every institution and organization in the African American community. According to Marcia Dyson, even though African American women comprise 75 percent of the congregation in Black Churches in the United States they make up less than 5 percent of the clergy.[14] Nevertheless, African American women possess enormous skills, talents, and abilities and their inability to utilize these strengths is a waste of human capital that the African American community and its institutions cannot afford. In order to combat the various institutional assaults on the African American family, the leadership abilities of all African American men and women must be available to the entire community. Dyson states that while "the Black church in America has historically been an incubator for Black-male leadership when it could assert itself nowhere else," today there are more opportunities for African American men to exercise power and authority and the need is no longer as great for the Black Church to provide this kind of sanctuary.[15] Recognizing severe career restrictions and opportunities still exist, these and other destabilizing factors that affect African American families stand a greater chance of being corrected with the collaborative efforts of African American men and women assuming leadership roles in the Black Church and other institutions within the African American community. Like others, Reverend Marcia Dyson cites the problems of families in crisis and disintegration, the criminalization of African American men and children, and so forth as reasons for utilizing the leadership capabilities, including knowledge and other resources, of African American women in the Black Church.

It is difficult to successfully challenge racial inequality in the larger society and other forms of inequities that are generally based on the assumption that those who occupy leadership or decision-making positions do so because of superiority that is generally purported to be based on intellectual superiority. If such is the argument for the existence of one form of superordinant-subordinant relationship, then it may serve the interests of those who subordinate individuals on the basis of race and sex to justify their actions by identifying the existence of a parallel paradigm, within the African American community, based on sex inequality, that is also predicated upon the belief that males are intellectually superior to females. Thus, those who monopolize wealth and power in the larger society based on race, sex, and class clearly derive support for their position by the existence of similar institutional arrangements within microcultural communities. Again, African Americans cannot allow unsound logic that perpetuates inequalities throughout the larger society to be accepted and to contribute to conflict, marital disruption and familial instability, and the inability to overcome systematic forms of race, sex, and class inequalities that are confronting African American families and their members. However, because African American women have agency, they are not helpless nor do they have to accept these traditional guidelines that limit the nature of their participation in churches that they helped to found and upon which their contributions depend.

Therefore, African American women must establish time-specific goals for assuming greater leadership in the Black Church and devise alternative means for spiritual growth, development, and expressions. These alternatives may include attending a different church or denomination that recognizes and respects the skills and abilities of African American women by providing opportunities for them to assume clerical positions, founding new churches that are more inclusive, and identifying men and women within the Black Church who share the belief that women should assume greater leadership roles and work with them to generate sufficient support to bring about significant policy changes to elevate African American women to clerical and other leadership positions in their own Black Churches and religious denominations.

4. Social policy must build on the strengths of extant African American families and other institutions and structures within the African American community.

It is important, for example, that the Faith-Based Initiatives and foster care system include the values, norms, and belief systems of African American families, including the use of kinship networks and informal social-support systems as well as the Black Church in order to ensure the viability of each. There is sufficient evidence that social policies and the policies and practices of societal institutions should be carefully assessed, as they may promote or prohibit the stability of African American families.

During the 1990s there were three national events that demonstrated the strength and resolve of African American families and their members to reaffirm their commitment to traditional values and beliefs in the importance of family, community unity, and self-determination. In effect there were three marches that occurred, The first, led by Minister Louis Farrakhan, the leader of the Nation of Islam, was entitled the Million Man March and was considered a day of atonement for African American men. Held in Washington, D.C., on October 16, 1995, the march attracted over one million African American men who made a commitment to improve their lives as well as those of their families and the entire African American community. Two years later, the Million Woman March took place in Philadelphia, Pennsylvania, on October 25, 1997. Over one million African American women arrived in Philadelphia to also rededicate themselves to revitalizing themselves, their families, and their communities through spiritual and community empowerment and unity.[16] Finally, the Million Youth Movement March was held in two cities, in New York City on September 5, 1998, and on September 7, 1998, in Atlanta, Georgia. These marches attracted thousands of youth who were encouraged by civil rights activists to utilize strategies to eliminate the economic isolation of African American youth and presented the need for them to become more economically empowered. The aftermath of these marches resulted in African Americans returning to their local communities with a great sense of determination to identify strategies and programs to address the many challenges that confront African American families and their members.

Clearly, such events reflect a genuine commitment on the part of numerous African Americans to revitalize their communities and to seek remedies for the institutional challenges that African American families encounter on a daily basis. However, the sheer magnitude of the problems that structural barriers present to African American families requires that the federal government assume greater responsibility for eliminating many of the institutional forms of inequality that continue to exclude African American families' participation from mainstream institutions. After all, it seems reasonable to expect that since African Americans are taxpayers their financial contributions be allocated to programs and services that will ameliorate conditions within their communities and reduce institutional resistance and structural barriers that, decades after the era of liberal social policy, continue to lead to their exclusion and subordination.

5. Strategies for expanding the participation of African Americans in institutions in the African American community and within the larger society should be identified.

Recognizing the need for institutions within the African American community to generate sufficient funds in order to fulfill their missions and to achieve their goals of ameliorating conditions facing African American families and their members, a dilemma is often encountered, as local and national organizations receive considerable support from corporations as opposed to the constituents they serve. While few can argue with the copiousness of resources of large corporations or their willingness to make charitable contributions to African American organizations, it has become increasingly the case that while membership in various civil rights organizations is possible, attendance at annual meetings, luncheons, dinners, and conferences is often cost prohibitive due to the exorbitant ticket prices. Ostensibly, corporations can afford such tickets, and even purchase entire tables, distributing the tickets they purchase as complementary to various employees. However, it is often the case that many African American families are unable to attend these events as they cannot afford to purchase an individual ticket, not to mention tickets for their entire family. Therefore, it is important that corporations be encouraged to give some of the tickets back to these civil rights organizations so that African American families who are members or interested in and committed to these civil rights organizations can feel a sense of belonging and ownership. In addition, it may also be the case that a separate fund should be set aside to make tickets available to African American families interested in attending these events. Special fundraising may also be pursued, and grants written for the express purpose of providing tickets to families who wish to attend these important forums and events.

While African Americans agree that they are entitled to the same opportunities as their white counterparts, many recognize that African American families are not playing on a level playing field because of slavery, as well as past and ongoing institutional racial discrimination. While contemporary forms of institutional racial discrimination must be eradicated with effective social policies and legislation, slavery is, according to many, the most egregious form of economic exploitation, which has bestowed immeasurable benefits upon descendants of slaveholders as well as immigrants who have come to this country and benefited from the free labor of enslaved Africans, who built and developed American institutions and wealth with their labor and brilliance. In the case of inventions, they were denied patents; therefore, it leaves little doubt that their inventions, many to facilitate the laborious work that they were required to perform, were appropriated by slaveholders, their business partners, and other associates. Moreover, there are numerous corporations that exist today that benefited directly from the free labor of enslaved Africans. In fact, there are insurance companies that sold life insurance policies to slaveholders for the enslaved Africans that they owned.

There has been a reparations movement for a considerable number of years. This movement has included the participation of many African Americans from laborers to professionals and businesspersons. In January 1989, Representative John Conyers, a Democrat from Detroit, Michigan, introduced a bill, H.R. 40. The purpose of H.R. 40 is to establish a Commission to Study Reparation Proposals for African Americans Act. Specifically, the bill calls for a discussion to acknowledge the injustice and inhumanity of slavery, a commission to study slavery and its subsequent racial and economic discrimination against freed former slaves, a study of the impact of slavery on African Americans living today in the United States, and a commission to recommend to Congress appropriate remedies to redress the harm inflicted on living African Americans. The movement has steadily gained momentum and held its first march on Washington, the Millions March for Reparations, on August 17, 2002. The demands of the reparation movement are for America to pay the descendants of formerly enslaved Africans for their free labor as well as punitive damages for the harsh and brutal treatment of their ancestors. In effect, reparations are intended to make amends for the injury inflicted on a specific group, in this case enslaved Africans and their descendants, for a number of reasons: Because wealth is generally inherited, and because African Americans were denied the 40 acres proposed in a bill by Representative Thaddeus Stevens, a Republican from Pennsylvania, which was not enacted by Congress. And because African American families who purchased and leased parcels of land following Emancipation were required to give the land back, as ordered by President Andrew Johnson, and many were physically removed from properties that they had purchased and leased, as these properties were returned to white former slaveholders. In addition, African Americans were never supplied the tools, equipment, and farm animals necessary to become integrated into the Southern agricultural economy. This was true despite the fact that the promise of 40 acres and a mule was not a government handout, as these families had toiled for endless hours and at the very least this was a miniscule form of payment for their labor; yet even this tawdry gesture was denied African Americans as they were forced through Black Codes to become the providers of virtually free labor through the sharecropping system, which placed them in a virtually inescapable cycle of poverty, very much like that which many African American families find themselves entrenched in today. The similarities are numerous, but essentially African American families have been extended credit in order to purchase the basic necessities of life but are denied the opportunity to earn a salary that will enable them to end their indebtedness. Instead, as the costs for these necessities increase (the cost of living), their incomes either stay the same or decrease, or they experience a slight increase in their income but never enough to rise out of poverty and their indebtedness.

In addition, the reparations movement has not defined what form reparations should take or how determinations will be made regarding the distribution of reparations. However, other cultures who have been wrongly treated, like the

Japanese who were interned in the United States during World War II, are cited as an example in which the American government attempted to pay Japanese Americans for enduring the pain and humiliation of internment. To this end, Randall Robinson provides a compelling argument for African Americans to receive reparations.[17]

It is also the case that the reparations movement has served as the impetus for several lawsuits that have been filed primarily against insurance companies that were known to derive financial benefits from the institution of slavery. It is projected that new lawsuits will be filed in the future, and some are expected to name the federal government as the defendant since the White House and other federal buildings and monuments were built by the labor of enslaved Africans. Representative John Conyers' proposed legislation is simply to result in a forum where reparations would be discussed. However, this bill has not been passed. Still, there is a growing commitment and involvement on the part of African American families to pursue reparations and receive the remuneration that their ancestors, whose slave labor is responsible for the tremendous wealth of this country, were denied.

6. A reassessment of traditional and contemporary value orientations within the contexts of the larger society and the African American community should create a synthesis that will serve as a moral imperative for African American families.

   Furthermore, those macrocultural value orientations that are detrimental to the stability and functioning capacity of African American families should not be adopted (i.e., competition and rugged individualism, according status based on income, education, and occupation, etc.).

7. New venues must be created for the national dissemination of key information on legislation, social, economic, and political events occurring on local, regional, and national levels, which are critical to the survival and progress of African American families.

   Every national civil rights organization should develop a one-hour weekly radio broadcast describing its activities and allowing for audience interaction, when it is economically feasible, using a toll-free telephone call-in, question and answer format.

### Institutional Responsibility

Clearly, while microsystems within the African American community must play a major role in efforts to elevate the social and economic status of African American men, women, and children, institutions in the larger society that impact upon the lives of African American families must also make a commitment to ensure that constructive change occurs. In the past, the government's involvement in social-service delivery did not move beyond legislating that institutions ensure the civil rights of African Americans. Even in this regard, as Derrick Bell so cogently asserts, laws passed during the 1960s and 1970s were inadequate to protect African Americans and provide civil rights for them collectively. Little changed in this regard during the 1980s, 1990s, and twenty-first century have occurred. Handling matters of racial discrimination on an individual rather than a systematic basis represents a less than suitable method of remedying past injustices and curbing invidious social inequities. Moreover, as Bell suggests, the mere fact that in our society the burden of proof lies with the victim makes eradicating institutional racial discrimination an arduous task. That African Americans are faced with proving not only covert but overt racial discrimination only confounds the issue of seeking redress for the purpose of ameliorating social and economic conditions for African American families. And when one considers the economic constraints of the majority of African American families, challenging racial discrimination, whether in housing or employment, is a difficult undertaking at best. Even for those willing to persevere, individual efforts to obtain the equal treatment necessary to enhance their life chances are a highly uncertain endeavor, the outcome of which, even if positive, in no way guarantees that others are any less likely to experience the same treatment.

Because of the exorbitant costs and imposed structural barriers to individuals seeking redress for civil rights violations, efforts to file class action lawsuits should be given serious consideration. Class action litigation may provide a more effective approach to civil rights violations and may generate more resources, such as similar cases, corroborating witnesses, and evidence, increasing the likelihood of retaining qualified attorneys to provide legal representation in these cases.

Given past experience, changing societal institutions requires considerably more than the type of legislation passed during the 1960s and 1970s. Laws must go beyond mandating that rudimentary principles of fairness be met; they must also serve as an edict that the equitable treatment of African Americans and other racial and ethnic minorities should occur on a systematic basis. Thus, any evidence of a violation of an individual's civil rights should warrant intense scrutiny to prevent further unfair treatment of minorities. When civil rights violations are proved, penalties should entail substantially more than monetary forms of retribution. The violators should demonstrate through a long-range plan how they will safeguard the rights of African Americans and other protected groups.

Over the past 25 years anti–civil rights laws have been enacted to eliminate and dilute earlier civil rights laws enacted during the 1960s and 1970s. However, despite their success, existing civil rights legislation alone cannot accomplish the eradication of structural barriers that make upward mobility difficult for African American families. Therefore, in conjunction with legislation, members of racial and ethnic groups must use networks to coordinate their efforts to provide critical information to their members regarding ways to access various institutions. Members of informal networks internal to various institutions and organizations must gather information regarding institutional needs and goals (i.e., job opportunities and business contracts for goods and services). This information must be channeled through external networks and disseminated on a local level. Because institutional forms of racial discrimination occur throughout the country it is essential for African Americans to own media that can provide venues for the dissemination of information to African American families regionally and nationally. Since I proposed that African American media outlets, particularly those that serve as a repository and clearinghouse for information, be established in the earlier edition of his book, there are now more syndicated radio stations that cover events, activities, and issues that affect the African American community. Later in this chapter I provide a more thorough discussion of the development of these media outlets and their status in the twenty-first century

### Measuring Success

One major flaw in liberal social policy was the amorphous nature of its goals. With the broad goal of eradicating poverty, disagreement over the extent to which social and economic programs were successful is understandable. However, quantitative measures alone are no reliable indicator of the overall effectiveness of these efforts. For example, the number of families in poverty before the government's expanded role in the delivery of social services, compared to the number in poverty at the end of the 1970s, reveals an overall decrease in poverty. However, considerable disagreement continues to exist over whether this decrease should be interpreted as constituting success. In this regard, the issue is whether the goal of alleviating poverty should have been more clearly defined. In other words, is the fact that fewer families had incomes below the poverty level, more than 20 years after poverty programs were implemented, a real measure of the effectiveness of liberal social policy? Or should we take into account the inordinate number of families whose incomes hover just above this arbitrary figure? When we consider the inordinate number of families, particularly African American families, who make up the working poor, with incomes slightly above the government-established poverty level, can we say that liberal social policy was effective? Moreover, the growth in joblessness and the cyclical nature of poverty and unemployment often mean that adult members of African American families who are employed for one full year may be unemployed or working in part-time employment for the next two or more consecutive years. In essence, such families, while the adult members are engaged in full-time employment, are able to afford the basic necessities of life and to occasionally make purchases many middle-class and upper-middle-class families take for granted, like going to a movie, attending a concert, buying books and magazines, dining out at restaurants, and even eating at fast food restaurants. However, with little notice these adult family members may be faced with unemployment due to deindustrialization. This feast or famine standard of living has become increasingly common for African American families over the past 25 years and is both frustrating and destabilizing. Having limited or no control over one's employment, which is tantamount to lacking job security, should result in African American adult family members ensuring that they have more than one source of income. Hence, two sources of income have become an imperative for African American adults who head families. While one may have full-time employment, involuntary part-time employment has become a necessity to meet financial obligations and to provide another source of income should one source of employment cease. However, in the interest of rearing and supervising children it is important whenever possible to seek part-time or temporary (seasonal) employment either in one's home, within close proximity to one's home, or in an environment that permits children to accompany their working parents. Some part-time employment in which adult male and female family members engage includes hair braiding, selling various goods or merchandise, providing child care, mowing lawns, seamstress services, typing, tutorial services, piano lessons, evening janitorial services cleaning office buildings (where children are often allowed), driving for courier services, repairing automobiles if not prohibited by city ordinances, and driving taxis, not to mention cosmetology services and barbering, which require licenses. There are also temporary services that hire adult family members on a seasonal basis, such as income tax preparation, companies taking inventory, and recreation centers hiring employees for summer programs teaching tennis, swim lessons, arts and crafts, dance lessons, and so forth.

Moreover, the absence of short-term goals and objectives made it difficult to determine the effectiveness of certain policies and administrative practices. Thus, programs were permitted to continue relatively unchanged because administrators were left with the task of defining success. In some instances, where decisions of this nature were made internally, one obvious inclination was to maintain programs that were of dubious benefit simply to justify the organization's existence. Therefore, the jobs of service providers were secured at the expense of effecting changes that would have eliminated the program. In addition, establishing short-term, measurable goals is not synonymous with the all-too-frequent method of measuring program success annually, based on the number of recipients the program or agency serves.

Admittedly, the number of individuals who benefit from diverse services is an important indicator of the capacity of a program to reach those in need. However, quantitative figures that reflect the scope of service delivery should not be interpreted as a measure of success. What is equally important is not merely how many individuals receive a service but the effect that the program has on enhancing the overall status and level of functioning of an individual or group. For example, an increase in the number of African Americans receiving educational grants and loans is likely to increase the enrollment of African Americans in institutions of higher education but may do little to reduce other barriers that preclude African Americans from graduating. In this regard, a number of interrelated goals should be established and measured independently and interdependently to determine the overall impact of educational programs designed to increase the number of African Americans who are admitted to and expected to graduate from colleges and universities. All social and economic programs must be developed with agreement relative to what constitutes favorable outcomes. This agreement should take place between policymakers, administrators, and program participants.

In this decision-making process, academicians and others with a history of involvement in and knowledge of social and economic programs should play a key advisory role. Previous social policies designed to improve the status of African American families have been formulated and implemented as though they would last forever. Accordingly, their sponsors have assumed that social and economic programs would be available at optimal levels until the economic status of African Americans and poor families in America indicated that the need no longer existed. Such an open-ended approach to effecting social equity is unrealistic and does not allow for the integration of criteria to measure success during various stages of service delivery. Moreover, this method of formulating and administering social and economic programs generates cultural anxiety among program participants, as well as the general public. This open-ended nature of social and economic programs gave rise to the ideas that African Americans have received enough to account for past injustices and that today, because no de jure segregation exists and much of the civil rights legislation of the 1960s and 1970s is still available, it is not uncommon to hear white academicians and nonacademicians say that America is now a color-blind society. Therefore, these individuals contend that there is no longer a need for liberal social policies and social and economic programs designed to ensure equality of opportunity based on race. In addition, the unpredictable duration of social and economic programs makes participants and members of society at large subject to political manipulation. In essence, politicians have been given a free rein to play on the fears and desires of both advocates and opponents of liberal social programs. Establishing concise, time-specific goals is clearly a more tenable and viable way of bringing about needed social change for African American families.

### Building on the Strengths

Future attempts to develop a social policy capable of elevating the status of African American families should embrace the assumption that African American families and institutions within the African American community are composed of disparate structures that represent adaptations for survival. And like other institutions throughout society, they possess positive as well as negative qualities. If social and economic initiatives are to be effectual, the strengths of institutions in the African American community must be recognized, enhanced, and integrated into those efforts. Perhaps the most glaring error in the past was the generalization by policymakers—with substantiation from select scholars—of social problems affecting subpopulations of African Americans to African American families in general. Ignoring invaluable strengths and deemphasizing survival strategies employed by African American families, the Black Church, African American–owned businesses, and African American schools served to attenuate positive advances for African American families. Furthermore, this narrow, ethnocentric approach to liberal social policy contributed to the decline of those institutions that before the 1960s had been responsible for African American social and economic progress.

There is sufficient evidence that ethnic and racial cultural groups that have advanced to a position of economic power have done so in part through group solidarity and cooperation. Moreover, they have become integrated on an economic level but have retained a strong sense of cultural identity and pride. African American leaders involved in the civil rights movement in the 1960s were aware of the importance of African American families acknowledging and maintaining a sense of commonality of interests. Because of this, they placed emphasis on the strengths of African American families. Historical images, which depicted African Americans as intellectually and culturally inferior, were discarded and replaced with positive imagery of African American men, women, and children.

Today, many in the hip-hop generation are making positive contributions toward elevating the status of African Americans through music that applauds all complexions and frequently extols brown skin tones and those of a darker hue. They are also affirming natural hairstyles, braids, and African headdresses or head coverings in men and women. These artists include Erykah Badu, India Arie, Musiq, D'Angelo, Jill Scott, and Eric Benet. There are also rappers making contributions toward redefining African American males and females and the African American family, like Common, Mos Def, and the Roots. The music of these artists continues to reaffirm African American culture by emphasizing physical qualities that are valued in the African American community like large buttocks, breasts, smiles, and rounded shapes. It is important that emphasis continues to be placed on changing the language immediately, making it racially neutral and racially sensitive, whether it is linguists or the many artists proficient in varied verbal art forms in the African American community that must take on this important task. It is important that African American families rear their children by informing them, "Do not try to neutralize a word that carries a negative connotation, eliminate the use of the word forever or replace it and then withhold rewards for those who continue to use the consensually agreed upon negative terms."

Such was the case with words that were gender biased and affected the livelihoods of many women in the United States, keeping them from competing for jobs occupied primarily by men; therefore, these positions were at the high end of the salary scale because they were male intensive by tradition. A mailman is now a mail carrier, a fireman is called a firefighter, a chairman is a chairperson, and hurricanes, considered unpredictable and temperamental, are given both male and female names. Racially biased words and phrases that must be replaced include black magic, black listed, black balled, black mailed, white lie, the black sheep in the family, a dark day in American history . . . and so forth.

It is difficult to conceive of a social policy that can significantly improve the status of African American families that does not utilize existing resources in the African American community. Considering that the Black Church continues to be the most economically wealthy and independent institution in the African American community, any social policy designed to help African American families that does not give the Black Church a central role is inconceivable and likely to meet with failure. Moreover, the familiarity of the Black Church with social and economic spheres means that the Black Church can provide guidance and direction in the area of African American economic development. Because of the widespread nature of the racially biased institutional practices of law enforcement agencies to target African American families and their members for racial profiling and the growing number of video documented tapes of police brutality that, in many instances, continue to result in law enforcement officers not being charged and convicted of this criminal behavior, it appears that African American families must turn to the Black Church for leadership in bringing these policies and practices that are disturbing and destabilizing to families and the African American community in its entirety to a halt. To successfully effect meaningful change in this institutional practice is likely to require that African American clergy collectively meet and develop a strategy for approaching white clergy who are members of the same denominations or ministerial alliances or who are of different religious persuasions. They may wish to include those white clerics who have a high degree of visibility and public support for their ministries. African American clergy must inform white clergy of the ongoing and systematic nature of these practices and how they occur (i.e., shopping while black, flying while black, vacationing while black, driving while black, etc.). It is essential, however, at this time that African American clergy petition white religious leaders to take a stand against racial profiling and police brutality. Perhaps African American clergy will formulate some recommendations of venues and forums that may be appropriate if white clergy indicate a willingness to address their parishioners and followers regarding the injustices and social, economic, and spiritual costs borne by those who are the victims of these practices. An exchange of information by these ministers on methods that are likely to be most effective and a time frame for these strategies to be employed should produce a positive outcome, as many of the parishioners in white churches are law enforcement officers as well as state and national congressional representatives who are in key positions to influence meaningful policies that will greatly diminish this conduct. It is important to look for leadership in the Black Church, as many African American civil rights leaders have emerged from the ministerial ranks of Black Churches, such as the Reverends Adam Clayton Powell, Martin Luther King Jr., Jesse Jackson, Andrew Young, Al Sharpton, and U.S. Congressman William Gray III, to name a few, suggesting that Black Churches are equally equipped to produce those who are adept and participatory in social, economic, political, and religious systems.

During the 1990s academicians began citing the emergence and growth of Black Megachurches, or churches with 3,000 or more members.[18] Many of these churches have within their membership some of the country's most upwardly mobile African American families and individuals, who have experienced success as high-level professionals and entrepreneurs. These same churches also have members who represent every socioeconomic strata, including lower-income, working-class, and middle-class families. One of the problems facing these churches that span many denominations, some even being nondenominational, is space. Their existing inner-city buildings are generally inadequate to accommodate such large numbers of parishioners. The first level of response for many entailed holding two or more services every Sunday. Generally, there was an early morning service and the original service that commenced at 11:00 A.M. When this proved ineffective, along with other facilities within the church, to accommodate these large memberships, many Black Churches made a decision to move. And in many cases some churches decided to build a structure that would meet the many needs of their diverse membership. Many Black Churches have moved to newer buildings or have built churches within urban areas. However, these new buildings that house the church are frequently located on the periphery, or in outlying areas, of the city, where there is either limited or no mass transportation. Therefore, shuttles and vans are used to transport members and others interested in attending these churches to these outlying communities. A serious

problem has occurred with this particular and increasingly accepted practice of Black Churches. Relocating is having a tremendous impact on African American families in that the perception of many African American
families left behind is that their presence and participation is not highly
valued. In addition, these relocations leave inner-city African American
families without an extremely important traditional symbol, one that sig-
nifies hope, strength, and the sense of belongingness to a religious organization that their families, including previous generations, helped to
establish and develop. Thus, there is not only physical distance that is
created but social distance as well. This is obviously compounded by the
bifurcation of the African American community created by upwardly mobile African American families moving to suburban communities, taking
with them invaluable financial and informational resources regarding accessing and maneuvering societal institutions; strategies for overcoming,
resolving, and circumventing institutional racial discrimination; and viable social networks that provide the connections necessary to enable families and their members entrée into various institutions and organizations
that can facilitate upward mobility out of poverty and the working class
and can solidify a family's position in the middle class. Now, with several
Black Churches leaving the inner city, the bastion of hope, financial independence and assistance, and political power leaves African American
families whose mobility out of these poor communities is viewed as even
less probable given their lack of access to material and nonmaterial resources. It is therefore crucial that when it becomes necessary for Black
Churches to move and build or purchase buildings that may be in urban
areas but are miles from the inner-city to retain those churches while adding another church. If the edifices that they are leaving are irreparable or
if maintaining these structures is cost prohibitive then another inner-city
church should be purchased. There is evidence of this practice in that there
are churches that own more than one building and where the senior pastor
preaches at each church on rotation. In these cases the church retains the
same name, but each church is referred to as Church number 1, Church
number 2, and Church number 3. This ownership of more than one church
is vital to the survival of African American families in inner-city communities who are oftentimes devalued by surrounding macrocultural institutions like schools and financial institutions, as well as by a
mainstream value orientation that assigns a lower status to those who do
not, like more affluent families, possess certain status symbols. Some have
argued that when a Black Church builds in a neighborhood that is at a
distance from the previous church that this does not present a problem as
it provides transportation to their new location. However, new families
moving into the inner-city neighborhood that housed the previous church
may be unaware that the church was once in their community. And if they
become aware of the church's existence they may be reluctant to travel to

a new church that they have never attended, especially if they identify the church's new location to be in close proximity to suburban or upscale communities that are comprised of people who they perceive as unable to relate to them and their circumstances, given that they have lifestyles and material possessions with which they are totally unacquainted. Suffice it to say that African American families who attend churches that were once located in the heart of the inner city and have since relocated to distant sections of the city are often viewed as disingenuous by inner-city African American families when upper-middle-class parishioners return to inner-city neighborhoods to give of themselves in the form of service. In many cases their former neighbors and church members perceive their volunteering in food pantries, tutorial programs, school supply dissemination, and used clothing flea markets as patronizing, for these are services that they provide themselves in their own communities. In the case, however, of workshops on starting small businesses, computer technology training, free tax preparation services, and so forth that many of these more affluent families provide to inner-city African American families under the auspices of the church, while they are needed, it is unlikely that these individuals are perceived as mentors or role models, as their involvement in the inner city is narrowly defined and temporal. This underscores the importance of keeping churches in inner-city communities, which also allows parishioners, including those who have themselves moved to suburban communities, to maintain their affiliation with inner-city churches and to retain the church family with whom their own families have interacted for generations, if they chose to do so. The departure of Black Churches from inner-city communities may also encourage upwardly mobile families, who were comfortable in their communities, to also relocate to reduce their travel distance to the church. In effect, when Black Churches move away from the inner city to remote sections of the city where mass transportation is restricted, taking with them members who make weekly or biweekly trips to inner-city community centers to impart their skills and information, they produce urban missionaries with valuable resources but whose motivation may be viewed as dubious and whose presence is often perceived with skepticism by inner-city residents.

## Dual Cultural Participation

One major factor that can lead to either the success or failure of social and economic programs is the need to develop a working relationship between members of the African American community and those within the larger society. That need can be filled by commissions, which would develop, monitor, and recommend changes in social programs. Because this ongoing relationship between these segments of the population is needed on a local, regional, and national level, such an aggregate would take on a tiered configuration. Mutual understanding and respect for both micro and macro systems is vital to the outcome of social and economic programs. An established body of representatives from government, the private sector, academia, the Black Church, other segments of the African American community, and the population at large is not a novel concept. However, such a group now has a wealth of knowledge on which to draw. This information was virtually unavailable in the 1960s and 1970s when similar associations were formed. However, race, sex, and class inequality has continued to adversely influence the composition of such organizations in the 1980s, 1990s, and the early twenty-first century. The differences in experiences speaks to the problem of racially integrated commissions working together effectively to address long-standing problems facing African American families, as one population experiences privilege while the other is confronted daily with pain. Though there may be a common goal, race is a major difference that often inhibits mutual collaboration unless it is addressed and attitudes, stereotypes, and biases are explored. In so doing white members of such organizations can become sensitized to the effects of race on social interaction and planning as well as policy making that is designed to reduce institutional racial discrimination and its effects on African American families. One factor that would differentiate any future eclectic organization, like the one I have described, is the imperative that they be convened long before the formulation of social policy to explore these and other factors that influence collaborative efforts such as these, including social policies that are produced by these entities. To do otherwise is likely to result in a lack of the ownership and commitment essential for a body charged with overseeing and providing ongoing input into the policies and practices of social and economic programs.

### Synthesizing Cultural Values

The current level of ambiguity and confusion, which exists throughout society, relative to redefining norms and values, is also prevalent throughout the African American community. African American families, like their white counterparts, are also affected by uncertainty surrounding what constitutes acceptable gender-role definitions. The lack of consensus regarding appropriate role behavior for husbands, wives, and children is apparent in efforts to determine which cultural values, normative within the larger society, are beneficial to the upward mobility of African American families.

Historically, African American children were socialized into two cultures, which in some ways were similar, while different in others. Policymakers and others whose views were represented by the normative paradigm insisted that African American families wishing to achieve had to adopt mainstream values and norms. As a consequence, increased numbers of African Americans who gained entrance into societal institutions were expected to discard cultural values and to replace them with those of the majority culture. Moreover, the growing number of schools that underwent desegregation and the increased availability of the electronic media exposed a larger percentage of African Americans to competing socializing agents. On one hand, African American parents and kin emphasized African American cultural values and norms, while schools, employers, and the media transmitted a cultural orientation that often was in direct conflict with that inherent in the African American community. During the 1960s values and norms within the larger society were collectively challenged. Before the culmination of this period of liberalism, African American values and norms were also expected to change. Policymakers and controllers of social institutions were usually included among those who believed it was no longer expedient for African American families to juxtapose their values and norms with those of the majority culture.

It has become apparent that certain values and norms within both cultural systems will increase the level of participation of African American families and their members in the larger society as well as in the African American community. African American families should retain the values that increase their overall levels of functioning without impairing or diminishing effectiveness in either sphere. Since it is not plausible to assume that African American families, or any families, should or could return to a bygone era, what is needed is a synthesis of values, norms, and behaviors that reflect the essentials of both cultures.

If the stability of African American families is to be enhanced and poverty and its concomitants are to be reduced, one of the most important values that must be retained is the African American family's propensity for interdependent relationships. The values of cooperative collectivism must take precedence over those of individualism, regardless of the purported benefits attributed to the latter. The importance of collectivism versus individualism exists not only on a short-term basis but has long-range implications for social and economic progress for African American families. As Harriette McAdoo has noted, unlike majority families, in African American families each successive generation must start anew. Usually African American families are unable to leave their offspring with the financial, material, and other critical resources that are necessary to give youth an edge on ascending the socioeconomic ladder. In order to effect a cultural synthesis in which salient norms, values, and behaviors are merged, the Black Church must serve as the initiator and vehicle for spreading emergent norms and values.

Because the 1960s encouraged the expression of divergent beliefs regarding individual rights versus institutional conformity, individuals can choose between numerous views. Consequently, irrespective of the belief system to which one subscribes or the behaviors that one exhibits, there is usually a segment of the population that will lend its support. This is particularly detrimental to youth, who are in need of specific guidelines for behavior. In addition, the multiplicity of prevailing values and beliefs means there are many role models for youth to emulate. In this regard, the Black Church and other established African American organizations such as the National Urban League and the NAACP must establish prescribed patterns of behavior, norms, and values for African American families and their members. Activities such as these have already been undertaken by the National Urban League in their efforts to reduce out-of-wedlock births among African American adolescents. These measures, along with the increased availability of contraceptives, have reduced teenage pregnancy among African American adolescents. However, out-of-wedlock births increased within the African American population due in part to the dearth of social policies that would increase the number of employment opportunities for African American males facing differential treatment in classrooms, low teacher expectations, and differential discipline based on race, whereby more severe and harsh forms of discipline have continued to be given to African American male students than white male students for the same rule infractions. These negative experiences contribute to the higher school dropout rate for African American males, leaving them with inadequate skills to meet the demands of today's labor market and to enroll in training and educational programs beyond high school that would increase their marketability. The absence of employment plays a major role in out-of-wedlock births, along with employer queue systems that place African Americans in the lowest queues for employment. One cannot ignore media images that encourage African American males, like other males in America, to avoid making commitments and prolong being single. It is also the case that the age group 20–24 is the one in which the largest percentage of women have children out of wedlock. This group, unquestionably, may feel the need to validate their womanhood and to affirm their worth by giving birth to a child, which they perceive as an achievement and the possibility of becoming the wife to the father of their child. However, numbers alone will not afford African American women this opportunity, as there is a genuine sex-ratio imbalance that precludes African American women in the marriageable ages from having an adequate number of African American males available for marriage.

### The African American Media: Bridging the Information Gap

In order for social policy and other social, political, and economic events within the African American community and the larger society to positively affect African American families, there must be a medium that will systematically transmit information to African Americans throughout the country. Over the past 25 years there has been unparalleled growth in computer technology. Used to obtain and exchange information, this is an invaluable vehicle for African Americans to apprise and remain informed of activities, events, ideas, and strategies that are pertinent to their families and communities locally, regionally, and throughout the world. However, a digital divide exists in that there is a significantly smaller number of African American families and their members who own computers and have access to the Internet, which is the avenue or the "highway" through which information is acquired and exchanged. By contrast European American families have disproportionate ownership of computers and information that they make available through paid subscriptions and employer-funded Internet access, an important benefit made available to employees, which many are able to share with their families. Approximately 98 percent of American households own a television, compared to 66 percent of homes that have a computer in the United States. In effect, this digital divide is only lessened in many communities by the availability of computers with Internet access through schools, but for entire families, local libraries are the primary providers of computers. These vital sources of information are seldom affordable by many families in the United States, including a disproportionate number of African American families, who are barely able to meet the basic necessities of life. And for these families television ownership is more likely to be their source of information, and this usually does not include cable television, for which there is a monthly cost that is usually unaffordable for poor families and those with incomes slightly above the poverty line.

Throughout the country, African American–owned and African American–oriented newspapers contain information primarily regarding local or at best regional activities. In many of these publications, information on national activities tends to appear in the form of editorials and commentaries. Although there are regional and national editions for specific African American–oriented newspapers, generally they are not available throughout the country without subscription. For more than 40 years, however, African Americans have relied on *Jet* and *Ebony,* two major African American–oriented magazines, for national news and events. These publications have bridged the information gap for African Americans residing in different regions of the country, informing African Americans of current and historical events and issues affecting the African American community. Many other African American–oriented magazines national in scope have been valuable but could not be sustained. Two magazines that have been contributed to the wealth of knowledge of African Americans, inspiring and motivating African Americans to address economic challenges and explore viable opportunities to create success individually as well as collectively for families, have been *Essence* and *Black Enterprise*. That is not to say that other national African American magazines reaching a sizeable number of Africa American readers have not been viable organs for the dissemination of information that have improved the lives of African Americans. However, *Essence* and *Black Enterprise,* unlike many of the other African American magazines that were geared toward and disseminated to a national readership, have been able to remain viable, overcoming the challenges within the popular magazine publishing industry in general and those that are unique to African American magazine publishers and entrepreneurs in general. Indeed, magazines are still reaching millions of readers on a monthly basis through subscriptions and newsstands. *Essence* magazine was cofounded by Edward Lewis and Clarence O. Smith in 1969 and is designed primarily for African American females. *Essence* is both informative and entertaining and has become one of the leading magazines featuring issues of importance to African American women. It contains articles that examine virtually every situation and issue affecting African American females in the United States, including male-female relationships, fashion, health, beauty, the work environment, parenting, and so forth. *Black Enterprise* was founded by Earl G. Graves Sr., chairman, editor, and publisher, in 1970. Its major focus is on economic issues of particular interest to African Americans, like entrepreneurship, African Americans in corporate environments, building wealth, investment portfolios, workplace issues, and so forth.

It is still the case that there is considerable emphasis placed on relying on the electronic media for information and entertainment, particularly television. Therefore, television remains a preferred medium for the majority of families in the United States. The same holds true for African American families. In fact, studies reflect that a greater percentage of the African American population views television than whites. Certainly, as I indicated earlier, there is a need for several nationally syndicated, African American–oriented television programs to provide news and commentary on social, political, and economic events. While such programs have been broadcast for years, generally they have been available only through cable networks, which are not as accessible as the major networks. In the 1990s, African Americans were provided a national television network, albeit cable, that broadcast and devoted its entire programming to African American–oriented issues and interests. Moreover, several nationally syndicated radio programs also came into existence in the 1990s with programming targeted to the African American community. These media definitely were welcomed and filled a tremendous service void as they transmitted information and news that affected African American families and their members from a local, regional, and national perspective. The call-in feature of many of these programs allowed the exchange of information and ideas as well as strategies that were being implemented by

African American individuals, families, and communities to confront and combat the invidious and horrific institutional forms of racial discrimination throughout the United States. The effectiveness of various endeavors and approaches was discussed.

Many of these programs integrate this informational component into their news broadcasts, while there is one nationally syndicated radio program hosted by Tom Pope that focuses primarily on issues affecting the African American community. This program also provides its listeners with a toll-free number, which permits the audiences, comprised largely of African Americans, throughout the country to discuss individual experiences with community-based and local governmental policies and practices and their impact on African American families and the entire African American community. Much of the information from authors and experts in diverse fields provides knowledge for the purpose of understanding as well as for application. And the momentum for marches and movements to stabilize and empower African American families and the entire African American community is fueled through these new and reliable venues.

It was also the case that BET, the Black Entertainment Network, once owned and operated by Robert Johnson, an African American entrepreneur, presented programming targeted to the African American audience. This programming, while disproportionately containing music videos primarily featuring hip-hop and rap, also included a jazz program, a gospel program, an evening talk show, a talk show addressing issues of concern to African American teenagers, and a Sunday talk show with a moderator and panel comprised largely of journalists who discussed current issues and problems germane to the African American community. Experts from various disciplines were also included in this program to provide an analysis of social, economic, and political issues. This network founded in 1980 eventually reached 71.9 million homes and was sold in 2001 for almost $3 billion to a white-owned transnational conglomerate known as Viacom, leaving the African American community without an African American nationally owned television network of this magnitude. However, Robert Johnson contends that he continues to be involved in the management of the network. Critics indicate concerns over the network's format, citing sparse programming that provides adequate news coverage and talk show programs that address events affecting the African American community, and an overrepresentation of music videos that present degrading visual imagery of African American females. These same complaints began to surface prior to the sale of BET but were attributed to the infantile stage in the development of the network. However, while that rationale was not without merit at that time its validity has substantially diminished given the reported assets of the megacorporation that now owns the network and the sufficient time it has had to become a more viable vehicle for purveying meaningful and relevant information regarding the plethora of issues, policies, and practices affecting African American families and other African American institutions and individuals. Instead, the programming has essentially remained unchanged and continues to allow a significant number of music videos, usually of the rap genre, that perpetuate negative stereotypes regarding African American males, females, and children. Here, the music moguls who own major record companies and control the music industry are responsible for perpetuating these negative cultural images and this stereotypical, racially biased information about African American families and their members. Even though the justification that is provided by artists who either speak or sing these demeaning lyrics is that they are simply presenting the life that they experienced being raised in poverty, there are other experiences that families and their children who live in poverty have that are reflective of traditional African American values, norms, and beliefs like sharing, compassion, spirituality, hard work, kinship and community support networks, and so forth. Why are these experiences omitted and those that portray African American young men as thugs and females as preoccupied with displaying their bodies and engaging in sex the central theme of vocal music and visual images? Moreover, rappers who refer to African American females using gender pejoratives and relate to them in the most degrading manner must be challenged. This skewed version of the life of African American poor families is generalized to all African American families and their members. Moreover, the same stereotypical messages are being perpetuated by the same privileged groups of individuals, as they have done historically, to maintain their image of innocence, stability, responsibility, and moral superiority, while projecting young African American males, females, and children as individuals who possess the exact opposite socially unacceptable attributes of a preoccupation with sex, sexual and financial irresponsibility, and other forms of what is deemed moral turpitude. Because much of this music and music videos is consumed and watched by those outside of the African American community they tend to perpetuate racial tensions among youth and adults, although some youthful supporters of this music purport that this type of music produces racial harmony. Because 60 percent of rap music is purchased by suburban white male teenagers, denigrating stereotypical information and images are damaging to African Americans who will usually work in subordinate positions to those who have been inculcated with these negative, demeaning, and unrepresentative images of African Americans. To believe that these artists have poetic license to say and write any lyrics that they wish is patently false, as was clearly indicated by the recording company's refusal to continue to sell a recording by the rapper Ice-T that included lyrics about killing cops. Therefore, there is little justification for this systematic denigration of African American families, their members, and the entire community of African Americans. It is also the case that economic exploitation is integral to the identification of artists who are willing to use such lyrics, as many tell of enormous hardships that they faced while being reared in poor families. To individuals whose lives have been enmeshed with struggling for day-to-day survival one must ask if they are more vulnerable to being the victims of economic exploitation and willing to use demeaning language, as a necessary compromise to escape the cycle of poverty, when so few legitimate avenues are available. This is particularly true as many of these artists report rising from poverty to unbelievable material privilege. In order to eliminate these demeaning cultural images and damaging, racially biased stereotypes of African American families and their members, African American institutions and organizations must demand that the recording industry replace these negative messages with those that are more positive and representative of African American men, women, children, and families. And since a disproportionate number of the consumers are white youth, African American families, churches, organizations, and associations must use public, private, suburban, and parochial schools to inform those who control these educational systems of the racially insensitive and derogatory nature of this music. It is likely that racially integrated meetings will permit the disclosure to predominantly white school administrators and teachers that they should inform these youthful consumers that many within the African American community find this music, irrespective of the race or ethnicity of the artist, to be culturally offensive and humiliating. These school superintendents should ask for the assistance of white parents, teachers, and administrators to ask their children to refrain from reinforcing the proliferation of these images and information by discontinuing being consumers of this type of racially defamatory music. African American families and institutions must also collectively develop similar methods to encourage greater institutional responsibility throughout the larger society. Such networking will also serve as a conduit for providing valuable information to ameliorate conditions for African American families and others who are marginal to or outside of the economic mainstream.

### Projected Social Policy Initiatives

Many activities necessary to redefine and replace current and previous forms of social welfare policy are already underway. The major problem with welfare reform in the 1980s is that it was extremely fragmented. The federal government's affinity for decentralization has led to states wielding greater influence over social programs. The idea of states having more responsibility for allocating federal funds to, and establishing guidelines for, social welfare services was expanded during the 1990s, as mandated by the 1996 Welfare Reform Act, and maintained in the twenty-first century under the George W. Bush administration.

There are various initiatives that are being undertaken by organizations to address the needs of impoverished families, especially African American families and other families of color who are confronted with the exacerbated effects of poverty, in the twenty-first century, particularly in the areas of housing and health care.

Because affordable housing is an issue of monumental proportions, the housing shortage, in conjunction with housing discrimination practiced by financial institutions, has resulted in a major disparity in home ownership for African American families compared to white families. Although these differences have existed in the past, had liberal social policies, especially fair housing legislation, been effective the disparity between African American and white home ownership may not have reached parity but would have been appreciably reduced by the twenty-first century.

There are essentially two major efforts that have the national goal of increasing home ownership, making it more available and affordable to African American, Hispanic, and other economically disadvantaged families. These two initiatives are being undertaken by the Fannie Mae Corporation and Habitat for Humanity International.

The Fannie Mae Corporation, a Fortune 500 company whose chairman and CEO is Franklin D. Raines, an African American, has established a program called the American Dream Commitment. The major component of this national program involves a collaborative effort with the public and private sectors to achieve a national goal of creating 4.6 million new home owners of color by 2009. Fannie Mae is making a $700 billion dollar investment available to an estimated 5 million households containing families of color. It should be noted that Fannie Mae has already demonstrated a commitment to eliminate racial disparities in home ownership in that their home financing to this population rose from $16.4 billion dollars in 1993 to $49.3 billion in 2001.

In this particular program, home ownership for African American families and other families of color is likely to increase due to flexible mortgage products that Fannie Mae and its partners are offering, such as contributions of as little as $500 dollars from the borrower toward closing costs and flexible qualifying guidelines that consider alternative sources of income such as part-time employment.

In addition, Habitat for Humanity International (HFHI) hopes to eliminate substandard housing and increase affordable housing to local communities through its program known as the Twenty-First Century Challenge. Their overall mission is to eliminate substandard housing and homelessness by building homes that are affordable and energy and resource efficient. They intend to sell homes to families who are ineligible for conventional financing. Their mortgages will be financed with no interest over a 20–30 year period. Prospective home owners are expected to make a $500 downpayment and contribute 300 hours of sweat equity toward the construction of their home and other homes, which must be completed in one year. Mortgage payments on completed homes range from $175 to $265 per month. These payments are reinvested to finance the further construction and acquisition of additional properties and building materials.

Another serious problem facing African American families is the existence of a dual health-care delivery system, one that provides health care only to individuals and family members who have private or employer-sponsored insurance or who have the financial capability of paying for their own health and medical care. Secondly, there is a capricious health-care delivery system that provides medical care primarily through public clinics and county hospitals. It is also the case that uninsured lower-income patients may seek and receive care at privately owned hospitals if they are experiencing a medical emergency, which legally obligates the hospital to treat the patient, or the hospital can elect to treat the patient if a nonmedical emergency exists. For many poor and working poor families homeopathic remedies are the norm rather than the exception as they rarely have monies available for medical care and medications needed to treat chronic and acute medical conditions. Clearly this is a fast-growing population due to the1996 Welfare Reform Act that resulted in many families losing their health coverage provided by Medicaid. Consequently, there is a rapid growth in and expansion of free health clinics throughout the United States. Many of these programs were established during the era of liberal social policy in the 1960s and 1970s and have now begun to attract large numbers of volunteers including physicians, nurses, dentists, social workers, lab technicians, and so forth. Some of these health clinics because of the HIV/AIDS medical problem also have syringe exchange programs.

There are also more mobile units providing prenatal care and mammographies. Moreover, the Black Church has been in the vanguard of providing annual health fairs that include blood pressure screenings and diabetes testing, because of the high percentages of African Americans with hypertension and Type II diabetes, along with other diagnostic services.

It is still the case that these noteworthy efforts are not sufficient to address the structural conditions that lead to the chronic socially and economically depressed status of African American families that are manifested in the stereotypical labels, denigrating cultural images and language, and racial, sex, and class inequality that is woven in the very fabric of American institutions. The fact that a major disparity exists between a small group of families and their members who are and have continued to monopolize societal resources is at the root of the problem. The fact that they use social policies and legislation to maintain their positions of privilege and use race, sex, class, and other superficial qualities to exploit and exclude families, particularly African American families, is becoming widely accepted. Their control of the media is no longer sustaining their veneer of innocence and the greed and avarice that serve as the motivating factors to ensure that social policies are formulated and implemented in their interests to perpetuate their positions of privilege. They have been quite successful, however, in influencing policies whether liberal, conservative, or centrists also known as neoliberalism (again a synonym for conservatism) that effectively result in institutions preserving their power and privilege while simultaneously perpetuating the poverty and continuum of privileges dispersed to families in other strata. Recognizing that classes are more likely since the past 25 years to reproduce themselves, it is quite apparent that African American families must continue to challenge and expose irregularities and inconsistencies, as meaningful change cannot happen at the local level or because of any one specific program.

The success of any one program is inextricably related to the effectiveness of national social and economic programs. Given that regional differences exist in the level of support that states allocate to social welfare services, the problem of poverty and its prevalence among African American families requires national attention. One state may put forth more effort to alleviate poverty among its residents, while another may choose to allocate less to economically disadvantaged families.

Clearly, social policy must assume a multifaceted approach to eradicate the social problems poor and African American families encounter. However, past methods have been relatively ineffective in reducing poverty or alleviating racial discrimination. Moreover, the failure of African American families to become economically independent can be attributed to the absence of a sound social policy void of political interests.

## CONCLUSION

A definite relationship exists between social policy and family structure. Given the dynamics and structures of institutions within the African American community and the erroneous assumptions that have given rise to both conservative or centrist and liberal social policy, it is no surprise that the response of policymakers in the 1960s was designed to offer a proactive institutional response for replacing systems considered weak and ineffective with systems perceived as more efficacious. Not only has liberal social policy failed to bring about social equity, it has served as the impetus for the decline of salient African American structures. Included among African American institutions that have shown signs of strain and erosion are African American two-parent families, extended families, African American–controlled educational institutions, and African American–owned businesses. The return to conservative policy in the 1980s has resulted in the resurgence of extended families, an increase in individuals with no familial structures, and the failure to abate the increase in the rate of African American family breakups. Moreover, after the initial efforts of liberal social policy began to erode African American families, the more conservative social policies of the 1980s only added to these problems as the few social and economic gains that were registered by African American families were rescinded, and by the 1990s and continuing in the twenty-first century an assault from many positions has been and continues to be targeted at African American families and their members. Because these assaults transcend social-class lines, one would anticipate that they would result in a concerted effort to resist and develop and share strategies to overcome these overt and covert institutional bombardments. In many ways this is occurring, but again, there must be more venues for the exchange of information detailing the methods that are being used by African American families, institutions, and individuals to deal with the reactionary forms of racism that have been mounting over the past 25 years. And the bifurcation of the African American community must continue to be addressed to prevent the future loss of human capital and sense of community or consciousness-of-kind that revitalizes unity and provides the energy and motivation necessary to combat the kinds of social policies that are capable of enriching those who are already privileged at the expense of exploiting those who are already socially and economically disadvantaged.

I conclude that neither conservative nor liberal social policy as formulated and enacted in the United States has offered substantial or sustained benefits for African American families. However, as in the case of liberal social policy, conservative social policy is not without some benefits. For example, conservative social policy in the 1980s has served to revitalize African American institutions, which are essential for African American progress. However, to the extent that conservative social policy has merit, it is not because of intent but effect. Analyzing the effects of liberal social policy on African American families was important to understanding its mystifying and enigmatic nature. The fact that liberal social policy contributed to many adverse changes that were overshadowed by modest gains is reason for concern. During the 1990s, with its continued conservatism known as centrism, much of the myths and the illusions were dispelled. And the twenty-first century has yet to produce any significant social policies to increase African American families' opportunities for equality in the social, economic, and political systems in the United States. In the case of conservatism or centrism, its effects on African American families, in terms of institutional exclusivity and rigidity, are overt. However, the unforeseen and subtle consequences of liberal social policy have an effect that is also devastating to the stability of African American families.

What we have gained from these experiences is a better understanding of the impact social and economic forces have on African American families and their members. Moreover, African American intellectuals, politicians, administrators, and leaders are more keenly aware of the measures that must be taken by the African American community and those that government and the private sector must take to bring about positive changes for African American families. There is little doubt that the wealth of knowledge gained over the past 30 years will have an indelible influence on the relationships between African American institutions, government, and the private sector.

Despite the dire social and economic conditions in the 1980s, 1990s, and the twenty-first century and the failure of liberal social policy (considered a bastion of hope by many), African Americans continue to strive to identify and develop means to strengthen the family and other institutions, demonstrating that African American families have the will to survive. Indeed, African American families, historically, have never occupied a position of passivity, but have been active agents influencing social policy to bring about change. Nevertheless, the extent to which African American families are able to survive and progress, not to mention to reach social and economic parity with white families in America, will not be determined by their efforts alone but will come through a national social policy that reflects a total commitment on the part of the African American community, the federal government, and the private sector that is initiated within the African American community. This must be demanded by African American families and institutions, as they develop alternative strategies to insist on redress for past injustices and to prevent future forms of racial, sex, and class discrimination. Moreover, African American families must develop and identify existing venues for successful strategies for obtaining remedies for ongoing institutional racial, sex, and class inequality. Finally, African American families must socialize their children to understand the overt and covert methods by which mainstream institutions are structured to reproduce social classes, yet provide them with viable strategies to render these discriminatory institutional policies and practices ineffective.

## NOTES

1. Robert Hill, "The 80's: What's Ahead for Blacks?" *Ebony*, January 1980, pp. 27–36.

2. Dennys Vaughn-Cooke, "The Economic Status of Black America—Is There a Recovery?" in *The State of Black America* (Washington, D.C.: National Urban League, 1984), p. 10.

3. Andrew Hacker, *Two Nations: Black, White, Separate, Hostile, Unequal* (New York: Ballantine Books, 1995).

4. Ibid., p. 13.

5. Susan M. George and Bette J. Dickerson, "The Role of the Grandmother in Poor Single-Mother Families and Households," in *African American Single Mothers: Understanding Their Lives and Families,* ed. Bette J. Dickerson (Thousand Oaks, Calif.: Sage Publications, 1997), p. 149.

6. Harriette Pipes McAdoo, "Upward Mobility Across Generations in African American Families," in *Black Families,* 3rd ed., ed. Harriette Pipes McAddoo (Thousand Oaks, Calif.: Sage Publications, 1997), pp.139–162.

7. Michael T. Hannan and Nancy Brandon Tuma, "Income and Marital Events: Evidence from an Income Maintenance Experiment," *American Journal of Sociology* 82 (May 1977): 1186–1211.

8. Joyce P. Jacobsen and Laurence M. Levin, "Looking at the Glass Ceiling: Do White Men Receive Higher Returns to Tenure and Experience?" in *Prosperity for All?* ed. Robert Cherry and William M. Rodgers (New York: Russell Sage Foundation, 2000), p. 217.

9. Randall Robinson, *The Debt: What America Owes to Blacks* (New York: Dutton, 2000), p. 8.

10. Mark Zepezauer and Arthur Naiman, *Take the Rich Off Welfare* (Tucson, Ariz.: Odonian Press, 1996), pp. 38–50.

11. Marita Golden, "White Women at Work," *Essence,* page 198; Ella L. J. Edmondson Bell and Stella M. Nkomo, *Our Separate Ways: Black and White Women Struggle for Professional Identity* ( Boston: Harvard Business School Press, 2001), pp. 137–158.

12. McAdoo, "Upward Mobility," pp. 139–162.

13. Evelyn Brooks Higginbotham, *Righteous Discontent: The Women's Movement in the Black Baptist Church, 1880–1920* (Cambridge, Mass.: Harvard University Press, 1993), pp. 68–69.

14. Marcia L. Dyson, "The Houses of Worship Our Mothers Built," *Essence,* May 2002, p. 232.

15. Dyson, "Houses," 2002.

16. Steve Stephens, "It Was a Day of Atonement in Local Churches As Well," *Columbus Dispatch,* 17 October 1995, p. 5B; and Lornet Turnbull, "Women Moved by Journey," *Columbus Dispatch,* 26 October 1997, p. 1A.

17. Robinson, *The Debt.*

18. Cheryl Townsend Gilkes, "Plenty of Room in a Changing Black Church," in *One Nation Under God? Religion and American Culture,* ed. Margie Garber and Rebecca L. Walkowitz (New York: Routledge, 1999), pp. 163–164; "The New Mega Churches," *Ebony,* December 2001, pp. 148–160.

# Bibliography

Aguire, Alberto, Jr., and David Baker. *Race, Racism and the Death Penalty in the United States*. Barren Springs, Mo.: Vende Vere Publishing Ltd., 1991.

Akbar, Na'im. "Our Destiny: Authors of a Scientific Revolution." In *Black Children*, edited by Harriette McAdoo and John McAdoo, pp. 17–20. Beverly Hills, Calif.: Sage Publications, 1985.

Aldous, Joan. "Wives' Employment Status and Lower-Class Men as Husbands-Fathers: Support for the Moynihan Thesis." *Journal of Marriage and the Family* 31, no. 3 (1969): 469–476.

Alexander, Bill. "The Black Church and Community Empowerment." In *On the Road to Economic Freedom: An Agenda for Black Progress*, edited by Robert L. Woodson, pp. 45–69. Washington, D C.: National Center for Neighborhood Enterprise, 1987.

Alexander, Chauncey A., and David N. Weber. "Social Welfare: Historical Dates." *Encyclopedia of Social Work* 17 (1977): 1497–1503.

"America's Underclass, Broken Lives: A Nation Apart." *U.S. News and World Report*, 17 March 1986, pp. 18–21.

Andersen, Margaret L., and Patricia Hill Collins, eds. *Race, Class and Gender*, 2nd ed. Belmont, Calif.: Wadsworth Press, 1998.

Anderson, Martin. *Welfare*. Stanford, Calif.: Hoover Press, 1978.

Anderson, Talmadge. "Black Enterpreneurship and Concepts Toward Economic Coexistence." *Western Journal of Black Studies* 6, no. 2 (summer 1982): 80–88.

Austin, Richard. "Under the Veil of Suspicion: Organizing Resistance and Struggling for Liberation." In *Police Brutality*, edited by Jill Nelson, pp. 206–209. New York: W. W. Norton and Co., 2000).

Axinn, June, and Levin, Herman. *Social Welfare*. New York: Dodd, Mead and Co., 1975.

Bahr, Stephen. "The Effects of Welfare on Marital Stability and Remarriage." *Journal of Marriage and the Family* 41 (August 1979): 553–650.

Bane, Mary Jo. *Economic Influence on Divorce and Remarriage.* Cambridge, Mass.: Center for the Study of Public Policy, 1975.

Barol, Bill. "The Eighties Are Over." *Newsweek,* 4 January 1988, pp. 40–48.

Beck, Allen J., and Paige M. Harrison. *Prisons in 2000.* Washington, D.C.: U.S. Department of Justice, 2001.

Bell, Carolyn. *The Economics of the Ghetto.* New York: Pegasus, 1970.

Bell, Derrick A., Jr. *Race, Racism and American Law.* Boston: Little, Brown, 1980.

Bell, Ella L. J. Edmondson, and Stella M. Nkomo. *Our Separate Ways: Black and White Women and the Struggle for Professional Identity.* Boston: Harvard Business School Press, 2001.

Berlage, Gai, and William Egelman. *Experience with Sociology.* Reading, Mass.: Addison-Wesley, 1983.

Berry, Mary Francis, and John Blassingame. *Long Memory: The Black Experience in America.* New York: Oxford University Press, 1982.

Billingsley, Andrew. *Black Families in White America.* Englewood Cliffs, N.J.: Prentice-Hall, 1968.

———. *Climbing Jacob's Ladder: The Enduring Legacies of African American Families.* New York: Simon & Schuster, 1992.

Billingsley, Andrew, and Amy Billingsley. "Negro Family Life in America." *Social Service Review* 39 (September 1965): 310–319.

Billingsley, Andrew, and Jeanne M. Giovannoni. *Children of the Storm: Black Children and American Child Welfare.* New York: Harcourt Brace Jovanovich, 1972.

"Blacks Get Less Aggressive Heart Attack Care, Study Finds." *Columbus Dispatch,* 10 May 2001, p. 12A.

Blackwell, James E. "Persistence and Change in Intergroup Relations: The Crisis upon Us." *Social Problems* 29, no. 4 (1982): 325–346.

Blakeslee, Sandra. "Poor and Black Patients Slighted Study Says." *New York Times,* 20 April 20 1994, p. B9.

Blassingame, John W. *The Slave Community.* New York: Oxford University Press, 1972.

Boykin, Wade A. "The Academic Performance of Afro-American Children," in *Achievement and Achievement Motives,* edited by Janet T. Spence, pp. 324–371. San Francisco: W. H. Freeman and Co., 1983.

Boykin, Wade A., and Brenda A. Allen. "Enhancing African American Children's Learning and Motivation: Evolution of the Verve and Movement Expressiveness Paradigms." In *African American Children, Youth, and Parenting,* edited by Reginald L. Jones, p. 115–162. Hampton, Va.: Cobb and Henry Publishers, 1999).

Boykin, Wade A., and Forrest D. Toms. "Black Child Socialization: A Conceptual Framework." In *Black Children: Social, Educational and Parental Environments,* edited by Harriette McAdoo and John McAdoo, pp. 33–51. Beverly Hills, Calif.: Sage Publications, 1985.

Caplow, Theodore. *Elementary Sociology.* Englewood Cliffs, N.J.: Prentice-Hall, 1971.

Chambliss, William. "The Saints and the Roughnecks." *Society* 2 (1973): 24–31.

"City May Order Housing for Poor." *Columbus Dispatch,* 28 March 1986, p. 1.

Cobb, Sidney. "Social Support as a Moderator of Life Stress." *Psychosomatic Medicine* 38 (1976): 300–314.

Coleman, Milton. "Reagan's 'Rising Tide' Is Sinking Blacks." *National Leader*, February 1984, p. 1.

Compton, Beulah Roberts. *Introduction to Social Welfare and Social Work*. Homewood, Ill.: 1980.

Cooke-Vaughn, Dennys. "The Economic Status of Black America—Is There a Recovery?" In *The State of Black America*. Washington, D.C.: National Urban League, 1984.

"Court to Congress: You Cut Budget." *USA Today*, 8 July 1986, p. 1.

Covington, Jeanette. "Round Up the Usual Suspects: Racial Profiling and the War on Drugs." In *Petit Apartheid in the U.S. Criminal Justice System: The Dark Figure of Racism*, edited by Dragan Milovanovic and Katheryn K. Russell. Durham, N.C.: Carolina Academic Press, 2001.

Crews, Douglas E., and James R. Bindon. "Ethnicity as a Taxonomic Tool in Biomedical and Biosocial Research." *Introduction to Clinical Medicine: Medical Humanities Anthology* (2001): 353–359.

Crosby, Faye, and Cheryl Van Deveer, eds. *Sex, Race and Merit*. Ann Arbor: University of Michigan Press, 2000.

Cross, Theodore. *The Black Power Imperative*. New York: Faulkner Books, 1984.

Cutler, D. M., E. S. Glaser, and J. L. Vigdor, "The Rise and Decline of the American Ghetto." *Journal of Political Economy* 107 (1999): 455.

Darity, William A., Jr., and Samuel L. Myers Jr. "Does Welfare Dependency Cause Female Headship? The Case of the Black Family," *Journal of Marriage and the Family* 46 (November 1984): 766–767.

———. "The Impact of Labor Market Prospects on Incarceration Rates." In *Prosperity For All?* edited by Robert Cherry and William Rodgers, New York: Russell Sage Foundation, 2000.

Darity, William A., Jr., and Samuel L. Myers Jr. with Emmett D. Carson and William Sabol. *The Black Underclass: Critical Essays on Race and Unwantedness*. New York: Garland Publishing Co., 1994.

DiMatteo, M. R., and R. Hays. "Social Support and Serious Illness." In *Social Networks and Social Support*, edited by Benjamin Gottlieb. Beverly Hills, Calif.: Sage Publications, 1981.

Drake, Clayton S. "The Social and Economic Status of the Negro in the United States." In *The Negro American*, edited by Talcott Parsons and Kenneth B. Clark. Boston: Beacon, 1965.

Du Bois, W.E.B. "The Function of the Negro Church." In *The Black Church in America*, edited by Hart M. Nelsen, Raytha L. Yokley, and Anne K. Nelsen, pp. 77–81. New York: Basic Books, 1971.

———. *The Souls of Black Folks*. London: Longsman Green, 1965.

Duncan, Greg J., and Saul D. Hoffman. "A Reconsideration of the Economic Consequences of Marital Disruption." *Demography* 22 (November 1985): 493–495.

Durose, Matthew R., and Patrick A. Langan. *Bureau of Justice Statistics, State Court Sentencing of Convicted Felons, 1998. Statistical Tables*. Washington, D.C.: U.S. Department of Justice, 2001.

Dyson, Marcia L. "The Houses of Worship Our Mothers Built." *Essence,* May 2002, p. 232.

"Economically Disadvantaged Make Up Bulk of Fiscal '76 Title I Clients." *Manpower Information Service* 8, no. 1 (September 1976): 8–9, 23–24.

Edelman, Marian Wright. "'The Sea Is So Wide and My Boat Is So Small': Problems Facing Black Children Today." In *Black Children,* edited by Hariette McAdoo and John McAdoo, pp. 72–82. Beverly Hills, Calif.: Sage Publications, 1985.

Ehrenreich, Barbara, and Karin Stallard. "The Nouveau Poor." *Ms.* 11 (August 1982): 217–224.

Elkins, Stanley. *Slavery: A Problem in American Institutional and Intellectual Life.* New York: Grosset & Dunlap, 1963.

Emerson, Richard M. "Power-Dependence Relations." *American Sociological Review* 27 (1962): 31–41.

"Employment and Training Reporter: 1982 Employment and Training Report to the President: Selected Tables." Washington, D.C.: The Bureau of National Affairs, August 23, 1982.

Evans, William L. *Race, Fear and Housing in a Typical American Community.* New York: National Urban League, 1946.

Feshbach, Muriel. "Dynamics in the AFDC Caseload 1967–Present." Washington, D.C.: Department of Health and Human Services, 1982 (unpublished report).

Fischer, Ann, Joseph Beasley, and Carl Harter. "The Occurrence of the Extended Family of Procreation: A Developmental Approach to Negro Family Structure." *Journal of Marriage and the Family* 30 (May 1968): 291–300.

Fleming, Jacqueline. *Blacks in College: A Comparative Study of Students' Success in Black and White Institutions.* San Francisco: Jossey-Bass, 1984.

Franklin, Anderson J., Nancy Boyd-Franklin, and Charlene V. Draper. "A Psychological and Educational Perspective on Blacking Parenting." In *Black Children: Social, Educational, and Parental Environments* (2nd ed.), edited by Harriette Pipes McAdoo. Thousand Oaks, Calif.: Sage Publications, 2002.

Franklin, Donna. *Ensuring Inequality: The Structural Transformation of the African-American Family.* New York: Oxford University Press, 1997.

Franklin, John Hope. *From Slavery to Freedom: A History of American Negroes.* New York: Alfred A. Knopf, 1948.

Frazier, E. Franklin. *The Free Negro Family.* Nashville: Fisk University Press, 1932.

———. *The Negro Family in Chicago.* Chicago: University of Chicago Press, 1932.

———. *The Negro Family in the United States.* Chicago: University of Chicago Press, 1939.

Furstenberg, Frank, Theodore Hershberg, and John Modell. "The Origin of the Female-Headed Black Family: The Impact of the Urban Experience." *Journal of Interdisciplinary History* 5 (spring 1975): 211–233.

Gans, Herbert, Jr. *The War against the Poor: The Underclass and Antipoverty Policy.* New York: Basic Books, 1995.

George, Susan M., and Bette J. Dickerson, "The Role of the Grandmother in Poor Single-Mother Families and Households." In *African American Single Mothers: Understanding Their Lives and Families,* edited by Bette J. Dickerson. Thousand Oaks, Calif.: Sage Publications, 1997.

Georges-Abeyie, Daniel. "Criminal Justice Processing of Non-White Minorities." In *Racism, Empiricism and Criminal Justice,* edited by Brian D. MacLean and Dragan Milovanovic. Vancouver: Collective Press, 1990.

Gilder, George. *Wealth and Poverty.* New York: Basic Books, 1981.

Gilkes, Cheryl Townsend. *If It Wasn't for the Women.* Maryknoll, New York: Orbis Books, 2001.

Gilkes, Cheryl Townsend. "Plenty of Room in a Changing Black Church." In *One Nation under God? Religion and American Culture,* edited by Marjorie Garber and Rebecca L. Walkowitz. New York: Routledge, 1999.

Glasgow, Douglas G. *The Black Underclass.* San Francisco: Jossey-Bass, 1980.

Gouldner, Alvin Ward. "The Norm of Reciprocity: A Preliminary Statement." *American Sociological Review* 25 (1960): 161–178.

Graham. Wilson K. "The Clinton Administration and Interest Groups." In *The Clinton Presidency First Appraisals,* edited by Colin Campbell and Bert A. Rockman. Chatham, N.J.: Chatham House Publishers, 1996.

Gray, Katti. "Take a Stand: Flying While Black." *Essence,* February 2001.

Gner, William, and Price Cobbs. *Black Rage.* New York: Bantam Books, 1968.

Gurin, Gerald, Joseph Veroff, and Sheila Feld. *Americans View Their Mental Health.* New York: Basic Books, 1960.

Gutman, Herbert. *The Black Family in Slavery and Freedom, 1750–1925.* New York: Pantheon Books, 1976.

Guzzardi, Walter, Jr. "Who Will Care for the Poor?" *Fortune,* February 1982, pp. 34–42.

Hacker, Andrew. *Money: Who Has How Much and Why?* New York: Scribner's, 1997.

———. *Two Nations: Black, White, Separate, Hostile, Unequal.* New York: Ballantine Books, 1995.

Hale, Janice E. *Learning while Black: Creating Educational Excellence for African American Children.* Baltimore: Johns Hopkins University Press, 2001.

Hall, Marcia L., and Walter R. Allen. "Race Consciousness among African American College Students." In *Black Students: Psychological Issues and Academic Achievement,* edited by Gordon LaVern Berry and Joy Keiko Asamen, pp. 174–176. Newbury Park, Calif.: Sage Publications, 1989.

Hamilton, Dona Cooper, and Charles V. Hamilton. *The Dual Agenda: Race and Social Welfare Policies of Civil Rights Organizations.* New York: Columbia University Press, 1997.

Hampton, Robert L. "Institutional Decimation, Marital Exchange, and Disruption in Black Families." *Western Journal of Black Studies* 4 (summer 1980): 134–135.

Handel, Gerald. *Social Welfare in Western Society.* New York: Random House, 1982.

Hannan, Michael T., and Nancy Brandon Tuma. "Income and Marital Events: Evidence from an Income Maintenance Experiment." *American Journal of Sociology* 82 (May 1977): 1186–1211.

Hare, Nathan. "The Frustrated Masculinity of the Negro Male." *Negro Digest,* August 1964, pp. 5–9.

Hare, Nathan, and Julia Hare. "Black Women, 1970." *Transaction,* November 1970, pp. 66–67.

Hayes, Floyd W. "The Political Economy, Reagonomics, and Blacks." *Western Journal of Black Studies* 6 (1982): 90.

Herrnstein, Richard J., and Charles Murray. *The Bell Curve*. New York: Free Press, 1994.

Herskovits, Melville. *The Myth of the Negro Past*. Boston: Beacon, 1970.

Higginbotham, Evelyn Brooks. *Righteous Discontent: The Women's Movement in the Black Baptist Church, 1880–1920*. Cambridge, Mass.: Harvard University Press, 1993.

Hill, Robert. "The Black Family: Building on Strengths." In *On the Road to Economic Freedom: An Agenda for Black Progress*, edited by Robert L. Woodson, pp. 71–92. Washington, D.C.: National Center for Neighborhood Enterprise, 1987.

———. "Economic Forces, Structural Discrimination, and Black Family Instability," in *Black Families*, edited by Harold E. Cheatham and James B. Stewart, pp. 87–105. New Brunswick, N.J.: Transaction Publishers, 1997.

———. *Economic Policies and Black Progress: Myths and Realities*. Washington, D.C.: National Urban League, 1981.

———. "The 80's: What's Ahead for Blacks?" *Ebony*, January 1980, pp. 27–36.

———. *The Impact of AFDC-UP on Black Families: Report for the Black Family Resource Center*. Baltimore: Baltimore Urban League, 1987.

———. "Self-Help Groups in the African-American Community: Current Organization and Service." University of North Carolina School of Social Work, University of North Carolina at Chapel Hill. Unpublished paper.

———. *The Strengths of Black Families*. New York: Emerson Hall, 1972.

Honig, Marjorie. "AFDC Income, Recipient Rates, and Family Dissolution." *Journal of Human Resources 9* (summer 1974): 302–322.

Hoover, Theressa. "Black Women and the Churches: Triple Jeopardy." In *Sexist Religion and Women in the Church*, edited by Alice Hagemen, pp. 63–76. New York: Association Press, 1974.

Hopkins, Thomas J. "The Role of Community Agencies as Viewed by Black Fathers." *Journal of Orthopsychiatry* 42 (1972): 508–516.

Jacobsen, Joyce P., and Laurence M. Levin, "Looking at the Glass Ceiling: Do White Men Receive Higher Returns to Tenure and Experience?" In *Prosperity for All?* edited by Robert Cherry and William M. Rodgers. New York: Russell Sage Foundation, 2000.

Jencks, Christopher. "Divorced Mothers, Unite!" *Psychology Today* 16 (November, 1982): 73.

Jenkins, Louis E. "The Black Family and Academic Achievement." In *Black Students: Psychological Issues and Academic Achievement*, edited by Gordon LaVern Berry and Joy Keiko Asamen, pp. 138–152. Newbury Park, Calif.: Sage Publications, 1989,

Jensen, Arthur R. "How Much Can We Boost I.Q. and Scholastic Achievement?" *Harvard Educational Review* 39, no. 1 (1969):123.

Jewell, K. Sue. "An Analysis of the Visual Development of a Stereotype: The Media's Portrayal of Mammy and Aunt Jemima as Symbols of Black Womanhood," Dissertation. Ohio State University, 1976.

———. "Black Male/Female Conflict: Internalization of Negative Definitions Transmitted Through Imagery." *Western Journal of Black Studies* 7 (spring 1983): 43–48.

———. "The Changing Character of Black Families: The Effects of Differential Social and Economic Gains." *Journal of Social and Behavioral Sciences* 33 (1988): 143–154.

―――. *From Mammy to Miss America and Beyond: Cultural Images and the Shaping of U.S. Social Policy.* London: Routledge, 1993.

―――. "Use of Social Welfare Programs and the Disintegration of the Black Nuclear Family." *Western Journal of Black Studies* 8 (winter 1984): 192–198.

―――. "Will the Real Black, Afro-American, Mixed, Colored, Negro Please Stand Up? Impact of the Black Social Movement, Twenty Years Later." *Journal of Black Studies* 16 (September 1985): 57–75.

Joe, Tom, and Cheryl Rogers. *By the Few for the Few: The Reagan Welfare Legacy.* Lexington, Mass.: Lexington Books, 1986.

Joe, Tom, and Peter Yu. *The "Flip" Side of Black Families Headed by Women: The Economic Status of Black Men.* Washington, D.C.: Center for the Study of Social Policy, 1984.

Johnson, Dirk. "A Leap of Fate." *Newsweek,* 20 January 2003, p. 34.

Johnson, Wayne. *The Social Services: An Introduction.* Itasca, Ill.: F. E. Peacock Publishers, 1982.

Jones, Reginald. *African American Children, Youth, and Parenting.* Hampton, Va.: Cobb and Henry Publishers, 1999.

Kantrowitz, Barbara, and Pat Wingert. "What's at Stake." *Newsweek,* 27 January 2003.

Katz, Michael B. *Improving Poor People.* Princeton, N.J.: Princeton University Press, 1995.

Kendall, Diana. *Sociology in Our Times,* 2nd ed. Belmont, Calif.: Wadsworth Press, 2000.

*Killing with Prejudice: Race and the Death Penalty in the U.S.A.* New York: Amnesty International U.S.A., 1999.

Klinkner, Philip A. "Bill Clinton and the Politics of the New Liberalism." In *Without Justice for All: The New Liberalism and Our Retreat from Racial Equality,* edited by Adolph Reed Jr. Boulder, Colo.: Westview Press, 1999.

Kornblum, William, and Joseph Julian. *A Custom Edition of Social Problems,* 2nd ed. Englewood Cliffs, N.J.: Prentice-Hall, 1998.

Kozol, Jonathan. *Savage Inequalities: Children in America's Schools.* New York: Crown Publishers, 1991.

Kramer, Morton, and Nolan Zane. "Projected Needs for Mental Health Services." In *The Pluralistic Society: A Community Mental Health Perspective,* edited by Stanley Sue and Thom Moore, pp. 47–76. New York: Human Sciences Press, 1984.

Kunjufu, Jawanza. *Countering the Conspiracy to Destroy Black Boys.* Chicago: African American Images, 1995.

Laham, Nicholas. *The Reagan Presidency and the Politics of Race: Pursuit of Colorblind Justice and Limited Government.* Westport, Conn.: Praeger, 1998.

"Landmark Study Finds Capital Punishment System Fraught with Error. *Columbia (New York) News,* 16 June 2002, p. 1.

Landry, Bart. *Black Working Wives: Pioneers of the American Family Revolution.* Los Angeles: University of California Press, 2000.

Landry, Bart. *The New Black Middle Class.* Berkeley: University of California Press, 1987.

Landsburgh, Therese W. "Child Welfare: Day Care of Children." *Encyclopedia of Social Work,* 17th ed. Washington, D.C.: National Association of Social Workers, 1977.

Leavy, Walter. "Is the Black Male an Endangered Species?" *Ebony*, June 1983, pp. 41–46.

Lefley, Harriet P., and Evalina W. Bestman. "Community Mental Health and Minorities: A Multi-Ethnic Approach." In *The Pluralistic Society: A Community Mental Health Perspective*, edited by Stanley Sue and Thom Moore, pp. 116–148. New York: Human Sciences Press, 1984.

Leibow, Elliot. *Tally's Corner*. Boston: Little, Brown, 1966.

Levitan, Sar A., and Clifford M. Johnson. *Beyond the Safety Net: Reviving the Promise of Opportunity in America*. Cambridge, Mass.: Ballinger Publishing Company, 1984.

Levy, Leo, and Louis Rowitz. *The Ecology of Mental Disorders*. New York: Behavioral Publications, 1973.

Lewis, Oscar. *The Study of Slum Cultures*. New York: Random House, 1968.

"Life Below the Poverty Line." *Newsweek*, 5 April 1982, p. 25.

Lincoln, C. Eric. "Black Studies and Cultural Continuity." *Black Scholar* (October 1978): 12–18.

MacDonald, J. Fred. *Blacks and White T.V.: Afro-Americans in Television Since 1948*. Chicago: Nelson-Hall, 1983.

Maguire, Lambert. *Understanding Social Networks*. Beverly Hills, Calif.: Sage Publications, 1983.

Mann, Coramae Richey. *Unequal Justice: A Question of Color*. Bloomington: Indiana University Press, 1993.

Manns, Wilhelmina. "Supportive Roles of Significant Others in African American Families." In *Black Families*, 3rd ed., edited by Harriette Pipes McAdoo, pp. 198–213. Thousand Oaks, Calif.: Sage Publications, 1997.

Martin, Thad. "The Black Church: Precinct of the Black Soul." *Ebony*, August 1984, pp. 154–158.

Massaquoi, Hans J. "The New Racism." *Ebony* 51, no. 10 (August 1996): 56–60.

McAdoo, Harriette Pipes. "Black Mothers and the Extended Family Support Network." In *The Black Woman*, edited by La Frances Rodgers-Rose, pp. 125–144. Beverly Hills, Calif.: Sage Publications, 1982.

————. "Patterns of Upward Mobility in Black Families." In *Black Families*, edited by Harriette Pipes McAdoo. Beverly Hills, Calif.: Sage Publications, 1981.

McCray, Carrie Allen. "The Black Woman and Family Roles." In *The Black Woman*, edited by La Frances Rodgers-Rose, pp. 67–78. Beverly Hills, Calif.: Sage Publications, 1982.

McElvaine, Robert. *The Great Depression: America, 1929–1941*. New York: Times Books, 1984.

McGhee, James D. "The Black Family Today and Tomorrow." In *The State of Black America*, pp. 1–15. New York: National Urban League, 1985.

Mead, Lawrence. *Beyond Entitlement*. New York: Free Press, 1986.

Meeks, Kenneth. *Driving while Black: What to Do if You Are a Victim of Racial Profiling*. New York: Broadway Books, 2000.

Meriwether, Louise. "Teenage Pregnancy." *Essence*, April 1984, p. 96.

Merton, Robert K. "The Unanticipated Consequences of Purposive Social Action." *American Sociological Review* 1 (1936): 894–904.

Miller, Seymour Michael. "The American Lower Classes: A Typological Approach." In *Blue Collar World*, edited by Arthur B. Shostak and William Gomberg. Englewood Cliffs, N.J.: Prentice-Hall, 1964.

Milovanovic, Dragan, and Katheryn K. Russell. "Petit Apartheid." In *Petit Apartheid in the U.S. Criminal Justice System: The Dark Figure of Racism*, edited by Dragan Milovanovic and Katheryn K. Russell, pp. xix–xxi. Durham, N.C.: Carolina Academic Press, 2001.

Moles, Oliver C. "Marital Dissolution and Public Assistance Payments: Variation among American States." *Journal of Social Issues* 32 (winter 1976): 87–101.

Mott, Frank L., and Sylvia F. Moore. "The Causes of Marital Disruption among Young American Women: An Interdisciplinary Perspective." *Journal of Marriage and the Family* 41 (May 1979): 355–365.

Moynihan, Daniel P. *Family and Nation*. New York: Harcourt Brace Jovanovich, 1987.

———. *The Negro Family: The Case for National Action*. Washington, D.C.: U.S. Government Printing Office, 1965.

Murray, Carolyn Bennett, and James S. Jackson. "The Conditioned Failure Model Revisited." In *African American Children, Youth, and Parenting*, edited by Reginald L. Jones, p. 51. Hampton, Va.: Cobb and Henry Publishers, 1999.

Murray, Charles. *Losing Ground: American Social Policy, 1950–1980*. New York: Basic Books, 1984.

Naisbitt, John. *Megatrends: Ten New Directions Transforming Our Lives*. New York: Warner Books, 1982.

National Center for Health Statistics. "Infant Deaths and Infant Mortality Rates, by Age and Race and Hispanic Origin in the United States." *National Vital Statistics Report* 49, no. 12 (9 October 2001).

———. "Life Expectancy at Birth by Race and Sex, 1940–2000." *National Vital Statistics Reports* 49, no. 12 (9 October 2001).

Nelson, Jill. "Introduction." In *Police Brutality*, edited by Jill Nelson, pp. 9–13. W. W. Norton and Co., 2000.

"The New Mega Churches." *Ebony*, December 2001, pp. 148–160.

"1984 *Black Enterprise's* Top 100 Black Businesses." *Black Enterprise*, June 1985, pp. 87–105.

Nirode, Jodi. "Paying a Steep Price: Blacks More Likely than Whites to Turn to High Cost Lenders." *Columbus Dispatch*, 4 June 2001, p. A5.

Nirode, Jodi, and Stephanie Brenowitz. "A Dream Denied: Even with High Incomes, Blacks Face a Tough Time Getting Home Mortgages." *Columbus Dispatch*, 3 June 2001, pp. A1, A9.

Nobles, Wade. "Africanity: Its Role in Black Families." *Black Scholar* 9 (June 1974): 10–17.

"Officer Is Indicted in Beating That a Bystander Videotaped," *New York Times*, 18 July 2002, p.18.

"One Giant Step for Washington." *U.S. News and World Report*, 23 December 1985, pp. 18–19.

Orfield, Gary. "America Lacks Equal Opportunity," *Los Angeles Times*, 26 December 1993, p. 5.

———. *Desegregation of Black and Hispanic Students from 1968 to 1980* (Mass.: Joint Center for Urban Studies, 1982).

Orfield, Gary, and Susan E. Eaton. *Dismantling Desegregation: The Quiet Reversal of Brown v. Board of Education*. New York: New Press, 1996.

Parsons, Talcott. "Age and Sex in the Structure of the United States." *American Sociological Review* 7 (1942) .

Parsons, Talcott, and Robert F. Bales. *Family, Socialization and the Interaction Process.* Glencoe, Ill.: Free Press, 1955.

Pattison, E., D. Francisco, P. Wood, H. Frazier, and J. Crowder. "A Psychosocial Kinship Model for Family Therapy. "*American Journal of Psychiatry* 132 (1975): 1246–1251.

Peters, Marie Ferguson. "Historical Note: Parenting of Young Children." In *Black Families,* 3rd ed., edited by Harriette Pipes McAdoo, pp. 167–171. Thousand Oaks, Calif.: Sage Publications.

Pinkney, Alphonso. *The Myth of Black Progress.* New York: Cambridge University Press, 1984.

Piven, Frances, and Richard Cloward. *Regulating the Poor: The Functions of Public Welfare.* New York: Vintage, 1971.

Pollack, E. S. "Monitoring A Comprehensive Mental Health Program." In *Comprehensive Mental Health: The Challenge of Evaluations,* edited by L. M. Roberts, N. S. Greenfield, and M. H. Miller. Madison: University of Wisconsin Press, 1968.

Quirk, Paul J., and Joseph Hinchcliffe. "Domestic Policy: The Trials of a Centrist Democrat." In *The Clinton Presidency First Appraisals,* edited by Colin Campbell and Bert A. Rockman. Chatham, N.J.: Chatham House Publishers, 1996.

Rainwater, Lee. *Family Design.* Chicago: AVC, 1965.

Rainwater, Lee, and William Yancey. *The Moynihan Report and the Politics of Controversy.* Cambridge: M.I.T. Press, 1967.

"Reagan's Polarized America." *Newsweek,* 5 April 1982, pp. 17–18.

Reed, Adolph, Jr., ed. *Without Justice for All: The New Liberalism and Our Retreat from Racial Equality.* Boulder, Colo.: Westview Press, 1999.

"Report of the Department of Health and Human Services before the Subcommittee on Public Assistance and Unemployment Compensation." 23 June 1982 (unpublished report).

Roberts, Dorothy. *Shattered Bonds: The Color of Child Welfare.* New York: Basic Books, 2002.

Robinson, Randall. *The Debt: What America Owes to Blacks.* New York: Dutton, 2000.

Rodgers-Rose, La Frances, ed. *The Black Woman.* Beverly Hills, Calif.: Sage Publications, 1982.

Rodman, Hyman "Family and Social Pathology in the Ghetto." *Science* 161 (1968): 756–762.

Ross, Heather L., and Isabel V. Sawhill. *Time of Transition: The Growth of Families Headed by Women.* Washington, D.C.: Urban Institute, 1975.

Roth, Dee, Jerry Bean, Nancy Lust, and Trian Saveanu,. *Homelessness in Ohio: A Study of People in Need.* Columbus: Ohio Department of Mental Health, 1985.

Rothman, David J. *The Discovery of the Asylum.* Boston: Little, Brown, 1971.

Ryan, William. *Blaming the Victim.* New York: Vintage, 1971.

Scanzoni, John H. *The Black Family in Modern Society: Patterns of Stability and Security.* Chicago: University of Chicago Press, 1977.

———. "Black Parental Values and Expectations of Children's Occupational and Educational Success: Theoretical Implications." In *Black Children,* edited by

Harriette McAdoo and John McAdoo, pp. 113–122. Beverly Hills, Calif.: Sage Publications, 1985.

Schecter, Patricia A. *Ida B. Wells-Barnett & American Reform: 1880–1930.* Chapel Hill: University of North Carolina Press, 2000.

"Senate, 93–3, Votes Welfare Revision Mandating Work." *New York Times,* 17 June 1988, p. A-l.

"Small Business Financing Hits Record High, Point of Beginning, 2000." Small Business Administration, 2000.

Smith, Preston. "Self-Help, Black Conservatives and the Reemergence of Black Privatism." In *Without Justice for All: The New Liberalism and Our Retreat from Racial Equality,* edited by Adolph Reed Jr. Boulder, Colo.: Westview Press, 1999.

Smith, Stephen Samuel. "Education and Struggle against Race, Class and Gender Inequality." In *Race, Class and Gender,* 2nd ed., edited by Margaret L. Andersen and Patricia Hill Collins, pp. 289–304. Belmont, Calif.: Wadsworth Press, 1995.

Sowell, Thomas. *The Economics and Politics of Race.* New York: William Morrow and Co., 1983.

Spanier, Graham, and Paul Glick. "Mate Selection Differentials between Blacks and Whites in the United States." *Social Forces* 58 (March 1980): 707–725.

Spratlen, Thaddeus H. "The Continuing Factor of Black Economic Inequity in the United States." *Western Journal of Black Studies* 6 (summer 1982): 73–88.

Stack, Carol. *All Our Kin: Strategies for Survival in a Black Community.* New York: Harper & Row, 1974.

"Still More Billions for Food Stamps." *U.S. News & World Report,* May 1980, p. 7.

Steele, Claude M. "Expert Tesitimony in Defense of Affirmative Action." In *Sex, Race and Merit,* edited by Faye J. Crosby and Cheryl Van Deveer, pp. 124–125. Ann Arbor: University of Michigan Press, 2000.

Steinberg, Stephen. "Occupational Apartheid in America." In *Without Justice for All: The New Liberalism and Our Retreat from Racial Equality,* edited by Adolph Reed Jr.. Boulder, Colo.: Westview Press, 1999.

Stephens, Steve. "It Was a Day of Atonement in Local Churches As Well." *Columbus Dispatch,* 17 October 1995, p. 5B.

Sudarkasa, Niara. "African American Families and Family Values. In *Black Families,* 3rd ed., edited by Harriette Pipes McAdoo, pp. 30–38. Thousand Oaks, Calif.: Sage Publications, 1997.

———. "Interpreting the African Heritage in Afro-American Family Organization." In *Black Families,* edited by Harriette Pipes McAdoo, pp. 37–53. Beverly Hills, Calif.: Sage Publications, 1981.

Swinton, David. "Economic Status of Blacks, 1985." In *The State of Black America.* New York: National Urban League, 1986.

Tatum, Beverly Daniel. *Why Are All the Blacks Kids Sitting Together in the Cafeteria?* New York: Basic Books, 1997.

Taylor, William L. "Access to Economic Opportunity: Lessons Since Brown." In *Minority Report: What Has Happened to Blacks, Hispanics, American Indians and Other Minorities in the Eighties?,* edited by Leslie W. Dunbar New York: Pantheon Books, 1984.

Thomas, Evan, and Stuart Taylor Jr. "Center Court." *Newsweek,* 7 July 2003, pp. 46–47.

Toliver, Susan. *Black Families in Corporate America.* Thousand Oaks, Calif.: Sage Publications, 1998.

Tolsdorf, Christopher. "Social Networks, Support and Coping: An Exploratory Study." *Family Process* 15 (1976): 407–417.

*True Colors.* Northbrook, Ill.: Coronet/MTI Film and Video, 1993.

Tucker, William. "Kindness Is Killing the Black Family." *This World,* January 1985, p. 7.

Turnbull, Lornet. "Women Moved by Journey." *Columbus Dispatch,* 26 October 1997.

U.S. Bureau of the Census. *America's Black Population: 1970 to 1982. A Statistical View.* Special Publication, P-10/POP 83-1. Washington, D.C.: U.S. Government Printing Office, 1983.

———. *Attendance Status of College Students 15 Years Old and Over by Age, Sex, Year and Type of College, Race and Hispanic Origin, October, 2000.* 1 June 2001.

———. "Current Population Reports." U.S. Department of Labor, 1984 (unpublished report).

———. *Current Population Reports.* Series P-20, No. 388. Washington, D.C.: U.S. Government Printing Office, 1984.

———. *Current Population Reports 2000. America's Families and Living Arrangements, Population Characteristics.* Washington, D.C.: U.S. Government Printing Office, 2001.

———. *Educational Attainment of People 25 Years and Over by Nativity and Period of Entry, Age, Sex, Race and Hispanic Origin in the United States. Detailed Tables.* March 2000.

———. *Family and Nonfamily Household Type by Race and Hispanic Origin of Householder.* March 2000.

———. *Historical Income Tables—Families.* 2000.

———. *Living Arrangements of Black Children Under 18 Years Old: 1960 to Present.* 29 June 2001.

———. *Living Arrangements of White Children Under 18 Years Old: 1960 to Present.* 29 June 2001.

———. *Major Occupation Group of the Employed Civilian Population 16 Years and Over by Sex and Race and Hispanic Origin.* March 2000.

———. *Noncash Benefits Received by Households by Selected Household Characteristics, Race and Hispanic Origin, and Poverty Status: 2000.* November 2001.

———. *The Social and Economic Status of the Black Population in the United States: An Historical View, 1790–1978.* Series P-23, No. 80. Washington, D.C.: U.S. Government Printing Office, 1979.

———. "State of the Nation's Housing 2000."

———. *Statistical Abstract of the United States. National Data Book and Guide to Sources.* Washington, D.C.: U.S. Government Printing Office, 1984.

———. *Statistical Abstract of the United States. National Data Book and Guide to Sources,* 106th ed. Washington, D.C.: U.S. Government Printing Office, 1986.

———. *Type of Family, Black Families by Median and Mean Income: 1967 to 2001.* March 2001.

———. *White Non-Hispanic Families Median and Mean Income: 1987 to 2001.* March 2001.

U.S. Department of Health and Human Services. "Statistical Report on Medical Care: Recipients, Payments, and Services." Health Care Financing Administration, 1984 (unpublished report).

U.S. Department of Health, Education and Welfare. *Findings of the 1973 AFDC Study: Part 1.* Washington, D.C.: National Center for Social Statistics, 1974.

U.S. Department of Housing and Urban Development, Superintendent of Documents. *1979 Statistical Yearbook.* Washington, D.C.: U.S. Government Printing Office, 1979.

U.S. Department of Labor. *Labor Force Status of the Civilian Population 16 Years and Over by Sex and Race and Hispanic Origin.* March 2000.

———. *WIN Handbook.* No 318. Washington, D.C.: U.S. Government Printing Office, 1984.

U.S. Social Security Administration. *Aid to Families with Dependent Children. Social Security Bulletin. Annual Statistical Supplement.* Washington, D.C.: Department of Health and Human Services, 1982.

Vander Zanden, James W. *Sociology: A Systematic Approach.* New York: Ronald Press Company, 1970.

Vaughn-Cooke, Dennys. "The Economic Status of Black America—Is There a Recovery?" In *The State of Black America.* Washington, D.C.: National Urban League, 1984.

Verbrugge, Lois M. "Marital Status and Health." *Journal of Marriage and the Family* 41 (May 1979): 267–285.

Weinberg, Meyer. *A Chance to Learn.* Cambridge, England: Cambridge University Press, 1977.

Weitzman, Lenore. "The Economics of Divorce: Social and Economic Consequences of Property, Alimony and Child Support Awards." *UCLA Law Review* 28 (1981): 1228.

"What Must Be Done About Children Having Children?" *Ebony,* March 1985, p. 76.

*Who Will Care When Parents Can't?: A Study of Black Children in Foster Care.* Washington, D.C.: National Black Child Development Institute, 1989.

Will, George. "Will Wrongly Sees Need To Link Crime, Ethnicity." *Columbus Dispatch,* 19 April 2001, p. 12A.

Williams, J. Allen, Jr., and Robert Stockton. "Black Family Structures and Functions: An Empirical Examination of Some Suggestions Made by Billingsley." *Journal of Marriage and the Family* 35 (February 1973): 39–49.

Williams, Walter E. *The State against Blacks.* New York: McGraw-Hill, 1982.

Wolfgang, Marvin E. *The Culture of Youth.* Washington, D.C.: U.S. Government Printing Office, 1967.

Wolkon, George H., Sharon Mornwaki, David Mandel, Jeraldine Archuleta, Pamela Bunje, and Sandra Zimmerman. "Ethnicity and Social Class in the Delivery of Services: Analysis of a Child Guidance Clinic." *American Journal of Public Health* 64 (1974): 709–712.

Woodson, Robert L. "A Legacy of Entrepreneurship." In *On the Road to Economic Freedom: An Agenda for Black Progress,* edited by Robert L. Woodson, pp. 1–26. Washington, D.C.: National Center for Neighborhood Enterprise, 1987.

Yoon, Jane. "Republican Plan for Children Too Hard to Swallow." *Yale Herald, Inc.*, 1995.

Zastrow, Charles. *Introduction to Social Welfare Institutions: Social Problems, Services and Current Issues.* Homewood, Ill.: Dorsey Press, 1982.

Zepezauer, Mark, and Arthur Naiman. *Take the Rich Off Welfare.* Tucson, Ariz.: Odonian Press, 1996.

# Index

## About the Author

K. SUE JEWELL is a sociology professor in the Department of African American and African Studies at The Ohio State University. She received the B.A. and M.A. from Kent State University and the Ph.D. in sociology from The Ohio State University. She has published the book, *From Mammy to Miss America and Beyond: Cultural Images and the Shaping of U.S. Social Policy*, as well as many articles. Her research is concentrated in the areas of social policy; race, gender, and class issues; the African American family; African American children; social inequality; and cultural imagery. She has also conducted research and evaluation in mental health and substance abuse.